The Official  Bible

THE OFFICIAL

eBaY™

BIBLE

■ The Most Up-to-Date, Comprehensive
How-to Manual for Everyone from First-Time Users
to People Who Want to Run Their Own Business

JIM "GRIFF" GRIFFITH

GOTHAM
BOOKS

GOTHAM BOOKS
Published by Penguin Group (USA) Inc.
375 Hudson Street, New York, New York 10014, U.S.A.
Penguin Books Ltd, Registered Offices: 80 Strand, London WC2R 0RL, England
Penguin Books Australia Ltd, 250 Camberwell Road, Camberwell, Victoria 3124, Australia
Penguin Books Canada Ltd, 10 Alcorn Avenue, Toronto, Ontario, Canada M4V 3B2
Penguin Books (N.Z.) Ltd, Cnr Rosedale and Airborne Roads, Albany, Auckland 1310, New Zealand

Published by Gotham Books, a division of Penguin Group (USA) Inc.

First printing, June 2003
10   9   8   7   6   5   4   3   2   1

Gotham Books and the skyscraper logo are trademarks of Penguin Group (USA) Inc.

LIBRARY OF CONGRESS CATALOGING-IN-PUBLICATION DATA has been applied for.

ISBN 1-592-40007-8

Printed in the United States of America
Set in Sabon with Frutiger
Designed by Victoria Hartman

This book is printed on acid-free paper. ∞

To the millions of eBay members
who have helped make eBay what it is today

CONTENTS

ACKNOWLEDGMENTS

I would like to thank the following: My esteemed eBay colleagues Kristin Seuell, Brett Healy, Jim Davis, and Henry Gomez, whose support was crucial in getting this project off the ground. Joni Evans and Lisa Shotland of William Morris and William Shinker, Lauren Marino, and Mark Roy at Gotham Books for showing me the ropes and providing advice and counsel; Patti (Louise) Ruby, Matt England, Rodney Hill, John Tillinger, Chris Byrne, Rob Stanger, Joanna Ross, Joan Wing, Mary Lou Song, Matt England, and Josh Lewis for their support and encouragement; and finally, Mike Winslow for putting up with the whole darned process.

Very special thanks to the following eBay members who contributed their tips and stories: Craig M. Keller, Sr., Craig Knouse, Tim Heidner, Tom Reddick, Julie Douglas, Pam Withers, Heather Luce, Mike Ford, Leah Lestina, Karen Gray, Anita Leather, Melissa Fiala, Brenda Bienlein, Tim Burnett, Robert Sachs, Barry Lamb, Peter Cini, Deanna Rittel, Bill Cawfield, Mike Driscoll, Tina DeBarge, Bob Bull, Laurie Liss, Kim and Chris Hecker, Chris Spencer, Terry Wagner, Lori Taylor, Linda Huffman, Sharon Marcacci, Dave Rayner, and Pat Fulton.

INTRODUCTION

On the morning of May 10, 1996, a friend sent me an email. At the time, I was living in Vermont, dividing my day between administrative duties for a nonprofit arts organization known as The Carving Studio, some residual mural painting left over from my once-flourishing decorative painting business, and buying, building, and reselling computers.

In short, I was going broke.

My online friend knew I was searching for a hard-to-find memory chip. He had just stumbled upon a new Web site called eBay, where he had discovered that the very part I needed was for sale there in an auction format. I immediately clicked the URL he had copied into the body of the email and found myself at a plain, gray-background Web site with a logo on the top the page that announced "AuctionWeb—eBay Internet."

With a little easy searching, I soon found the chip and put in a bid of $15. (Two days later, I would win the item for $10—a bargain.) I had finally found the part for which I had been searching. Excited by my find, I was soon exploring the rest of the site, looking for more treasure on which to bid, when I came across a page called "the AuctionWeb Bulletin Board."

[Listings] [Buyers] [Sellers] [Search] [Contact]

The AuctionWeb Bulletin Board

This page contains messages left by AuctionWeb registered users. You can use this bulletin board to communicate with the rest of the AuctionWeb community. Only the most recent **100** messages will be kept. (This used to be higher, but this page became too slow.)

User: wgtaylor (175) **Date:** 04/04/97 **Time:** 16:47:19 PST	Dan, Just scroll up to the top of this page, right under "The Auction Web Bulletin Board" and click on user feedback forum. It will give you instructions from there.
User: antique(93) **Date:** 04/04/97 **Time:** 16:46:31 PST	Dan, there is a link to the user feedback forum just above the boxes where you just entered your question. 8^) Aunt Patti
User: dwboynton (1) **Date:** 04/04/97 **Time:** 16:43:29 PST	How do I pass feedback, positive or negative. Can't seem to find the right niche..... Dan
User: wgtaylor (175) **Date:** 04/04/97 **Time:** 16:35:09 PST	Hey Donna, You sing pretty good...I really like the "Oldies" but don't you ever do "Country"?
User: wgtaylor (175) **Date:** 04/04/97 **Time:** 16:31:25 PST	Phillip, Sounds like your server to me.. Nancy
User: gypsy13 (4) **Date:** 04/04/97 **Time:** 16:24:05 PST	Hey out there, am I the only one who cannot contact a seller through "ask the seller a question"? Every time i try, it goes to the e-mail page, I compose the message, try to send it, but it never goes anywhere. Is the problem eBAY's or netcom (my server) Thanks for any help Phillip

The original eBay chat board was nothing fancy—just a simple message board where anyone could submit a text-only post for the rest of the world to read and to which anyone else could post a response.

I watched for a few hours as new eBay users posted their questions and a few regular eBay experts provided answers. Here was a group of friendly buyers and sellers having a grand time chatting and sharing expertise—a genuine online community! Unable to resist the fun, I jumped in and started posting my own eBay-related questions, making acquaintances with other regular posters and learning a lot about buying and selling on eBay. Within weeks and with the help of generous eBayers chat denizens, I had mastered the finer points of buying and selling and started answering questions like an old eBay pro.

The ultimate pro, AuctionWeb creator Pierre Omidyar, usually stopped by the chat board in the evenings to say hello and chat about new features he was considering for his "hobby" site. He would even answer a few queries about listing procedures or policies. I was immediately struck by Pierre's good-natured chatting style, encyclopedic computer knowledge, and genuine concern for eBay users.

During the next few weeks, inspired by Pierre, I slowly patched together my own online persona "Uncle Griff"—a hybrid of Miss Manners, Dame Edna Everage, Maude from the 1971 cult film *Harold and Maude,* along with a bit of Norman Bates thrown in for "balance."

Uncle Griff's primary mission on the chat board—besides chewing the online scenery—was to establish and maintain decorum and civility by dint of his own exemplary online behavior and slightly weird sense of humor. With the torch of his perfect manners held aloft, Uncle Griff embarked on a valiant crusade to lead the huddled eBay chat-board masses out of the darkness of messy, tear-ridden misunderstandings—which often escalated in to all-out flame wars—onto the lofty plateau of polite and productive eBay discussion.

For a while, it was great fun, but although the "Uncle Griff" avatar was outwardly a jolly and well-adjusted—if somewhat bizarre—old coot, in truth, my offline life was coming apart and by late September, with savings depleted and no prospect of gainful employment in sight, I sank into a severe and paralyzing depression.

I thought it was a typical male midlife crisis but it proved to be much more serious. I would later learn that I had been suffering from regular bouts of clinical depression for most of my life, but just like many sufferers of this pernicious disease, I had proudly resisted acknowledging or addressing my condition.

Unable to rouse myself out of bed, "Uncle Griff" unceremoniously disappeared one day from the AW Bulletin Board.

After a few weeks, with the support of concerned friends, therapy, and medication, I was able to return one morning to my studio. My landlord, an understanding man, had been patient about the back rent, but not so the utility companies. The studio heat and electricity had been shut off.

Standing alone in my cold, dark space, I considered my options. Although technically "on the mend," I would still need a job in order to crawl out of debt and pull my life together. But who in their right mind would ever hire an undereducated, middle-aged, previously-self-employed-now-flat-broke gentleman with a very left-of-center sense of humor?

It was the low point of my life.

Then, the phone rang.

"Hello?"

"Hello, is Uncle Griff there?"

"Who wants to know?"

"This is Jeff Skoll from eBay. Pierre is here with me. We are looking for Uncle Griff."

I remember thinking that I must have not paid my AuctionWeb bill.

"Uncle? Where have you been?"

"I had, uh . . . a cold. Is something wrong?"

"No, not at all. We were concerned. We've been watching Uncle Griff's antics for the last few months. We really think he's terrific. Then he just disappeared. We don't want Uncle to disappear again, so we were wondering if we could pay you to keep him around."

" . . . "

"Uncle? You still there?"

"Work for eBay?"

"Are you interested?"

Interested? Jeff and Pierre had thrown me a lifesaver. I grabbed it.

"Yes!"

We settled on a fair hourly wage, worked out a schedule of sorts, and by the end of the call, I was eBay's first official customer-support rep—answering emails and chatting on the boards, and all from West Rutland, Vermont.

Seven years, and a lot of changes, later, I am still with eBay, except that my job title has changed to "Dean of eBay Education" and I am living in California instead of Vermont. Although I now travel around the country and the world spreading the word about eBay to the experienced and uninitiated, I am still teaching others how to use eBay every other weekend at one of our eBay University seminars. (More on eBay University later in this book.)

EBAY CHANGED MY LIFE—IT CAN CHANGE YOURS!

It sounds like a cliché but it's absolutely true—eBay changed my life. eBay has changed or enhanced the lives of literally millions of folks who, like me, stumbled one day upon this incredible revolutionary Web site and, as either buyers or sellers or both, found themselves suddenly taking control of their lives in ways they had never imagined were possible.

Over the past six years, through email and face-to-face, literally hundreds of eBay members have shared their own awe-inspiring eBay stories with me. Some of these stories are brief tales of the "Good Samaritan" who helped someone get started with their eBay listings. Others border on the miraculous—how finding eBay helped salvage a career or a business on the verge of collapse and ruin. People have met on eBay and were later married. One woman bought her entire wedding on eBay.

Others who once felt they were too incompetent or just plain too dumb to ever learn how to get online were motivated by the eBay juggernaut and finally mastered that damnable computer their son or daughter had given them and were soon buying and selling along with the other millions of registered eBay users.

Today, over 60 million buyers and sellers around the world have jumped on the eBay train; an impressive number indeed, but by my reckoning that leaves several hundred million still unaccounted for.

Are you one of the unaccounted?

- Your friends and relatives all use eBay and you want to join in the fun, but just the very thought of computers gives you the willies.

- You've heard the buzz and checked out eBay once or twice but are over-whelmed by the sheer numbers of items for sale on the eBay Web site.

- You are currently selling on eBay but you want to improve your eBay skills with more tips, tricks, and eBay seller secrets.

If any of the above fits your situation, then this book is for you!

By combining the eBay knowledge I have garnered since 1996, the tips and tricks of other savvy eBay experts, and the astonishing tales of people whose lives have been forever changed by eBay, I've put together this comprehensive how-to manual for using eBay—one that I hope will inspire you to take those first steps toward successful eBay buying and selling, and reward you with the confidence and the satisfaction that come from learning and applying, firsthand, a new and exciting set of skills.

Buyers! We'll take you step-by-step through the eBay registration process and show you how to effectively browse and search the eBay site; with lots of information on how to safely bid and buy, both for yourselves and your families.

Sellers! You'll take better digital pictures; write professional item listings with HTML; learn how to put together a new eBay business and how to promote it effectively.

Don't think you can do it? Think again.

Over the last seven years, I've witnessed thousands of folks just like you get the "eBay knack," and all it took was encouragement, a little humor, and step-by-step instructions in plain English.

I *know* you can do it!

What are we waiting for? There's treasure to discover.

Let's get started!

HOW TO NAVIGATE THE OFFICIAL EBAY BIBLE

The Official eBay Bible can be read from cover to cover or used as a reference. I have tried to include a wide range of information to benefit both the brand-new computer user and the seasoned eBay expert.

This book is divided into two sections. Section One is primarily for eBay buyers. However, whether you want to buy or sell on eBay—if you are a brand-new computer user, start with Section One. Section Two is most definitely for eBay sellers.

Experienced computer and Internet users can start anywhere or use the index at the end of the book to look up specific topics.

The Official eBay™ Bible

Buying
the eBay Way!

Let's Get Started

You are about to enter a wondrous universe called eBay—a place where you can hunt for and buy treasure; sell the contents of your attic; or maybe finally follow that old dream of yours and start your own online business—all the while meeting and chatting with other eager eBay traders in your hometown, your state, or from halfway around the globe. But first, a little history. . . .

The eBay Phenomenon

Shopping!

Whether it's at garage sales or malls, through mail-order catalogs or the Shopping Channel, in Middle Eastern souks, at auctions, bazaars, swap meets, flea markets, or even the stock market: we humans love to shop! Shopping and acquiring are a basic a part of human nature. We can't get enough of them. Our uniquely human passion for barter and trade is what sets us apart from the rest of the animal kingdom. In fact, we've been bartering goods since before recorded history, so it's no surprise that some of the earliest surviving examples of human writing—Sumerian cuneiform V-shaped impressions on clay tablets—are receipts.

There have been watershed moments in the history of human commerce, starting with the invention of the wheel, agriculture, water-powered mills, and currency, through the creation of the first steam engines, assembly lines, and flight, but in the 1990s a completely new conduit for commerce appeared—one so revolutionary in scope that in just a few short years, it changed forever the way that humans traded with each other.

The Internet provided anyone with a computer and a telephone line access to a rapidly growing universe of millions of Web sites from around the globe offering a wide array of information, news, entertainment, and most important, goods.

At first, the Internet was considered suitable only for the exchange of information such as email and bulletin boards, but in 1993, with the creation of a graphics-capable tool called the World Wide Web, the idea of the Internet as a venue for commerce took hold, especially as the first trickle of Internet pioneers grew overnight into a virtual stampede of new users. Where there are people, there's trading.

In the early summer of 1995, the commercial and social potential of the Internet was on the mind of Pierre Omidyar, a computer programmer living and working in San Jose, California.

Most commercial Web sites up to 1995 were just online variations of the off-line merchant-customer model, where a single company offered merchandise for sale at a set cost. These Web sites were only slightly more exciting than mail-order catalogs.

Pierre had an idea.

Why not create a Web site where buyers and sellers could trade directly with each other, much like an old-time flea market, using an auction format?

The concept was simple. The World Wide Web could provide a market "space" where sellers could list items and where buyers could browse for and buy these items, just like a flea market—except, whereas the traditional flea market was limited to one geographical location, the Web was truly worldwide in scope. This would be real Internet trading—people trading with other people online, through their computers, from the comfort of their homes, from anywhere around the world.

Pierre immediately set to work. Working alone and in his spare time (he had a day job, after all), it took him only a few weeks to complete a design and write the software that would run his new Web site.

The actual design of the site was simple.

Using a unique email address as an "identifier," anyone with something to sell could, through his or her home computer and an Internet connection, upload an item description and title to the site. Anyone who visited the site and found the item—either by searching on keywords or by browsing the list of item titles in various categories—could then submit a bid for that item.

Bids would be accepted by a proxy system, that is, instead of having to sit on the listing to rebid every time someone outbid him, the bidder could instead submit a maximum bid amount—the highest amount he was willing to pay—and the system behind the Web site would execute his maximum bid on his behalf, protecting his interest until either the listing ended or another bidder submitted a bid amount higher than the first bidder's proxy. It was a simple but brilliant and efficient way to import the traditional auction format to this new medium.

The most brilliant aspect of all: the buyer and seller would complete the transaction without the direct involvement of the Web site! The seller would send payment instructions to the high bidder, and the high bidder would send payment. The seller would then mail or deliver the item to the high bidder.

Pierre called his new Web site "AuctionWeb–eBay Internet." The Auction-Web site went "live" on Labor Day, 1995. Pierre's only initial marketing effort was to post a simple announcement that month on Usenet:

```
From: Pierre Omidyar <pierre@shell1.best.com>
Subject: SHOPPING: Free Interactive Web Auction
Date: 1995/09/27

AuctionWeb
----------

  "The most fun buying and selling on the web!"

  * Run your own auction
  * Bid on existing auctions
  * New listings added daily!
  * Fast, fun, and FREE!

  * AuctionWeb doesn't sell anything - we just provide the service.

Try it out!

  <URL:http://www.ebay.com/aw/>


--
Pierre Omidyar    Home page: http://www.ebay.com/pierre.shtml
pierre@ebay.com   Free Web Auction:   http://www.ebay.com/aw/
```

(The "AuctionWeb" name was dropped in favor of just "eBay" in September of 1997.)

The first eBay Web site was totally devoid of fancy graphics, colors, icons, or logos. It was as thrilling as a gray paper box:

```
Auction Web
        [Menu]  [Listings]  [Buyers]  [Sellers]  [Search]  [Contact/Help]  [Site Map]
```

Welcome to today's online marketplace...	**Welcome to our community.** I'm glad you found us. AuctionWeb is dedicated to bringing together buyers and sellers in an honest and open marketplace. Here, thanks to our <u>auction format</u>, merchandise will always fetch its market value. And there are plenty of great deals to be found!
...the market that brings buyers and sellers together in an honest and open environment...	**Take a look at the listings.** There are always several hundred auctions underway, so you're bound to find something interesting. If you don't find what you like, take a look at our **Personal Shopper.** It can help you search all the listings. Or, it can keep an eye on new items as they are posted and let you know when something you want appears. If you want to let everyone know what you want, post something on our <u>wanted page</u>. If you have something to **sell,** start your auction instantly.
Welcome to eBay's AuctionWeb.	**Join our community.** Become a registered user. Registered users receive <u>additional benefits</u> such as daily updates and the right to participate in our user feedback forum and the bulletin board. Please **read on** about the AuctionWeb vision...

What does the word "eBay" mean?

Earlier on in Pierre's career, he made a trip to Sacramento in order to incorporate all of his current and future business endeavors under a single "holding company" using a favorite name—Echo Bay. However, much to Pierre's disappointment, the clerk at the state capital office informed him that someone else had already incorporated a California business using "Echo Bay." Thinking fast, he came up with "e-bay."

The clerk checked. The name "ebay" had not yet been incorporated.

The rest is history.

In the months immediately following the launch, a few hundred people stumbled across eBay and began listing items for bid; at first mostly computer parts, used items, and a smattering of collectibles.

Throughout 1996, news about Pierre's little Web site began to spread across the Internet. Each day, more and more sellers came to eBay, liked what they saw, and added their merchandise to the expanding list of items for bid. The increasing number and variety of items brought more curious buyers looking for a possible bargain. As more items were sold, so even more sellers would come to

AuctionWeb and list even more items, bringing even more new buyers, and so on, until the number of eBay users began to expand at an almost exponential rate.

By the fall of 1996, there were close to 10,000 registered users on eBay.

In May of 1997, the 1 millionth item was sold on eBay (a *Sesame Street* Big Bird figure).

For the first two years of its existence, the astonishing growth in both eBay members and eBay items was due entirely to word of mouth. By the end of 1998, there were over 2 million registered eBay users. Sellers were listing 3.4 million items per month.

In 1998 eBay went public. This new American pastime—buying and selling on eBay—had attracted the attention of not only Wall Street but the general public as well. By 1999, "eBay"—the brand—was recognizable enough to be a regular feature of David Letterman's Top Ten List and a punch line in *New Yorker* cartoons. eBay was a bona fide cultural phenomenon.

The number of registered users grew to 10 million by the end of 1999, and eBay sellers were listing nearly 10 million items a month.

By the end of 2001, the number of eBay users stood at over 40 million, with eBay sellers listing a staggering 31 million items each month.

Starting in earnest in early 2000 and continuing to the present, the eBay Inc. team, led by CEO Meg Whitman, has extended the eBay reach across the globe as new language and culturally distinct eBay Web sites were opened in Britain, Australia, France, Italy, South America, and Korea.

As of the end of 2002, the trading statistics were astonishing. On eBay . . .

> Someone buys a vehicle every 1.7 minutes.
> A diamond ring is purchased every six minutes.
> A digital camera sells on the site every ninety seconds.
> People buy ten CDs and five videos every minute.
> Someone purchases a PC every thirty seconds.
> A pair of men's shoes sells every twenty-one seconds.

Looking back, given the extraordinary timing, the brilliant simplicity of the idea or business model, and how seamlessly it fit the promise of the Internet, the birth and subsequent phenomenal success of eBay now seem to have been inevitable. Pierre's idea of a Web site for person-to-person trading was an idea whose time had clearly arrived. But that's not the entire picture.

A person-to-person trading site is nothing without the "persons" who do the trading. eBay's success and popularity are due in large part to the dedication and hard work of those individual buyers and sellers who use it every day. These folks make up the core of the eBay Community.

That's the story of eBay so far. It's most definitely not the end of the tale. From Pierre's simple idea—a Web-site trading outpost—eBay has grown into the biggest human commerce phenomenon of the last hundred years of trading.

Welcome to eBay!

Using eBay—The Basic Tools

In order to use eBay, you will need two basic computer tools: a Web browser and an email application.

WEB BROWSERS

All computers come with at least one version of a Web browser. The two most popular models of Web browsers are Microsoft Internet Explorer and Netscape.

All of the illustrations and examples in this book use Internet Explorer (IE). However, with just a few minor adjustments, you can easily adapt them to Netscape Navigator or any other Web browser.

You can start Internet Explorer on your computer by looking for the blue *E* icon on your computer desktop:

When you first start up your Web browser, the first page that shows up is the default home page. The first thing we are going to do with your Web browser is change the preset default home-page to the eBay home page. That way, every time you connect to the Internet, the first Web page displayed will be eBay.

CHANGING YOUR WEB BROWSER'S DEFAULT HOME

Position your mouse cursor inside the Address box and highlight the text within the box by clicking the left mouse button two times.

Begin typing the address for the eBay home page, **www.ebay.com**. The old text will automatically be replaced by the text you type.

Press the Enter key on your keyboard or click the Go button to the very right of the Address window:

This will bring up the eBay home page in your browser window.

On the Command Menu, click on Tools and then from the drop-down menu, Internet Options.

This will display the Internet Options box. In the top third of the box, there is a section labeled "Home page." The URL (Web address) for the current page displayed in your Web browser will show in the Address box. Click the Use Current button.

Then click the OK button on the bottom of the Internet Options window.

eBay is now your default home page! Every time you open a new browser window by clicking on the Internet Explorer icon, the first page you will see will be the eBay home page.

You can change your "home page" at any time by following the above steps.

GRIFF TIP! Throughout this book, you will see suggestions to "go to" a particular Web address like **http://www.ebay.com.**

To "go to" any Web page address in this book, repeat step one, type in the Web address (make sure to type it exactly as shown), and then press the Enter key on your keyboard.

Basic Web Page Navigation

HYPERLINKS

Navigating from one Web page to another is a snap.

If you look at the eBay home page, you will notice that many of the lines of text are a blue color and underlined. If you move your mouse over this blue, underlined text, the mouse cursor changes from a little arrow to a tiny hand with a pointing index finger.

These changes indicate that the text underneath the mouse cursor is a **hyperlink.** The task of hyperlinks is to take you to another location, either within the current Web page or to a completely different Web page. You ask the hyperlink to do its task by clicking the mouse directly on the hyperlink.

Try moving your mouse cursor over one of the hyperlinks on the eBay page. Also, when you do move your mouse over a link, watch as the Web address for the Web page to which the link leads appears in the IE status bar on the bottom of the IE window.

Once your mouse cursor is over a hyperlink, move to the Web page represented by that link by clicking the left-hand button on your mouse. Depending on the speed of your Internet connection, the page whose hyperlink you clicked will start to appear in the IE window.

BACK AND FORWARD BUTTONS

Clicking a link will move you forward to that page. To move back to the previous Web page, look for and click the Back button located on the menu bar at the top of the IE window.

To move forward again to the clicked page, click the Forward button (located directly to the right of the Back button).

THE IE ADDRESS BOX

As I mentioned in the previous Griff Tip, if you know the address for a Web page, you can type it into the box labeled Address at the top of the IE window.

Remember that the quickest way to type text into any text entry box is to click twice anywhere inside the box to highlight the existing text and to then start typing the new text. (Many folks don't believe the highlighted text is going to disappear, so they press the Delete key on their computer keyboard before they start typing. This is an unnecessary step.)

CHANGING YOUR WEB BROWSER'S COOKIE SETTINGS

In order to use most eBay Web pages to their fullest, your Web browser needs to be able to accept **cookies.**

Cookies are simple text files stored on your computer to which a Web site will write your chosen preferences. For example, the first time you visit a Web site like **www.moviephone.com** looking for film locations and schedules for your city, the Movie Phone site will "remember" your city preferences by storing them in a cookie file. On your return to Movie Phone, the Web site will read the contents of the cookie and immediately display the pages for your city, saving you the trouble of navigating there. eBay's most popular features must use cookies in order to work properly. Two of the most important (but by no means the only) eBay features that use cookies are the **Sign In** feature and the **eBay Picture Services** feature (iPix). If your Web browser is not set to accept cookies from eBay, you will not be able to use either of these features properly.

Here are the steps for making sure that your Web browser is set up to accept cookies from eBay.

For Internet Explorer Versions 5.0 and Below

Go to the menu bar on **Internet Explorer** (the menu bar is the list of commands on the top of any Windows application) and look for the option for **Tools.** Select it and then click "**Internet Options . . .**"

In the next window, select the top tab for "Security" and make sure the icon for **Internet** is highlighted. Then look for and click the button for "Custom Level . . ." at the bottom of the window.

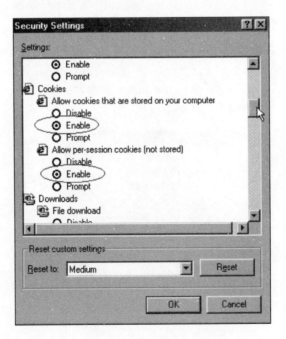

This will bring up the **Security Settings** window. Scroll down and look for the section for **Cookies**. Make sure that either the **Enable** or the **Prompt** option is checked for both "Allow cookies that are stored on your computer" and "Allow per-session cookies (not stored)."

NOTE: Selecting **Enable** will allow all sites you visit to place a cookie on your computer.

Click **OK** (the Security Settings window will close), then click **Apply** and **OK** on the **Internet Options** window.

For Netscape

In a Netscape browser, select the option for **Preferences** under the menu command for **Edit**.

In the **Preferences** window, highlight the option for **Advanced** in the left-hand panel. Make sure that the option for **Cookies** is set to either **"Accept all cookies"** or "Accept only cookies that get sent back to the originating server."

Click **OK**.

Now you can use all of eBay's time-saving features!

For Internet Explorer Versions 6.0 and Above

On the Internet Explorer toolbar, click on **Tools** and then click the menu item for "Internet Options . . ."

In the resulting **Internet Options** window, select the **Privacy** tab and click on the button labeled **"Edit"** in the **Web Sites** frame (located at the bottom of the window)

This will bring up the **Per Site Privacy Actions** window, where you can add Web sites by name and either **Allow** or **Block** their cookies.

NOTE: In order to use eBay correctly and efficiently and in order to have access to all of eBay's user features, you MUST allow cookies from **www.ebay.com**.

Type in **www.ebay.com** in the window marked **"Address of Web site:"** and click the button marked **"Allow."**

Once you have added the Web sites for which you wish to allow or block cookies, Click the button marked **OK** and then, in the **Internet Options** window, click the Button marked **OK**.

EMAIL

As a form of communication, email has nearly supplanted the handwritten letter. It's quick to send and receive and it's easy to keep track of. It's incredibly well suited for sending out one mailing to one, two, or, curses! several hundred people all at once. Email calls upon the sender's learned and practiced ability to write clearly and unambiguously.

In short, email is a blessing and a curse. Email is also an absolutely critical tool for using eBay and the Internet. You cannot utilize the Internet's fullest potential without using email, and to do so you will need an email account.

An email is part of every ISP's (Internet Service Provider) service package. Outlook Express is the email application that comes built in with all versions of Internet Explorer. It can handle all your basic email needs, including your eBay email.

Free Web-Based Email Accounts

Web-based free email accounts are one of the most popular methods of sending and receiving email, mostly because, well, it's free, but also because web-based email is accessible from anyplace on earth where there is an Internet-connected computer, be it your friend's house, an Internet café in Italy, or from your laptop while on the road.

There are literally hundreds of free email accounts to choose from. Two of the most popular are:

Yahoo!
Hotmail

You can find hundreds of others online at **http://www.emailaddresses.com**.

AOL Email

As of this writing, AOL email doesn't always display hyperlinks as active, "clickable" links. If someone sends you the address of a Web page and that address is static text, not clickable, you will have to **copy and paste** the Web page address from the email body to your Web browser's address box in order to view the page.

Save Your Email!

Saving your old in and out emails is a wise habit to acquire, especially when you start buying and selling on eBay. You will receive and send many emails to sellers and buyers as your activity on eBay increases, and you very well may need to access them sometime long after the transactions have closed.

If you are new to computing and the Internet, it can be overwhelming at first venture, but with just a little perseverance, you will master Web browsers and email in no time.

Here's an email from eBay member Craig M. Keller, Sr.:

Uncle Griff,

I am one of those "older farts." . . . I wanted nothing, and I mean NOTHING to do with computers, when we first got them in at work. I fought and fought against using them. When in 1999 due to a serious illness I was forced to leave work and retire, my daughter (bless her heart) said that she was going to email me a joke or cartoon every day on my wife's computer and that I had to read it.

*One day, my wife came home from her job and said that if while I was reading my joke of the day, I wanted to check out the neatest site, try **www.ebay.com.** Well, let me tell you, my whole life changed on that day. I found a whole new world out there in cyberspace and I have learned not only great things to buy, but I now do quite a bit of selling. . . .*

Believe you me, without eBay to go to each day, I would have sooner or later went out of my mind after being forced to stay at home.

I have had an operation, in 2001, that now lets me pretty much do everything I used to do before the illness, but I'll never give up eBay.

Craig did it. So can you!
Let's get you registered on eBay.

Registering on eBay, Step by Step

THE COMPLETE PROCESS

You will need to register on eBay in order to bid or buy, sell, or use the other various eBay features like feedback or chat. Even though you don't need to be registered to browse for treasure on eBay, we might as well get ourselves registered.

Registering on eBay is fairly straightforward. It involves three simple steps:

Fill in your information (name, address, etc.) and choose your eBay User ID and password.
Agree to Terms.
Receive confirmation email and confirm your registration.

To begin, go to the eBay home page, **www.ebay.com,** and look for the button on the top of the eBay home page labeled "register now."

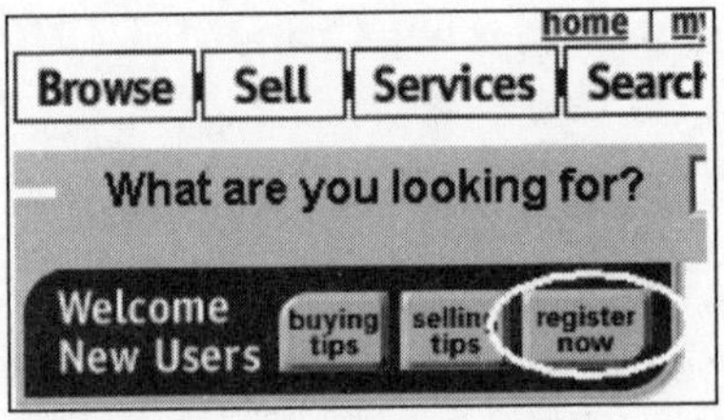

This will bring you to the page for Step 1 of the three-step registration process.

Step 1—Enter Information

On this page, enter your contact information.

> Full name
> Address
> City
> State (from the drop-down list)
> Zip Code
> Country
> Primary phone number
> Secondary phone number
> Email address

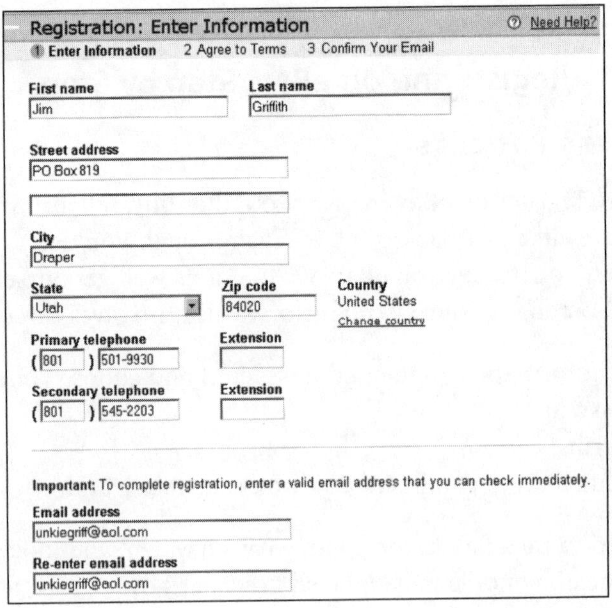

You will need to enter your email address twice to make sure there are no typed mistakes in the email address itself. An incorrectly typed email address would prevent you from finishing the registration process, since the email address you provide in this step is the address to which eBay sends the all-important confirmation email in Step 3 of the registration process. If it goes to the incorrect or a nonexistent email address, you will not be able to complete the registration process.

At the bottom of the same page, create a User ID and password, and select a secret question and answer. (If you forget your password, you'll be asked the secret question and you'll need to answer the question correctly in order to receive a new password.)

```
Create your eBay User ID
unkiegriff
Example: rose789 (Don't use your email address)
Your User ID identifies you to other eBay users.

Create password

6 character minimum
Enter a password that's easy for you to remember, but hard for others to guess. See tips.

Re-enter password


Secret question                          Secret answer
What street did you grow up on?    ▼
You will be asked for the answer to your secret question if you forget your password.

Date of birth
April        ▼    05   ▼   Year 19


Continue >
```

Choosing an eBay User ID and Password—Tips

Your eBay User ID is the "handle" by which all other eBay members will recognize you on the site. Your User ID will show up on the pages of your items for sale, next to your bids, on your feedback profile, on your About Me page, and anywhere you chat online on eBay. Since this is going to be your official handle (you may actually become famous by this User ID!) it is crucial that you create one that is absolutely perfect for you.

If you are primarily a bidder, you may want to create an eBay User ID that reflects your buying passions. For example, if you collect balls of string, a good ID might be "ballofstringlover" (At this writing, this User ID is unclaimed!)

If you are a seller, choose something that hints at your business. If your business name were Say It With Widgets, then perhaps "sayitwithwidgets" would be a good choice. (Do not use **"www.sayitwithwidgets.com,"** as the system is set to reject any User ID that is a Web site address.)

Whatever you choose, do keep it easy to remember. Complicated combinations of letters and numbers are not easy to remember. If you are a seller, this can be an obstacle for your future eBay customers. Shorter User IDs are easier to recall and notice.

Avoid punctuation. If you attempt to create a User ID and it comes back as already in use, you may find that adding a period at the end will allow it to go through. However, as a seller, you will end up with confused bidders who may think you are someone else. Best that your User ID is as unique as possible.

Every User ID on eBay is displayed in lower case, regardless of how you type it in the box. Certain combinations of letters and numbers in lowercase can look ambiguous in a viewer's Web browser. For that reason, avoid User ID choices that include directly adjacent combinations of the letters *I, L,* and the number 1. Also avoid choices that include directly adjacent combinations of the letter *O* and the numeral 0.

You cannot use your email address as a User ID. Initially, it was possible for eBay users to name their email addresses as their User IDs. This was changed in 2001. But all those folks who were using an email address as their User ID before the policy change were "grandfathered" into the new policy, that is, they were allowed to continue to do so.

This no-email-address-for-a-User-ID policy was implemented to discourage bulk emailers from using software to harvest the eBay site for new email addresses to add to their spam lists. Although it hasn't totally prevented the harvesting, it has made it more difficult for harvesters to do so successfully.

A word about passwords . . .

Never take an obvious word or phrase as a password! For example, don't use a common name, or your eBay User ID. The best passwords are a combination of random letters and numbers. Another solution is to use a word or words that have special meaning to you, surrounding them with numbers that also relate to something in your life. Either way, avoid writing the password down unless you positively cannot memorize it.

Like eBay User IDs, eBay passwords are always reduced to lower case. Therefore, in order to avoid confusing yourself, you might as well use only lower case in your password.

Once you have finished entering all the requested information, click the Continue button.

If your email address is through a pay service like your ISP, you will go directly to Step 2—Agree to Terms.

However, if your email address is with one of the thousands of free email account services such as hotmail.com, yahoo.com (or, in our example, mail.com), you will see a message stating that you will next see a Web page requesting a credit- or debit-card number, name, and billing address.

Since most free or Web-based email accounts do not verify the identity of their subscribers, eBay makes this step necessary in order to verify that the name and address you have provided for your registration are valid (by matching the registration name and address with the name on the card and billing address for the credit or debit card.)

If you do not wish to provide a credit card, and you have an email address that does not come from one of the free, Web-based email services, click the link for "enter a different email address." This will take you back one page so you can edit the email address field.

NOTE: Make sure that the credit- or debit-card billing name and address matches the contact information you provided for the registration. Your credit card will not be charged, nor will it be used for any future billing purposes. eBay uses the billing address and name for the card to match against the name and address you provided for your contact information. The credit card number itself is not kept by eBay. This is important to note because, later, if you register an eBay Seller's Account, you will be asked for a credit card again, which eBay will, at that time, store on your eBay Seller's Account.

Step 2—Agree to Terms

In order to use the eBay site, you must first agree to the eBay User Agreement and Privacy Policy. Take a few moments to read through them and print them out (by clicking the links for Printer-friendly User Agreement and Printer-friendly Privacy Policy).

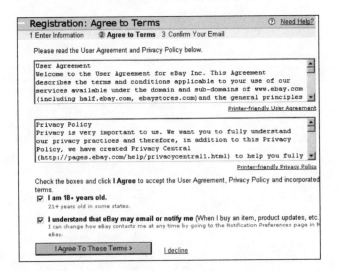

If you have never registered with an online service, you may be unfamiliar with user agreements (also known on other Web sites as Terms of Service agreements).

User agreements are binding contracts. They list the dos and don'ts for both you, the registered user, and also for eBay. The eBay User Agreement is pretty extensive and comprehensive. If you read it carefully, you will get a very clear picture of what responsibilities, activities, and conduct eBay expects from all registered members.

GRIFF TIP! Never take a Web site's User Agreement for granted, including ours. The information contained in the User Agreement can prove invaluable later on. You can always review the text of the eBay User Agreement at **http://pages.ebay.com/help/community/png-user.html**.

Read each section of the User Agreement and check off all of the boxes on this page. All of the boxes must be checked in order to complete your registration!

You also must check the boxes for "I am 18+ years old" and "I understand that eBay may email or notify me." Once you have done so, click the button labeled, "I Agree to These Terms >."

Step 3—Confirm Your Email

This screen informs you that you need to go check your email.

I used an AOL account to register, so I will open my AOL email for **unkiegriff@aol.com**

Here is the email in my AOL New Mail box.

I open it and click on the button for "Complete eBay registration."

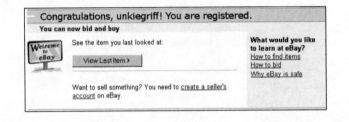

And the registration process is complete!

GRIFF TIP! If your email doesn't display clickable links (AOL, for example), you can go directly to the "User ID and Password" page by going to the eBay Site Map:

On the site map, look for a link labeled "Confirm registration" on the eBay Site Map under the section for Registration in the top middle column of links.

This will take you to the following page, where you enter your email address and the confirmation code contained in the confirmation email.

Changing Your Contact Information

Should you someday move to a new address, you will need to change the address for your eBay registration information.

You can change your contact information at any time by going to your "My eBay" page. The link for "My eBay" can be found on the top of any eBay page.

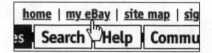

Click the link. If you are not currently signed in, you will be prompted for your eBay User ID and Password. Enter them and click the Sign In button.

Once you are on your "My eBay" page, look for and click the tab for "Preferences" and in the box marked "Personal Information," look for and click the link labeled "Update My Registration Information" under the Address Information heading.

On the next page, make the necessary changes and click the Change Registration Information button.

Review the information to make sure it is accurate. If you are satisfied, click the Submit button.

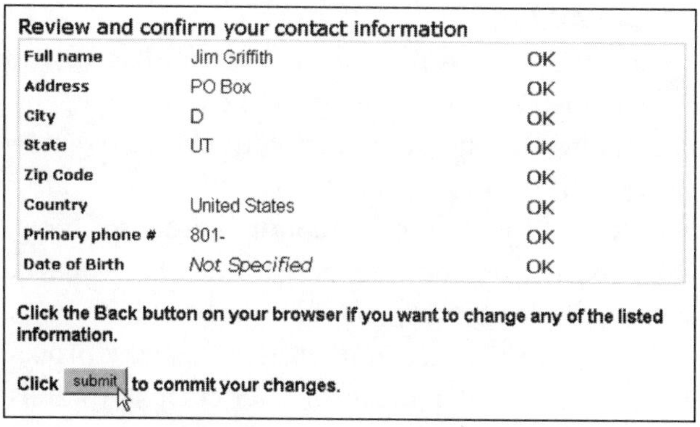

Review and confirm your contact information		
Full name	Jim Griffith	OK
Address	PO Box	OK
City	D	OK
State	UT	OK
Zip Code		OK
Country	United States	OK
Primary phone #	801-	OK
Date of Birth	*Not Specified*	OK

Click the Back button on your browser if you want to change any of the listed information.

Click submit to commit your changes.

Your new contact information is now recorded.

Changing Your User ID, Email Address, or Password

You can change your eBay User ID, your registered email address, and your eBay password from your "My eBay" Preferences page as well.

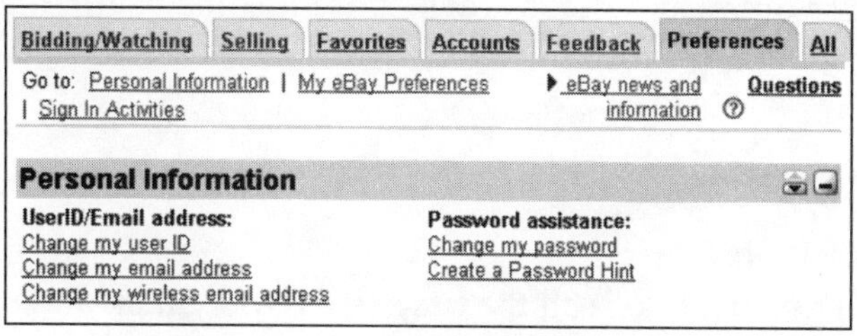

Bidding/Watching	Selling	Favorites	Accounts	Feedback	Preferences	All

Go to: Personal Information | My eBay Preferences   ▶ eBay news and   **Questions**
| Sign In Activities   information ⓧ

Personal Information

UserID/Email address:
Change my user ID
Change my email address
Change my wireless email address

Password assistance:
Change my password
Create a Password Hint

Look for the links on that page for changing your User ID, password, or contact information.

Changing your eBay User ID, email address, or password is nearly as easy as changing your contact information. However, there are some important points you need to know about each.

Changing Your User ID—Tips

When you change your User ID, your old User ID becomes "locked" for a period of thirty days, after which anyone can claim it! Therefore, you should give serious consideration to any changes you make to your current User ID, since once abandoned, you may not be able to get it back.

You can only change your eBay User ID once every thirty days.

Each time you change your eBay User ID, an icon-sized pair of sunglasses will appear next to your new eBay User ID for a period of thirty days.

Changing Your Email Address

You can change the email address for your registration at any time and as often as you like. However, you cannot change it to one that is currently or was previously registered on eBay. If the system rejects your choice of a new email address, you probably registered it sometime in the past and forgot that you had done so.

IMPORTANT! Never register a new account in order to change your email address! If you have established a good feedback profile (more on feedback later) and a noted presence as a seller or bidder, you will not be able to move your feedback from the old account to the new account! Instead, use the process on your "My eBay" page to change your email address for your current, established account.

Changing Your eBay Password

Although you should not need to change your eBay Password, there are cases where doing so is prudent. For example, if you ever suspect that someone has obtained or deciphered your password, you should change it immediately. Again, always create a password that is not obvious. Don't use your pet's name. Create a combination of random letters and numbers. Memorize and avoid having to write it down. If you must write it down, store it somewhere safe and secure. A bank safe-deposit box, for example.

TROUBLESHOOTING

I Forgot My Password!

It happens. Don't panic. I do it all the time. There is a quick and easy process for obtaining a forgotten eBay password. Go to the eBay Site Map.

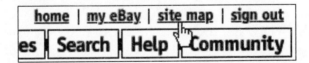

Look on the Site Map for the link labeled, "I Forgot My Password."

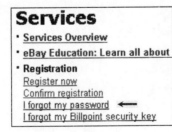

Click it and follow the instructions from there.

I Forgot My User ID!

You can always use your email address in place of your eBay User ID—they are interchangeable. If you use your email address to bid on an item, your User ID will appear after you place your bid.

GRIFF TIP: If you want to recall your eBay User ID without bidding on an item, click on the Search link on the top of any eBay page.

On the sub–navigation bar, click on Find Members.

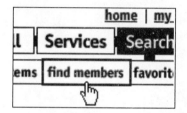

Scroll down to the Feedback Profile section of the page, enter your email address, and click Search.

Feedback Profile
View the Feedback Profile of another member

jimgriffebay@yahoo.com   [Search]
User ID of member

How many feedback comments do you wai
◉ 25 ○ 50 ○ 100 ○ 200 ○ 500

The eBay User ID tied to this email address will appear at the top of your Feedback eBay ID card.

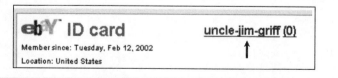

ebY ID card   uncle-jim-griff (0)
Member since: Tuesday, Feb 12, 2002   ↑
Location: United States

2

The eBay Web Site

Navigating the eBay Web Site—A Road Map

The eBay Web site is big. No, that's not quite accurate. The eBay Web site is humongous. Not counting the 12 million–plus separate pages for each item listed on eBay, there are hundreds of other pages containing virtual warehouses of information about eBay. Finding one's way around eBay can sometimes be a daunting task.

But don't despair. You will find navigating eBay is a snap once you have a good grasp of how certain eBay Web pages are grouped together, what they contain, and how they are interconnected.

Let's start with the most important navigation tool, the eBay Navigation Bar.

THE EBAY NAVIGATION BAR

Found at the top of every eBay Web page, the eBay Navigation Bar is gateway central to all areas of eBay.

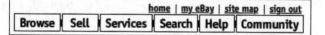

Think of the eBay Navigation Bar as Signpost Central, showing you the route and direction to every single possible place on eBay you might wish to visit.

Whenever you are lost or are searching for a particular area of the eBay Web site, use the navigation bar and the four hyperlinks over the navigation bar to quickly get your bearings.

These are the hyperlinks on the top of the eBay Navigation Bar:

home | my eBay | site map | sign out

These four links point to the four most popular Web pages on eBay Inc.

The eBay home page
Your "My eBay" page
The eBay Site Map
The eBay Sign In page

All of these pages are described in greater detail farther on in this chapter.

Below the links are the boxes that make up level one of the eBay Navigation Bar. When clicked, each of these boxes will take you to the respective main page for "Browse," "Sell," "Services," "Search," "Help," and "Community." In addition to taking you to the main topic page, clicking any one of the boxes will expand the eBay Navigation Bar down one level to display the sub–navigation bar for that topic.

The eBay Navigation Bar has two levels: a top level with six topics and a sub-level for each of the six top-level topics. For example, by clicking the box for "Browse," you are taken to the eBay Main Categories page, where you can view a slightly more expanded view of the main categories on the eBay home page.

home | my eBay | site map | sign in
Browse | Sell | Services | Search | Help | Community
categories | regions | themes | stores

The sub–navigation bar under "Browse" displays four more choices related to browsing eBay: categories, regions, themes, and stores. "Categories" is the current page. "Regions" displays the Local Trading page.

Click on each of the links on the navigation bar and explore each link on the resulting sub–navigation bar. Once you are familiar with these pages, you will be an eBay navigation expert!

Let's look at each of the other links after Browse on the navigation bar.

Subtopics for Sell

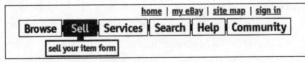

home | my eBay | site map | sign in
Browse | Sell | Services | Search | Help | Community
sell your item form

The **"sell your item form"** is where you go to start listing an item for sale or bid.

Subtopics for Services

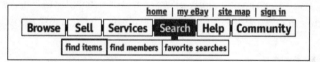

The **"overview"** page contains several links to some of the most popular eBay member services.

"registration" leads to the registration page

"buying and selling" takes you to a hub page for specific buyer and seller tools and tutorials.

"my eBay" is a repeat of the my eBay link on the top line over the Navigation Bar.

"about me" is where you go to create your free eBay home page that's all about you, your business, your collecting or selling interests, etc.

"feedback forum" takes you to a hub page containing all feedback-related links.

"rules & safety" page contains an overview of all the links related to customer-support departments, eBay policies, and special protection and security services.

Subtopics for Search

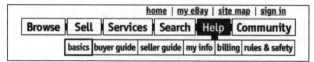

Click on **"find items"** to search by item number, seller, and bidder.

The **"find members"** link leads to a page with forms for learning another user's User ID, contact information, feedback profile, etc.

"Favorite searches" points directly to the "favorites" page in your "My eBay."

Subtopics for Help

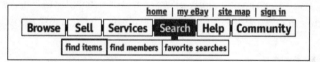

Clicking the Help link will open a pop-up window where you can navigate to any of the other topics under Help on the sub–navigation bar.

Subtopics for Community

				home	my eBay	site map	sign in		
Browse	Sell	Services	Search	Help	Community				
overview	news	chat	newsletter	library	charity	eBay store	about eBay		

The Community "**overview**" page contains all the links related to community, chat, news and announcements, etc.

The "**news**" link takes you to a page containing links to all the news-related pages, press releases, important events, etc.

"**chat**" goes right to the chat board hub page from which you can navigate to any of over ninety separate chat areas.

The contents of the latest online newsletter can be viewed by clicking the "**newsletter**" link.

The "**library**" contains online articles. The material is varied in topic, but they all relate to eBay buying and selling.

For shopping at or selling for a charitable cause, the "**charity**" link will take you to the eBay Charity Home Page.

You can find cool eBay gear, toys, collectibles, and books in the "**eBay-o-rama.**" "eBay-o-rama" also has its own navigation bar to help with finding and purchasing items in the eBay store.

The "**About eBay**" page is eBay's corporate hub page, with links for recent press releases, a company overview, eBay contact information, investor relations, the eBay Foundation, and job postings for open positions at eBay.

THE SIGN IN PAGE

Although you don't need to supply an eBay User Id and password in order to view items, item categories, or to search for items using keywords (Title Search), you will need to supply your User ID and password in order to bid, sell, or visit your "My eBay" page. In order to eliminate the need to keep entering them over and over, eBay provides a one-time sign-in feature.

To sign in, just click the link on the top of any eBay page for "Sign In."

This will take you to the following Sign In page:

Enter your eBay User ID and Password in the boxes provided. To keep your-self signed in indefinitely, check the box for "Keep me signed in on this computer unless I sign out." Then click the Sign In button.

Now you won't have to reenter your eBay User ID and Password each time you bid or list an item, leave feedback, or use your "My eBay" page.

GRIFF TIP! You can change your Sign In preferences using your "My eBay" page. We discuss the "My eBay" page in depth later on in this chapter.

NAVIGATING THE EBAY HOME PAGE

Go to: **http://www.ebay.com**. Many eBay members make the eBay Home Page their browser's start or home page so that it is the first Web page they see when they start their Web browser. Instructions on how to do this are in Chapter 1.

The basic layout of the eBay home page currently looks something like this:

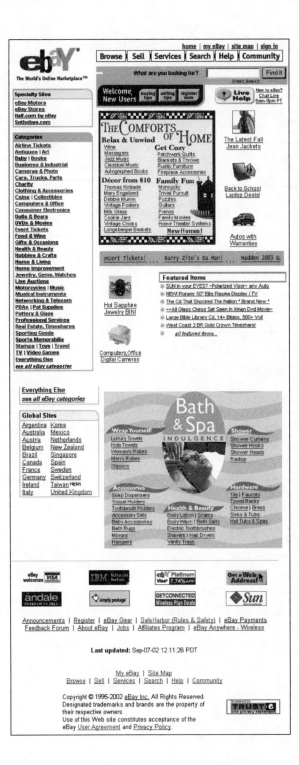

The eBay home page includes a section for searching by keyword at the very top of the page, a place to register in the Welcome New Users section, and a link to the eBay Featured Items (covered in more depth in a following chapter). At the bottom of the home page there are links to third-party service providers.

There's also a series of text links at the bottom of the page:

Announcements | Register | eBay Gear | SafeHarbor (Rules & Safety) | eBay Payments
Feedback Forum | About eBay | Jobs | Affiliates Program | eBay Anywhere - Wireless

These may come in handy someday, so remember where you saw them. One of my favorites is the About eBay page.

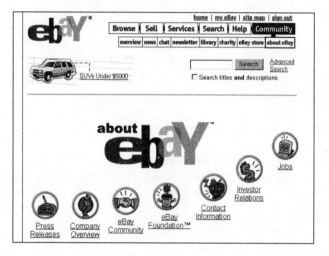

This is the page to visit to read recent eBay press releases, as well as to learn more about eBay Inc., the eBay Foundation, the eBay Community, and current job openings at eBay.

NAVIGATING WITH THE EBAY SITE MAP

Although not the prettiest page on eBay, the eBay Site Map can be the most helpful. Nearly every page on the eBay site can be reached by a link on this page. Think of the site map as your eBay "index" page. If you are ever unable to find a certain eBay page using other navigation methods, don't give up! Try looking on the site map. If it's an eBay page, it's probably on this list.

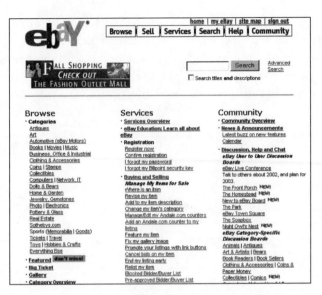

I make it a habit to stop at this page first whenever I can't find a certain eBay Web page. I am always certain to find it again, starting from the site map!

NAVIGATING THE EBAY CATEGORIES—CATEGORY HIERARCHY

There are nearly eighteen thousand separate eBay categories. In order to make navigating them easy, all eighteen thousand are arranged in a hierarchy structure according to topic.

There is more than one way to view the eBay category hierarchy. The most obvious and most popular method is to start from the list of top categories in the left-hand column on the eBay home page.

The links listed on the left under "Categories" represent the top-level categories of the eBay categories.

Navigating eBay categories is a breeze. By clicking any one of these top-level categories, you are directed to that category's "home page" where you can find a list of links for subcategories related to the top-level category. For example, here is a partial view of the "home page" for the Clothing and Accessories category.

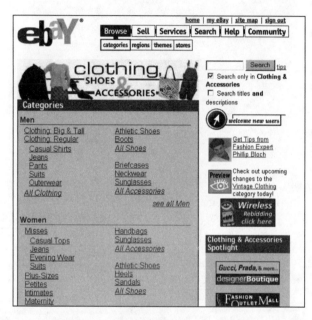

From here, you can view the home pages for any of the Clothing and Accessories subcategories by clicking on their links:

> Women
> Girls
> Infants
> Men
> Boys
> Wedding Apparel

Or you can click on the link for "*see all Clothing and Accessories categories.*" Let's click the link for "Women."

We are now on the Clothing and Accessories: Women home page. From this page, all of the third-level categories are displayed. To view the items in any of the subcategories, just click its corresponding link. Let's click on "Heels, Pumps."

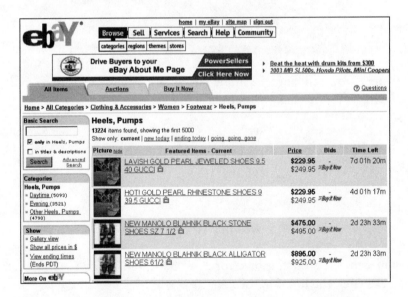

From here, you can start browsing through the category for women's heels and pumps.

GRIFF BROWSING TIP! The Heels, Pumps subcategory page above shows that there are 11,047 items currently listed within this subcategory. It would take several hours to scroll through that many items looking for that special shoe in your size.

You can easily filter these 13,224 items to, say, those that will fit you, by entering your shoe size in the box labeled "Basic Search" and leaving the box for "only in Heels, Pumps" checked. Let's say that I am a size six and a half. Most sellers of shoes will indicate a half size with a decimal point, but some will use fractions. I will enter the following (6.5,6½) into the Basic Search box so that my search will harvest both instances:

Now I only have to browse through 328 items that will all match my shoe size! (We'll dive deeper into the finer points of searching eBay in the next chapter.)

If you plan on revisiting this or any other category, you may want to make it one of your Favorite Categories in "My eBay" (see the "My eBay" section later in this chapter for more information about "My eBay" Favorites.)

eBay Category Overview

Under each of the many main categories on the home page, there are countless subcategories, all grouped together by type, brand name or make. A quick way to view all the subcategories for a top-level category is to go to the Category Overview page.

You can get there from the Site Map

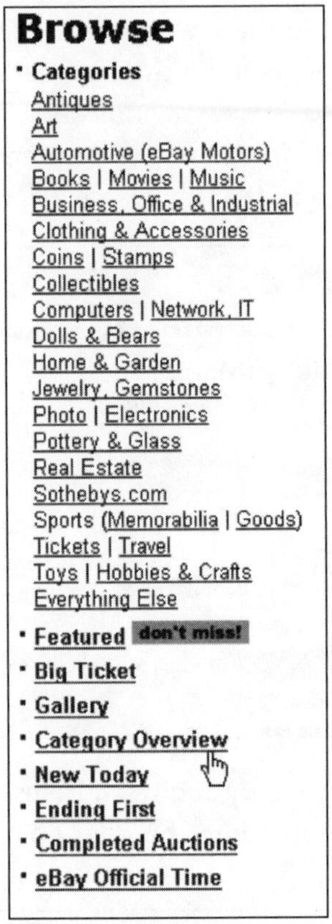

		home	my eBay	site map	sign out
Browse	Sell	Services	Search	Help	Community

Browse

- **Categories**
  Antiques
  Art
  Automotive (eBay Motors)
  Books | Movies | Music
  Business, Office & Industrial
  Clothing & Accessories
  Coins | Stamps
  Collectibles
  Computers | Network, IT
  Dolls & Bears
  Home & Garden
  Jewelry, Gemstones
  Photo | Electronics
  Pottery & Glass
  Real Estate
  Sothebys.com
  Sports (Memorabilia | Goods)
  Tickets | Travel
  Toys | Hobbies & Crafts
  Everything Else

- **Featured** `don't miss!`
- **Big Ticket**
- **Gallery**
- **Category Overview**
- **New Today**
- **Ending First**
- **Completed Auctions**
- **eBay Official Time**

You can also get there from the navigation bar

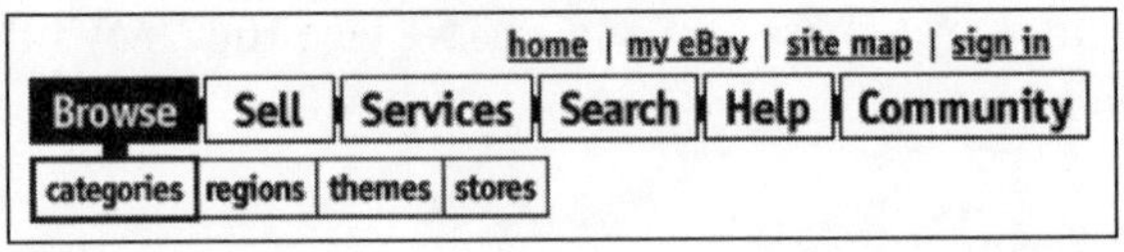

		home	my eBay	site map	sign in
Browse	Sell	Services	Search	Help	Community
categories	regions	themes	stores		

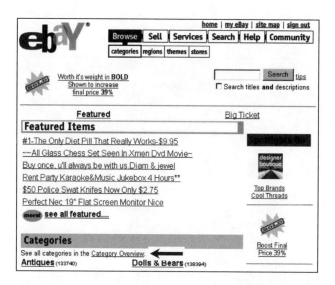

In the first few years of eBay, the Category Overview page displayed the entire hierarchy of categories, but as they have grown in number (now approaching eighteen thousand categories in total!) we have divided them up into separate overview pages for each top-level category. The numbers in parentheses next to each category are the actual number of items for sale in that category.

To select a category to view, click on one of the links on the first Category Overview page:

By default, the first category displayed is Antiques:

Under the main category for Antiques, there is a plethora of related subcategories, for example, Antiquities, Maps, Atlases, Furniture, Rugs and Carpets, etc. Some of these have one, two, and in the case of Silver, three subcategory levels.

The Category Overview page is an excellent way to search for those sublevels in the category hierarchy that contain items of interest to you.

NAVIGATING THE EBAY ITEM DESCRIPTION PAGE

We've seen how browsing through categories can take us to specific subcategories where we can more easily find particular treasure that piques our interest. On eBay, all items are displayed in a list. Currently, we are looking at a category list for Antiques > Rugs, Carpets.

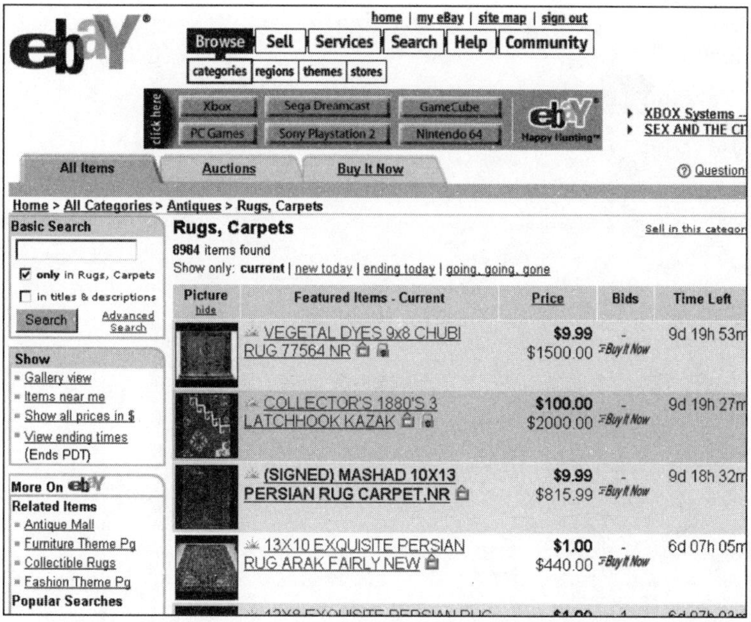

(Later we will cover search lists that look almost exactly like category lists. Item titles are displayed the same way in both.)

Each item title in a category list is a clickable link. To view an individual item, you simply click on the item title wherever it appears in a category or search list. I searched through the Rugs, Carpets category pages and found this intriguing gallery picture and title.

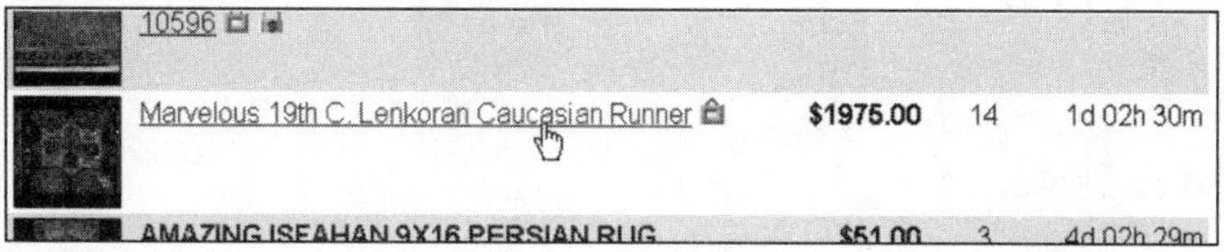

Clicking on the title will open up the Item Description Page for that particular item.

There are four major sections to every Item Description page.

Title
Description
Payment
Bidding

A typical Item Description page looks like this:

home | my eBay | site map | sign out

Browse | Sell | Services | Search | Help | Community

item view

Marvelous 19th C. Lenkoran Caucasian Runner
Item # 903760368

Antiques:Rugs, Carpets

Currently	US $1,975.00 (reserve not yet met)	First bid	US $500.00
Quantity	1	# of bids	14 bid history
Time left	1 days, 2 hours +	Location	Arlington, VA
		Country/Region	United States /Washington
Started	Sep-01-02 17:33:23 PDT	Mail this auction to a friend	
Ends	Sep-06-02 17:33:23 PDT	Watch this item	
		Featured Plus! Auction	
Seller (Rating)	haroz (238) ★		
	view comments in seller's Feedback Profile	view seller's other items	ask seller a question		
High bid	o_mandarim (411) ★		
Payment	Money Order/Cashiers Checks Personal Checks Other online payment services		
Shipping	Buyer pays for all shipping costs. Seller ships internationally (worldwide).		
Seller Services	Sell similar item		
Item Revised	To review revisions made to this item by the seller, click here .		

Seller assumes all responsibility for listing this item. You should contact the seller to resolve any questions before bidding.
Auction currency is U.S. dollars (US $) unless otherwise noted.

Description

This spectacular 19th century Lenkoran runner is a riot of color. The field has three Lenkoran calyx medallions alternating with two gabled rectangular medallions similar to those of Fachralo Kazak rugs. These are all separated by pairs of smaller octagonal "Turkmen" style medallions. Size is 42 by 117" (107cm x297cm).

Colors are marvelous, all natural, bright, well saturated. This has what I think of as the "Genge" color palette. It has two different hues that are apparently derived from cochineal, or perhaps from combining cochineal and madder (one of these is a more typical darker cochineal color, the other is a lovely plum). These colors are not uncommon in Lenkoran rugs. The pictures here were all taken outside in natural light (not direct sun) with a Nikon Coolpix 950, and appear on my monitor to be close to reality.

The pile is very good, probably virtually original length, over much of the rug. The dark brown/black is shorter due to dye corrosion. This gives a nice three-dimensional effect to the outer blue and black reciprocal border. This is also the ground color of the field, and some of this dark background has been repiled. There are 3 or 4 small rewoven areas in the field and at one corner (click link for picture 10 below); these small repairs are very professionally done and are hard to find from the front.

The sides and ends are original. One end has most of the original end finish, in which there are black and green strips of soumak weave (about a half inch altogether-this shows in one of the detail pictures), and then the warps are plaited into a flat braid, about three quarters of which is intact. The other end has some remnants of the soumak and is otherwise just warp fringe at the edge of the pile. The side finish is a three cord flat selvage wrapped with green, blue and red tightly-spun wool. These side finishes are original and mostly still present, but worn and a tattered in some places, and in need of some repair. I will happily answer any questions.

On Sep-02-02 at 09:16:19 PDT, seller added the following information:

Pay me securely with any major credit card through PayPal!

Payment Details	Payment Instructions
See Payment Instructions and item description, or contact seller for more information.	See item description or contact seller for more information.

Bidding

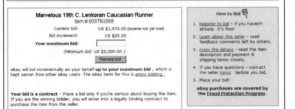

Marvelous 19th C. Lenkoran Caucasian Runner
Item # 903760368

Current bid:	US $1,975.00 (reserve not yet met)
Bid increment:	US $25.00
Your maximum bid:	

(Minimum bid: US $2,000.00)

Review bid

eBay will bid incrementally on your behalf **up to your maximum bid** , which is kept secret from other eBay users. The eBay term for this is proxy bidding .

Your bid is a contract - Place a bid only if you're serious about buying the item. If you are the winning bidder, you will enter into a legally binding contract to purchase the item from the seller.

How to Bid

1. Register to bid - if you haven't already. It's free!
2. Learn about this seller - read feedback comments left by others.
3. Know the details - read the item description and payment & shipping terms closely.
4. If you have questions - contact the seller haroz before you bid.
5. Place your bid!

eBay purchases are covered by the Fraud Protection Program.

The **Title** section of the Item Description Page, directly under the bar containing the item's title, is where you find the basic information about the item, such as the current high bid, time and date of the listing's closing, and so on.

The Title section of the page also contains links to view the bid history for that item, to send an email to the seller, to view the seller's other listings, and to mail the listing to a friend.

The **Description** section is just below the Title section. The seller provides everything that appears in this section, including text, pictures, and any fancy layout or graphics. There is no limit to how much text or how many pictures a seller can include within the Description section.

Underneath the Description, you will find the **Payment** section, which displays the payment options the seller selected for this item.

Finally, the **Bid** section is where you enter the amount of either your bid or, if the seller provided a Buy It Now option for instant purchase and you decide simply to buy the item outright without bidding, the Buy It Now price.

"My eBay"

There is no other page on eBay that provides such a fantastic array of services for the individual buyer or seller as "My eBay."

From your "My eBay" page, you can keep track of all your current and recent bidding and selling activity; your feedback; your eBay favorite searches, sellers, and stores; as well as your eBay email notice preferences, your account setup, your contact information, and the custom "My eBay" preferences as well.

To go to your "My eBay" page, simply click the link for "My eBay" located on the top of any eBay page.

If you have not signed in yet, you will be prompted to do so. Fill in your User ID and password and click the Sign In button.

Your "My eBay" page will show seven separate clickable tabs along the top of the page:

By clicking any of these tabs, you will bring up the associated page.

Since I am primarily a buyer, I tend to use the Bidding/Watching, Favorites, and Feedback pages the most.

Let's take a look at the Bidding/Watching page first.

NOTE: The default setting for displaying data in a My eBay page is two days back. You may view activity for any number of days up to thirty by changing the number in the box next to the appropriate section.

Items I've Bid On

Items I'm Bidding On (2 Items)

√ = Items you're currently winning   ✗ = Items you're not currently winning
Multiple Item Auctions (Dutch Auctions) do not use color coding.

All item details

Item #	Start Price	Current Price	My Max Bid	Qty	# of Bids	Start Date	(PST) End Date	Time Left
Old Lead Couple on Bench								
1764043984	$2.99	$2.99 √	$15.67	1	1	Sep-02	Sep-09 19:13:49	2d 3h 30m
ca.1870 bidjar-garrus-wagireh ca.1870								
905207160	$1.00	$1,100.00 ✗	$657.89	1	11	Sep-06	Sep-13 08:32:12	5d 16h 49m
Page total: (Items I'm winning)	$2.99	$2.99	$15.67	1	1			

< Previous ‖ Showing Items 1 - 2 of 2 ‖ Next >
Back to top ↵

All of your current bids will show in this section, with each item on a separate row. One of the best uses of this section is to check your maximum bid amounts.

In addition, any listings where you are a bidder but have been outbid will show the bid amount in red as an alert so that you can consider a new bid.

Items I've Won

Items I've Won (1 Item)

▶ Show items for past [2] days [Go]   (30 days max)   ☐ 🔖 Save this setting

Select (all)	Item #	(PST) End Date	End Price	Qty	Seller	Next Steps / Status	Leave Feedback
☐ PORTLAND MAINE GENERAL STORE LEDGER 1876							
	902472818	Sep-06 12:36:03	$91.00	1	saznj	Paid 🖼	Leave Feedback
[Delete] selected items							
		Page total: (Items I've won)	$91.00	1			

< Previous ‖ Showing Items 1 - 1 of 1 ‖ Next >
Back to top ↵

Directly under your current bids, you can view the items that you have won. The fields for Items You've Won show you the End Price, the quantity, the seller's User ID (which, if you click it, will display the seller's email address), the status of the transaction (paid, request total, total requested, etc.), and a Leave Feedback link for each transaction.

Items I Didn't Win

Items I Didn't Win (0 Items)

▶ Show items for past [4] days [Go]   (30 days max)   ☐ 🔖 Save this setting

No items currently appear within this section. If you can't see any items, try increasing the number of days in the "Show items..." box above and then click the Go button.

Back to top ↵

This section displays items where you were a bidder but were outbid and subsequently the listing closed, with you as a losing bidder. This is helpful in that you can use the links to the right of the item title to view that seller's other current items or view similar items.

Items I'm Watching

Finally, we reach one of my favorite features of the Bidding/Watching page.

Sometimes, I find intriguing items that I may wish to bid on later instead of now. Each item page has a link to click to put the particular item on your "My eBay" watch list.

The link above shows that currently, I am watching thirteen items. The limit of items allowable on one watch list is thirty.

Here is a watch list for my account on September 07, 2002.

You can delete items from your watch list by checking the box to the left of the item number and then clicking the Delete button.

You can go directly to an item on your Watch list by clicking the item title or the Bid Now button for that item on the far right-hand corner.

The other columns display the current bid amount for the item and the closing date and time.

Additionally, if you check the appropriate setting for Item Watch Reminder in your email notification, you will receive an email once a day, alerting you to the items on your watch list that are set to close within the next twenty-four hours so you can go make a bid before it's too late!

> **GRIFF TIP!** As a constant eBay bidder, I would be lost without the "My eBay" Bidding/Watching page. If you are primarily a bidder, I urge you to make this page one of your favorite places and make a habit of visiting every time you come to eBay.

TRACKING YOUR EBAY SELLING

The "My eBay" Selling page is similar to the Bidding/Watching page except that instead of tracking bids and a Watch list, it tracks an eBay seller's Current and Closed listings.

Select (all)	Item #	(PST) End Date	Last Sale	End Price	Qty	High Bidder(s)	Next Steps/Status	Payment Reminder	Feedback	Relist
19th Century American Redware Ovoid Jug										
☐	903152205	Sep-05	--	$202.50	1	debbie653	Invoice Sent	Available in 3 days	Leave Feedback	Relist
19th C. American Redware Ovoid Jug										
☐	903159645	Sep-05	--	$51.00	1	ragmandon	Invoice Sent	Available in 3 days	Leave Feedback	Relist
19th C. American Redware Storage Jar										
☐	903168707	Sep-05	--	$38.75	1	themomms	Paid	Available in 3 days	Leave Feedback	Relist
19 Cent American Redware Ovoid Jar										
☐	903173112	Sep-05	--	$53.00	1	chie993	Invoice Sent	Available in 3 days	Leave Feedback	Relist
Page Totals: (Sold items)				$345.25	4					

We cover the "My eBay" Selling page in greater depth in Section Two of the book. For now, just keep it in mind.

The next "My eBay" page is Favorites, which is definitely my favorite! On this page, you can select up to four favorite categories to display; you can save up to fifteen title searches for easy access, three of which you can select to receive one-a-day email alerts whenever new items are listed that match one of up to three of your possible fifteen saved searches criteria; and finally, you can save a list of your favorite sellers or stores.

Since my "My eBay" Favorites page is rather full, I have broken it up into separate screens to better illustrate each section:

You can add categories to your Favorite Categories list by clicking the "Add/Change Categories" link. To delete categories from the list, check the box next to the category you wish to delete and click the Delete button.

Directly below the Favorite Categories section you'll find the Favorite Searches.

To add a "Favorite Search" to your list, click on the link labeled "Add new Search" on the top right-hand side of the table.

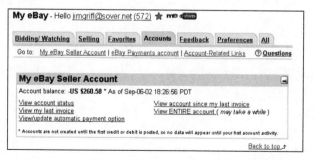

To delete a search, check the box next to it and click the Delete button.

You can select up to three of your saved Favorite Searches for daily email alerts by checking the box on the far right-hand column on the same line as that search and then clicking the Submit button.

We delve deeper into the intricacies of Search (both creating and saving) in a later chapter.

TRACKING YOUR EBAY ACCOUNTS

The "My eBay" Accounts page is used by sellers to track the fees they are charged for selling. We explore this page in greater detail in Section Two of this book, "Selling the eBay Way!"

TRACKING FEEDBACK

When you use eBay to buy or sell something from another eBay member, both of you can leave a public record of your transaction, indicating your satisfaction (or lack thereof) with the other party.

These comments are called feedback. Each eBay member has a feedback profile easily reached for viewing by clicking the number in parentheses next to any member's eBay User ID.

We discuss the intricacies of eBay Feedback in a later section. For now, note that viewing your feedback and the feedback you need to leave can all be accomplished most easily using "My eBay." On your "My eBay" page, click the tab marked "Feedback."

My eBay - Hello jimgriff@sover.net (572) ☆ me ‹stores›

| Bidding/Watching | Selling | Favorites | Accounts | Feedback | Preferences | All |

Go to: My Feedback

? Questions

Leaving Feedback Links

Need to leave feedback? Find all listings from the past 90 days that need your feedback.

[Leave Feedback]

▸ Review and respond to feedback about me
▸ See all feedback I have left about others

ebY ID card jimgriff@sover.net (572) ☆ me ‹stores›

Member since: Monday, May 20, 1996
Location: United States

Summary of Most Recent Comments

	Past 7 days	Past month	Past 6 mo.
Positive	1	8	93
Neutral	0	0	0
Negative	0	0	0
Total	**1**	**8**	**93**
Bid Retractions	0	0	0

My Feedback (669 Items)

User: saznj (1119) ☆   Date: Sep-06-02 12:55:18 PDT   Item: 902472818
Praise: LIGHTNING FAST PAYMENT AND EXCELLENT COMMUNICATION! THANK YOU JIM! A++++++++++++

User: tdovnn (304) ☆ ‹stores›   Date: Aug-26-02 08:43:11 PDT   Item: 1372574274
Praise: VeryFastPayment, Ebay Asset. Hope to have business with Thanks((((A+++++)))))

User: alex~z (425) ☆   Date: Aug-25-02 06:21:15 PDT   Item: 1372624360
Praise: Fast response and payment - thank you! A+++ reliable buyer!

User: rosavpc (948) ☆ me   Date: Aug-18-02 17:04:33 PDT   Item: 2123292455
Praise: Fast payment, great communication, fast and friendly emails. Great buyer. A+!!

User: corrieloom (90) ☆   Date: Aug-15-02 21:16:31 PDT   Item: 895737407

The "My eBay" Feedback page displays all the feedback left for you, with the most recent on the top of the list. (You will be so proud the day you get your first feedback. I have heard from new members who wept with joy when they got theirs. We have some very emotional members.)

GRIFF TIP! There is one extremely important tool on this page that bears highlighting. At the top of the "My eBay" Feedback page is a box labeled "Leaving Feedback Links."

My eBay - Hello jimgriff@sover.net (572) ⭐ me stores

Bidding/Watching Selling Favorites Accounts Feedback Prefe

Go to: My Feedback

Leaving Feedback Links
Need to leave feedback? Find all listings from the past 90 days that need your feedback.

[Leave Feedback] ⟵

▶ Review and respond to feedback about me
▶ See all feedback I have left about others

In the box, "Feedback-Related Links," there is button labeled "Leaving Feedback Links." This will take you to a page containing the following text and button:

Find all transactions
Find transactions completed in the past 90 days for which you have not left feedback yet.

[Find all transactions in the past 90 days]

Clicking the button takes you to the following page:

You have 14 feedback comments to leave.
Showing comments 1 to 14.

Find User [   ] [Go!]   Find Item# [   ] [Go!]

User ID	Item#	Item	Ended
weakfish (sesqui1926@aol.com) (2269) ⭐	2122614896	MA LAWRENCE HOOD SCHOOL	Jul-25-02 19:39:50 PDT

Is your comment positive, negative or neutral?
○ positive ○ negative ○ neutral ● **Don't leave feedback now**

[   ]
Your comment (max. 80 characters)

| **saldixie** (nhdixie1@aol.com) (383) ⭐ | 2129416353 | Congregational Church & YMCA Lawrence Mass | Aug-08-02 11:20:54 PDT |

Is your comment positive, negative or neutral?
○ positive ○ negative ○ neutral ● **Don't leave feedback now**

[   ]
Your comment (max. 80 characters)

| **laboheme1** (laboheme1@earthlink.net) (2224) ⭐ me stores | 2132236503 | VINTAGE IRRIDESCENT RED SUSPENDERS I DEADSTOCK | Aug-24-02 07:34:57 PDT |

Is your comment positive, negative or neutral?
○ positive ○ negative ○ neutral ● **Don't leave feedback now**

[   ]
Your comment (max. 80 characters)

You can now scroll down this page, entering feedback comments for all those listings you select.

This little-known and little-used feature makes leaving feedback an easy task as opposed to a confusing chore.

Do make a note of this feature for later reference. This and the fine art of leaving and receiving feedback are examined in depth in an upcoming chapter.

SETTING YOUR EBAY PREFERENCES

Your eBay registration has many possible facets. All eBay member registrations include a User ID, an email address, a password, and contact information. In addition, if you are a seller you will either have a credit card on file or will have been ID verified. You may also choose to receive or to decline various types of email from eBay. All of these are grouped together as your eBay Preferences. You can change these preferences at any time by clicking the Preferences tab in "My eBay."

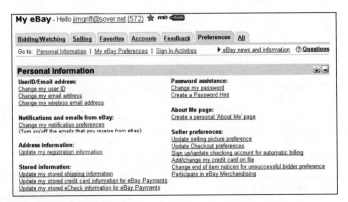

This is an extremely handy page. Here, you can read up on eBay news, view and change your Personal Information, create your About Me page (covered later in the book), and update or change your Selling information.

You can also customize the way your "My eBay" page is displayed.

Finally, you can configure your Sign In Activities preferences. Note one of the settings above:

> **You have *not* selected the following activities:**
>
> **Preferred Sign-in Method**
> • eBay User Id and password

I want to change this setting to keep me signed in to eBay until I sign out, otherwise I will automatically be signed out after a certain period of time.

To make the change, I click the link on the top left-hand side of the Sign In Activities table:

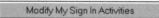

This takes me to the following page:

> **Edit your sign in options**
>
> **Sign in options**
> ☑ Bidding and buying – Remember my User ID and password for bidding and buying
> ☑ Selling – Remember my User ID and password for selling
>
> ☑ Keep me signed in on this computer until I sign out (Available only when you select the eBay preferred sign in method below.)
>
> Note: For your protection, updating personal information or financial information will always require that you enter your User ID and password.
>
> **Display Settings**
> ☑ See email addresses when viewing User IDs – if you are involved in a transaction. Learn more
>
> **Preferred sign in method**
> I prefer to sign-in to eBay using:
> ⦿ eBay User ID and password
> ○ Microsoft Passport
>
> Save changes
>
> Cancel

I checked the box next to "Keep me signed in on this computer . . ." and click the Save Changes button.

Now when I Sign In to eBay, my computer will stay signed in until I decide to Sign Out.

One very important link to mention on the Preferences/Setup page is the "Change my notification preferences" link.

Notifications and emails from eBay:
Change my notification preferences
(Turn on/off the emails that you receive from eBay)

Click it to view the next page:

Billing Emails

✔ **Invoice**
Send me monthly invoice.

Billing Emails Delivery Format
◉ Get Text-Only Email
○ Get HTML Email

Legal and Other Emails

Note: These may take up to 14 days to be updated. Delivery format varies.

☐ **User Agreement Changes**
Notify me if the current User Agreement changes.

☐ **Privacy Policy Changes**
Notify me if the current Privacy Policy changes.

☐ **Special Promotions, Offers and Events**
Send me notices from eBay about special offers for eBay members.
Note: if you are a PowerSeller, unchecking this box excludes you from PowerSeller Marketing Communications.

⑤ **Sothebys.com Promotional Updates**
Send me promotional updates on special auctions and events through email and direct mail from Sothebys.com in accordance with Sothebys.com Privacy Policy.
Click to subscribe/unsubscribe.

☐ **eBay Product Surveys**
Send me occasional surveys to help eBay evaluate new features and proposed changes to eBay services.

Other Contacts

Note: These may take up to 14 days to be updated.

☐ **Telemarketing Calls**
I would like to receive calls from eBay regarding eBay-related products and services.

☐ **Direct Mail**
Send me eBay product and service related direct mail (through the postal service).

[Save my Changes]   [Cancel]

This page contains a long list of possible email notices you can receive. You can choose to receive any one of them by checking the box next to the option. Leave that box unchecked if you do not want to receive a particular type of email notice.

Once you have checked or unchecked the options of your choice, click the Save My Changes button on the top of the page to reset your email preferences to your new preferred settings.

The Feedback Forum

To the first pioneering eBay buyers and sellers back in late 1995 and early 1996, the infant eBay Web site proved to be a nearly perfect trading platform, where individuals could trade with each other directly through the time-old tradition of the auction format.

An enterprising new eBay seller could set up listings in a matter of minutes, and within days that seller would be completing successful transactions, usually with a buyer whom she had never met. As eBay's founder, Pierre Omidyar, stated on the old Web site, it was all truly based on trust. A seller trusted that a high bidder would honor her bid and send payment and a buyer trusted a seller to send him the merchandise.

The system had one glaring deficiency: After an eBay sale was completed, the buyer and seller had no mechanism for telling the world how the transaction went. You could complete many transactions, but no one else on eBay would know that you were someone who could be trusted based on your prior successful transactions.

And so it was that within about six months after the introduction of the eBay/AuctionWeb, Pierre created a system where members could leave comments about other eBay members from whom they had bought or sold.

READING FEEDBACK

Simply put, the eBay Feedback Forum is a mechanism whereby a registered eBay member could leave a public comment about any other registered eBay member. All feedback left for a member can be viewed by clicking the number in parentheses next to that member's user ID wherever the User ID appears.

jimgriff@sover.net (572) ⭐ me 〈stores〉

You can also view feedback for a member by clicking on the Search link on the eBay Navigation bar, then clicking Find Members.

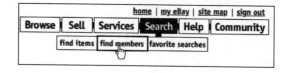

home | my eBay | site map | sign out
Browse | Sell | Services | Search | Help | Community
find items | find members | favorite searches

Scroll down the page to the Feedback Profile box and enter that member's User ID or email address.

Either way will take you to that member's Feedback Profile. Here is my Feedback Profile:

The Feedback Profile page consists of three parts: overall profile makeup, ID card, and a paginated list of all the comments ever left for that member.

Three important facts about eBay Feedback:

1. From the beginning of the Feedback Forum, there have been three types of comments from which a member can select: positive, neutral, and negative. Besides the type of comment, a member can also type a text comment of up to eighty characters.

2. Everyone who starts out on eBay begins with a feedback rating of zero. Each positive feedback comment left for another member increases his feedback rating (the number in parentheses) up one point. Each negative

decreases his rating one point. A neutral comment does not count for or against a person's feedback rating.

3. The same user can increment or decrement another user's feedback score only one point in either direction. A user can leave successive comments for the same user (if he has future transactions with that person) and those comments could be a combination of positive and negative, but they will not move the other user's feedback score up or down more than one point.

HOW TO READ A FEEDBACK "OVERALL PROFILE MAKEUP"

Here is the "overall profile makeup" for my eBay registration:

> **Overall profile makeup**
> **659** positives. **572** are from unique users and count toward the final rating.
>
> **10** neutrals. **10** were converted from users <u>no longer registered</u> .
>
> **1** negatives. **1** are from unique users and count toward the final rating.

Since May 20, 1996, I have received a total of 659 positive comments in my feedback profile. Five hundred seventy-two are from unique users. Eighty-seven of the 588 positive comments were from users with whom I have had more than one transaction. An eBay member can only increment another eBay member's feedback score once. Any subsequent feedback left for that member will not raise that member's score. Thus, though the comments for these 87 positive feedbacks are displayed on the long list of feedback comments, they do not count toward my total score.

I received 1 negative (way back in 1996).

I also have 10 neutrals, all of which were once positive comments that were converted to neutral when the members who left them were suspended by eBay. This is an old feature and is no longer in effect.

In its original incarnation, the ability to leave a comment for another eBay member was unlimited. You could leave a comment for anyone just to tell the rest of the world just how wonderful he or she was. Unfortunately, it was also possible to leave unlimited negative feedback comments for another eBay member, deserved or not. Although the majority of community members maintained only the highest standards of conduct on the Feedback Forum, a few bad apples did cause otherwise innocent eBay members some major headaches.

For a short time, a remedy to this problem was implemented that effectively wiped out the score of any suspended eBay member. The comments remained but the type was changed from negative or positive to neutral.

Still, this remedy proved to be only a partial panacea. Since fairness dictated that *all* of the feedback, both positive and negative, left by a suspended member be changed to neutral, many eBay members would wake up one day and see that their feedback score had *decreased* overnight.

As always, eBay members came up with the best solution: tie all feedback to an eBay transaction. And so eBay eventually agreed to limit the ability to leave feedback to only the buyer and seller of a closed listing. At the same time, the policy of changing the feedback for suspended users to neutral was abandoned. As shown by my overall makeup, evidence of this old policy is still displayed for some longtime members.

FEEDBACK ID CARD

A member's Feedback ID card tells you many things about that member. For example, when she became a member, if she uses ID Verify,* and the country from which she registered.

Also, the Summary of Most Recent Comments breaks down how many of what type of comment the member has received in the last week, the last month, and the last six months.

Notice the link for Bid Retractions. All bid retractions a member makes are listed on a page accessible via the Bid Retraction link in the ID Card.

Just below the card are four links, one for visiting the "My eBay" Store, one for my Auctions, one to view my ID History (where you can view any previous User IDs I used for this account), and one to view all Feedback I have left for others.

---

*ID Verify is an eBay feature that uses a third party to cross-check the information a user provides and verifies that information for accuracy. The ID Verify feature is covered in Section Two.

FEEDBACK COMMENTS

Below the ID card and the overall profile makeup, all of the feedback comments for that member are listed.

By default, comments are displayed twenty-five per page. You can change the number of comments displayed per page by scrolling down to the bottom of the first page of comments and selecting from the options provided:

The numbers in parentheses are the individual pages of twenty-five comments each. You can navigate to any of these pages by clicking the page number.

In addition, there is a link here for "leave feedback" for me and a link to "Respond to comments."

Let's break down the information contained within one feedback comment:

The comment above was left by har1986 on April 3, 2002 at 8:12 Pacific Standard Time. The comment was about item 707217972. You can view the item itself by clicking the item number. The item is only viewable as long as the link is clickable (about ninety days). The *B* indicates that I was the buyer in this transaction.

Another more recent enhancement to the feedback system was the ability for members to comment on feedback left for them. The comment appears directly under the original feedback comment for that item.

jimgriff@sover.net (572) ⭐ me stores	Apr-01-02 14:34:02 PST	152316903
Praise : Extremely satisfied with this transaction. Perfect item. Thanks!		
Response by guyb62 - Knows what he wants! A REAL PRO!! Thanks alot!		

In addition, the person who left the comment can also respond to the recipient's response. This allows for some back and forth between two members.

LEAVING FEEDBACK

A buyer or seller can leave feedback for any eBay member with whom he has a closed eBay transaction. There are two ways to begin: from the closed item page and from "My eBay." The process for leaving feedback using "My eBay" is described earlier in this chapter in the "My eBay" section.

Leaving Feedback from the Closed Item Page

The Closed Item page is simply the item page for a closed listing or Buy It Now item. You can get to a Closed Item page via item number, from your completed item list in Search as Bidder or Seller, or from your "My eBay" Bidding/Watching page.

On the Title section of every eBay Closed Item page, there will be an Icon you can click to leave feedback for the other party in the closed transaction:

THE IMPORTANCE OF FEEDBACK

All eBay members place enormous importance on their feedback. On eBay, feedback is considered by most to be the currency of an eBay member's reputation. Feedback promotes accountability and good trading ethics among all eBay members, buyers and sellers alike.

Feedback Protocol—Who Goes First?

For most members, leaving feedback is a crucial duty. However, there is no set protocol regarding who should leave feedback first. Normally, the seller leaves it for the buyer once the seller has received the buyer's payment. The buyer never leaves feedback until she has received the item. Over the past few years, I have noticed that many sellers will not leave feedback for a buyer until the buyer has done so for them, an unfortunate trend. Still, it really doesn't matter who leaves feedback first as long as someone does so.

Keep a Civil Tongue!

The vast majority of all eBay transactions end with satisfied buyers and sellers. However, if by some chance you need to leave a less-than-positive comment, don't do so in anger! Remember that feedback left cannot be removed (except under specific circumstances outlined later). It never pays to leave a belligerent comment. State your case clearly and concisely. A general rule of thumb: Never post a feedback comment you would be ashamed to show your mother.

Positive Feedback

If you do your homework and bid with trusted eBay sellers who provide professional, easy-to-understand, comprehensive item descriptions and payment/shipping terms as well as clear photos of their items, all of your eBay transactions should be flawless. Let the world know by leaving your trading partner a glowing positive feedback.

eBay member Craig Knouse provided a few examples of simple but concise positive comments.

"Item was even better than described. I'm very pleased with this deal."
"Thanks again, I'll be happy to refer more eBay customers to you in the future."
"Thanks for the opportunity to buy this outstanding item. You really made my day!"
"I was very impressed by this seller's professionalism and commitment. Thanks!"

A few tips:

Use as many of the eighty character spaces as you can. With a little ingenuity, you can get a lot of praise and information into eighty spaces.

Leave out punctuation. It takes up valuable room from the eighty-character-limit space that is better served with actual words.

Avoid using any part of a member's contact information, like his name or phone number.

Never post an email address or Web address in a feedback comment.

Negative Feedback—the Last Resort

Your eBay transaction didn't go as smoothly as you'd hoped. The item arrived broken or was not as described. The seller used soiled packing materials. The bidder or seller hasn't responded to your emails. The item or payment is late in arriving. The receipt shows that the shipping cost was a lot less than what the seller charged you.

Stop. Take a deep breath. The world is not a perfect place. Sometimes things go awry. Sometimes, sellers make mistakes.

Only leave negative feedback as a last resort. Contact is crucial! Email the other party and, using all the diplomatic skills you possess, try to work out a solution. Let her know your concerns.

The item arrived broken? Many sellers buy insurance as a habit. Contact him via email. Let him know the item arrived damaged.

The item isn't as described? Even those sellers who state "no returns" will exhibit more flexibility if you state your case with respect and with no aggression.

The packing materials were soiled or the packing was imperfect. Let the seller know your feelings in a polite and helpful email.

Your bidder or seller hasn't responded? A faulty email system or address could be the culprit. Request the contact information (phone number) of the other party and give him a call.

The item or payment has not yet arrived? Email the seller or buyer and let her know. No delivery system is perfect.

You feel you were overcharged for shipping? Let the seller know (again, in a polite and nonaggressive email) and perhaps suggest that she state her shipping terms more explicitly in her descriptions so that bidders will not be unpleasantly surprised by the higher-than-necessary shipping costs.

As always, be polite. Nine times out of ten, you will find that diplomacy, civility, and tact are more effective at resolving difficulties than a hasty negative comment.

If all of the above fail and you have to leave negative feedback as a last resort, keep in mind what longtime eBay member Tim Heidner ("just_ducky") has to say about leaving negative feedback:

1. Never, under any circumstances, leave feedback when you are angry. Take a break and think about what you want to say. Don't be a hothead. It can scare away future users.
2. Don't embellish. Stick to the facts.
3. Keep it within your transaction. Don't bring up other problems this person has had. You don't know the circumstances regarding other feedback left for this person. It might not be true.
4. Don't use profanity. We are adults. Profanity only shows how immaturely you react in a situation.
5. Be respectful. Remember this is still a person. It is possible to leave negative feedback in a respectable way.

Communication is a two-way street. How you say something may tell a story about someone else, but it could speak volumes about you.

The majority of feedback left on eBay is positive, but occasionally a customer or seller may not be pleased with his trading partner's behavior and will let the world know with a neutral or negative comment. In most cases where someone has left a negative comment, the other party will respond in kind.

Over the past five years, I have fielded many an email from an unhappy person who is distraught to have received what he believes to be an undeserved negative comment. A "retaliatory" negative feedback comment may sting at first, but it is a necessary risk that all eBay members must assume if feedback is to work as originally and currently intended.

Feedback is intended to act as a public record between you and your trading partner. If you are a good eBay buyer or seller, your feedback will reflect that fact clearly to all who view it, even if your feedback contains the occasional negative comment. That one recent negative may glare out at you, but in the eyes of other eBay members it doesn't change your previous string of positive comments, and that is what counts: the sum total of all your comments.

I hear from many people who flatly tell me they will never leave a negative comment, no matter how well deserved, for fear of receiving a negative in kind. These folks are more concerned with keeping their feedback unblemished. On first consideration, who could blame them? However, there is a dangerous flaw in this strategy.

Feedback is not a beauty contest. If you should have an unpleasant experience with another eBay member and you do not leave appropriate feedback fearing retaliation, you may keep your feedback lily white but you are doing a grave disservice to the rest of the eBay community. There are two important reasons for always leaving appropriate feedback.

One. You read a feedback profile of another eBay member and decide, on the basis of her total lack of negatives, to go ahead and bid on her item. Subsequently, you discover that the seller is not very customer oriented and is prone to anger and rudeness in her emails to you. Wouldn't you have appreciated a warning about this seller's rudeness? Why did no one leave a previous feedback alerting you to this seller's lack of good business manners? Because they were afraid that if they did, the seller would leave a negative in kind for them. Outcome? That bad guy wins.

Two. People really are basically good. It's true. Still, sometimes it is up to us to help bring out this innate goodness, especially for those buyers or sellers whose eBay activity could use some gentle correction. By leaving constructive critical feedback in the form of a neutral or, when necessary, a negative, you help educate and, hopefully, reform the buyer or seller so that she can learn from the experience.

EBAY MEMBER TIP! Not all sticky situations call for negative feedback. You have to use common sense and good judgment. Tom Reddick, ("treddick"), an eBay member since 1998, makes a good point in advising when not to leave negative feedback:

"As a buyer I have received a few things that were not as described but the losses were small and I did not leave a negative feedback. And I did not get any in return. It is important to leave feedback to warn others in serious situations, but it is also smart to consider the long-term consequences of racking up lots of negatives because you 'negged' someone over a small oversight or a misunderstanding over a three-dollar item."

EBAY INC. AND FEEDBACK

eBay will not edit or change a feedback comment under any circumstances. No exceptions. Don't even think about it. That's why it is so important to make sure you leave comments carefully, especially negative comments.

eBay will, however, remove a feedback comment, but only under very specific circumstances. To view the Feedback Removal Policy, click on the Navigation Bar Help link and then click on Rules and Safety. Under the list of links for Policies, look for and click the Feedback Removal Policy.

There are some important detailed rules and guidelines regarding how to properly leave feedback in the Trust and Safety chapters of this book.

ANOTHER AMAZING EBAY TESTIMONIAL

Before we move on, take a look at this post to one of the eBay chat boards. It's from eBay User auntiem:

SINCERE GRATITUDE AND HEARTFELT THANKS

auntiem71 (176)

1:53 P.M. June 16, 2001

I just wanted to tell you how thankful I am for eBay. My husband had a severe stroke seven years ago, at age forty-four. It left him with aphasia/apraxia and comprehension difficulties. He had all but closed himself off to the world. He was afraid people would laugh at him and think he was stupid. I bought a computer a few years ago, hoping he would try to use it. Well, after months of failed attempts, he finally mastered the basics. In the meantime, I had gotten "hooked" on eBay thru my brother-in-law. I started selling some of my dolls to make some extra money. My husband eventually learned to navigate eBay also, a slow process for him. It has been many months now and he has become quite a pro! He had been an automotive machinist, so naturally our house is packed with car parts. He decided he wanted to start selling his 'treasures' on eBay! He gets the parts ready and gives me the information and I type up the listings for him.

Here is the part I am grateful for. He has started talking to people, is more outgoing, and has confidence in himself! He realizes that he is not worthless just because he cannot get the words out of his mouth or that he takes a long time to do something that other people finish in a short time. He has always been excellent where cars are concerned, and now knows he still has this knowledge and always will. Thank you everyone for listening to me. I just needed to express my thanks.

3

Shopping on eBay—
Find it!

What Can I Buy on eBay?

Well, what are you looking for?

eBay seller Linda Huffman ("lindyfrommindy") found a small wooden beer sign at a local yard sale. After dragging it home, her husband nixed her plan on hanging it in their family room. She put it aside in her "eBay" pile.

"I finally got around to photographing it and listing it and I was surprised at the interest in this corny Pabst Blue Ribbon sign."

She was most pleased when the winning bidder contacted her with profuse thanks. It seems he had been searching everywhere (Internet, yard sales, flea markets) for a long time trying to find this particular sign.

"His dad had owned one just like it and for years it had decorated their family's basement until it was destroyed in a fire. His dad had passed away, and being able to have this memento of his childhood in his own home now was very important to him. The money I made selling this item was small, but knowing I had reunited someone with an item they valued more than money was priceless."

Just about anything you can imagine is probably available right now, this very minute, on eBay. From the old stalwarts of collectibles and computers to

73

A 1960 Cadillac

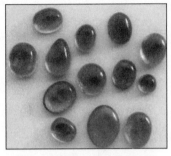

Thirteen Colombian emeralds

A complete computer system

A used ten-burner commercial
Garland restaurant stove

A new men's Armani suit

A new cello

A new glass chess set

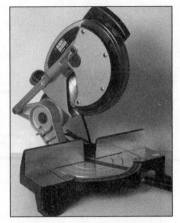

A new Black & Decker miter
saw

A John Deere bucket loader

A Lalique vase

Lucille Ball's childhood home in upstate New York

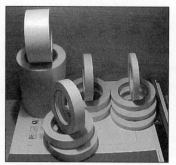

A box of brand-new masking-tape rolls

A pet-door kit

A new Pierre Cardin luggage set

A fifties Pink Poodle suitcase

clothing, jewelry, cameras, and farm machinery, to real estate, houses, cars, planes, boats, event tickets, services, and on and on . . . you can find it on eBay.

In just a few minutes of random browsing on eBay, I found all the items shown on these two pages.

If you can think of it (and it's legal), you probably can find it on eBay.

Last year I received an email from an eBay User named Julie who actually found most everything for her wedding on eBay!

Let me tell you a little about myself. I am a working mom. My fiancé works and has two kids and so do I. . . . I started going to eBay because of the great deals my fiancé and I got on computer parts for my whole family. . . . I want this day to be so special. I plan to keep everything for the girls when they get married. We even found real champagne glasses on eBay. . . . Most of what I bought I got from eBay. . . . I bought a wedding topper on eBay that cost $25 including shipping. It was completely custom made. . . . the prettiest cake topper I have ever seen. The seller runs her business off of eBay. . . . My wedding is going to be totally elegant.

I owe my thanks to all the people who I have purchased things from. . . . One deal early in the game changed everything about the wedding. . . . I was bidding on four bridesmaid dresses . . . in the listing [the seller] stated that they were a pastel blue. Well, when I got them, they were a pastel green. She did offer to take them back. I had already bid on some other high-dollar things in dark blue based off of the dresses. Anyway, my fiancé and I discussed this problem and I was busy sending out emails frantically the next day to the sellers. I didn't know if I was going to be able to have these good people change the color from blue to green, but I had to try. . . . Our wedding colors are now emerald-green and white. . . . I have met some wonderful friends on eBay. . . . eBay has been very good to me, and my fiancé is impressed with the deals that I have made.

Of course, the trick is, like Julie, to know how to find what you are looking for. With over 12 million items up for bid or sale at any given moment, finding that special object (like an entire wedding) can seem a formidable task. However, by utilizing some or all of the following helpful tips, you'll be an expert eBay searcher in no time!

To begin, there are two primary methods of finding items on eBay—browsing and searching.

BROWSING EBAY

By "browsing," I mean the Internet equivalent of old-fashioned "window shopping," much like taking a leisurely stroll through a mall or the old downtown of your hometown, scanning the windows of the shops, not exactly sure what it is you are looking for but hoping that something will catch your eye. Or maybe you have a pretty good idea of the type of item you want, so you focus on specific stores offering this type of item.

Browsing on eBay is much the same thing. There are two ways to browse on eBay. A buyer can browse through:

eBay Categories
eBay Stores

BROWSING THE EBAY CATEGORIES

All items on eBay are placed somewhere in the eBay category hierarchy. As of this writing, there are thirty-four top-level categories. The folks at product development on eBay don't usually add more top-level categories, but there are always new subcategories showing up based on eBay buyer and seller requests.

You can view the top-level categories on the eBay home page or on one of the several Category Overview pages. Here is the list of top-level categories as they currently appear on the eBay home page:

Categories
Airline Tickets
Antiques | Art
Baby | Books
Business & Industrial
Cameras & Photo
Cars, Trucks, Parts
Charity
Clothing & Accessories
Coins | Collectibles
Computers & Office
Consumer Electronics
Dolls & Bears
DVDs & Movies
Event Tickets
Food & Wine
Gifts & Occasions
Health & Beauty
Hobbies & Crafts
Home & Living
Home Improvement
Jewelry, Gems, Watches
Live Auctions
Motorcycles | Music
Musical Instruments
Networking & Telecom
PDAs | Pet Supplies
Pottery & Glass
Professional Services
Real Estate, Timeshares
Sporting Goods
Sports Memorabilia
Stamps | Toys | Travel
TV | Video Games
Everything Else
see all eBay categories

Let's say you are looking to buy something old and rare. You would probably want to start out by clicking on the link in the category list for Antiques. This will bring you to the Antiques category home page.

By starting your browsing on the Antiques home page, you have reduced the number of items to browse from the 12 million–plus total items available on eBay at any given moment to about 300,000 that were specifically listed by sellers in the Antiques categories. Note: The seller determines under which category her items will appear when she lists the item.

The Antiques home page contains subcategories for specific types of antiques. Select and click on a link for a subcategory of your choice and you will be directed to "page one" for all items that are currently listed under that subcategory. For example, I like to search for oriental rugs, so I would click on the Rugs, Carpets link and start my browsing from there. Let's dissect this page!

The most prominent features are the three tabs on the top of the page marked "All Items," "Auctions," and "Buy It Now." The default view is for "All Items." Clicking the "Auctions" tab will display only those listings that are listed in the auction format. Clicking the "Buy It Now" tab will display only those listings where the seller has listed the item with a "Buy It Now" option.

This newer feature is a boon to the many eBay buyers who prefer to skip the auction format and shop only for those items that they can buy immediately.

Under the tabs there is a series of links showing the location of the subcategory Rugs, Carpets in the overall category hierarchy.

You can move up the hierarchy by clicking any of the links. We'll stay with Rugs, Carpets for now.

Directly under the subcategory name you will find the number of total items currently listed in this category. When this screen shot was captured, the number of New Today items was 885.

"New today" is one of four sorting options for the entire category. The four links are located under the number of items found.

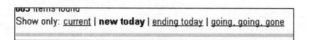

Selecting "current" shows all the items in the subcategory sorted by newest items first.

Selecting "new today" shows only the items that were listed in the last twenty-four hours, sorted by newest items first.

Selecting "ending today" displays only those items that are ending within the next twenty-four hours, sorted by items ending soonest first.

Selecting "going, going, gone" displays only those items that are ending within the next five hours, sorted by items ending soonest first.

Scroll down to the bottom of this category list page. In the right-hand corner under the "Go to page . . ." box, you'll find a very important bit of information in very tiny text.

This indicates the date and time that this category was last updated. When items are listed on eBay, they do not immediately appear in their categories. Instead, they are held aside until the eBay system updates that particular category, at which time all items in the "holding pen" are added to the category. This process is called "indexing" and it occurs once every 30 to 120 minutes.

On the left-hand side of the page you will find other filters for viewing the contents of a category.

The Basic Search box allows you to search the current category using keywords. (The mechanics of Search are discussed in depth in the next section of this chapter.)

In the Show box, there are four options: "Gallery View" for viewing only those items for which the seller provided a Gallery image; "Items near me" for viewing only those items from the category that are located in your area; "Show all prices in $" for viewing all current prices in dollars; and "View ending times," which toggles the "time left" field to ending date and time. Clicking the Gallery View link gives us this version of the category:

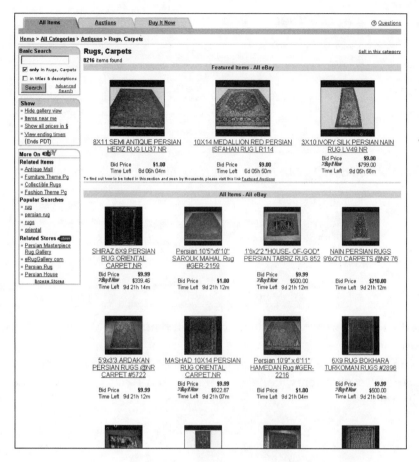

(Note that Gallery View shows all items that are currently listed in the category.)

The second link in the Show box is for "Items near me."

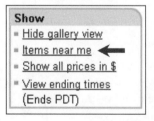

Clicking this link will take you to a page for selecting the metropolitan area nearest you:

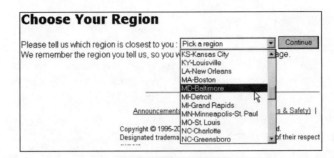

I have selected MD-Baltimore. Clicking Continue shows the following:

Rugs, Carpets	
174 items found in **MD-Baltimore**	
Picture <u>hide</u>	**Current Items - Current**
	SUPER FINE 1950s PERSIAN KASHAN 8.2*12.5@NR
	SUPER FINE PERSIAN GARDEN DE BAKHTIARI 5*8@NR
	SEMI ANTIQUE PERSIAN SAROUK(SAROUGH) 10*13@NR
	SUPER 1950s PERSIAN MAYMEH JOSHEGHAN

At the time, there were 174 item located in Baltimore listed in the Rugs, Carpets category.

Below the Show box, there's a box labeled "More on eBay," containing suggestions for Related Items, Popular Searches, and Related Stores based on the category topic.

In Related Items, you will find other theme pages related to the category.

Popular Searches are the most popular keyword searches that other browsers use in this category.

The last section of the "More on eBay" box, "Related Stores," displays a random selection of eBay Stores for sellers offering items similar to the items in the category. We'll discuss eBay Stores in greater detail later in this section.

For now, let's move to the actual item titles as shown in the category itself.

Directly under the bar containing the last update information is a bar labeled Featured Items.

Featured Items · Current

If you are viewing the category by "current" items, as we are doing above, the tab will read "Feature Items—Current."

Directly below are all the Featured Plus items. When the sellers of these items listed them to eBay, they selected a special option for "Featured Plus." It costs the seller $19.95 to have an item appear as a Featured Plus. The benefit of Featured Plus is that these items will always appear on the top of page one of their category view as well as within the category pages themselves.

The Featured Items section usually fits on the first page of the category—but for the more populated categories, it can extend two or three pages into the list of category pages. At the end of the Featured Items, the All Items section begins. The shot below shows the end of the Featured Plus item list and the beginning of the All Items list:

NOTE: An item that appears in the Featured Items section of a category will also appear in the All Items section as well.

Each time a category is updated, items that were listed after the previous update are added to the top of both the Featured and All Items sections, in chronological order according to the actual time that the seller submitted them. Items are added to the top of each list and are scrolled down and onto the next page as new items are added after them. Think of it as a tall stack of plates with new plates constantly added to the top of the stack.

You can probably see why sellers who list their items so that they appear in the Featured section are at an advantage over those who do not. The items in the Featured section are always on the first or second page of every category for current view, and on eBay, where there are sometimes hundreds of pages of items, it pays to be on the top of the stack!

On the left-hand side of the category list, you should see "Gallery" thumbnail images for those items where the seller opted to employ a Gallery picture.

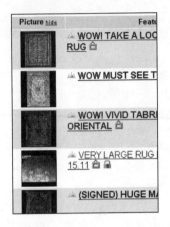

Gallery pictures allow us browsers to scan through the category items more efficiently. It's also an excellent way for sellers to promote their items. A title may be descriptive and enticing, but as we all know, a picture is worth a thousand title keywords!

Not all the items in the category list will have Gallery thumbnails. For those items where the seller did not opt for a Gallery image but supplied photos, there will be a camera icon.

If you scroll down the page and see no Gallery images at all on the page, click the link at the top of the column labeled "Show picture."

You can toggle back and forth between the "Show picture" and "Hide Picture" views. This can be helpful if you are on a slow Internet connection and don't want to wait for Gallery images to download.

If there is no Gallery thumbnail and no green camera icon to the left of an item title, then the seller may not have provided pictures for the item. This is not always the case. The only way to tell for sure is to click the item title to open the item description page.

To the right of the Gallery thumbnail or the camera icon is the item title as provided by the seller.

hide	Current Items - New Today	Price	Bids	Listed
	CREAM FLORAL 10x2 NAIN RUNNER 77514 NR 🗋 🔒	$9.99 $300.00	- *Buy It Now*	Sep-08 10:25
	Vegetable Dye Afghan War Rug NO RES 🗋 🔒	$1.00 $265.00	- *Buy It Now*	Sep-08 10:23
	Persian 11'8" x 8'11" HAMEDAN Rug #GER- 62 🗋 🔒	$1.00	-	Sep-08 10:20

You may have noticed that there are many different styles of titles. (In the Sell It section of this book, we describe the pros and cons of different title composition styles.)

The next column is labeled "Price" and shows the current price of the item as of the last category index update.

The column after this is labeled "Bids" and indicates the number of bids received as of the last category index update. A Buy It Now (BIN) icon indicates the seller listed the item with a Buy It Now format. If someone bids on the item (and the reserve, if any, has been met), the BIN icon will disappear and the number of bids will show in the space.

If you find an item that interests you, you can click either the Gallery image or the item title to open up the Item Description Page.

Item Specifics—a Recent eBay Feature

eBay recently introduced a new sorting tool for some categories that allows you to filter the items in the categories using something called "Item Specifics." Currently, this feature is limited to a few select categories like, for example, "Art, Folk Art."

In the Folk Art category, there is a box on the left-hand side labeled "Folk Art."

Inside this box you select options from a series of drop-down lists for one or more of the following "item specifics" filters:

> Type
> Age
> Country/Region
> Min Price
> Max Price

You can also combine these item specific filters with a keyword search by using the Basic Search box directly above it to refine your keyword search for items in Folk Art.

Item specifics have two view modes; simple and advanced. Advanced is the default. To select "simple mode," click the link at the bottom of the box.

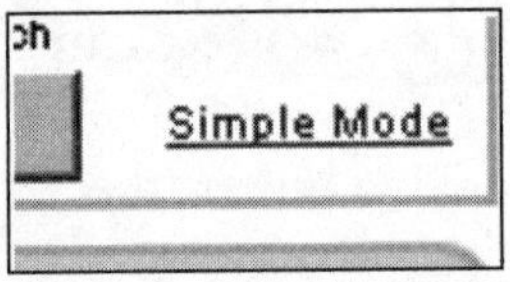

Item Specifics like those in the Folk Art box display by default in Simple Mode. Simple Mode provides fewer options than "Advanced" Mode and presents them as links as opposed to lists in drop-down boxes.

At this writing, Item Specifics are available in a few select categories such as Art, Event Tickets, Men's Clothing, PDAs (Personal Digital Assistants), and Watches.

BROWSING BY EBAY STORES

eBay Stores are a way for sellers to offer their customers both auction and fixed-price merchandise on eBay through an online storefront. To browse, search, and buy on eBay Stores home page, go to the eBay home page and click the link at the top of the left-hand column marked eBay Stores.

This will take you to the eBay Stores home page:

You probably have noticed that the eBay Stores home page looks very similar to the eBay home page.

Another way to browse eBay Stores containing items related to the category you are in (for example, Rugs, Carpets) is to look for the "Browse Stores" link in the Related Stores box for that category.

You can also get to an individual eBay Store by clicking on the red Stores icon next to a seller's User ID. (Only those sellers who have set up an eBay Store will display the Stores icon.) You can also get to that seller's eBay Store by clicking the link for "Visit my eBay Store!"

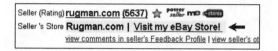

Browsing through eBay Stores is much like browsing through categories. To select a category to browse, click on one of the top-level categories in the box on the left of the eBay Stores home page:

Stores Categories

Antiques
Art
Books
Business, Office & Industrial
Clothing & Accessories
Coins
Collectibles
Computers & Office Products
Consumer Electronics
Dolls & Bears
Home & Garden
Jewelry, Gems & Watches
Movies & Television
Music
Photo & Optics
Pottery & Glass
Real Estate
Sports
Stamps
Tickets & Travel
Toys & Hobbies

For the sake of consistency, let's select the Antiques & Art eBay Store Category by clicking on the link in the box for Antiques & Art. This brings up the eBay Stores Antiques category home page.

The eBay Stores Antiques category home page looks similar to the regular eBay Antiques category home page. The major difference between the two is that the Store home page, instead of displaying individual items, displays the separate eBay stores containing items related to the Antiques category.

As with the Antiques category home page, we can delve deeper into the category by choosing a selected subcategory from the hierarchy displayed in the Store category box on the left-hand side of the Web page:

Let's select our favorite Antiques subcategory, Rugs and Carpets.

Search Stores

All eBay Stores within a subcategory can be search and sorted—searched by keyword for all listings or just "Buy It Now," using titles or titles and descriptions. (More in the next section.)

They can also be sorted by number of items in the individual stores or alphabetically. Notice that the default sort lists all eBay Stores, starting with the store containing the highest number of items at the top. The links for switching from the default sort to an alphabetical sort are located at the bottom of the Search Stores box.

SEARCHING EBAY

Although casually browsing eBay categories and eBay Stores can be a fun and often rewarding way to hunt down treasure, it's not the most efficient option in that it takes time and effort to scan through so many items. However, if you have a specific type of item in mind, there is an efficient and popular method for locating those items using "Search"!

There are seven ways to search for items on eBay.

Search (Title)
Advanced Search (Title and more)
Item Number
Seller
Bidder
eBay Stores
Completed Items

All of these search options are quickly accessible simply by clicking the link marked Search on the navigation bar located on the top of any eBay page. This will take you to the eBay Search—"find items" Web page.

The Search—"find items" page looks like this:

Note that all seven "Search" options are listed as clickable tabs across the top of the Search box.

Let's start with the first tab, "Search" (otherwise known as Searching by Title or Title Search)

Searching by Title—Title Search

By far the most popular method used to hunt for items on eBay is to use keywords in a Title Search.

Title Search, by default, searches the titles that sellers create for their items. To use Title Search, you type a keyword, or some keywords, that relate to the type of item for which you are searching, into the box provided in many areas on eBay.

The system then searches all items (depending on your choice, within a single category or all of eBay) and returns those that match your search.

The Search tab shows not only a text entry box for entering a keyword but several other optional text entry and drop-down boxes to help you tailor or restrict the returned results of your Title Search. The optional boxes are fairly self-explanatory:

Words to Exclude
Add words to exclude from your search results.

Search in Categories
Select a specific category to which you wish to limit the search.

Price Range
Here you can specify a price-range high and low amount for filtering returned results.

Item Location
Limit your search to a major US metropolitan area.

View Results
There are three possible choices: All Items (displays all items—gallery and non-gallery alike), All Items with Item Number (displays all items matching the other search criteria and displays the item number in a column before the Item title), and Gallery Items Only (displays only those items for which the seller has added a Gallery image).

Sort By

Select an option here to sort the returned list of items by Items Ending First, Newly Listed Items, Lowest Prices First, and Highest Prices First.

We will use some of these options in a later example. For now, let's focus on the nuances and tricks of creating effective Title Searches.

A Simple Title Search

Let's say you are looking for Beatles-related items. One way to find all the Beatles items on eBay is to type in the word *beatles* in the Title Search text entry box and then click the Search button.

This Title Search will return a list of all items that have the word *beatles* in their titles. At the time of this writing the total number of "beatles" items was 12,452.

Picture hide	Item Title	Price*	Bids	Time
	THE BEATLES Discography Price Guide CD ROM	$11.70	1	
	Doris Troy Jacob's Ladder 45 The Beatles	$4.95	1	
	THE BEATLES CARTOON BAND PRINT	$9.99	-	
	DISC MAG 28/4/73 BEATLES F/ C + INT	$2.65	2	
	The Beatles CARTOON BAND print 9 x 12	$7.99	-	
	BEATLES ANTHOLOGY HARDCOVER BY THE BEATLES	$29.99	-	

You probably noticed that this page bears a remarkable resemblance to a category list page, with a few differences.

The sort options are different. Title Search results search options are:

ending first | newly listed | lowest priced | highest priced

Also, there is a new box on the left-hand side of the page labeled Matching Categories, containing several links to items related in some way to the keyword that you used for searching. This is eBay's way of subtly suggesting other possible items of interest.

Tailoring a Simple Title Search

Twelve thousand four hundred fifty-two "beatles" items may be more than you care to wade through. Many of these items, although related to the Beatles, may not be on your treasure-hunt list.

For example, say you are looking for only old vinyl Beatles albums, not CDs or CD-ROMS or songbooks or videos. You can tailor your search by entering these words into the "Words to Exclude" box back on the Title Search.

This reduces the number of items to 11,533—still too many items to browse quickly.

Lets add *book* and *poster* to the exclusion list:

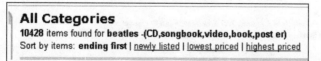

This trims the number of returned results to 10,428; still too many to browse efficiently.

All Categories
10428 items found for **beatles** -(CD,songbook,video,book,post er)
Sort by items: **ending first** | newly listed | lowest priced | highest priced

We need to filter this search down even more.

Lets add some words to include, instead of exclude. We know we are looking for Beatles albums. What other words besides *album* would a seller use to describe such an item? *LP, album,* and *vinyl* come to mind. But how do we add them?

Go back to the Search page and type in the following:

Beatles (lp,vinyl,album)

This is a more advanced search method. The words in parentheses form an "OR" part to the search. What this does is look for all items that have *beatles* and *lp* OR *beatles* and *vinyl* OR *beatles* and *album*.

Add to this Title Search the following excluded words—*CD songbook video book poster*—and all of the results that contain any one of these excluded words will be filtered out of the search.

All Categories
1728 items found for **beatles (lp,vinyl,album)** -(CD,songbook,video,book,post er)
Sort by items: **ending first** | newly listed | lowest priced | highest priced

Picture hide	Item Title
🖼	THE BEATLES WHITE ALBUM RUSSIAN

The results for this more detailed Title Search number 1,728 items. This is a much easier number to scroll through. However, we could continue to tweak this search by adding keywords to the OR list or the excluded list and reduce the number of results to an even more manageable amount of specific items.

Once you have tailored a Title Search to your liking, you can save it on your "My eBay" Favorites page by looking on the top of the first page of returned results for the link labeled "Save this search."

All Categories
1728 items found for **beatles (lp,vinyl,album)** -(CD,songbook,video,book,post er)   Save this search
Sort by items: **ending first** | newly listed | lowest priced | highest priced

Picture hide	Item Title	Price*	Bids	Time Left
🖼	THE BEATLES WHITE ALBUM RUSSIAN	$29.01		14m

- **Try as many related keywords words as possible.** What keywords would you use to describe the item if you were selling it?
- **Use more than one specific keyword to target your search.** As we have seen above, *Beatles poster* will return fewer and more targeted listings than a search for *Beatles*.
- **Use conjunctions and articles *(and, or, the, a)* carefully.** Use *and, or, the* only if you're searching for items containing these words. For example *Tommy James and the Shondells* or *Truth or Dare* or *A Beautiful Mind*. If the number of returned matches is too high, retry the search minus the conjunction or article.
- **Use punctuation only when required.** For example, you'll be successful if you search for *Elvis T-shirt* (correct punctuation with hyphen) or *Elvis tee shirt* (correct wording without hyphen). But don't try *Elvis: T-shirt* (unnecessary colon) or *Elvis-tee-shirt* (incorrect hyphen).
- **Use an asterisk (wild card) to include plural forms of nouns and alternate endings.** If searching for *diamond rings* doesn't return enough matches, find more items with very little overlap by entering *diamond ring**.

  Using the asterisk, you can also search for items with multiple endings. For example: Beatles man* would return items such as Beatles manager, Beatles mania, Beatles Nowhere Man, etc.
- **Increase your results by selecting the "Search *titles* and *descriptions*" option.** Search always looks in the *title* of the items for sale to find the keywords that you specify. You can find many more items by searching both the *title* and *description* for each item. Just click on the option to "search titles **and** descriptions" under the search box.
- **Search for exact phrases using quotation marks (" ").** Typing *"Statue of Liberty"* or *"Gone With the Wind"* inside quotes will find items with **those exact words in sequence.** Without the quotation marks, you could wind up with many other listings containing the words *statue* or *liberty*.
- **Use the minus sign (–) to narrow your search.** antique –lamp tells the search engine to include the word *antique* but not *lamp*. Remember there's no space after the sign (e.g. –card, –teddy).
- **Sort your results by starting date, ending date, or price.** After you see the results of your search, you can use the sort menu to rank these items by starting date, ending date, or bid price. The drop-down sort menu is right above your search results.

SEARCH COMMAND CHART

Here is a summary of all the advanced search commands available to you:

To search for	Use the Command:	Example:
One word **AND** another	Use space between words	**baseball autograph** Returns items with the words baseball **and** autograph in the title
One word **OR** another	(word 1,word 2) *Attention: No spaces after the comma!*	**(baseball,autograph)** Returns all items with the words baseball **or** autograph in the title
EXACTLY these words	"word 1 word 2"	**"baseball autograph"** Returns items with **exactly** the words baseball and autograph, in that specific order, separated by a space, in the title
One word **BUT NOT** another	– (minus symbol) *Attention: No spaces after the minus sign!*	**baseball –autograph** Returns items containing the word *baseball* and will **exclude** all items containing the word *autograph* in the title
One word **BUT NOT SEVERAL** others	–(word 1,word 2,word 3) *Attention: No spaces after the minus sign or the comma!*	**baseball –(autograph, card,star)** Returns items containing the word *baseball* and will **exclude all** items containing the words *autograph, cards,* and *star* in the title
Any words starting with a **SPECIFIC SEQUENCE OF LETTERS**	* (asterisk symbol)	**base*** Returns items with **words starting** with "base" such as *baseball card, baseball cap,* and *iron bases.*

Continued

Words **OUT OF A GROUP**	@1 word1 word 2 word 3	**@1 baseball autograph card** Returns items containing **two out of the three words** specified. This example will return items containing the words *baseball* and *autograph, baseball* and *card,* or *autograph* and *card* in the title. You can try searching for 3 words out of 4 by using @2 in the beginning of the command.
One word **ALONG WITH AN ADVANCED SEARCH**	**+** (plus symbol) *Attention: No spaces after the plus sign!*	**@1 baseball autograph card +star** Returns items containing two out of the three words specified **plus** the word star in the title.

- **For the closest matches, specify a date, color, or brand.** For example, to find a particular Barbie item, don't just type *Barbie* in the search box. If you are looking for a Barbie dress made in the 1960s, enter: *Barbie dress 196**. If you want only red dresses, type: *Barbie red dress*. The trick is to be specific and use a narrowly defined search!

You can also use any of these commands to search item descriptions by clicking on the option to "Search titles and descriptions" under the search box.

Title Searching Tips (Smart Search)

Misspellings
Most sellers take great pains to ensure that their title keywords are spelled correctly. Then there are a few sellers for whom spelling has always been a challenge. These sellers often spell keywords incorrectly. This can decrease the potential of a high price for that item, since the misspelling will prevent the item from appearing in most title search results—bad news for the seller but good news for the crafty eBay treasure hunter (that's you!).

An effective way to take advantage of these unfortunate spelling errors is to regularly run title searches using the most common misspellings of the appropriate keywords. For example:

Singular/Plural

There are many types of items that sellers may list as plural or singular. As shown above in the Effective Title Search Tips from eBay, the use of the singular root of a word, along with the wild-card asterisk in place of the *s* or *es* for the plural, will return both singular and plural forms of a specific keyword.

Creating a Custom-Tailored Title Search—
Another Example Using Item Location

Sometimes, a search on one or two keywords will return many results unrelated to your search. If you plan on searching for this particular item on a regular basis, it's wise to tailor and save the search for future use. First, let's explore how to custom-tailor a title search.

Let's say I was looking to purchase a good used grand piano from a local seller here in Salt Lake City. I would start by going to the Search page and entering the words *grand piano* in the Search Title box. I would also select UT—Salt Lake City from the Item Location drop-down box.

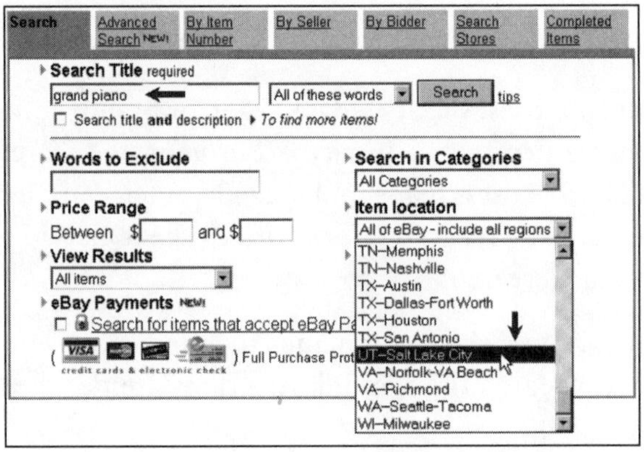

After I click the Search button, the eBay Search engine returns the following results:

There were no actual grand pianos for sale in the Salt Lake City area at the time I ran this search; however, there were lots of sterling silver piano charms.

Still, someone located in the Salt Lake City area is bound to put up a real grand piano for sale on eBay someday. I will want to be informed if they do. Instead of running this search manually every day, I can save it in my "My eBay" favorites page and elect for the eBay email system to alert me when a seller in the Salt Lake City area lists an item matching my title search criteria. First, let's tailor the title search to remove the unwanted charms, etc.

Back on the Title Search page, I entered the following words into the box labeled "Words to Exclude": *charm miniature "sterling silver"*

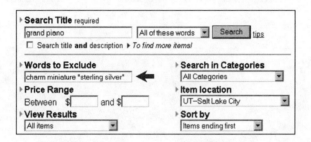

I put quotes around the words *"sterling silver"* in order to force the title search engine to treat the two words as a single phrase.

After I clicked the Search button, the following results were returned:

All Categories
2 items found for **grand piano** -(charm,miniature,"sterl ing,silver") in **UT–Salt Lake City**
Sort by items: **ending first** | newly listed | lowest priced | highest priced

Picture hide	Item Title
	Musicale Black Baby Grand Piano ..MINT
	Small Wood Baby Grand Piano - Works! *Buy It Now*

As it happens, both of these items are actually toy pianos. I could add the word *toy* to the "Words to Exclude" list, but since neither of these particular listings use the word *toy* in their titles, the system still would not have filtered these two listings out. Perhaps two or three unrelated items are an acceptable error level for us (it is almost impossible to create a perfect custom-tailored title search), so let's next save the search for future use.

Saving a Search with "My eBay"

Once you have tailored a title search to your liking, you can save it for quick and easy reference in your "My eBay" Favorites page. To do so, look toward the top of the Title Search results page for a link labeled "Save this search."

Click the "Save this search" link. If you are not currently signed in, the eBay system will request that you do so. After you've signed in (or if you were already signed in), the tailored search will be added to your "Favorite Searches" on the Favorites page.

If you want to receive an email alert each time an item is listed that matches the title search criteria for this individual saved search, look for and check the box in the fourth column marked "Email me when new items appear."

NOTE: You can save up to thirty separate "Favorite Searches" in My eBay. You can have up to three Favorite Searches checked for email alerts.

There are other ways of searching, using the eBay Search page. Some of them may come in handy for you in the future.

Advanced Search Tab

The Advanced Search tab page provides more options for tailoring a search than does the regular Search tab page.

Specifically, the "Refine your search" section contains a filter for Currency and for Type.

By selecting the default, "Any currency," your search will cover all eBay global sites including the US. If you select a currency from the drop-down box, your search will be limited to the eBay Country site for that currency. This option replaces the old "International Search" option.

Completed Items

The option for Type allows you to apply your search criteria to completed items only. This is an effective tool for researching recently closed eBay items to determine the value of items matching your search criteria.

Searching by Item Number

If you know an item's number, you can navigate to it in one click by starting at the eBay Search page and selecting the tab for "By Item Number," then typing in the item number for the item.

Click the Search button to go directly to that item page.

Searching by Seller

It is also possible to search for items listed by a specific seller or by keywords for specific multiple sellers.

On the eBay Search page, click the tab for "By Seller."

Search	Advanced Search NEW!	By Item Number	**By Seller**	By Bidder	Search Stores	Completed Items

Single Seller [_____] [Search]
View all a seller's items   User ID or email address of seller. ▸ *See your favorite seller's listings.*

Include bidder emails   ◉ No ○ Yes
(Accessible by Seller only)

Include completed items   ◉ No ○ Last Day ○ Last 2 Days ○ Last Week ○ Last 2 Weeks ○ All

Sort by   ○ Newest first ○ Oldest first ◉ Auction end ○ Current price

# of items per page [25 ▾]

Search Title [_____] [Search] *tips*
Find items by keywords for multiple sellers   ☐ Search titles **and** descriptions

Multiple Sellers 10 Sellers Maximum. Separate names by a comma.
[   ]

◉ Find items from these sellers.
○ Find items excluding these sellers.

You no doubt notice that there are various filtering options for this search. The first four filters are pretty self-explanatory:

Include bidder emails—This option is restricted to a seller searching on her own User ID for an inventory of her listings. This is a useful tool for garnering email addresses for the high bidders of each closed listing in order to send email notices.

Include completed items—Selecting one of the options here will limit the results to specific time criteria. Selecting "No" will return only active listings. Selecting "Last Day" will display all active listings with listings that have closed within the past twenty-four hours. You can extend the inclusion time back by selecting one of the subsequent options.

Sort by—This option allows you to presort the returned results by one of four choices: Newest first, Oldest first, Auction end, and Current price.

# of items per page—If you have a very slow dial-up Internet connection, you will want to leave this option to the default "25," since anything higher may take longer to display, especially if the seller has hundreds of items listed. If, however, you are lucky enough to have a quick connection through DSL or a T1 line, you may want to select a higher number of items displayed per page. Choose an amount per page from the drop-down box.

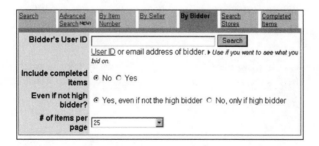

The second set of options for Search by Seller provides a method for searching via keyword (like with title search) by one or more specific sellers.

First enter keywords for a Title Search in the same manner you would for a regular title search. Then enter the eBay User ID for one or more eBay sellers. You can select to search for all items matching your title search, restricted to one or more sellers (up to ten); or you can elect to find all items matching your title search, excluding one or more sellers (again, up to ten).

Searching by Bidder

Just as you can search by seller, you can also search for items by bidder.

The options are similar to search by seller.

It is also possible to use a title search for searching eBay Stores.

The Search Stores page looks a lot like the first Search page, with a couple of differences:

> The "Search in Category" option is missing.
> There is an added Search for Stores by Store Name.

NOTE: The items that are specifically listed in eBay Stores are not included in a regular "Search Title" search. Use this title search to find those items.

As more and more eBay shoppers spend more and more time shopping eBay Stores for great items at good value, they are relying more and more on this option.

Completed Items Tab

By the time this book has gone to press, the Completed Items feature will have been moved to the Advanced Search tab (and the old Completed Items tab page will have been retired). To search completed items, use the "Type" option on the "Advanced Search" tab page as described in the previous section of this chapter for "Advanced Search."

Using these search tips, you can hunt for eBay treasure with the precision of a shark! Pam Withers, an avid eBay buyer, sent me the following story about finding a long lost item on eBay:

When I was about five, I received a wooden apple, as a gift. No big deal . . . but the apple contained a little wooden tea set. It was adorable . . . and I lost it! I had looked for many years (I am now fifty-four) to find one like it, to no avail. Then, one day, I asked about this little wooden apple tea set on eBay and was amazed to get a response. The funny part of this story is that my last name is Withers and so was the seller's. However, the seller thought that I was his daughter, who lived in the same town, and was just trying to play games! Imagine his (and MY) surprise after returning emails a couple times when we got to the bottom of the whole thing! I still laugh when I think about his response to my first email to him after learning that he had what I wanted. Thinking I was his daughter, he simply mailed back an email that said, "Why don't you come over and look at it?" After he received my response to that email, he emailed me again, explaining how he had been thinking I was his daughter. He was VERY embarrassed! . . . Call it luck or coincidence . . . he had the wooden-apple tea set and I bought it. By the way, even though we have the same last name, we are not related. Ain't life amazing?

Now that you know, like Pam, how to browse and search for your heart's desire, it's time to learn how, once you have found it, to bid for or buy it!

4

Shopping on eBay—
Buy it!

Most hard-core Internet users will agree—online shopping and, in particular, shopping on eBay, is the most fun anyone can have on a computer. The exquisite thrill of hunting for, bidding on, and winning your first eBay purchase never really fades, even after many years of eBay trading! I started buying on eBay back in 1996 and I have never stopped enjoying it, and I have a house overflowing with eBay-bought treasure to prove it.

You've discovered a priceless treasure you cannot live without. Your bidding finger is sweaty with anticipation. You gotta have it. You just can't wait to get a bid in.

Stop right there! You should never just rush in and bid or buy. To assure that your eBay buying experience is a safe and satisfying one, you must always do a quick bit of homework before you bid or buy.

eBay shopper Sharon Maracci had a bit of shock when she learned her eBay purchase was thousands of miles away.

I wanted to buy a discontinued Fisher Price toddler bed for my niece Molly. I had bid on several on eBay but was always outbid at the last minute. I couldn't afford to bid too much because I knew shipping would be very high.

Finally I was the high bidder for the bed by going over what I could afford, only to find out that the bed was all the way in New York. When I wrote the seller about my concern over shipping, she wrote back, "I actually am selling the bed because I'm moving. I just got a job offer from Cisco in Silicon Valley. If that's anywhere near you, I'll throw the bed in the moving van and you can get it when I arrive." I said sure.

Two weeks later, I got a call. The seller had been given temporary housing by Cisco in an apartment complex less than a mile from my house in Campbell. Now my niece is sleeping in that bed that came to her all the way from New York shipped courtesy of Cisco.

(And I have a REALLY cute picture of my niece in the bed!)

Sharon lucked out this time, as the seller of the bed was more than happy to accommodate her shipping problem (eBay sellers can be a very accommodating), but the lesson of the story is to always ask a seller about shipping details before you submit a bid or commit to an outright purchase. This is just one of the important items on our eBay Safe Trading Checklist below.

Before You Bid—A Safe Trading Checklist

It is important to learn a few things about any eBay seller before you commit to bidding on or buying an item from him.

Before we look at our bidder safety checklist, let's look at an item-description page for reference:

Here is a picture of the item:

Looks like something we might want to add to our collection of interesting things. Before we bid or buy, let's go over the top section of the item page using our Buyer Checklist:

READ THROUGH THE TOP OF THE ITEM PAGE CAREFULLY

I like to learn about the seller first.

READ THE SELLER'S FEEDBACK

To read a seller's feedback, click the number next to the seller's User ID.

Make this a habit. Before you do anything, before you read through the item description or start figuring how much you are willing to spend, and for heaven's sake, *before* you bid, always check the feedback profile for the seller first.

ebY ID card	theblueox (14963) power seller me stores		
Member since: Sunday, Mar 09, 1997			
Location: United States			
Summary of Most Recent Comments			
	Past 7 days	Past month	Past 6 mo.
Positive	215	1252	7636
Neutral	0	5	77
Negative	1	19	93
Total	**216**	**1276**	**7806**
Bid Retractions	0	0	0

This seller has excellent feedback. **NOTE!** Most high-volume sellers get the occasional negative feedback. It's important to take the negatives in context and as a percentage of the seller's total. This seller has less than one percent negative to positive—an excellent ratio indeed!

It's also worth noting that this seller has been a member of eBay since March 1997, which makes him an "old-timer."

The "gold" star next to the feedback number indicates that this seller is a "shooting star" seller (a feedback score of 10,000 to 24,999).

This seller is also a PowerSeller.

The PowerSeller program is for sellers who reach a certain level of monthly eBay sales.

READ THE SELLER'S ABOUT ME PAGE

Many (but sadly, not all) sellers have an About Me page. (All sellers should!) If a member has created an About Me page, there will be a little "ME" icon to the right of her feedback number:

Just click the "Me" icon to view that seller's About Me page.

You can learn a lot about a seller by what she tells you on her About Me page. Some sellers use their About Me page to advertise their standard payment, shipping, packing, and return policies.

WHAT IS THE "CURRENT" BID?

The amount shown as the value for "Currently" is the actual current bid price for the item. It changes each time a bidder submits a bid (with only one exception: A bidder cannot raise her own bid by rebidding.)

Any bid amount you are considering as your bid for the item must be greater than the amount shown for "Currently."

IS THERE A RESERVE?

Our seller is not specifying a reserve for our item of interest, but many sellers will place a Reserve Price on their item. The optional Reserve Price is the amount below which the item will not be sold. The Reserve Price is always private—only the seller knows the Reserve Price for his or her listing.

You can always tell if a listing has a Reserve Price by the indication next to the "Currently" amount, which will state either "(reserve not yet met)" or "(reserve met)." Here is one from a different listing:

Currently	US $39.95 (reserve not yet met)
Quantity	1
Time left	1 days, 23 hours +

This item's reserve has not yet been met. If the item were to close at this point, there would be "no sale"—that is, the seller is not obliged to sell the item and the high bidder has no claim on the item.

Currently	US $47.00 (reserve met)
Quantity	1
Time left	21 hours, 33 mins +

This reserve has been met. The item will end with a high bidder. The seller is obliged to sell to the high bidder at the end of this listing.

TWO IMPORTANT FEATURES OF RESERVE PRICE LISTINGS!

1. If, in a Reserve Listing, the bidder bids an amount lower than the reserve, the bid will increment up according to the rules for proxy bidding. Though the amount for "currently" will increase accordingly, the reserve indication will remain "(reserve not met)."

2. If a bidder should bid an amount equal to or greater than the reserve amount, the amount for "Currently" will rise to equal the amount of the reserve and the indication next to the amount will change to "(reserve met)."

Q. "Griff, why would a seller use a Reserve? Why doesn't the seller just start that bidding at the reserve amount?"

A. Because in most cases where the First Bid amount is equal to or near the market value of the item, very few people will actually bid.

It's all about psychology.

For example, a seller has a recognizable collectible that she will not consider selling for less than $100, and the item itself has a high-end book or market value of $125. The seller offers the collectible for bid on eBay without a reserve but with a First Bid amount of $100. Potential buyers for the item will be lukewarm at best about bidding on the item, since there is so little room for "play." Sure, the item is $25 lower than high market, but the smaller the margin for a possible bargain, the less likely any bidder is to jump in and bid.

If, however, the same seller offers the collectible item with a First Bid of $1 and a reserve of $100, potential buyers are more likely to bid because the possibility of a bargain is much greater, that is, at least the *appearance* of a possible bargain is greater. Remember, no one but the seller knows the Reserve amount. At a First Bid of $1, someone is more inclined to start the bidding.

Eventually, a second bidder will enter the fray and then something very interesting happens that I call "preownership delusion." Once a person has the high bid on an item, emotionally, he immediately begins to consider the item "his"—which is a delusion, since the seller is the owner of the item until the listing ends.

The strength of this "ownership delusion" is directly proportional to the bidder's desire to own the item. This desire increases once a new bidder outbids a high bidder. The previous high bidder irrationally feels as though he or she has been robbed. The first and strongest instinct of those who believe they have been robbed is to retrieve the item, in this case by rebidding until they are once again the high bidder.

This often starts a back-and-forth of "It's mine!" "No . . . it's MINE!" "Excuse me, I believe this is MY item you are attempting to win." "Yours? Au contraire, the item is most definitely MINE!" "What? Who do you think you are?" with both parties bidding and rebidding until, in the heat of battle, the reserve price is met and is even surpassed, with one person happily winning the item—sometimes for much more than she would have dreamed of paying if the same item were offered to her for direct sale at a comparable price.

Bidding becomes much more than just a fun way to shop. It turns into a life-and-death struggle between the champion and the vanquished, and nobody wants to be the vanquished.

Actually, the real champion in a case like this is the seller, who is more than pleased to watch two bidders fight for the honor of overpaying for an item.

Let's get back to the checklist.

IS THERE A BUY IT NOW OPTION?

Some listings will have two ways for a bidder to win the item. The old standard way is to bid for it and hope for the best. A newer format was introduced recently that allows a potential bidder to skip the bidding process and purchase the item directly for a price specified by the seller. This format on eBay is called "Buy It Now."

If the seller has provided potential buyers with the Buy It Now option, there will be a gray box directly under the amount of the current high bid. Inside the gray box will be text stating

In this example, the seller has provided the Buy It Now option with a Buy It Now price of $894.00. (See page 138 for how to "Buy It Now.")

The "Buy It Now for $894.00" option will immediately disappear if a buyer places any bid less than the stated Buy It Now price, in this example, $894.00. (A bid of $894 or higher will close the listing with a final price of $894).

If a buyer opts to pay a Buy It Now price, the listing will close and show the following:

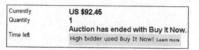

If a seller has opted to have a Buy It Now price and a Reserve Price for the listing, the text will state:

In this instance, the Buy It Now option will remain in place, even if bidding starts, as long as the bidding is below the seller's reserve price.

In some cases, the Buy It Now price might be equal to or lower than the maximum bid amount you are willing to pay for the item. In that case, it might be smart to simply Buy It Now!

HOW MANY ITEMS IS THE SELLER OFFERING IN THIS LISTING?

The number in the Quantity field shows the number of lots the seller is offering. In this case, there is a "1," which indicates "one lot." Note that "one lot" can mean one piece or a lot of two or more pieces.

Currently	US $2.99	First bid	US $2.99
Quantity	1 ←	# of bids	0 bid history
Time left	5 days, 1 hours +	Location	Illinois
		Country	United States
Started	Sep-08-02 18:33:59 PDT	✉mail this auction to a friend
Ends	Sep-15-02 18:33:59 PDT	👀watch this item

The number shown for Quantity determines what type of selling format is in force. A numeral 1 indicates a standard eBay proxy bidding format. Any other number besides 1 indicates a Dutch Auction format.

The procedures for each selling format are different. We discuss them in detail later in this chapter.

HOW MUCH TIME IS LEFT?

You can determine when the item closes by looking for the Time Left field directly under the Quantity field. In addition, the actual closing date and time are displayed next to the Ends field.

Currently	US $2.99	First bid	US $2.99
Quantity	1	# of bids	0 bid history
Time left	5 days, 1 hours + ←	Location	Illinois
		Country	United States
Started	Sep-08-02 18:33:59 PDT		✉mail this auction to a friend
Ends	Sep-15-02 18:33:59 PDT		👓watch this item

When did the listing start and when does it end (close)?

The time and date in the Started field shows the exact date and time (PST) the listing went "live." The Ends shows the exact date and time the listing will close.

Currently	US $2.99	First bid	US $2.99
Quantity	1	# of bids	0 bid history
Time left	5 days, 1 hours +	Location	Illinois
		Country	United States
Started	Sep-08-02 18:33:59 PDT ←		✉mail this auction to a friend
Ends	Sep-15-02 18:33:59 PDT		👓watch this item

WHAT IS THE FIRST BID?

The First Bid for an eBay listing is the amount set by the seller at which the bidding will begin. It is displayed on the right-hand side of the listing page, just under the title description bar.

Currently	US $2.99	→ First bid	US $2.99
Quantity	1	# of bids	0 bid history
Time left	5 days, 1 hours +	Location	Illinois
		Country	United States
Started	Sep-08-02 18:33:59 PDT		✉mail this auction to a friend
Ends	Sep-15-02 18:33:59 PDT		👓watch this item

The First Bid is the lowest acceptable amount to start the bidding. The amount displayed as the value for the First Bid will never change, even after bids are made for the item. That way, anyone can always see what the First Bid for the item is (if there are no bids yet) or was (once someone has submitted a bid).

If you are the first bidder for an item, the amount of the Current High Bid will be the same as the First Bid.

NUMBER OF BIDS

This number displays the actual number of bids placed on this item. It does not necessarily show the actual number of bidders, since a bidder may bid more than once.

Currently	US $2.99		First bid	US $2.99
Quantity	1	→	# of bids	0 bid history ←
Time left	5 days, 1 hours +		Location	Illinois
			Country	United States
Started	Sep-08-02 18:33:59 PDT		✉mail this auction to a friend	
Ends	Sep-15-02 18:33:59 PDT		👀watch this item	

There is a link to the right of the number that will show you the actual bid history for this listing to date. It will not show actual bid amounts until the listing closes. Click the link to view the Bid History.

WHERE IS THE ITEM LOCATED?

The seller's location can be a crucial factor in determining how much it's going to cost to ship the item to you. The Location field for the seller can be found directly under the First Bid field. The Country field is located under the Location field.

Currently	US $2.99		First bid	US $2.99
Quantity	1		# of bids	0 bid history
Time left	5 days, 1 hours +	→	Location	Illinois
		→	Country	United States
Started	Sep-08-02 18:33:59 PDT		✉mail this auction to a friend	
Ends	Sep-15-02 18:33:59 PDT		👀watch this item	

Unfortunately, some sellers do not use the Location field to specify exactly where they are located. However, the Country field is mandatory and does indicate the country in which the seller resides or does business.

Note the two links under the Location field. One is for mailing a friend a copy of the URL for this listing. The other is for adding the item to your "My eBay" watch page.

Directly under the seller's User ID are three links.

view comments in seller's Feedback Profile | view seller's other items | ask seller a question

The most important of the three is the last one: "ask seller a question." Click this link to open a Web email form.

Ask Seller a Question form

Requesting information about the item and the seller helps ensure a successful transaction.

- Use this form to ask the seller a question regarding their listing.

Enter your questions and send an email to theblueox:

To:	theblueox
From:	jimgriff@sover.net
Bcc to myself:	jimgriff@sover.net
	☑ Uncheck if you do *not* want to send a copy of this email to yourself
Subject:	**Question to seller regarding eBay Item # 1766157833**
Item:	Britains #591 Dairyman with Pails
Message:	

Enter up to 4000 characters. HTML cannot be displayed.

- theblueox will receive an email from eBay with your email address displayed as the return address so that he/she can contact you.
- Transactions that take place through eBay provide you access to valuable services including the ability to leave feedback, free insurance, integrated payment methods, escrow, and dispute mediation.

Send message   Clear form

You can use this form to communicate directly with the seller.

The last part of Title section of the Item Description Page displays *extremely important* information! Besides showing the high bidder's User ID (if there has been a bid, which there has not been for this listing . . . yet!), it also shows which types of payment the seller accepts and where the seller will consent to ship the item.

High bid	---
Payment	Money Order/Cashiers Checks. Personal Checks. Visa/MasterCard. See item description for payment methods accepted
Shipping	Buyer pays fixed shipping charges. Seller ships internationally (worldwide).

The seller will usually restate within his item description, in detail, all of his payment and shipping terms, but make it a habit to read this section as well.

Finally, the two links for "the Revise item | Sell similar item" are for the seller.

Seller Services	Revise item	Sell similar item
Item Revised	To review revisions made to this item by the seller, click here .

If there have been revisions to the listing prior to any bids being made, you can click the link for "review revisions."

NOTE: Sellers cannot revise an item once it has received a bid!

That covers the top section of the item description page. Let's read the actual (seller-supplied) description.

READING AN ITEM DESCRIPTION

While I was with eBay Customer Support, I learned the two biggest bidder mistakes, which are:

> Failure to read a seller's feedback profile before bidding
> Failure to read carefully the seller's item description before bidding

We showed you how to avoid mistake number one in the section before this one. Let's dive into how to avoid mistake number two.

The seller supplies all of the text found between the Description bar and the Payment Options/Payment Instructions bars. You simply *must* make it a habit of carefully and thoroughly reading everything the seller has provided in the way of a description, payment options, shipping and handling charges, return policies, any bidder restrictions, etc.

If you have questions or concerns about the item or the seller's policies, you must email the seller for a clarification before you bid. Hold off bidding on or buying an item until the seller has answered your questions to your satisfaction. You can always place the item in your "My eBay" Watch List for access later, once the seller has answered your questions and concerns to your satisfaction.

Here is the seller's description for the item on which we plan on submitting a bid.

The description of the actual item is fairly brief, but it accurately describes the item, and when read along with the picture the seller provided, I get a good idea of the item's condition.

EXAMINE THE ITEM PICTURES!

Here is the picture of the item:

Note that the seller provides the option for viewing a bigger version of the picture simply by clicking on the picture itself.

Are the pictures of the item an adequate representation?

Most sellers understand the importance of clear, sharp, well-lit photos of their items. If the item you are viewing has less-than-perfect photos, email the seller and ask him or her for some better shots (and please do mention this book as an excellent guide for taking perfect eBay item pictures. Thank you).

This seller's picture is clear, focused, and shows the item in close-up. It's a good picture.

Are There Views of the Item That You Would Like to See?

Often, a seller will provide photos of all aspects of an item. Sometimes she doesn't. For example, I might like to see the back of this figure.

If there is a view aspect of the item that you need to see before you make your bid, again, email the seller and ask for a photo of that particular aspect. For example, I once found a beautiful chest of drawers on eBay. The seller provided excellent pictures of the chest, including the back, underside, top, and bottom. However, I needed to see a photo of the drawer sides, specifically the method used to join the sides of the drawer to the drawer front, in order to determine if the chest was handmade or machine made. I emailed the seller asking if he or she could send a photo of the drawer sides, and they happily agreed. The photos proved that the chest was indeed handmade, and I bid accordingly. In the end, I didn't win the chest. I was sniped! (Outbid in the final minutes.)

CHECK THE SELLER'S PAYMENT AND SHIPPING OPTIONS AND POLICIES (TOS—TERMS OF SERVICE)

This seller has provided a comprehensive set of shipping and handling terms.

> **SHIPPING:**
>
> **Our Terms:**
>
> **IMPORTANT!!** We charge for insurance on all orders. If you wish to decline it, you must email us. Insurance is 70 cents per $100 for US, $1.00 per $100 for International. We do NOT use the post office, we do use a private insurance agent.
>
> **International Customers Please Read** We do everything humanly possible to make sure your order is delivered to you BUT we can not work miracles. Countries like Mexico, South Africa, Netherlands have a higher rate of non-delivery than other countries. INSURANCE is $1.00 per $100 and is HIGHLY recommended. We will NOT refund non-delivered orders with no insurance. Further, some shipments we are requiring to be recorded delivery. We do ALOT of international business so your satisfaction is important to us. We use USPS because of the inexpensive shipping rates but tracing international shipments requires many steps--so keep that in mind when contacting us about the status.
>
> Shipping is by priority mail and UPS. We charge $1.00 handling charge on all pckgs except postcards. We combine orders on a daily basis--WE NO LONGER COMBINE SHIPMENTS PAST ONE DAY. Books go media rate unless noted. Average shipping rate for priority/UPS for a small item is $5.00. For Books its $3.00. Postcards are $1.00 up to 6 cards. We do not make money on shipping--we break even because we have to pay for labor and materials. We do NOT ship surface mail internationally. Do not bid if this is the method you want--we ship airmail only.
>
> Payments are due within 10 days of auctions close. 14 for international orders. We accept Checks, Money Orders, Cash by registered mail, Visa, Mastercard, Paypal, Bidpay and Billpoint. If Payment is not received timely, we do reserve the right to void the auction and resell the item. We do leave feedback on these transactions and follow up with Ebay. If you do not intend to pay, please do not bid.
>
> We do ship timely, however, some orders with many items may be delayed a day or two while we pull. Upon receiving your order, you have 3 days to contact us for a return if the product is not up to expectations. We are human and make mistakes so if there is anything wrong with the order, please contact us and we will correct it or resolve the problem.
>
> Please contact our customer service email at Threedtv@aol.com if you have any questions.

What Type of Payment Does the Seller Accept?

There are several ways to pay for an eBay item.

Credit Cards
Money Orders
Checks
Cash

Sellers are usually very clear about which of the above they accept. The first place to look for a seller's payment options is in the top section of the listing page as shown above. But there should also be some indication inside the item description.

If the seller has not provided details about accepted payment methods, remember to ask her for details, *before you bid!* (Use the "ask seller a question" email feature as described above.)

Credit Cards

Most eBay sellers accept credit cards for payment, either through an online payment service like PayPal (more on PayPal in the next chapter) or through their own merchant account.

Using a credit card on eBay is the quickest and safest way to pay for an item. Check with your credit card issuer for details regarding the buyer protection they provide.

Electronic Check

Most online payment services like PayPal will provide secure electronic check as a buyer payment option. Online payment services also will back up electronic checks for their full amount.

Money Orders

Most (but not all) eBay sellers will accept a money order for payment. Again, don't assume. If the seller doesn't state his terms, ask first before bidding.

Paying with a money order is not as quick as with a credit card, nor does a money order offer the buyer the same protection as a credit card.

Checks

Besides money orders, many (but not all!) sellers will also accept a check as payment for an eBay item. Sellers who accept checks usually specify a "waiting period" of three or more days in their item description before they will ship the item. This is to allow ample time for the check to clear their account.

Cash

Some sellers will accept cash for payment.

It is always a bad idea to send cash through the mail. eBay doesn't prevent sellers from stating "cash" as a payment option, since in some situations cash would be acceptable (for example, if you arrange with the seller to pay for an item in person).

Does the Seller Offer Escrow?

Online escrow is a valuable third-party service to help protect both buyer and seller. If a seller offers escrow, you will find the indication at the top of the item page as well as sometimes within the seller's item description.

Here's how eBay's preferred escrow service, **www.escrow.com**, works.

First, the buyer and seller agree to the terms of the escrow transaction. This may include a number of days for the buyer to inspect the item, shipping information, and who pays the escrow fee.

The buyer then sends payment to escrow.com, who then verifies and processes the payment. Once the payment has been verified (cleared), escrow.com authorizes the seller to ship the merchandise to the buyer.

Once the buyer receives the item, he has the previously agreed-upon number of days to inspect and accept the item. Once he informs escrow.com that he accepts the item, escrow.com pays the seller.

Online escrow can offer great peace of mind for certain types of eBay transactions. If you are looking at possibly buying a big-ticket item like an expensive car, piece of jewelry, or work of art, and the seller for the item has little or no feedback, then you may want to ask him if he would consider using online escrow should you be the high bidder or buyer when the listing closes. Always ask the seller about using escrow *before* you bid!

Of course, many newer eBay sellers, realizing that their lack of a feedback history on eBay may give pause to otherwise eager potential bidders or buyers, will offer the escrow option in their listing description, but note: eBay sellers are not required to accept escrow! It is a seller choice. If a seller does not offer it explicitly, contact the seller to inquire about possible escrow as a payment option *before you bid*.

Sellers who offer escrow services will have various terms for sharing or not sharing the costs of using an online escrow service. Again, make sure you understand who is bearing what costs for using escrow *before you bid!*

Does the Seller Accept Returns?

Most anyone who sells online realizes that a buyer cannot know if she is truly happy with an item until that item is actually in her hands. No one wants to be stuck with an item she doesn't like.

Most, but not all, sellers understand this reality of online buying and will offer a reasonable return and refund policy. Make sure to check for a seller's return policy before you bid. If the seller has not provided a return policy, send him an email inquiry.

The best return policy is one that offers you your full money back for any reason whatsoever, no questions asked, no return fees. The worst return policy is none at all. A seller will usually indicate "no returns" by stating that the item is sold "as is." Bid if you must on such an item, but always remember, "Caveat emptor!" (Latin for "Buyer beware!") You bid at your own risk!

The majority of sellers offer something in between. Some sellers will accept returns but will charge you a fee for doing so. Make sure you fully understand the seller's return policy before you submit your bid.

Does the Seller Ship Internationally?

Although the eBay community of buyers and sellers extends around the globe, some eBay sellers (mostly based on the US site) will not ship items outside of the US. These sellers will usually state this fact clearly within their terms.

If you are an eBay buyer based outside of the US, make sure that the item's seller is agreeable to shipping internationally *before you bid*.

Another option for non-US buyers is to establish a contact within the US (a friend or family member) who will accept delivery of eBay items on your behalf.

OTHER SELLER TERMS OF SERVICE

Does the Seller Have Special Requirements for Buyers?

For example, some sellers prohibit bidding by eBay members who have a certain number of negative comments in their feedback profile or hidden feedback. (Users can opt to hide all their feedback comments. Their feedback number will still display. Not recommended.

Sellers are free to employ this type of restriction based on feedback.

Does the Seller Have Specific Time Limits for Receiving Payments?

eBay sellers are usually quite specific about how long they will wait for contact and payment from you, the buyer. Read these specifications before you bid!

Still Have Questions? Ask the Seller!

If you go through the checklist and you still have questions about the item or the seller's terms, ask the seller *before you bid*.

ONLINE PAYMENTS—THE SAFEST WAY TO SHOP ON EBAY

The best way to ensure your security as an eBay buyer is to give preference to items where the seller accepts online payments through PayPal or some other similar payment service.

During the first few years of Internet commerce, many folks had reservations about using their credit cards online. Many feared that enterprising thieves would break into an online transmission in order to hijack the credit card information for their own use.

Today, most e-commerce Web sites employ a special form of transmission for sensitive data like credit card numbers. This special form is called Secure Socket Layer or SSL. SSL uses an extremely secure type of data encryption that makes it virtually impossible for anyone to break into an SSL transmission of data.

Without getting extremely technical about how SSL works, all you need to know about any e-commerce Web site's security is that they provide SSL for you. How do you tell if a Web site is using SSL?

First, check the Web site's own text, especially on the page or pages where you are asked to enter your credit card information. If they are using SSL, they will state the fact clearly on this page for your peace of mind.

Second, check your Web browser's status bar (the little bar along the bottom of the Web browser) and address window (where the current Web page's URL or address is displayed.) If the page you are viewing is employing SSL technology, there will be a little yellow padlock showing on the far right-hand side of the browser status bar.

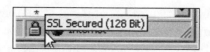

Another way to determine if the current page you are viewing is using SSL technology is to look at the URL or address for the page. The URL for the page can be found in the little window on the top of your Web browser marked "address" or "location." URLs usually start with **"http://www ..."** The URL for a SSL page will start with **"https:// ..."**

You Found It! You Checked It Out . . . Let's Bid!

Congratulations! You've done your homework and are now ready to bid for the item (or, if the item is offered with the "Buy It Now" format, buy it outright.)

Let's cover basic bidding first.

BIDDING

There are two bidding formats in use on eBay: the Proxy format and the Dutch Auction format. First, Proxy Bidding.

eBay's Proxy Bidding System

The majority of items listed on eBay in a bidding format (as opposed to those listed exclusively with the fixed-price "Buy It Now" format) are using the default eBay Proxy Bidding system.

The Proxy Bidding system is not at all complicated. To begin, let's use a real-life example to illustrate the concept of proxy bidding in an offline auction.

What are Friends For? (If Not to Act as Proxies?)

You are I are old friends who have met at an offline auction. Some dear old richer-than-King-Tut grandma has passed away and her loving family, unable to agree on how to split up her worldly goods, has decided to call in a local auctioneer to sell it all—money being easier to split than worldly goods. (Too bad none of the heirs uses eBay or bought this book—they could have sold it all online!)

There's a wonderful old oriental rug at the auction that you desperately want for your living room, but the auctioneer isn't putting it up for bid until noon and you have to leave at 11:45 A.M. to meet a client, fifteen minutes away. (By the way, you're a real-estate agent.)

Oh, what to do! You can't leave your client hanging. But you simply MUST have this rug!

Thinking quickly, you lean over and ask in a whisper if I might be willing to bid for you in your absence.

"Why, dear old friend, of course I would! How much are you willing to spend?" I whisper back.

You look around quickly to see if anyone is listening. They are. You think fast.

"I will write it down so no one hears it."

You rummage in your bag for a slip of paper and pen, find them, and, using your thigh as a desk, scribble a figure. You then hand the slip of paper to me. I read, *Bid $1,000 and not a single penny more. Destroy this immediately!*

I silently mouth, "No problem. Consider it done!"

I have just agreed to act as your "proxy," that is, I will bid for you in your absence.

At noon, the auctioneer puts up the rug as promised. He asks for an opening bid of $100. Someone else starts the bidding. The auctioneer accepts the bid of $100 and asks for a bid of $125—$25 being his choice of increment. Your best friend and proxy, me, springs into action. I raise my hand and enter the fray with a bid of $125.

Thus it begins. The auctioneer calls out for a bid of $150 and sure enough, another bidder bids. I rebid $175. The bidder bids again, $200. I rebid $250. And so on it goes back and forth between us as we battle it out to see who will pay the most. Suddenly, the bidding stalls out at $550. The other bidder has reached her limit! The auctioneer roars, "I have five hundred fifty. Do I hear six hundred? Six hundred? Going, going . . . gone! Sold to the handsome man in the back row for five hundred fifty dollars!"

You, my dear old friend, arrive back at the auction at 12:30 and I rush up to meet you in order to share the good news.

"I got it for five hundred fifty dollars!"

You are deliriously happy. You have sold a house and your dear old friend, me, has successful acted as your proxy. You bearhug me with joy. You were willing to pay $1,000 but your plucky proxy, me, got it for you for only $550. (I don't charge a percentage. After all, we *are* dear old friends.)

Bidding on eBay is nearly identical to our example above, except instead of me acting as your proxy, eBay does.

Let's use the real eBay listing we visited earlier to illustrate the process, step by step.

We know that the starting bid is $2.99. The current bid is zero.

We've read the Title and Description sections, viewed the pictures, and made sure we've read the seller's terms of service. Now we have to settle on the maximum price we are willing to pay.

After due consideration, I decide we are willing to pay up to $12.39 *and not a penny more.*

Now, I could bid the $2.99 starting bid amount and then check every few minutes to see if a new bidder has placed a bid so you can outbid them; or you could simply submit a proxy bid, much as you did at the real live estate auction, but instead of me acting as your proxy, the eBay system will! You only need to decide on a maximum amount you will pay for the item (just as in the live auction) and once you have, you then submit it as a bid. The eBay system will act as I did for you at the live auction. The eBay system will rebid every time someone outbids you, up to the exact amount you submit as your bid (your "proxy" bid.) If no one bids over the amount of your proxy, you win the item for the current high bid. If someone bids more than your proxy, you lose or, better put, don't have to shell out any dough.

Going back to our example, I scroll down to the bottom of the Item Description Page to the Bidding section.

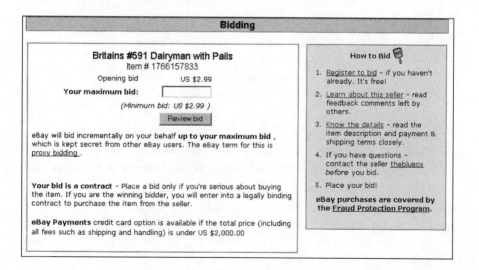

I type my absolute maximum bid amount, $12.39 in the box labeled "Your maximum bid" at the bottom of the page.

Britains #591 Dairyman with Pails
Item # 1766157833
Opening bid   US $2.99
Your maximum bid: 12.39
(Minimum bid: US $2.99)
Review bid

Then I click the "Review bid" button to go to the Review Bid page.

eBaY
Confirm and Place Your Bid
Confirm that your bid is correct and then place your bid.
Britains #591 Dairyman with Pails
Item # 1766157833
Your current bid: $2.99
Your maximum bid: $12.39

eBay User ID
jimgriffi@sover.net (Not jimgriffi@sover.net? Change User ID)
Password
Forgot your password?
☑ Remember my User ID and password for bidding.
Place Bid >   Back to item

Reviewing this information, we see two fields labeled

Your current bid
Your maximum bid

The current bid shows what the current high bid will be, once you actually submit your bid and *if the current high bid for the item ($x) is the maximum proxy amount of the current high bidder.* This point is important. The actual outcome of your bid is not known in the Review Bid page—it can only be known once you have committed to your bid by actually submitting it.

Here are some additional important facts about proxy bidding:

Bid Increments
The following bid increments are used by the eBay Proxy Bidding:

Current Price	Bid Increment
$ 0.01 – $ 0.99	$ 0.05
$ 1.00 – $ 4.99	$ 0.25
$ 5.00 – $ 24.99	$ 0.50
$ 25.00 – $ 99.99	$ 1.00
$ 100.00 – $ 249.99	$ 2.50
$ 250.00 – $ 499.99	$ 5.00
$ 500.00 – $ 999.99	$ 10.00
$1000.00 – $2499.99	$ 25.00
$2500.00 – $4999.99	$ 50.00
$5000.00 and up	$100.00

Tie Bids

In cases where a tie bid is submitted, the current high bid is given to the tie bidder who bid first. That is, if you submit a maximum bid equal to the current (hidden) maximum bid for an item, the current high bid will jump up to the current bidder's maximum bid amount and the earlier bidder will show as the current high bidder.

Bidding and Reserves

If one or more bidders bid amounts less than the seller's hidden reserve, the bidding proceeds like any other proxy listing (with the indication next to the current price stating "reserve not met").

Once a bidder submits a bid equal to or greater than the seller's hidden reserve, the current high bid "jumps" to the reserve amount. From there, the bidding again proceeds like a regular proxy bidding listing (with the indication next to the current price changing to "reserve met").

PROXY BIDDING STRATEGIES

Always give serious consideration to the absolute maximum you are willing to pay for an item. In this case, you decide that you would not pay a penny more than $1,000. This means that should you be outbid for $1,000.01 (rare but possible), you will not whine at losing out for a penny. If you can picture yourself at the item's closing and you are spitting and kicking at being outbid for one cent and you can also picture yourself saying, "Darn it! I would have paid $1,000.02!" then you are telling yourself a big fat lie when you say your maximum is $1,000, because your real maximum is $1,000.02.

The solution? Settle on an absolute maximum and stick to it. Think, *If someone outbids my maximum by even a penny, then I will breathe a sigh of relief at not having to shell out more than my maximum.*

Sniping

As a bidding strategy and tool, the eBay Proxy Bidding system works like a charm. You simply determine a maximum amount you are willing to pay for an item, bid that amount, and walk away. The Proxy Bidding system will execute your bid and will protect your high-bidder position by outbidding all new bids using the lowest increment possible until and if someone bids an amount higher than your proxy bid.

There is, however, another popular bidding strategy known in eBay parlance as "Sniping," that is, waiting until the very last moments of an item listing and then submitting a maximum bid mere minutes or even seconds before the listing closes. It's a heart-pounding, sweat-inducing roller coaster ride and not for the faint of heart.

Does sniping work? Sometimes, but all potential snipers should consider the possible risks. If you are the type of person who tends to get caught up in the frenzy of last-minute bidding to the extent that you suffer a momentary lapse of common sense and end up insanely bidding much more than you would have under more relaxed circumstances, then sniping may not be for you. Remember, regardless of when you bid, the rules of the bidding format still apply. Someone equally as caught up as you might snipe an insane bid amount just a few pennies short of your insane bid amount, in which case you will be the proud winning—albeit overpaying—bidder.

Also, your success at sniping depends to some extent on the speed of your Internet connection. The slower the connection, the less likely your chances of success.

What about these Sniping software and services I see advertised? What are they? Do they provide an advantage? Sniping software or a sniping service snipes your bids for you. You enter the item number, the time you want your bid submitted, and the amount of your bid. The software or service supposedly does the rest. The only possible advantage that sniping software or a sniping service provides is it allows a sniper to be somewhere else at the end of the listing (like in bed asleep) and in the case of a service, they may have the advantage of a high-speed Internet connection that is faster than yours.

NOTE: As of this writing, eBay does not prohibit or condone the use of sniping software or services. Use them at your own risk!

A Popular Sniping Method

Determine a safe but effective snipe time. If your Internet connection is super fast, you can usually get away with waiting until the last few seconds to snipe. If instead your connection is slow, you may have to snipe sooner rather than later.

To make a more accurate determination of the time it might take over your connection, visit any listing set to close in the next hour. Note the time shown for "Time left."

Currently	US $18.50 (reserve not yet met)
Quantity	1
Time left	22 mins, 28 secs

Refresh the window and note the new "Time left."

Currently	US $18.50 (reserve not yet met)
Quantity	1
Time left	22 mins, 23 secs

The difference in seconds is the minimum amount of time you should wait before the listing closes to submit your snipe bid. In the example above, this would be five seconds. Thus, my snipe bid should be submitted no later than "Time left—05 secs."

Determine a snipe bid amount. Snipers tend to use high snipe-bid amounts as an offensive move against other snipers. Although chances are good that you, as a sniper, won't actually have to pay your high snipe amount should you win the item, it is possible you might get stuck if someone snipes you with a bid just under yours.

Open a Web browser window and navigate to the item you wish to snipe. Do this five minutes or more before a listing is set to close.

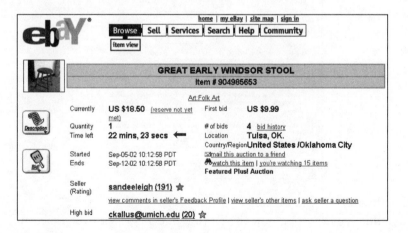

Once the item is displayed, open another copy of the window with the item by simultaneously pressing the Ctrl and N keys on your computer keyboard.

(You can also open a copy of the window by clicking File, New, Window on the Web browser's menu command bar.)

In this copy of the window, enter a bid amount in the Your Maximum Bid text box.

Click the Review Bid button.

Leave this window open on the Review Bid page with the Place Bid button showing.

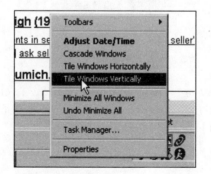

Arrange the two Web browser windows side by side. You can drag the windows and resize them with your mouse. Another quick way to do this is to open both windows. (Make sure any and all other programs or applications are closed or else they will tile as well.) Then, right-click anywhere on the Windows task bar. Select Tile Windows Vertically.

This will display the two open browser windows side by side like so:

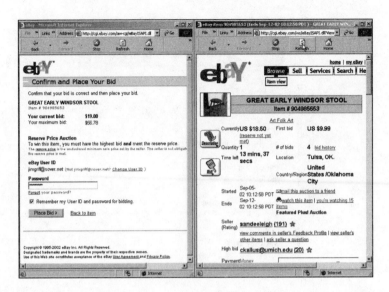

Make sure the second window is opened to the Review Bid page and that it shows the Place Bid button clearly.

Use the first window to watch the time wind down by refreshing the page at regular intervals. Click the browser's Refresh button to refresh the page:

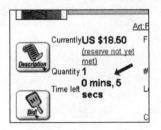

When the Time Left shown in the first window is close to or at your predetermined Snipe Time from step two, quickly move your mouse to the second window and click the Place Bid button.

Window one shows 5 seconds left! Time to snipe!

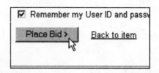

Click that Place Bid button!

Congratulations, Sniper! Now, cross your fingers and hope you've won. (I did not actually snipe the example item.)

eBay member Bill Cawlfield told me an amazing tale of sniping from a most unusual location . . .

Well, I had to have this one radio, about three years ago. The item was going to end while I was flying. This was long before sniper programs. So, not thinking about having someone else snipe for me, I decided to snipe from a plane on the way from Denver to L.A.

The connection was just awful in those days, maybe 7,600 baud. I finally loaded the item page, turned off all graphics, and counted down the seconds, not daring to hit refresh because that would tie up the reload too long.

I hit Bid and then refreshed, which took another couple of minutes. . . . I won!!

It proves that speed does not count, only the size. Sniping from thirty-five thousand feet. A new meaning of the mile high club.

Dutch Auction Bidding—How It works

Counter to a popular newbie misconception, the eBay Dutch Auction format is not reserved for selling wooden shoes, tulips, or windmills.

Whereas the Proxy Bidding format is used for listings with one single lot up for sale, the Dutch Auction format is used for selling multiple identical items in one listing.

Dutch Auction bidding does not work like Proxy Bidding. When you bid on a listing using the Dutch Auction format, you still bid an absolute maximum amount you are willing to pay, but you also select a quantity. For example, in a Dutch Auction, someone is offering 10 identical gold-tipped fountain pens. You want to buy two of them and you don't want to pay more than $30 apiece.

You would state your bid as $30 with a quantity of 2.

The maximum amount you submit for your bid is the amount that shows on the Dutch Auction bidding history page.

Most Dutch Auctions are for vast quantities of a single item, for example, backpacks. In the example shown below, the seller is offering 50 new grandfather clocks.

Odds are very slim that all 50 clocks will be purchased in this listing. For example, in a previously completed Dutch Auction by the same seller, we see that only 4 bids were made for a quantity of 50 clocks:

Checking the "See Winning Bidders List" we find that 4 individual eBay bidders purchased 4 grandfathers clocks (one to each bidder) at $109.99 each.

eBay Dutch Auction High Bidders for
6' 4" GRANDFATHER CLOCKS - BLOWOUT ONLY $109! (Item # 2048031866)

Currently	$109.99	First bid	$109.99
Quantity	50	# of bids	4 (may include multiple bids by same bidder)
Time left	Auction has ended.		
Started	Aug-21-02 18:10:07 PDT		
Ends	Aug-31-02 18:10:07 PDT		
Seller (Rating)	av8tor@flash.net(10859) me		

View page with email addresses (Accessible by Seller only)   Learn more.

Dutch Auction High Bidders (View Bid History | Leave Feedback)

User ID	Item Price	Quantity	Date of Bid	Payment
dotlej227756(8)	$125.00	1	Aug-31-02 10:11:47 PDT	Buyer: Pay Seller: Send an invoice
lynda1799(0)	$110.00	1	Aug-31-02 16:29:36 PDT	Buyer: Pay Seller: Send an invoice
sstargardt(1)	$109.99	1	Aug-23-02 08:13:37 PDT	Buyer: Pay Seller: Send an invoice
shockedp(3)	$109.99	1	Aug-27-02 16:39:59 PDT	Buyer: Pay Seller: Send an invoice

The highest bidder bid $125.00. Though it was unnecessary for the bidder to bid more than the $109.99 starting amount, his higher bid was a way to better guarantee that he would win a clock. Note that although this bidder bid $125, he only pays the lowest successful bid amount, which is $109.99.

Note that only if all 50 clocks had been spoken for at $109.99 and a new bidder wished to purchase, he would have had to bid $110.00 and the lowest bidder on the list (determined by the time of bid where all bid amounts are equal) would have been pushed off the Winning Bidders List.

Points To Keep in Mind about Dutch Auction Bidding:

Dutch Auction bid amounts are not kept secret during the listing. The amount you bid is the amount that shows in the bidding history immediately after you bid.

Your Bid Value is calculated as the amount of your bid times the quantity of items for which you have bid. For example, the Bid Value for a listing where you bid $30 for two items is $60. A rebid by a Dutch Auction bidder must have a Bid Value greater than his or her previous bid. Thus, if I bid for two items at $30 apiece, my bid value is $60. If I rebid in this listing, my Bid Value cannot be equal to or lower than $60. Thus, I could not bid $31 for one item. This automatic restriction is intended to prevent one bidder from tying up all the items in a Dutch Auction and then rebidding for a lower quantity at the last moment of the listing.

The Bid History for a Dutch Auction shows everyone who has bid, successful or not. The Winning Bidders List shows the current successful bidders for the item.

Regardless of their actual bid amounts, the winning bidder(s) in a Dutch Auction all pay the same final price (known as *the lowest successful bid*) times the quantity they each bid for. The lowest successful bid is the amount bid by the last bidder on the Winning Bidders list. In our example above, everyone shown on the list of winning Dutch Auction Bidders would pay the lowest successful bid, in this case, $109.99.

Buy It Now—How It Works

For all their fun and excitement, bidding formats are not for everyone or for every buying situation. Sometimes, a seller wants to move an item fast. He or she may not want to wait three or more days for the item to sell. Sometimes, a buyer may want to purchase an item immediately and not wait for three or more days for an item listing to close.

To meet both needs, eBay instituted a fixed-price format called Buy It Now.

Buy It Now is fairly simple. All items that offer the Buy It Now option will have a Buy It Now icon next to their title in both category lists and Title Search lists results.

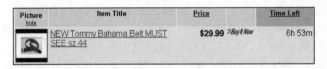

When you open a Buy It Now item's description page, you may see a box like the following (if no bids have been submitted for the item or, if the item was listed with a reserve, the reserve has not been met).

NEW Tommy Bahama Belt MUST SEE sz 44		
Item # 956698232		
Clothing & Accessories:Men:Accessories:Belts		
Currently	**US $24.99**	First bid **US $24.99**
	Buy It Now for **US $29.99** This option disappears once a bid is placed.	
Quantity	1	# of bids **0** bid history
Time left	**6 hours, 49 mins +**	Location **Please check my othe**

To Buy It Now, scroll to the bottom of the page and look for the Buy section next to the Bid section.

Bidding

NEW Tommy Bahama Belt MUST SEE sz 44
Item # 956698232

Bid	Buy
Opening bid: US $24.99	**Buy It Now for US $29.99**
Your maximum bid: [ ]	Learn more
	This option disappears once a bid is placed.
(Minimum bid: US $24.99)	
[Review bid]	➜ [Buy It Now]

eBay will bid incrementally on your behalf **up to your maximum bid** , which is kept secret from other eBay users. The eBay term for this is proxy bidding.

Buy It Now ends this listing. This option disappears once a bid is placed. Learn more

Click the button, read the review screen, and click the second Buy It Now button. It's yours. No bidding, no wondering if you will win it.

Confirm and Place Your Bid ⓘ Need Help?

New to eBay?	or	Already an eBay user?
If you want to bid on this item, you'll need to register first.		Confirm that the price is correct and then buy this item.
		NEW Tommy Bahama Belt MUST SEE sz 44 Item # 956698232
Registration is fast and **free**.		**Buy It Now Price** $29.99 shipping/handling may apply
		Your purchase is a contract
[Register >]		Buy only if you're serious about the item. You will enter into a legally binding contract to purchase the item from the seller.
		eBay User ID
		jimgriff@sover.net
		You can also use your registered email.
		Password
		********
		Forgot your password?
		☑ Remember my User ID and password for bidding.
		[Buy It Now >] Back to item

Whether you bid on the item and won it or bought it outright using Buy It Now, the next step is to pay for it. We cover how to pay for an item in the next chapter.

Congratulations! Your purchase has been confirmed.
NEW Tommy Bahama Belt MUST SEE sz 44 (Item #956698232)

jimgriff@sover.net, please review the seller's payment instructions below, then send your shipping and payment information to the seller.

[Continue >]

Payment Details		**Payment Instructions**
Item price	$29.99	<font color="red">PLEASE EMAIL YOUR
Shipping and handling	$5.00	NAME/ADDRESS AND METHOD OF PAYMENT AS SOON AS YOU WIN THIS AUCTION. THANK YOU!</font>

5

Shopping on eBay—Pay for It!

Congratulations, winning bidder/buyer! You've bought your first item on eBay! Get out your pocketbook—it's time to complete the transaction. But first, I want to share a story sent to me that illustrates the generosity and kindness typical of eBay members.

eBay seller Terry Wagner ("sheop") lives in New Jersey with her husband and three little girls. Terry lost her Internet-based job a few years ago. At the same time, she learned that she had a rare blood disorder that makes her feel constantly fatigued along with daily dizzy spells, leg and hand cramps, and pounding headaches.

By 2001, Terry was in a constant pain. Her disability was cut off. Her dad was fighting bladder cancer and her mom was recovering from heart surgery. Then came the terrible events of September 11. Terry had previously worked at the World Trade Center and she lost many old friends in the attacks.

"I knew people who never came home. I cried for days and days and still cry when I think about it."

Christmas 2001 looked bleak at best. She was hunting for affordable gifts on eBay when she came across a beautiful but expensive quilt—a perfect gift for her mother. Terry emailed the seller to ask if she had less expensive quilts. The seller wrote back and told Terry that she did indeed and would be happy to hold one for her.

"After a few weeks, I had to write her back and explain that I still couldn't afford the quilt and was so sorry for leaving her hanging."

Two days later, Terry received an email with the subject line of "Ho, ho, ho! We want to send you the quilt!" The seller had told her husband about Terry and, as the seller explained to Terry, "He took money out of his pocket and said, 'Send her the quilt!'"

The seller insisted Terry send her address so she could send the quilt to her in time to give to her mom for Christmas.

"She sent not only the quilt for my mom, but a small gift for me and a small gift for my thirteen-year-old daughter who had written her to thank her for making us all so happy!"

Terry and the generous seller correspond regularly and have exchanged family photos as well.

"I just can't get over the kindness. This is not the first person that I have met via eBay who has turned out to show what true human spirit is all about! Life continues to be a struggle. I'm in pain every day, but my friends on eBay keep me smiling."

Completing the Transaction

Many sellers offer detailed instructions on how to complete a transaction for their item by including payment options and shipping and handling amounts in their item descriptions. In fact, some sellers will actually provide a link to a listing management service where you can immediately view an invoice for the item and select a payment method.

Other sellers provide little or no information on how to complete the transaction.

If you did your homework by either reading the item description carefully or emailing the seller before you bid or bought the item, you should at least have a good idea of the following:

The amount due for shipping/handling
The types of payment the seller accepts

Here are four examples of eBay sellers' shipping and payment terms taken from descriptions of actual eBay listings:

> HIGH BIDDER **pays $29.99 UPS shipping cost within the continental USA. Alaska & Hawaii $10.00 more. No International orders, please. No APO/FPO Addresses. Cashier's Checks, Money Order, or use your credit card with either PayPal, BidPay.Com. NY State Residents must add 8.25% Sales Tax to final total.**

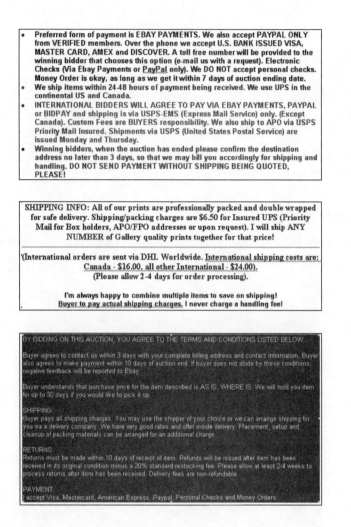

- Preferred form of payment is EBAY PAYMENTS. We also accept PAYPAL ONLY from VERIFIED members. Over the phone we accept U.S. BANK ISSUED VISA, MASTER CARD, AMEX and DISCOVER. A toll free number will be provided to the winning bidder that chooses this option (e-mail us with a request). Electronic Checks (Via Ebay Payments or PayPal only). We DO NOT accept personal checks. Money Order is okay, as long as we get it within 7 days of auction ending date.
- We ship items within 24-48 hours of payment being received. We use UPS in the continental US and Canada.
- INTERNATIONAL BIDDERS WILL AGREE TO PAY VIA EBAY PAYMENTS, PAYPAL or BIDPAY and shipping is via USPS-EMS (Express Mail Service) only. (Except Canada). Custom Fees are BUYERS responsibility. We also ship to APO via USPS Priority Mail Insured. Shipments via USPS (United States Postal Service) are issued Monday and Thursday.
- Winning bidders, when the auction has ended please confirm the destination address no later than 3 days, so that we may bill you accordingly for shipping and handling. DO NOT SEND PAYMENT WITHOUT SHIPPING BEING QUOTED, PLEASE!

SHIPPING INFO: All of our prints are professionally packed and double wrapped for safe delivery. Shipping/packing charges are $6.50 for Insured UPS (Priority Mail for Box holders, APO/FPO addresses or upon request). I will ship ANY NUMBER of Gallery quality prints together for that price!

'(International orders are sent via DHL Worldwide. International shipping costs are: Canada - $16.00, all other International - $24.00).
(Please allow 2-4 days for order processing).

I'm always happy to combine multiple items to save on shipping!
Buyer to pay actual shipping charges. I never charge a handling fee!

BY BIDDING ON THIS AUCTION, YOU AGREE TO THE TERMS AND CONDITIONS LISTED BELOW:

Buyer agrees to contact us within 3 days with your complete billing address and contact information. Buyer also agrees to make payment within 10 days of auction end. If buyer does not abide by these conditions, negative feedback will be reported to Ebay.

Buyer understands that purchase price for the item described is AS IS, WHERE IS. We will hold you item for up to 30 days if you would like to pick it up.

SHIPPING:
Buyer pays all shipping charges. You may use the shipper of your choice or we can arrange shipping for you via a delivery company. We have very good rates and offer inside delivery. Placement, setup and cleanup of packing materials can be arranged for an additional charge.

RETURNS:
Returns must be made within 10 days of receipt of item. Refunds will be issued after item has been received in its original condition minus a 20% standard restocking fee. Please allow at least 2-4 weeks to process returns after item has been received. Delivery fees are non-refundable.

PAYMENT:
I accept Visa, Mastercard, American Express, Paypal, Personal Checks and Money Orders.

By contrast, here is an example of a listing description where the seller hasn't included any shipping or payment terms.

Description
The catalogue is from a comprehensive exhibition held at Craftsman Farms in Parsippany, New Jersey from November 15, 1992 to January 31, 1993. Extensive photos of exceptopnal pieces of furniture with emphasis on rare, early material & signatures. Production and text by A. Patricia Bartinque including commentary and essays from other knowledgeable people. This is an unused, new copy published by Turn of the Century Editions.

If you were interested in purchasing this item, you would have to email the seller for more information. This seller would do her potential customers a great service by putting some shipping and payment information into the description.

CONTACT THE SELLER

Usually, once an eBay listing has closed, the seller will send an email to the winning bidder or buyer with exact payment instructions. However, there is no set
protocol for who should email whom first. As a bidder, instead of waiting for the
seller to contact you, you should always email the seller immediately after the
listing has closed. If the seller hasn't included an actual price for shipping, provide your shipping address in the email and your preferred method of payment
so the seller can calculate shipping and respond with an amount.

ASK SELLER A QUESTION

As we mentioned in the previous chapter, whenever you have a question or doubt
about an item, email the seller. Use the Ask Seller a Question link on the Item Description page.

The Ask Seller a Question form looks like this:

Fill in your message and click the Send message button. Your message will be
emailed to the seller with a blind carbon copy sent to your own email address for
your records.

Regular Email

You can also email the seller from your own email application.

eBay-member email addresses are not displayed on the site. However, once a listing has closed, the high bidder and seller for that listing can "see" each other's email addresses. To view the seller's email address, navigate to the closed listing and click on the seller's User ID or go to the Sign In preferences page in your "My eBay" Preferences/Set Up and check the box for:

Display Settings

☑ See email addresses when viewing User IDs – if you are involved in a transaction. Learn more

---

Regardless of which method you use for contacting the seller, you can never be too conscientious or detailed in your message.

Provide the seller with all the information he or she will need in order to formulate a total amount due that includes shipping. To this end make sure you provide the following in your email:

The item number and title
Your eBay User ID
The item price
Your shipping address
Your preferred method of payment (from the options provided by the seller)

PAYMENT OPTIONS

All eBay sellers offer at least one of the following four possible payment methods:

Credit/Debit Cards
Electronic Checks
Money Orders
Checks

Credit Cards

Before 1998, any eBay seller who wished to accept credit card payments had to apply and pay for a special merchant account with the credit card company.

With recent introduction of online credit-card payment services like PayPal, anyone can accept credit cards without the expense or hassle of setting up a merchant account at a bank.

Opening a PayPal account is easy. Just go to **www.paypal.com** and follow the instructions for New Account.

Make it a habit in your search for treasure on eBay to give preference to those items whose sellers accept payment through PayPal or have an excellent feedback history. Using your credit card to buy online affords you the highest possible level of security. It's also the quickest way to pay for an item. That means it's not only the safest way to pay for the item, but it's also the fastest way to get your item shipped to you, since most sellers will ship an item the same day payment is received.

Electronic Checks

Along with credit cards, online payment services like PayPal also provide a second option for payment: the electronic check.

Electronic checks are an alternative for those buyers who have a checking account but do not use credit or debit cards. PayPal electronic checks are protected for up to the full amount transferred, making it as safe a payment method as a credit card.

Money Orders

Although paying with a money order is very old fashioned, many sellers offer them as either one of a selection of payment options or, in some cases, as the only payment method they will accept!

Make it a habit to write the item number and the seller's eBay User ID in the memo section of the money order, and make sure to keep your money order receipt in a safe place in case you need it later.

Checks

As a payment method, checks are less popular than they were in the early days of eBay. It's easy to see why, as more and more eBay sellers are accepting credit cards. Still, there are those sellers who will only accept checks or money orders.

If you pay for an item using a check, make sure to keep a record of the check in your checking account register. Although not as secure or fast as paying with a credit card, a canceled check is considered ample evidence of your having paid for an item.

As with a money order, make sure you put the item number and seller's User ID in the check's memo field.

Cash?

Cash as payment would be appropriate if you plan to pay for and pick up the item yourself, for example, if you bought something on eBay from a seller in your location.

Never send cash through the mail. Should something go wrong (the seller doesn't receive the cash or you don't receive your item), you will have no record of payment and, consequently, no avenue of redress.

EBAY'S CHECKOUT FEATURE

Many eBay sellers will provide you, the buyer, with the eBay Checkout feature. Checkout facilitates the last steps of an eBay transaction by collecting all of the payment and shipping information and options into one central place.

Not all sellers take advantage of eBay's Checkout feature. If the seller does use Checkout, the closed listing page will display a "Pay Now" button:

Click the button to begin the Checkout process. Depending on how the seller has configured Checkout, you may see the following screens.

Select your Shipping Address or add a new address:

My Shipping Adresses

Select

Jim Griffith
123 Smart Ducky Lane
Quackville, OH 88888 , USA

Edit

You can add, edit, or remove address in your address book.

Your preferred zip code or country will be shown to the sellers once an item ends.

Or enter a new address

Contact name:

Address:

City:

State/ Province:

ZIP/ Postal Code:

Country: United States

Primary phone number:
optional   ex. 408-555-1212

☑ Make this my preferred shipping address

☑ Show this page every time I checkout.

Add Address & Continue >

Enter the Payment and Shipping Total:

Checkout: Shipping & Payment Information

① Shipping & Payment   2 Submit Payment

Ship to

Jim Griffith
123 Smart Ducky Lane
Quackville, OH 88888 , USA

Change shipping address

Enter the total and select a payment method. Then click the **Continue** button below. Your address and payment information will be emailed to you and the seller.

Item	Price	Qty	Subtotal
Genuine Leather Western Belt Sz. Extar Large			
#958335103	$12.00	1	$12.00

Enter total
(include S&H and other fees) $ [   ]

Ensure the total you enter is accurate. Seller reserves the right to accept the total you submit.

- OR -

▸ **If you are unsure what to pay, you can ask seller for total.**

Payment method
(Please select)

    Credit Card
    Electronic Check
    Other

Use eBay Payments for Full Purchase Protection!

Payment instructions   Seller says:

    Payment instructions not
    specified by seller.

Note: The seller has not provided a payment address for this item. If you plan to mail payment to the seller, you may want to request this address from the seller.

Message to seller
(optional)

[   ]

You should not put credit card numbers or other confidential numbers into this box as this message will be sent to the seller via email.

[Continue >]

This is where you would enter the total amount, including shipping and handling (if not provided, contact the seller for a total).

You also select your payment method on this screen. Again, the options for payment provided in Checkout will differ from seller to seller. (If you elect to use a credit card, you may be prompted on the next screen to either enter the information for a credit card or select from one or more credit cards you previously placed on file with the online payment service.)

Next, review the payment information:

Checkout: Review Payment Information

1 Shipping & Payment   ② **Submit Payment**

Item	Price	Qty	Subtotal
Genuine Leather Western Belt Sz. Extar Large			
#958335103	$12.00	1	$12.00

Shipping & handling		$2.50
Sales tax		$0.00
Total		**$14.50**

Shipping address   Jim Griffith

123 Smart Ducky Lane
Quackville, OH 88888
United States
888-555-1212
Change shipping address

Payment method   Credit Card 🔒
Visa ending with 6921
Change to electronic check | Change credit card

Payment Instructions   Seller says:

Message to seller
(optional)

Submit >

eBay Payments Help

Review your order and click the **Submit** button below. A confirmation email will be sent to you and the seller.

Click the button and you're finished paying!

Checkout: Completed

Congratulations! Your payment has been sent to the seller.

| Seller: smiles9 (6944) | | | 09/12/2002 |

Shipping to   **Billing information**

Jim Griffith   Jim Griffith

123 Smart Ducky Lane   123 Smart Ducky Lane
Quackville, OH 88888   Quackville, OH 88888
United States   United States
888-555-1212   888-555-1212

Item	Price	Qty	Subtotal
Genuine Leather Western Belt Sz. Extar Large			
#958335103	$12.00	1	$12.00

Shipping & handling		$2.50
Sales tax		$0.00
Total		**$14.50**

GRIFF TIP: Since each seller will have different payment options, shipping totals, etc., always follow the individual Checkout instructions contained within any of the above windows to request a total or pay for the item.

NOTE: At the time I was writing this, eBay had announced the acquisition of PayPal and the eventual dissolution of eBay Payments (BillPoint), so by the time you read this, the Checkout feature may look a bit different.

BID AND PURCHASES MANAGEMENT WITH "MY EBAY"

The "My eBay" Bidding/Watching tab—there is simply no better tool for tracking your current bids and completed items within the last thirty days.

You can read more about "My eBay" in Chapter 2.

COMPILING AND ARCHIVING LISTINGS
WHERE YOU ARE THE WINNER

It's smart to save a copy of all your winning bids on eBay. You never know when you might need the copy. For example, if you sell the item later, you may need some documentation to show how much you paid for it. A copy of your payment receipt plus a printout of the Item Description page should prove more than adequate proof of price and date of sale.

This simplest archive consists of printed copies of each item description page where you are the buyer. To make a print record, navigate to an item description page, let it load completely (look for "done" on the status bar on the bottom of the browser window), then print out the listing page by selecting File, Print on your Web browser's command bar.

It helps to have a color printer.

To save a soft copy, you can save any item page by clicking the File, Save As commands on your Web browser's menu command bar.

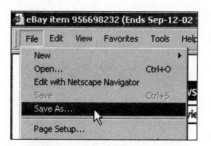

When you save the file, in the Save box, choose: "Save as Type: Web Page, complete 9*htm,*html" and note where you save it. (We are saving ours on our desktop.)

GRIFF TIP! Some sellers have limited Web server space for their pictures. Once one of their listings ends, they tend soon after to delete the picture files from their Web server space in order free up space for pictures of new listings. Consequently, it is not uncommon to visit a completed listing and find the images are all missing and in their place are little boxes with red *x*'s. Therefore, if you wish to archive a closed listing as hard or soft copy and you want to include the pictures of that item, you should do so as soon as possible after the item closes before the seller has deleted the picture files.

If there is an eBay Picture Services image that you want to save as a file and only the thumbnail for that image is showing on the item page, you need to do the following.

Save the entire page per the previous instructions.
Click on the selected thumbnail to open the bigger copy of that image:

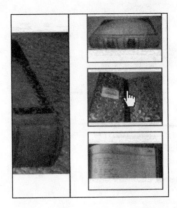

Hover your mouse cursor over the image. A small box with four icons will pop up on the upper left-hand corner of the picture. Click on the icon for "Save this image."

In the Save Picture dialog box, navigate to the same folder created by the "Save As Web Page, complete" when you saved a complete copy of the page. Ours is on our desktop, and the folder uses the item title within its folder name.

Click on the folder to open it.
Click the Save button.

Repeat the above steps for each image you want to save for future use.

UNPACKING YOUR ITEM

You've contacted the seller and paid for the item. The seller shipped the item to you.

Finally, the package arrives and you are giddy with delight. In fact, no small part of the appeal of regularly shopping on eBay is waiting for the UPS, FedEx, or USPS deliveryman to drop off your treasure. Your first impulse is to rip the package open.

But wait. If the item is fragile or expensive, you may want to go get your camera and maybe a friend or family member before you open the package, especially if the item inside the package is breakable.

As you open the package, have your friend or family member photograph the process with a minimum of three shots. One shot of the package before you open it; one shot of the package as you are just finished opening it; and finally, one shot of you lifting the item out of the package.

Even better, use your video camera if you have one. Either way—photos or video—you want to create a record of your opening the package and inspecting the item.

Why the record? Why, for insurance, of course! If, for whatever reason, the item was damaged, either before or during transit, the photos or video could prove invaluable when submitting a claim with the delivery service.

EMAIL THE SELLER . . . AGAIN!

As a common courtesy, let the seller know that the package arrived and that you are pleased with it.

If you are not pleased, or if the item arrived damaged or never arrived, let them know. Any good eBay seller will usually bend over backward to assist with insurance claims or missing packages.

LEAVE FEEDBACK

Based on how your experience went with the seller, leave appropriate feedback to let the rest of the eBay world know.

6

Special Bidding and Buying Considerations

In the previous chapters, we've covered almost every aspect of bidding, buying, and paying for goods offered by eBay sellers. Almost everything.

There are some specialty eBay items and categories that bear closer scrutiny.

Buying Big Stuff on eBay

When most folks think of "eBay," they tend to think of things that can fit in a cardboard box: toys, collectibles, clothing, pottery, small pieces of furniture, etc. Although many of the items for sale on eBay are indeed small enough to ship through the post, more and more, eBay sellers are putting up big items for bid and sale.

EBAY MOTORS—CARS, TRUCKS, BOATS, ETC.

eBay is the perfect place to buy a car. Car sellers range from the individual owner to used, new, and classic car dealerships.

All things "automotive" have their own special area of eBay called "eBay Motors." This includes cars, trucks, motorcycles, boats, ATVs, campers, snowmobiles, buses, and aircraft. Also for sale in the eBay Motors site are accessories for all of the above, as well as manuals, collectibles, tools, parts, and apparel.

You can get to eBay Motors from the home page:

Although the eBay Motors site is just slightly different in design, the basic layout of the site is identical to the rest of eBay. Categories are on the left-hand side of the page and include every aspect of all things automotive, nautical, and aeronautical.

Searching, bidding, and paying for items on eBay Motors is just like for the rest of eBay, with a few special considerations.

Some eBay Motors sellers have special payment terms, such as a percentage deposit immediately at the end of the listing. As always, make sure you read the seller terms carefully and that you fully understand and accept them before you bid. When in doubt, contact the seller for information and clarification.

If you are buying a car, boat, or any other similarly heavy item on eBay Motors, you will probably be more involved in the shipping aspect of the item than you might be for nonautomotive items. Unless the big item is near your location, you will have to arrange and pay for shipping. If the item you are interested in will need to be shipped, you should determine a close estimate of the shipping costs before you bid.

Most eBay Motors sellers provide, within the item descriptions, links to various third-party auto shippers who can help you, prebid, to figure shipping costs from the car's current location to your location.

Under the section for Motor Services, eBay also provides some suggestions for shippers, as well as for insurance, warranties, and registration options.

eBay might not jump to mind when you are hunting for a new home or property, but as of this writing there are over three thousand listings in the eBay Real Estate category, ranging from residential homes to businesses.

Also as of this writing, all items in the eBay Real Estate category are "non-binding." The real estate listings look and feel just like other eBay listings, and anyone may submit a bid; but the owner is not obliged to sell to the high bidder.

However, this is changing. As eBay obtains the proper licenses for each state, real estate listings for those states will become binding. Check the eBay site for more information and updates as they are announced.

When considering buying or bidding on real estate on eBay . . .

More so than with non-real-estate listings, always get as much information as possible before you bid. If the house or property is listed by an individual, email her for more pictures, etc.

Whenever possible, arrange to view the property before bidding.

For more information, visit the Real Estate Rules page. From the eBay home page, look for and click the links for Real Estate:

This will take you to the Real Estate home page. Once there, click on the link for Residential:

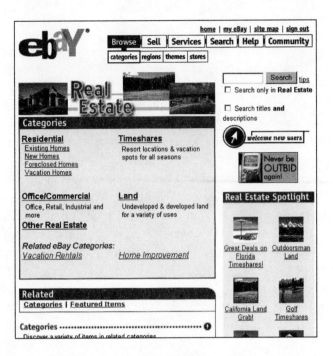

On the Real Estate: Residential home page, look on the lower right-hand side for links to Helpful Resources:

INTERNATIONAL BUYING

eBay may have started out as a small hobby site in San Jose, California, in 1995, but in just eight short years, it has expanded to cover the globe!

As of this writing, over fifty countries are now represented on eBay on nineteen separate eBay International sites.

You can navigate directly to any of the International eBay sites from any of the links on the bottom left corner of the eBay home page.

Global Sites	
Argentina	Korea
Australia	Mexico
Austria	Netherlands
Belgium	New Zealand
Brazil	Singapore
Canada	Spain
France	Sweden
Germany	Switzerland
Ireland	Taiwan
Italy	United Kingdom

Although instantly recognizable by the eBay logo and colors, each international eBay site has its own distinct look and feel and language.

The majority of eBay transactions at **www.ebay.com** take place between North American buyers and sellers. However, as eBay continues to expand around the world, folks from other countries are searching both their own eBay sites and the US eBay site.

Any registered eBay member can search for and bid on items listed on any of the eBay International sites. The only requirement is some ability to read and understand the description and terms for the item. For example, there are loads of fabulous items listed on the eBay Italia site:

If you have some grasp of Italian and the seller is not averse to shipping the item to your location, then by all means, bid away!

Searching

You can include all countries, a selected country, or all English-speaking countries by using the Advanced Search feature located under the Search link on the eBay Navigation Bar:

If you want to limit your search to those countries that will ship to your country location, first make sure the "Available to country selected" radio-button is checked. Select your country location from the drop-down list. This will limit the search results to all listings where the sellers are willing to ship to your country.

This search will limit the results to only those where the seller will ship to the US.

To limit your search for items sold from a specific country, click on the "Located in country selected" radio-button and pick the appropriate country from the drop-down list. **NOTE:** Even though you have limited your search to a specific country, read seller's descriptions carefully to make sure she will ship to your country.

To find items available to (or located in) the US from all sites in addition to the English site default, click on the "Search English language sites" check box to remove the checkmark. (To restore the default, click the check box again and the checkmark will reappear.)

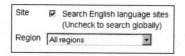

Currency

When you are shopping on an International eBay site, the items listed will show bid amounts in the currency of that country. It helps to have a basic understanding of the conversion rate between the two countries.

On eBay, you can see the current bid price of an international item in your currency by looking on the top of the item description page next to the seller-specified currency:

Currently	**EUR 180.00** *(approx. US $158.27)*
Quantity	**1**
Time left	**9 days, 20 hours +**

NOTE: This feature only displays the price in both your currency and the seller's currency when you have accessed the item through the eBay US Advanced Search box.

You can also get a more accurate currency-conversion amount by using one of the several online currency conversion and calculating sites, such as: **http:// www.bloomberg.com/markets/ currency/currcalc.html.**

Keep in mind that should you win an item listed on an International site, you are obligated to pay the seller the final bid amount in the currency of the seller's country. The closest estimate of the final bid price is shown using red font in parentheses next to the high bid. Use this figure when writing a check, making a wire transfer, or using your credit card.

PayPal will make the conversion for you automatically with no extra input on your end.

Credit card issuers will convert currency automatically from dollars into the foreign currency of the international eBay seller. You only need to know the correct amount in dollars for the final bid price.

For electronic checks handled directly by your bank, your bank will convert the currencies for you. Again, you need only let them know the amount in dollars.

As for international money orders or checks, you will have to find out from the seller how to make out the amounts so they are properly converted.

PAYMENT OPTIONS

If the seller accepts online credit-card payments, pay using your credit card. Most international sellers now have access to some type of online payment service. PayPal, for example, is now available to sellers in countries around the world.

If you have a preferred method of paying and the seller doesn't offer that method in his item description, suggest it via email to the seller, *before you bid!* Otherwise, understand that you are obligated to use one of the payment methods specified by the seller in his item description.

An international money order is a workable alternative for those listings where the seller doesn't or cannot offer an online credit-card payment option. Note that the USPS has a limited number of foreign countries where USPS international money orders are accepted. Check with the USPS site for more information (**www.usps.com**).

Remember to include any and all shipping costs and any additional fees/taxes with your payment.

Shipping Costs and Methods

International shipping costs are dependent on one or more of the following factors:

- The weight and dimensions of the packaged item
- The method of shipment (ground, next-day air, etc.) and the shipper (UPS, International Post, FedEx, etc.)
- Seller location
- Buyer location

In addition to shipping costs, buyers are usually responsible for any additional costs like duties, taxes, and customs clearance fees.

To calculate shipping for UPS shipped items, visit the **UPS Quick Cost Calculator** at: **http://www.servicecenter.ups.com/ebay/ebay.html#qcost**.

FedEx also has a rate calculator page at: **http://www.fedex.com/us**.

Taxes

In most instances, as a US buyer purchasing from an International seller, you will not be liable for taxes. If you are unsure, email the seller and ask about taxes before you bid.

Language

It's overstating the obvious, but if you are interested in bidding on or buying an item from a French-speaking seller on the eBay France site, it would probably be a good idea that you have some fluency in French.

If you don't, you may want to email the seller first, in English, asking politely for a description in English.

There are Web sites that can help you translate text or an entire Web page from one language to another. One of the more popular is BabelFish: **http://babelfish. altavista.com.**

GRIFF TIP: Translation Web sites can be helpful in getting the gist of information from an item description, but they aren't perfect! They tend to translate word for word with no regard for idioms and colloquialisms. This can result in translated sentences that do not make sense or, worse, mean something other than what they appear to mean.

Customs

The duty rate for many items bought online is usually zero. However, you should never assume this is always the case.

All goods brought into another country must clear that country's customs. In some cases, a customs duty may apply. If so, the recipient of the item is liable for the duty.

The sender is responsible for filling out a customs form for the item before the item is shipped. Again, not all items incur a customs duty. It can depend on the country, the value of the item, the type of the item, and the type of delivery. For example, it is much less complicated to send an item via International Post as opposed to a courier service (private shipping company). There is usually no duty for most items of a value less than $200 sent via International Post. In any case, make sure that the seller provides you with a receipt on her letterhead for customs, indicating the age and value of the item. The transaction value can usually be based on the price the buyer actually pays the seller. Depending on the item, you may need to make an export declaration or acquire an export license.

The US Customs Web site has a page devoted to Internet Transactions: **http://www.customs.ustreas.gov/impoexpo/impoexpo.htm.**

REGIONAL TRADING—BUYING LOCALLY!

Another way to buy big things is to do so locally. eBay provides tools and filters to limit your category view and search results to only those items that are listed by sellers located in your metropolitan area.

Regional trading comes in very handy for:

- Hard-to-ship items like cars, appliances, and furniture
- Fragile or breakable items like glassware, computers, and chandeliers
- Items of local interest like tickets and real estate

There are two methods for finding items listed in your local area:

- Browsing from your regional home page
- Searching regionally

Browsing from Your Regional Home Page

Navigate to the Local Trading home page from the eBay Navigation Bar by clicking Browse and then Regions:

This brings you to the Local Trading page:

From here, you can select your region by clicking the link for it. Let's click Salt Lake City:

Detroit	Rochester
Grand Rapids	Sacramento
Greensboro →	Salt Lake City
Hartford	San Antonio
Honolulu	San Diego
Houston	San Francisco

This takes us to the Salt Lake City region home page:

These regional home pages contain a listing of all the top-level eBay categories except that each one will only display items that were listed from the selected region—in this case, Salt Lake City.

Searching regionally

Another method for searching eBay with all results limited to a single region is described in detail in the Find It chapter. Let's review it here:

Click the Search link on the eBay Navigation Bar:

In the Search window, click the box for "Item location." Scroll down to and click your region.

Once you have selected a region, create your search using keywords and select any appropriate options for Words to Exclude, Price Range, etc.

All of the results of your Search will be filtered to show only those items matching your search criteria and listed in UT—Salt Lake City.

There's one more very important eBay buyer-related chapter in this book: eBay Guidelines, Rules, and Help for Buyers.

eBay Guidelines, Rules, and Help for Buyers

eBay Buyer Guidelines and Rules

All members of the eBay Community have a responsibility to ensure that their buying, selling, and chatting activity on the site is conducted within all eBay rules and guidelines. During my time with eBay Customer Support, the lion's share of the buyer mistakes and subsequent difficulties I have seen were due to ignorance of these rules and guidelines.

You can avoid difficulties of this sort by reading through the eBay rules and guidelines. Included in this chapter are the most basic topics regarding bidding and buying rules and guidelines. Everything in this chapter can also be found on the eBay site in the Rules and Safety pages.

You can reach these pages from the eBay Navigation Bar by clicking "Help."

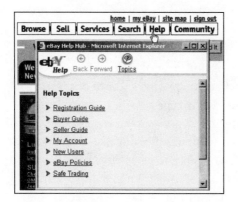

On the resulting pop-up window (the eBay Help Hub page), look for the links for "Safe Trading" and "eBay Policies."

A BUYER CHECKLIST

Much of the grief and frustration in the world is traceable back to someone, somewhere, who makes a few innocent assumptions and who then forges ahead, only to find himself unexpectedly enmeshed in chaos and confusion—realizing all too late that his initial assumptions were, in fact, false.

This holds true for eBay members as well. Whenever shopping on eBay, never assume! A fully informed eBay shopper is a happy eBay buyer. This means asking questions, doing research, and informing yourself of the eBay rules regarding bidding and buying.

Here is a basic checklist for the responsible eBay Buyer:

Ask First

If a seller isn't clear in her listing about the condition of an item or her own payment and shipping terms, ask her before you bid.

Research

If you are unsure about an item's value, condition, or authenticity, ask or research before you bid. For the actual condition or authenticity of an item, always ask the seller first. For value, use the eBay chat boards or search the Internet to do some price comparison. Seek out those folks on the topic-specific chat boards who are experts in their fields and ask them about a particular item.

Check Feedback and Leave Feedback

Although I have mentioned it many times throughout the preceding chapters, it bears repeating: Make it a habit to always check a seller's feedback, even before you read his item description or look at the item pictures! And don't just rely on the feedback number. Page through the list of comments left for that seller so that you can best determine what type of seller he is.

There is no rule stating that you must leave feedback for sellers. However, the giving and receiving of feedback is a lot like the sport of logrolling; it takes co-operation on the part of both parties in order for it to work.

If you want to establish your own sterling feedback history, you will often have to take the initiative and leave positive feedback first.

Keep Your eBay Password to Yourself!

Never grant access to your eBay account to anyone except maybe your spouse, and only if you trust him or her implicitly. Under no circumstances should you ever grant access to your children. No matter what the circumstances may be in your defense, you are responsible for any and all activity conducted using your eBay User ID and you, as the account holder, will be held responsible in the event that your account is employed for nefarious or illegal activity on eBay.

NOTE: eBay will *never* send you an email asking for your password, credit card number, or other personal or financial information, nor will eBay ever ask you to reconfirm a previously confirmed registration. If you receive an email that appears to have come from eBay and the email requests that you provide any of your personal information in a reply or instructs you to visit a Web site to supply any of your personal information, you should immediately report the email to eBay.

Use a Secure Method of Payment

Look for those listings where the seller takes credit or debit cards or provides a wire-transfer or electronic-check option through PayPal. Give these listings preference. Yes, there are many good, honest sellers who do not accept credit cards. If you simply must have her item, make sure her feedback is acceptable to you and read up on her return policy. If a seller doesn't have a refund policy on his item page, "Ask First" before you bid.

Avoid Questionable Activity

There are specific bidding activities that are prohibited on eBay. It is your responsibility to know what these prohibited activities are and to avoid employing them. You can find a comprehensive list of questionable and prohibited activity by clicking on the Help link on the eBay Navigation Bar and clicking the link for "eBay Policies" (as described earlier.)

eBay Rules for Buyers

The following describe the more common buyer infractions and how to avoid them.

- **Transaction interference.** Defined as: emailing buyers in an open or ended transaction to warn them away from a seller or item. If you have had an unsatisfactory experience with a seller, you can let the rest of the eBay community know by leaving appropriate feedback.

- Contacting a seller and offering to purchase the listed item outside of eBay. This is a violation of eBay rules and policies. It is definitely not in keeping with the spirit of eBay.
- **Bid Retraction.** You can, as a bidder, retract your bid in any eBay listing that has not yet ended. The link for retracting a bid can be found on the bottom of the My eBay page for Bidding/Watching.

> **Buying-Related Links**
>
> **Bidding information**
> New to eBay' tutorial
> Buyer's Guide
> Tips for buyers
> Bidding basics
> Bidding Frequently Asked Questions
> Retracting a bid ⬅
> What to do after the auction ends

It's OK to retract a bid if . . .

- You accidentally enter a wrong bid amount. For instance, you bid $99.50 instead of $9.95. (If this occurs you will need to quickly reenter the correct bid amount.)
- The description of an item you have bid on has changed significantly.
- You cannot reach the seller. This means that you have tried calling the seller and his or her phone number doesn't work, or you have tried emailing a message to the seller and it comes back undeliverable.

It's NOT OK to retract a bid if . . .

- You change your mind about the item.
- You decide you can't really afford it.
- You bid a little higher than you promised yourself you'd go.
- You only bid to uncover the seller's reserve amount or the current high bidder's maximum bid. (This is a serious offense that could result in the suspension of your eBay registration.)

Special Retraction Rules

If you place a bid before the last twelve-hour period of the auction:

You may retract that bid before that last twelve-hour period, but only for exceptional circumstances. You will not be allowed to retract that bid during the last twelve-hour period of the listing.

If you place a bid during the last twelve-hour period of the listing:

You will be allowed to retract the bid for exceptional circumstances, but only if you do so within one hour after placing the bid.

If you are not allowed to retract your bid during the last twelve-hour period of the listing, you may contact the seller to request that your bid be canceled. The seller will have the discretion whether to cancel your bid. When you retract a bid before the last twelve hours of a listing, you will eliminate all bids you have placed for that listing. If you are correcting a bid error, you will have to bid again. When you retract a bid within the last twelve hours of the listing, you will eliminate only the most recent bid you placed. Bids you placed prior to the last twelve hours will not be retracted. Your total number of bid retractions in the past six months is displayed in your Feedback Profile on the bottom of the page in the ID Card section:

eBay will thoroughly investigate bid retractions, and abuse of this feature may result in the suspension of your eBay account.

Unwelcome Buyer

Defined as bidding or buying in violation of the terms set forth by the seller in the listing description. Some examples:

- Seller states she ships to "home country" only and the buyer is outside the stated shipping area.
- Seller states she will not accept bids from members who have negative feedback.
- Bidder rebids after the seller has canceled his bid and requested he not bid on or purchase her items. (Sellers have every right to reject bids from certain bidders for whatever reason they choose. A bidder who has been asked to not bid must comply with that seller's wishes.)
- Bidder uses a second eBay registration to bid on an item after his first registration has been blocked by a seller.

Bid shielding

Defined as the deliberate use of secondary User IDs or other eBay members to temporarily raise the level of bidding and/or price of an item to extremely high levels in order to protect the low bid level of another bidder.

Shill bidding

Defined as using secondary User IDs or other eBay members to artificially raise the level of bidding and/or price of an item. Additionally, to avoid the appearance of being involved in this activity, family members and individuals living together, working together, or sharing a computer may not bid on each other's items.

Feedback Offenses

If you are not happy with the item, contact the seller and let him know *before you leave negative feedback!* It's always best to try to work out a solution with the seller first. If you and the seller are unable to reach a solution agreeable to both parties, then consider dispute resolution through a third party like Square-Trade (**www.squaretrade.com**).

Leave negative feedback only as a last resort.

Never use profanity or vulgar language in your feedback comments or responses to others.

Never include any part of another user's contact information in a feedback comment or response. This includes names!

Never post a Web or email link in a feedback comment or response.

Non-Paying Bidder (NPB)

When you bid on and win or buy an item on eBay and subsequently do not pay the seller for that item, you become what is known in eBay parlance as a "Non-Paying Bidder" or NPB for short. (We used to call them Dead Beat Bidders. Some sellers still do.)

A bid is binding on eBay. Winning the bid and then not following through with the transaction is against eBay rules.

When a buyer does not pay for his item, the seller can file a report with eBay requesting a credit for the Final Value Fee for that item. As part of this credit request process, the seller will be prompted to select a reason for making the credit request. If the reason selected is "buyer backed out," a Non-Paying Bidder mark will be made against your account.

Chronic NPBs run the risk of receiving scathing negative feedback. In addition, upon receipt of a third Non-Paying Bidder report, that bidder is suspended from eBay.

AVOID BIDDING ON QUESTIONABLE ITEMS

During your quest for treasure on eBay, you may stumble upon an item whose legitimacy or legality may be questionable and indeed, there are many categories of items and specific items that sellers may not offer on eBay. Some of these prohibited items are no-brainers—controlled substances, nuclear weapons—but others are not so obvious.

Did you know that the sale of bear parts is not allowed on eBay? Bear rugs, paws, heads, organs, and so on, are legal to sell everywhere in the United States save for one state, California. The black bear is the California state animal. It is illegal in California to trade in bear parts. eBay is headquartered in California, and chooses to apply this prohibition against the sale of bear parts across all of eBay.

There is a list of prohibited items on the eBay website at: **http://pages.ebay.com/ help/community/png-items.html**.

Navigate to this page by clicking the Help link on the eBay Navigation Bar, and then click the Rules and Safety link on the sub–navigation bar. This takes you to the Rules and Safety Overview page. Look for and click the link on this page labeled "Items that may not be allowed for sale."

REPORTING QUESTIONABLE ACTIVITY OR ITEMS

There is a process in place on the eBay Web site that eBay members can use to report questionable activity or items directly to eBay Customer Support.

The process begins on the eBay Help pages (as described above).

1. Click the link on the eBay Navigation bar for Help.
2. This will bring up the main topic pop-up window. Click the link for Getting Started>Getting Help>Customer Support.
3. Click through the subsequent windows till you find the link for contacting eBay and follow the instructions from there.

Within a matter of minutes of sending your report, you will receive an auto-acknowledgement email from Customer Support to confirm the receipt of your email report. Once the report is investigated thoroughly, eBay Customer Support will send you an email with the outcome of the report.

DISPUTE RESOLUTION

Most eBay sellers, especially the more successful sellers, know how important it is to put the needs of the customer first. These sellers are a dream to buy from.

You can tell if a seller is a customer-first seller by checking her feedback and her item description.

Even so, you may someday find yourself in a dispute with a seller and fault or blame may be impossible to assign. Don't get angry. Keep your mind focused on your goal: resolving the dispute as soon as possible and putting the transaction behind you. NO OTHER GOAL IS WORTH PURSUING! Any warlike behavior like "getting even," "one-upmanship," "tit-for-tat" . . . all are pointless in the end and only contribute to the world's vast pool of ill will. They certainly won't get you a resolution.

In the event of a dispute with a seller, remember to stay calm and civil.

Even though you and I know that the customer is always right, some sellers are not convinced. It doesn't mean that they are bad sellers—just that they haven't quite gotten the picture yet. Help them. Never lose your temper. Keep your emails polite and nonprovocative. If you resist the temptation to start screaming in an email, the seller will be more likely to listen to your complaint and your suggestions for resolution.

Offer to work out the dispute with the seller. If the seller is agreeable, there are third-party dispute arbitration services like SquareTrade that can help.

www.squaretrade.com

SquareTrade is a third-party fee-based service that will assign a professional, qualified arbitrator to listen to both sides of the dispute before issuing a best remedy for the dispute. In most instances, the SquareTrade arbitrator can assist you and the other member reach a solution that is agreeable to both parties.

Many sellers sign up with SquareTrade as a matter of good business. By signing up with SquareTrade, these sellers agree to a certain standard of conduct on eBay. Sellers who join with SquareTrade will display the SquareTrade icon in their item descriptions:

LAST RESORT—THE EBAY FRAUD PROTECTION PROGRAM

If all your attempts to resolve the dispute have failed (email, phone, Square-Trade), and if the dispute involves a transaction where you are the buyer and if one of the following is true:

The item did not arrive in the condition pictured or stated on the item page. The item did not arrive at all—you may want to use the eBay Fraud Protection Program.

All registered eBay members are eligible for coverage under the eBay Fraud Protection Program. Most items on eBay are covered for up to $200 (minus $25 to cover processing costs). Please note: The maximum reimbursement for any claim is $175. For example:

If the item price is $500, you are eligible to receive $175;
If the item price is $100, you are eligible to receive $75;
If the item price is $26, you are eligible to receive $1.

To learn how the eBay Fraud Protection Program works and to determine if your situation warrants reporting through the programs, click on the Help link on the eBay Navigation Bar.

In the eBay Help Hub pop-up window, click on the links for Buyer Guide, Trusting the Seller, and Payment.

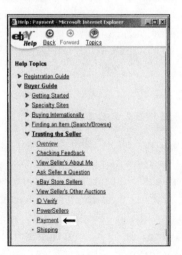

On the Help page for Payments, scroll down to and click the link for eBay's Fraud Protection Program.

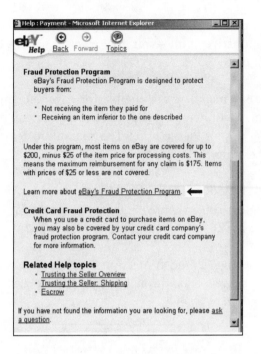

HOW TO GET HELP ON EBAY

Although I have tried my best to make this book as comprehensive as humanly possible—covering every imaginable aspect of eBay and more—it would be impossible to anticipate everything that could possibly happen on eBay. You may find yourself with an issue or question that this book does not address (Heaven forefend!). The following pathways to eBay Help should address these rare instances.

FINDING HELP ON THE EBAY WEB SITE

As discussed in the "Navigating eBay" chapter, there is a mountain of information about all things eBay on the eBay site itself. Most of it is pretty easy to find.

Most of eBay's Help pages are contained in special pop-up windows called the eBay Help Hub. You can activate them by clicking any of the links labeled Help, wherever they appear on the eBay site. The most common starting point for Help is the Help link on the eBay Navigation Bar. If you click it, you will see a version of the following window.

There is a list of main Help topic links in the first eBay Help Hub pop-up box:

> Registration Guide
> Buyer Guide
> Seller Guide
> My Account
> New Users
> eBay Policies
> Safe Trading

You can always return back to these seven topics no matter where you are in the Help windows by clicking the link for "Topics" at the top of the window.

Start on the appropriate topic and click through the subtopics related to your question. When you find yourself in an area containing content related to your question, read through it to find a possible response.

If you don't find a response that addresses your particular question, click through the subtopic windows.

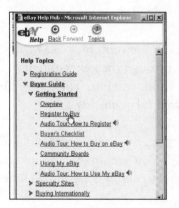

Topics indicated with the "dot" will usually contain a link labeled "If you have not found the information you are looking for, please ask a question."

This will bring up a Web form for sending email to Customer Support.

NOTE #1: Most, but not all, the subtopic pages will display this link. You may have to do a little hunting through the help content in order to find one that will open an email Web form window. Hint: The image above showing Bidder Tips shows how to reach the Web form quickly.

NOTE #2: In order to use the eBay Help pages, your Web browser must be configured to run JavaScript. If you are unable to view the Help pop-up windows, go to page 251 to learn how to configure your Web browser to use Java scripts.

EBAY EDUCATION

eBay is dedicated to helping new and experienced eBay members alike learn how to use the eBay site more effectively. To this end, there are two ongoing eBay educational initiatives available to all eBay members.

eBay On-Site Tutorials

For those eBay members who desire a detailed explanation of how to bid, how to sell, etc., there are excellent real-time basic tutorials available on the eBay site.

To get there, type the following into your Web browser's address window and press Enter: **http://pages.ebay.com/education**.

eBay Education is divided into six separate areas; each one indicated by a clickable icon.

There are tour pages for Selling, Buying, How to Register, and How eBay Works. In addition there are links to the eBay Workshops and eBay University.

eBay Workshops

eBay hosts a series of regularly scheduled eBay Workshops on specific eBay topics such as "Trust and Safety" and "How to Sell 45 Records on eBay." These workshops are presented in a moderated chat-board format with a guest "speaker" answering real-time questions from eBay members.

You can see the current schedule of Chat Workshops by visiting the About Me page for workshopevents, **http://members.ebay.com/aboutme/workshopevents**.

If you have questions related to specific aspects of selling, you should check the Workshop schedule on a regular basis.

If you are interested in hosting a workshop in your particular field of interest, send an email to **bo@ebay.com**.

Community Discussion Boards

Chat boards played an important role in the formation and growth of eBay, and they continue to do so today.

eBay started out with one chat board called the AuctionWeb Bulletin Board. It was a place where a new eBay member could come to learn from eBay veterans, among many topics, how to list an item for sale, how to create and host digital pictures, how to pack an item correctly, and how to find the best deals on packing materials.

It was also a place where folks could meet and chat about nearly anything.

Over time, this one board grew into two, then three, and then four. Today, there are over eighty separate chat areas on eBay, each one dedicated to a special topic or aspect of buying, selling, or collecting.

These discussion boards are often a source of excellent help and information provided by other eBay experts themselves. I urge you to visit them by clicking on the Community link on the eBay Navigation Bar and selecting the link for either Forums or Chat Boards.

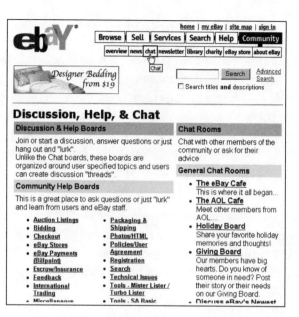

The discussions can become pretty raucous at times, but it's all in good fun. Find a topic that interests you and either lurk (read the posts without participating) or get involved and ask a question, introduce yourself, or help answer questions.

You will find instructions on how to use the chat forums—how to post, how to search, the rules of conduct, and so on—by clicking any of the links on the various chat pages.

eBay member Deanna Rittel has this to say about the eBay Chat forums:

I truly enjoy the chat boards on eBay. I usually "hang out" at the Town Square but have been known to wander over to the others occasionally. I've learned more on them than I ever thought I would and sometimes more than I ever needed to! In three days I had three different items that I needed to identify. In each case I literally had the item identified in less than five minutes. There are very knowledgeable and helpful people willing to help at the drop of a pin.

Just last week I posted on the Town Square that I was looking for a couple of specific "state" quarters for my two children who are collecting them. Everyone went through their change and located the ones I needed within minutes. We had been looking for them for weeks—a couple of months at least! One specific poster emailed me directly—he offered to send my children "mint uncirculated" coins every time they come out. He collects them also and told me he would love to make my children happy and complete their collection for them. These quarters only come out every few months and only five are issued each year. So these will take quite a few more years to complete. He said it was worth the money to make them happy. We have already received the quarters I had originally been looking for from some wonderful individuals on Town Square, and we also received the first "shipment" from the poster who is completing their collections. No one wanted to be reimbursed—I TRIED! My children are just absolutely thrilled, and to quote my six-year-old daughter, "Mom, have you ever met such a nice people? They aren't like those people who call you at work!" I work at an insurance company, if that tells you anything—I guess she really listens to my horror stories—LOL!

Finally—I would like to say that the eBay community is truly that—a community. There is always someone around on the boards to answer a question when you have one, make you laugh when you need to, offer a shoulder to cry on, and of course, there is always a good dose of controversy when you need a good argument!

eBay University

In June of 2000, eBay started a program called eBay University. An eBay U seminar consists of a day-long series of one-hour classes or workshops on all aspects of buying and selling on eBay. The seminars are held in a different city approximately every two weeks throughout the year. Attendance at a single eBay U varies from about five hundred to a thousand eager new and experienced eBay buyers and sellers.

eBay instructors are hired and trained by eBay to lead the various workshops. Currently, I instruct one or two of the workshops.

eBay University seminars are incredible experiences for both the instructors and attendees. Whether you are a brand-new eBay member or a seasoned old-time eBay expert, I urge you to check the eBay U schedule and see if we are coming to your town soon.

Course Locations	Come to a day-long class in your town taught by eBay experts. At eBay University, you'll soon discover that almost anything you can imagine can be found (and sold) on eBay. Fun, fast and easy, you'll be buying and selling like a pro in no time at all.
Boston, MA July 20, 2002	
Albuquerque, NM July 20, 2002	**Course Description**
Sioux Falls, SD July 27, 2002	Learn how to browse and search eBay for bargains and hard to find items. Learn the basics of selling and some advanced tips too. Learn the basis of HTML and how to add photos to your listings to make auctions more profitable. Learn why eBay is a safe place to do business. Get all your eBay questions answered. Meet other eBay users in your community. All this happens in a fun classroom atmosphere with other eBay enthusiasts. This class is taught by eBay experts who plan to share tips and tricks along with age-old wisdom of using the site. You'll spend the day in an interactive, personalized classroom setting and leave ready to conquer the world of eBay.
Sydney, Australia July 27, 2002	
Kansas City, MO July 27, 2002	
San Antonio, TX August 3, 2002	
St Louis, MO August 10, 2002	
Charlotte, NC August 10, 2002	
Milwaukee, WI August 24, 2002	**eBay Education**
Portland, OR September 14, 2002	`online seminars & recorded events` Listen and watch recorded events taught by eBay experts.
Raleigh, NC	

It's an excellent way to pick up a few tips, pass on your suggestions to eBay staff face-to-face, and meet other eBay members (who are without a doubt the most enthusiastic and fun group of people I've ever had the pleasure of meeting).

eBay Live

In June of 2001, eBay hosted its first user conference in Anaheim, California. The event, called "eBay Live," was attended by over five thousand eBay members of all ages and occupations from across the continental United States.

eBay Live 2002

The three days of peace, love, and trading—featuring parties, workshops, vendor booths, guest speakers, special events, and panel discussions with eBay executive staff—was such a hit that we hope to make it a regular yearly event.

Check the eBay Calendar of Events for more information about future eBay Live and other eBay events. Go to the Community link on the eBay Navigation Bar, which takes you to the Community Overview page. Click the link for Calendar.

That will take you to the current calendar of eBay events.

Here's where we'll be!

- Also check out our complete list of events for more details.

September

Sunday	Monday	Tuesday	Wednesday	Thursday	Friday	Saturday
1.	2.	3.	4.	5.	6.	7.
8.	9.	10.	11.	12.	13.	14. eBay University
15.	16.	17.	18.	19.	20.	21. eBay University
22.	23.	24.	25.	26. Long Beach Coin Expo	27. Long Beach Coin Expo	28. eBay University / Long Beach Coin Expo
29. Long Beach Coin Expo	30.					

October

Sunday	Monday	Tuesday	Wednesday	Thursday	Friday	Saturday

You've reached the end of Section One. Section Two deals with the fine (and simple!) art of eBay Selling.

Selling
the eBay Way!

"How do I get started selling on eBay?" This is definitely the most frequently asked question I hear. The eBay selling process is actually quite easy to grasp . . . once you have listed your first item. It's the first item that can overwhelm the new eBay seller into a state of total paralysis. Don't panic. Listing your first item on eBay will be a snap now that Griff is here to help guide you through the entire process, step-by-step. Not everyone was so lucky. Take Dave for example.

In January of 1996, business owner Dave Rayner suffered a serious back injury, costing him his business and livelihood. By March of that year, he and his wife were barely surviving off a combination of their diminishing savings and the meager wages she earned working at a grocery store twenty miles away from their home.

The night that Dave discovered eBay, he stumbled upon the eBay chat board and found eBay founder Pierre Omidyar chatting with others. Pierre personally welcomed Dave to eBay. Dave noted Pierre's email address.

Dave needed to replace the malfunctioning computer mouse. He turned to eBay in order to find a quick replacement.

"I found an item listing featuring PS 2 mice with a starting bid of $1. Wow, that's a bargain, and it was a Dutch Auction to boot, so I bid for two mice at a top bid of a buck."

Dave watched the listing for a full day until the final seconds passed and the listing closed with him as a high bidder for two brand-new mice for $2. Or so he thought.

"I got an email from the seller stating: 'CONGRATULATIONS! YOU'VE WON 2 LOTS of MICE for 400 DOLLARS!!'"

Dave was dumbfounded. He discovered that he had misread the item description and was indeed the proud owner of two lots of two hundred mice at one dollar apiece for a total of $400!

Dave went into a panic. His wife and he had only $600 left in their savings account.

"I knew my wife would go through the roof when I told her what I'd done. I emailed Pierre for help."

Within a day, Dave received a reply back from Pierre suggesting that Dave contact the seller to see if they might work out a solution. In the meantime, Dave had noticed an advertisement in a computer magazine for a company in Maine that was selling the very same type of computer mice that Dave had purchased on eBay. "I called the company and asked if they'd be interested in buying four hundred mice. The guy on the other end said he would take them off my hands."

The gentleman offered Dave $8 apiece for the mice for a total of $3,200, which, after subtracting the initial $400 cost to the eBay seller, left Dave with a profit of $2,800!

Elated and relieved, Dave emailed Pierre to inform him of the tale's happy ending.

"Pierre told me if I could turn deals like that, I'd never have a problem selling on eBay. I started selling a week later, after winning another mouse. . . . You see, I sold ALL of that two-lot batch and forgot to keep one out for myself!"

Dave continued buying and selling on eBay for another year. In 1997, he started an image hosting service called AuctionPix, which is today a profitable and popular image-hosting solution for thousands of other eBay sellers.

Dave has never looked back.

"I will always remember that day I opened the box to see four hundred mice staring back at me, knowing that not only had I turned a disaster into a profit but also had a chance to meet one of the nicest people in the online world—Pierre, founder of eBay!"

1

Selling Set Up, Step by Step

You have one thing you want to sell, you want to sell it quickly, and you don't have time to take a three-day course in eBay Selling 101. These next few chapters are for you.

FOLLOWING THE STEPS

Selling your first item on eBay can be broken down into seven steps:

Before the Sale
> Step 1. Set up an eBay Seller's Account (one-time step)
> Step 2. Take a Picture of the Item
> Step 3. Write an Item Description
> Step 4. List the Item on eBay

After the Sale
> Step 5. Accept Payment
> Step 6. Pack and Ship the Item
> Step 7. Leave Feedback

How long will it take to list my first item?

If you use a digital camera to take a picture of your item for Step 2, and if you follow the proceeding chapters carefully, the four "Before the Sale" steps for listing your very first eBay item can take as little as forty-five minutes to one hour. Using a print-film camera will add from one to several hours onto this time, depending on how quickly your local film developer does his job.

The listing process moves much faster once you have listed a few items.

How long will it take to sell my first item?

Your first eBay item could sell on the first day you list it, if you provide the "Buy It Now" format as a bidder option; or, if you use the standard bidding format, it will take three, five, seven, or ten days to sell your item, depending on the item listing duration you select.

How long will it take me to receive payment for my first item?

Receiving payment for your item After the Sale can take as little as a few minutes if you use PayPal to accept credit card payments from your buyer, or it can take as long as a week or more if you only accept mailed checks or money orders.

In this chapter, we will start you on your way to eBay selling by first walking you through Step 1, "Seting Up an eBay Seller's Account."

Selling on eBay, Step 1— Setting Up an eBay Seller's Account

In order to sell at something on eBay, you need to be a registered eBay user. If you are not yet registered, follow the instructions in Section One, Chapter 1—"Let's Get Started." Once you are registered, you are ready to set up an eBay Seller's Account. The process is fairly simple and quick.

In order to set up an eBay Seller's Account, you must provide eBay with a credit card and bank-account information, or you can utilize the ID Verify feature (provided to eBay by Equifax).

SETTING UP A SELLER'S ACCOUNT WITH A CREDIT CARD AND BANK ACCOUNT INFORMATION

As always, start at the eBay Navigation Bar:

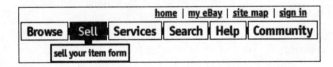

Click on the "Sell" link. This will bring you to the "Sell Your Item—Sign In" form. Look for the section labeled "New to selling?" You will find a link there for "Create a seller's account."

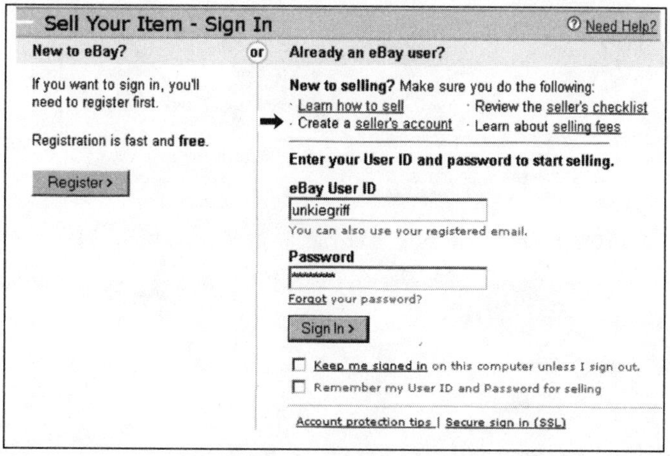

Click this link to begin setting up your eBay Seller's Account. Don't be confused by the next screen. It is another "Sign In" form like the first one, but this one is specific to setting up a seller's account.

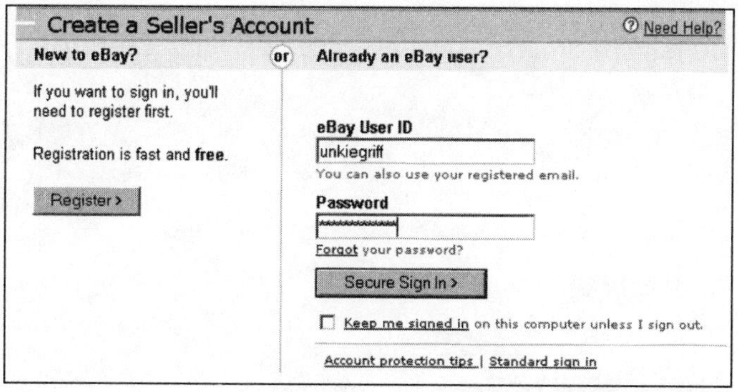

Enter your eBay User ID and password, and click Secure Sign In.

This will take you to the "Create a Seller's Account" page. It is divided into three separate steps. In step one, you enter a credit- or debit-card number and billing address as well as a bank account number, bank name, and routing number.

home | my eBay | site map | sign out

Browse | Sell | Services | Search | Help | Community

Create a Seller's Account

1 Verify your identity

Your credit/debit card and bank account information will be placed on your eBay account within 24 hours of receipt and is protected by the industry standard **SSL** encryption. All information is required and is kept confidential in accordance with eBay's Privacy Policy.

- Your credit/debit card and checking account information is used to verify your identity. (why is this required?)
- It's free to create a Seller's Account. Learn more

Enter Your Credit Card/Debit Card Information

Credit card/debit card number	Credit Card: Visa, MasterCard, American Express, Discover. Debit Card: Visa, MasterCard. eBay Welcomes **VISA**
Expiration date	Month: [– ▼] Day: [– ▼] Year: [– ▼] Leave day as --, if day on credit/debit card is not listed
Your name on card	

Please enter your billing address as it appears on your credit card bill statement:

Billing address	
City	
State/province	
Zip/postal code	
Country	United States ▼

Enter Your Bank Account Information

eBay Payments enables you to accept credit card and electronic checks from your buyers on eBay. Payments will be automatically deposited into your checking account.

Sample Check - U.S. Account (lower left corner)   View Non-U.S. Account Checks

⑆ 739811823 ⑆   632   0173136142⑈

The Bank Routing number is 9 digits between the ⑆ ⑆ symbols	The check number should match the number in the upper-right corner	The Checking Account number is usually to the left of ⑈. If check number is left of account number, ignore check number

Note: These three sets of numbers may appear in a different order on your check.

Account owner	First name MI Last name
Country of account	United States ▼
Bank name	You can find the Bank Routing # and the Checking Account # on the bottom of your check, as shown above.
Bank routing #	
Checking account #	
Retype Checking account #	

In the second step you select your preferred method for paying eBay seller fees.

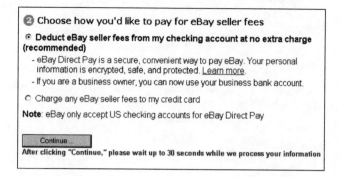

If you opted for paying your eBay fees through eBay Direct Pay, you will see the following screen:

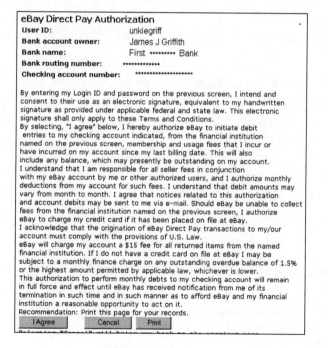

If you opted for paying your eBay fees with a credit card, you will see the following screen.

Follow the instructions from here to finish creating your eBay seller's account.

NOTE: At the time of this writing, eBay had purchased the online payment service PayPal. Although I don't know exactly what PayPal integration into the seller-account setup process will look like by the time this book goes to print, it should be clear and easy to follow.

TROUBLESHOOTING

If for some reason eBay is unable to verify the bank or credit-card information you provided, you will see one of the following error screens.

This inability to verify your bank and credit-card information could be due to one or more causes. Most likely, eBay is unable to connect to your bank or credit-card issuer for verification. The solutions are to:

1. Try another credit card and bank account
2. Try again later (my least favorite)
3. Use ID Verify to verify your eBay Seller's Account information

SETTING UP AN EBAY SELLER'S ACCOUNT USING ID VERIFY

If your bank account information could not be verified or if you would rather not provide a bank account or credit card to verify the information for your seller's account, you can use the ID Verify process instead.

ID Verify is a service provided by Equifax. For $5, your information is sent to Equifax for verification and accuracy. If you choose to verify your seller account information using ID Verify, click the link for ID Verify as shown in the previous figure. This will take you to the following screen:

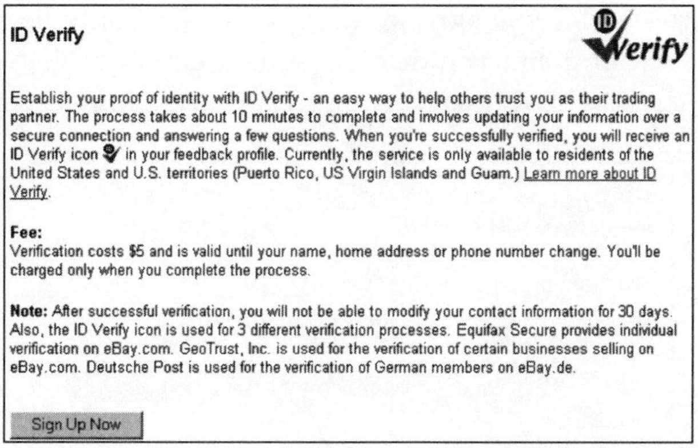

Click the Sign Up Now button. Sign In for ID Verify on the next screen.

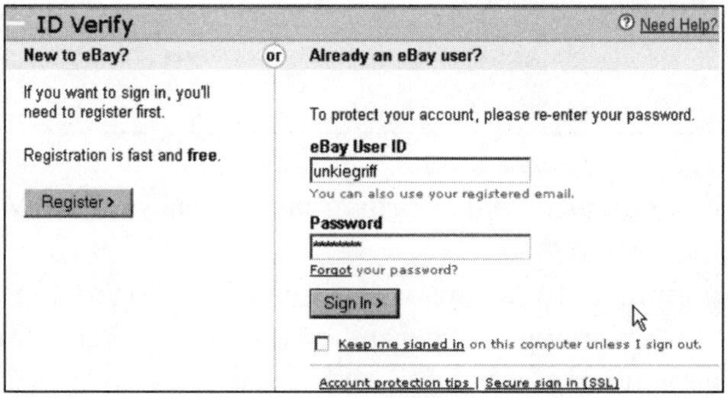

This will take you to page 1 of the ID Verify process.

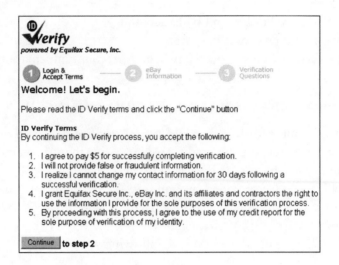

Read the terms and if you agree to them, click the Continue button. In Step 2, you may enter your contact information as requested or, if the fields are already filled in, accept what is displayed or make corrections if necessary.

(I've blocked out my personal information for this example. Make sure yours is complete and accurate.)

Click the Continue button. This will display the information as you entered it. Make sure that everything is accurate, or else the ID Verify process will not verify your contact information.

On the next page, fill in the requested information for your address, social security number, and driver's license.

Click the Continue button to move to Step 3 of the ID Verify process.

In this step, you need to select the correct entry for each question. The questions are based on your current loans, with information that only you should know.

1. Your credit file indicates you may have a mortgage loan, opened in or around September 1999. Please choose the credit provider for this account from the following options.
- BANK OF AMERICA
- COMMERCIAL CREDIT CORP
- G.E. CAPITAL
- MORGAN STANLEY DEAN WITTER
- NONE OF THE ABOVE

2. Please choose the range within which your monthly payment falls for the previously referenced account. The amount requested is the amount on your lender's statement including principal and interest, taxes and insurance, if applicable. If you make bi-weekly payments, multiply that payment by 2.17 to calculate the monthly payment.
- $1100 - $1199
- $1200 - $1299
- $1300 - $1399
- $1400 - $1499
- NONE OF THE ABOVE

3. Your credit file indicates you may have an auto loan/lease, opened in or around September 2001. Please choose the credit provider for this account from the following options.
- AMERICAN HONDA FINANCE CORP.
- GMAC
- NICHOLAS FINANCIAL
- WASATCH MOUNTAIN FCU
- NONE OF THE ABOVE

4. Please choose the range within which your monthly payment falls for the previously referenced account. If you make bi-weekly payments, multiply that payment by 2.17 to calculate the monthly payment.
- $975 - $1024
- $1025 - $1074
- $1075 - $1124
- $1125 - $1174
- NONE OF THE ABOVE

ebaY Verify powered by **Equifax Secure, Inc**

1 Login & Accept Terms — 2 eBay Information — 3 Verification Questions

INTERACTIVE QUERY

- The following questions are required as a security measure to protect you from someone else attempting to get verified with your information.
- This information is pulled from your consumer credit history and only you should know the right answer. If a question or a choice is not relevant to your status choose the option: "None of the above".
- Your information is secured!
  The information you supply below is used solely to confirm its accuracy for verification purposes.
  - Your additional personal information will not be stored by eBay or added to existing Equifax database.
  - The transfer of your information is protected by secure 128-bit encrypted SSL connection
  - Your credit score will not be affected.

Submit Request   Reset Fields

ID Verify is safe
- Protected by a secured SSL connection
- Information solely used for this process
- Your credit score will not be affected

Your personal Information
- Used to check against existing record in your credit file
- True verification - only you will know the right answer

For further assistance call Equifax M-F 8:00am-5:00pm PST 1-888-532-0179

Select the correct responses and click the button. You will see the next page:

ebaY Verify powered by **Equifax Secure, Inc**

1 Login & Accept Terms — 2 eBay Information — 3 Verification Questions

Thank you.

Please click the button below to return to eBay and find out if you have been successfully verified.

Continue

Click the "Continue" button to see if the verification has gone through.

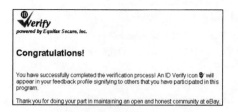

It has! You are now registered to sell.

GRIFF TIP: You can also start the ID Verify process by navigating to it from the eBay Navigation Bar. Click on the link for Services and then the link below it for "buying & selling."

Scroll down to the bottom of the Buying & Selling Tools page and look for the link for "ID Verify."

Congratulations! You have set up an eBay Seller's Account. Before we move on to the next chapter and take some pictures of a special item to sell on eBay, I want to share another remarkable eBay story sent to me by eBay seller Heather Luce.

Several years ago I was working at a countywide newspaper as the editor. It was a fun job, but it wasn't anything I was terribly passionate about. On the side, I was doing my artwork and creating costumes for people to pose in as reference for my paintings. The costumes were primarily Renaissance in design and my closets started to fill up. I began giving the costumes to friends and family, and after a while they told me, "NO MORE!" Apparently THEIR closets were starting to fill up too.

At that time, I had been to eBay a few times and had bought some small items. My experiences had all been pleasant, and on a whim I decided to try my hand at selling. I pulled out two of the costumes I had made, but had never used for any of my paintings, and listed them at $75 each, for seven-day listings. I still remember them: a milkmaid gown, "The Artiste," and a gold Italian Renaissance gown. Each gown sold for over $100 and I was instantly addicted. For four weeks I made new gowns and listed them while working full-time at the newspaper. (I was also a full-time nontraditional college student as well.) At the end of four weeks, I had made more money from the gowns I had sold on eBay than from my regular full-time job. I knew that I had found my passion, and two weeks later I quit my job and plunged full-time into the world of Renaissance Costuming.

That was almost two years ago and my business has grown leaps and bounds. I now have a wonderful Web site and a customer base from all around the world. In fact, just today I sent a gown to Australia and last week I was contacted by a woman from Germany who wants a new Renaissance gown as well. I've costumed actors from Renaissance Faires—Even "Queen Elizabeth" (aka Ms. Flores)! I get emails all summer long from people claiming, "I saw one of your gowns at my Renaissance Faire last weekend!"

It's been a huge struggle. During this time frame I was still going to college full-time and was also going through a divorce. There were times when I was worried that eBay wouldn't be enough and I would have to give up my "dream" job as a costume designer. But eBay has never failed me. My business has grown from a hobby to a full-time professional career and shows no signs of slowing down.

None of it would have been possible without eBay.

eBay allows average, everyday folks like me the opportunity to realize dreams. It puts us in touch with people from around the world for mere pennies. Nowhere else can you get as much advertising for your dollar—and be extremely successful in the process. eBay is a forum that allows people with ALL interests to shop in one convenient place. It allows for competitive pricing, and most important to me, it allows sellers a chance to really get to know their customers.

I have made some of the most wonderful friendships through eBay. (I swear, I have the nicest customers in the WORLD!)

I heard that eBay was going to open storefronts a few weeks before they made them open to the public. The week before they opened, I took pictures and wrote up all the listings for my anticipated storefront. The morning they were made available to the public, I rose at 6:00 A.M. and got to work opening mine. It was terribly exciting and within weeks the orders started pouring in.

Everything I have done has all been due to eBay. Without eBay I would still be working at a job that was not my "passion." Now I wake up every morning, eager to get to work (which I can now do in my pj's!), and I spend all day and well into the night creating magnificent gowns. Something I have always loved doing. The rewards come in the form of ecstatic emails (and sometimes boxes of chocolate through regular mail) from my customers. (Have I mentioned that I have the BEST customers in the WORLD?)

Because of eBay I now work with a group of Renaissance-gown eBay sellers and we work to promote eBay as a whole and we share tips and tricks to provide our customers with the best service and quality garments possible. They are absolutely delightful to work with and we have all become good friends. . . .

2

Creating and Editing Digital Pictures of Your eBay Item

Chris and Kim Hecker ("theblueox") joined eBay in 1996, only nine months after Pierre launched the original site.

"It was a moment of inspiration when we stumbled upon eBay, thanks to my brother," Chris said. "My wife and I looked at each other, our mouths dropped, and we knew we had to give it a try. We were both looking for a way out of corporate America."

At first Chris and Kim listed a few collectible items they had purchased at local auctions. To their delight, all of the items sold. Thus began the Heckers' long and successful careers as eBay sellers.

They converted their Chicago basement into "the blue ox" headquarters, from which they now run a global operation selling vintage toys exclusively on eBay. Today, the Heckers are official eBay Power Sellers with an average of seven hundred items listed a week for everything from rare Hot Wheels cars to Pink Panther dolls.

Both Chris and Kim quit their "real" jobs to sell on eBay full-time. It could not have been an easy decision. No matter how much we might hate our current jobs, it takes real determination and, yes, courage to toss aside the security of a steady paycheck for the uncertain and scary world of self-employment. Not everyone who strikes out on the entrepreneurial road discovers instant riches—being your own boss has its own set of perils and trials—but nearly everyone I have ever met who has taken the plunge and started her own business on eBay admits that the experience has changed her life, sometimes in profound, sometimes in unexpected, ways but always for the better.

Having completed more than 16,500 unique transactions in the last seven years, with a 30,500 positive feedback score the Heckers have helped people around the world complete their toy collections, now and then ending searches that have lasted for twenty or even thirty years. They have learned, firsthand and on their own, the ins and outs of running a business, and though they are the first to admit that selling full-time on eBay takes a lot of work and time, Chris and Kim obviously love what they do.

They are the masters of their own destinies. They are eBay sellers!

What are "Digital Pictures"?

In order to define and explain what makes up a digital picture, we first need to define a film picture.

A **film picture** is a mechanical recording of visual information. It is created by focusing reflected light from an object or view, onto a piece of film. When the exposed film is put through a chemical developing process, it causes a reaction in the layers of chemicals on the film, re-creating the initial visual information reflected onto the film only as a negative of the original image. The negative is then converted into a print by a sort of reverse process of what happened in the camera. The image on the print picture is made up of microscopic bits of color, so fine, the eye cannot see them as separate dots but instead sees them as bands and areas of different color.

A **digital picture** is an electronic recording of light reflected off an object or scene that has been converted to, or created as, a digital computer file. In a digital image, the light from the camera lens (or from a scanned print) strikes a special recording device, which converts the light information into binary information (ones and zeros) and stores this information as a digital file, either within the camera or on your computer.

Why Do I Need Digital Pictures of My eBay Item?

You *will* need a picture of your item if you expect any success selling it on eBay. Items without pictures usually end up closing out with no bidders at all—a waste of time and insertion fees.

eBay buyers are a funny lot. They like to see what it is they are buying. Imagine that! As a seller, you must provide the best possible pictures of your wares if you want to generate any buyer interest at all. Your item pictures should be clear, focused, uncluttered, and as close a representation of your item as possible. In addition, they will need to be big enough to show all important details but, since they will be digital files, small enough to download through the Internet and onto the item page as quickly as possible.

To the newbie, the whole concept of digital images can seem overwhelming. In reality, creating, editing, and uploading digital images is a snap *if* you approach the subject methodically, step-by-step. After you have finished your first digital picture, creating more will be a piece of cake, I promise.

There are the two parts to "Quick and Painless eBay Picture Mastery":

1. Taking the Picture
2. Editing the Picture

The two parts are described in great detail in the rest of this chapter. Read through them carefully and you'll have a good image of your item ready for your first eBay listing in no time!

Taking the Picture—Selecting a Method

Before we start setting up the item for photographing, we first need to consider which of the three basic options for creating digital pictures we will use. Depending on what equipment you have at your disposal, you could:

1. Take a picture of the item with a regular camera and have a local **film developer** convert your prints or negatives directly into digital files on a CD-ROM
2. Take a picture of the item with a regular camera, have the film developed, and scan the prints of the item into your computer using a **flatbed scanner**
3. Take a picture of the item with a **digital camera**

Which one of the three options above is right for you? Let's discuss their pros and cons.

FILM DEVELOPERS

If you don't have a **digital camera** or a **flatbed scanner,** use a regular film camera to take pictures of your item and take the exposed film to your local **film developer**—one who can create digital files of your images either on floppy disk or

CD-ROM. Most local film and camera stores, national chain pharmacies, and even some supermarkets now offer this service.

PRO: Film developers are ideal for the first-time or occasional seller. No shelling out for, or mussing or fussing with, a digital camera or scanner. If time and budget are a concern, and you don't have access to a digital camera, go with the **film developer** option.

CON: As a long-term option, the costs of buying and developing film will prove to be counterproductive, since the money spent in just a few months on film and processing will have paid for a good digital camera. Also, as part of the developing process—whether by machine or person—irreversible decisions will be made regarding the tone, brightness, etc., of your image files. Usually this is not an issue, but occasionally the resulting digital pictures may not be entirely to your liking.

FLATBED SCANNERS

Flatbed scanners create digital images of flat or nearly flat items. You can skip the camera steps altogether if you are selling flat items (comic books, trading cards, coins, stamps, ephemera, autographs, etc.). For flat stuff, scanning as opposed to photographing will provide you with the highest image-file quality possible.

Simply place your flat item directly on the flatbed scanner. No cameras or developers. Of course, you can also scan print photographs of your item.

PRO: The perfect tool for flat things. Otherwise . . .

CON: Same as for film developers if you are scanning photos of your item. You will still be paying for film and developing.

DIGITAL CAMERAS

A digital camera works almost exactly like a film camera. It has a lens and a shutter and usually a flash, but instead of recording an image on film the digital camera transforms the incoming light of an image into a digital file and then stores the digital image on a small removable chip or disk. The digital image can then be transferred to your computer by inserting the chip or disc into your computer or by connecting special cables from your digital camera to your computer. (Each make and model of digital camera has a slightly different way of transferring digital image files. Consult your camera's user manual or guide for more details.)

PRO: Easy to use. If you can shoot pics with a film camera, you can shoot pics with a digital camera. Most good digital cameras are "point and shoot."

There's no waiting for film to develop. You have total control over the quality of your pictures. A digital camera can pay for itself in only a few months of regular eBay selling.

CON: Initial cost might be a burden to some new sellers. Still, good new and used digital cameras suitable for your eBay pictures are available for $200 up. Check eBay first before you buy.

WHAT TO LOOK FOR IN A DIGITAL CAMERA

There are so many different brands, models, prices, and levels of quality available in digital cameras that making a decision can be tough. What follows is my smart-shopping checklist for digital cameras:

Buy the Best You Can Afford

Although you don't need to buy the top-of-the-line digital camera to take excellent images for eBay, it never pays to scrimp when purchasing an electronic gadget of any type. Buy the very best your budget will allow.

1.2 Megapixels or Higher

Digital camera resolution is measured in something called "megapixels." A pixel is the basic unit of programmable color on a computer display or in a computer image or in a digital camera—the higher the megapixels, the higher the quality of the image. Most good digital cameras have a resolution of 2.0 or higher, but for eBay pictures, you can get away with a 1.2 megapixel resolution.

Look for Brand Names

For example, Sony, Nikon, Olympus, Kodak, Canon, Fuji, HP, Leica, Epson, etc. If you've found a great deal and it's for a brand name you have never heard of before, it's probably best to avoid it.

Macro Is a Must

Look for cameras with "macro" capability (the ability to get your camera an inch away from an item without losing focus). Macro is *the* digital camera feature that you will need when selling on eBay.

Zoom, Auto-Focus, and Auto-Exposure Come in Handy

Although not absolutely necessary, zoom, autofocus, and autoexposure can make your photography tasks much easier. Lucky for you, nearly every recent make and model digital camera has all three features built in.

"Used" Is OK

Buy "new" if possible, but don't rule out a used digital camera. You can find both new and used digital cameras at, oh, let's see . . . where might one find used digital cameras . . . ?

Look for the "Complete Package"

If buying a used digital camera, look for those deals where the seller provides the complete contents of the original package, including software, cables, and accessories. Owners who preserve all the original contents of the package usually take extra good care of their cameras.

For more detailed information about digital camera features, price, and picture quality, try the Digital Photography Review Web site: **http://www. dpreview.com.**

This most excellent site contains hundreds of detailed professional and user reviews of all the most popular digital cameras. They can help you decide which model is right for your needs and budget.

For the record, I am currently using a Sony DSC-F707 for all my eBay pictures and other fine photography projects.

Once you have selected which option works best for you, the next step in the process is to set up the item and photograph it. For our example, we will take pictures of several types of items using both a film camera and a digital camera.

TAKING THE PICTURE—SETTING UP THE ITEM

Selecting a Space

For one-time eBay sellers, any well-lit spot in your home or apartment will do just fine. Under certain conditions, you can also set up your shots outdoors.

GRIFF TIP: If you intend to sell regularly on eBay, plan on setting aside a small studio space somewhere in your home or business location dedicated to nothing but taking digital pictures.

Your eBay photography studio space can consist of nothing more than a movable table placed against a wall. The entire space needed should be two to four feet wide and eight feet tall. It will help with lighting if the walls of the space surrounding your studio area are painted white or at least a neutral color. Avoid spaces with walls or immovable objects painted a strong color, as they can "tint" the light reflected onto your item—usually an unwanted effect.

The table you use for placing your item to be photographed should be about two feet deep by four feet wide by forty-two inches high. If you plan on selling only small items, you can scale these dimensions down accordingly except for the table height, which, to save you from bending over for long periods of time, should be no lower than thirty-six inches.

For our setup example, we will be photographing a small pottery pitcher. I have set up a table, some halogen work lights, and a digital camera on a tripod.

On the table, I placed a box to bring the height up to about forty inches, then I draped a backdrop of dark blue cotton cloth over a piece of thin plywood, over the box, and down over the front of the table. (More on backdrops and lighting later.)

Setting up the Camera

Film camera or digital camera: the rules of picture taking are the same for both. If you have a tripod, use it. If not, find a sturdy flat surface upon which you can rest the camera. In a pinch, try holding the camera steady and hope for the best.

Regular eBay sellers: Invest in a tripod. You can buy one new for about $20–$40 and you can find excellent new and used tripods . . . on eBay!

Backdrops

Many eBay sellers do not use backdrops for their item picture. They instead simply plop the item on the nearest table or, in some cases, even the baby's crib! This can often lead to very interesting pictures.

It's hard to tell just what is for sale in the following picture. Is it the dinette set or is it that thing on the table? The seller at least took the time to show the newspaper they plan to use for packing the "thing."

You can avoid these sorts of embarrassing and unprofessional picture mistakes by using a solid-color backdrop to isolate and focus attention on your item.

A backdrop can be a solid colored piece of either paper, board, or cloth placed behind and under the item. As a rule, the backdrop's color should contrast with the color(s) and brightness of the item. For example, a pale item usually looks best on a dark background. A dark item usually looks best on a pale background.

Don't spend a fortune on backdrops! You can purchase fabric suitable for backdrops from any fabric store. Check the remnants bins for good deals. Look for matte-finished cotton or linen yardage in solid colors (no patterns!) and purchase a selection of muted colors. For most purposes, you can get by with two to three yards of forty-five-inch-wide cloth.

You can also find incredible bargains for remnants . . . on eBay, of course! Search eBay using "cotton fabric." Also search in eBay's Cameras & Photo category, using *backdrop* to find good deals on professional backdrop cloth and paper.

If you are photographing your item on the table against the wall, use push-pins to fasten the fabric or paper into place on the wall itself, or place a piece of poster board or thin plywood on the table against the wall and drape the backdrop over it (as in our example above). Make sure your backdrop covers both behind and underneath the item.

You may need to shoot very large items "in situ" or in place. If so, try to isolate the object as best you can from its surroundings. If the item isn't too large, place a large sheet of paper or cloth behind the item and follow the same rules below for lighting the object to its best advantage. Large bolts of scenic muslin work well. Again, try searching eBay's photography category.

If the item is too large to isolate, place it in the least conspicuous location (against a wall of a house or a tall hedge) and try to fill the camera viewfinder frame with as much of the object as possible.

Lighting Your Item

Inadequate lighting is a common digital-picture mistake. How do you determine if your item is inadequately lit? A good rule of thumb is to rely on your camera. Aim the camera at the item. If the camera's built-in light meter or flash indicator shows that a flash is needed, then add more lighting, either artificial or natural.

Indoor—direct lighting: For most situations, your item should be lit from two or more directions. Three or more clip-on lamps with 100-watt halogen floodlights will usually provide adequate illumination. Position the lights above and to the sides of the item. Make sure they are slightly in front of the item (avoid lighting from behind). Experiment with lighting positions. Move the lamps around to get the best positions and the right blending of light and shadows. Shadows are not always bad. For items with complex surfaces (carving, embroidery, etc.), a prominent shadow in one direction can help emphasize the surface texture. Still, for most situations, you will want to "wash" the item to be photographed with light sources crossing each other from opposite directions.

Indoor—indirect lighting: Some items may suffer from direct lighting. Examples might be glossy pottery or porcelain, glassware, shiny jewelry, or harsh white objects. In these cases, you may need to light the item indirectly with diffused or bounced light. There are a number of ways to accomplish this type of lighting. A quick and cheap way is to point the light sources away from the item and onto white or metallic sheets of poster board. You can even "bounce" strong light off a white ceiling. A more professional (and expensive) way is to use professional photography-studio-grade strobe lamps, light boxes, or reflective screens. These devices bounce and diffuse light off white or metallic material. The resulting diffused light illuminates the item without glare or harsh shadows.

NOTE: Reflected lighting usually takes more wattage to achieve the same level of illumination using direct lighting. Translation: Double or treble the number of lamps and 100-watt bulbs. Without using a light meter, you can always take a test shot to see if your lighting is adequate.

GRIFF TIP: Check your local hardware store for good lighting deals: I found two halogen work-light trees for $35 each. Each tree has two 150-watt halogen lamps bolted to a solid tripod-based, extendable pole. The combination of four 150-watt halogen lamps is more than adequate for most of my eBay photography needs.

ANOTHER GRIFF TIP: The light from halogen or tungsten incandescent lamps tends to be more hot (yellow or red) than cool (blue). This may distort the colors of your item.

You can adjust for this by using your digital camera's white balance feature, if it has one. (Check your camera's manual.) Otherwise, you may need to use blue gels over your light sources or slightly blue reflective surfaces to counter the strong yellow light. Some sellers like to use natural-spectrum light bulbs, since they produce roughly the same neutral white light of sunlight. Verilux makes a very good natural-spectrum light bulb.

Outdoor—direct and indirect lighting: Your indoor photography space should suffice for nearly all your eBay pictures, but in some instances you may find it necessary to take your item pictures outdoors.

When shooting outdoors, avoid placing the item in direct sunlight. Bright, harsh sunlight can wash out or distort certain colors and can also cast unwanted dark shadows. The north side of a house is usually a good spot for photographing your item outside, as north light tends to be more even and less harsh, especially on a bright, sunny day. A lightly overcast day offers the ideal outdoor light for taking item pictures.

GRIFF TIP: When shooting your item outdoors, you should isolate the background with something solid. Of course, you can and should experiment and try all types of compositions in your shots. If you are selling antique lawn furniture, it might look smashing against a privet hedge but not so smashing against the family minivan. The only way to know for sure is to experiment. For those who are unsure of their design talents, a solid background will always do the trick as a first or last resort.

Camera Settings

Resolution (digital cameras only): If you are using a digital camera, make sure that your camera is set to take medium- to high-resolution pictures. Resolution is usually described in pixels. The lowest resolution you should use is 640 x 480 pixels. For eBay pictures, you should not need anything higher than 1024 x 768 pixels. At that resolution, the resulting files will be very large, but we will be reducing the size of the files in the editing process.

Some digital cameras come with something called "email" resolution. This setting is for taking small pictures suitable for sending as attachments to email. Don't use this setting if it is lower than 640 x 480 pixels. As we will see in the editing process, you can always reduce the size of a digital picture, but you cannot increase the size without noticeable degradation of the image itself.

Auto-Exposure, Auto-Focus: Why make extra work for yourself? If your film or digital camera has autoexposure and/or autofocus, by all means, use them.

Flash: Avoid using a direct flash to take eBay pictures. The intense light from a camera flash can wash out the colors of your item and can also obliterate details. If your film or digital camera indicates you need to use the camera's built-in flash to light the item properly, you need to add more lamps and watts to your lighting scheme, as we discussed in the lighting section.

Macro: If you need to place your digital camera a few inches or less away from the item, make sure the camera's macro feature is enabled.

Consult your digital camera's user manual for more information on changing your camera settings for resolution, autofocus, autoexposure, flash, and macro.

Framing the Item in the Camera Viewfinder

We've draped a backdrop cloth down the wall and over the table. We have also set the lights, and the camera is set securely on its tripod. Finally, we have positioned the item on the table.

Time now to frame the shot and take the picture.

First, this item is taller than it is wide, so I will shoot it in portrait mode. I do this by turning my camera ninety degrees clockwise as shown here:

If your camera has a variable lens, set it to the widest angle. Position the camera and tripod in front of the item, usually no more than twenty-four inches away. (This varies with the size of the item you are photographing.) Adjust the height of the camera, using the tripod. Some items photograph best when shot straight on; others look better shot slightly from above. Try different angles and use the one that works best for your item. Our little pitcher looks best shot from slightly above, so I have raised the camera about a foot higher than the pitcher. While looking into the camera's viewfinder, move the camera away from or toward the item or, if your camera has zoom, zoom in or out until you have the item framed within the view window so that it nearly fills the frame.

Snap the Shot

Everything is in place. Lighting looks good. The item fills the frame. It's time to take the picture. Here is what this first shot looks like.

Not bad. Remember, the pitcher is taller than it is wide, so I repositioned my camera to take the shot in *portrait* format. When the digital image is displayed, it shows in the default *landscape* format. That's why it appears on its side now. Later in the editing phase, we will *rotate* the image clockwise ninety degrees.

Also, my digital camera's autoexposure was set so that the dark blue background actually appears almost black. I like it. We'll keep it.

GRIFF TIP: It's always best to get all your photography done in one session, so if you have two or more items to list on eBay, photograph them in succession.

I took two other shots of this pitcher; one of the other side and one of the underside to show the maker's mark. It always pays to show all aspects of your item, including flaws and imperfections!

We will use these pictures in our listing in the next chapter.

A LIST OF QUICK PICTURE-TAKING TIPS

Whether you use a digital camera or film camera to take the picture, you should always follow a few simple picture-taking rules.

- If possible, avoid holding the camera to take the shot. Use a tripod or place the camera on a sturdy, flat surface. This will help guarantee the image is in focus. You can find good deals on inexpensive tripods on eBay, of course.

- Don't take a picture of the item sitting on your kitchen table, where the rest of your fabulous 1970s-era kitchen will be in the picture (unless, of course, you are selling the kitchen). Isolate the item you are photographing by placing a solid-color cloth or paper backdrop behind it. As a general rule, if the item is light in color, use a darker background color. If the item is dark, use a lighter colored background.

- Lighting—Outdoors: Avoid photographing an item in direct sunlight. Bright sunlight can distort colors and cast dark shadows. If you must shoot outdoors on a sunny day, shoot the picture out of direct sunlight. A good spot is often the north side of a wall or building. An ideal time to shoot outdoors would be on a lightly overcast day.

- Lighting—Indoors: Avoid using a flash to take a picture of your item. Just like direct sunlight, it can distort colors and cause white spots on shiny objects. Instead, light your item either directly or indirectly as appropriate from three or more angles using ordinary halogen flood lamps. (You can correct any yellow cast caused by incandescent lights by either using your digital camera's "white balance" feature or later on during the image editing stage. Consult your digital camera manual for information on "white balance.")

- If you are using a digital camera, make sure it is set at a pixel resolution of 640 x 480 or higher. (Again, your digital camera's manual will explain how to change your camera's resolution.)

- Whenever possible aim your camera at the center of the item. Using zoom, or by moving the camera closer or farther away, position the item image in the viewfinder so that it fills the frame with as little background showing as possible.

- In some instances, you may find it best to position your camera at an angle slightly or greatly above the item, but generally, you should position the item and the camera so that the camera is perpendicular to the item (the item and camera are roughly the same distance from the ground).

Although you can usually get away with only one image, take more if necessary to show a variety of aspects for the image; close-ups, back of the item, etc. If the item has a flaw, make sure to take a picture of it!

Once you have taken the pictures and have copies of them as digital image files, you will need to get them into your computer for editing and uploading. The process for transferring digital pictures from the digital camera to the computer varies depending on the make and model of the camera.

Most digital cameras store their images on a removable memory chip or card that can be popped out of the camera and into a chip or card reader or, in some cases, right into your computer if it has the appropriate slot.

Some digital cameras also provide an option for transferring digital picture files from the camera to a computer via a specially provided cable. Consult the user's manual that came with your digital camera. It will explain the method you need to use for transferring digital pictures from your camera to your computer.

SAVING YOUR DIGITAL IMAGE FILES

When you move or copy your digital image files onto your computer, you should set up a special folder where you can safely store them. That way, they will be easier to find later.

Some cameras come with special software that will automatically set up special folders on your computer, into which it will transfer copies of the images on your camera. This feature can be a useful method for keeping your files organized.

You can also create a special folder for your eBay images. For information on how to create a new folder on your computer, consult your computer's operating system's Help section. For Windows, click Start, Help. For Macs, click the Help link on the top of the desktop window.

EDITING THE PICTURE (USING SOFTWARE)

Now that you've created digital images of your item and have moved them to your computer, you are itching to get them up on an eBay listing so you can start the sale of your item. Hold on. We aren't finished with the digital image process yet. We need to edit the image files first.

Many eBay sellers skip the editing part of the picture process. Big mistake. It is highly unlikely that your picture files are perfect as taken. Many will need to be rotated. Some will need cropping. Almost all will need resizing. In order to rotate, crop, or resize an image file, you will need image-editing software. There are many brands to choose from:

You can pay for top-of-the-line image-editing software like:

Adobe Photoshop
Jasc Paint Shop Pro
Corel Photo-Paint
Micrographx Picture Publisher

Or you can try less expensive alternatives like Irfanview, which is a freeware application available for download at **http://www.irfanview.com.**

We will use **Microsoft Photo Editor** for our image-editing software examples in this chapter. If you don't have Photo Editor, you can use a different application (like the terrific Irfanview program) and follow along with us. The basic editing commands used by Photo Editor are common to all versions of image-editing software.

Many, but not all, Windows users will have a copy of Photo Editor on their computer as part of the Windows operating system. Not sure if your Windows computer has a copy of Photo Editor? Here's how to check: For Windows, click on Start, Search and select "For Files or Folders . . . "

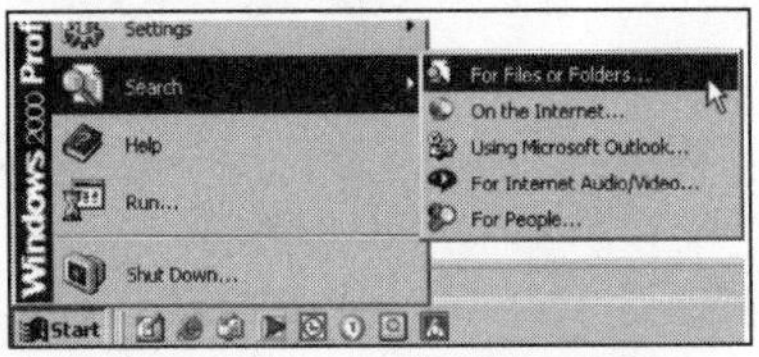

This will display the Search Results window. In the text entry box labeled, "Search for files or folders named:" type in: photoed.exe

Then click the Search Now box.

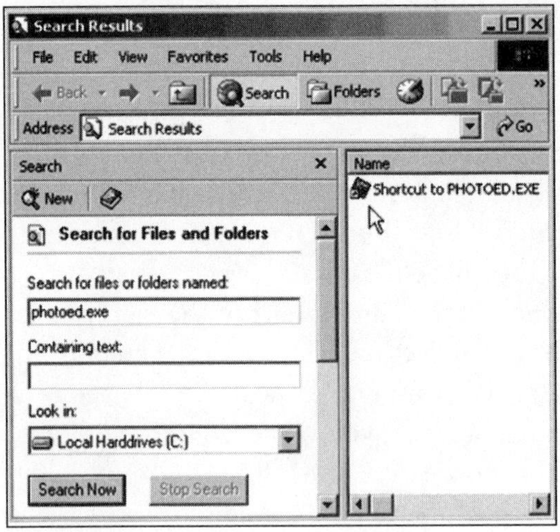

If your Windows computer has a copy of Photo Editor, the file icon for it will display as a search result in the pane on the right. If you see the icon for PHOTOED.EXE, hover your mouse cursor over the icon, click the mouse's right-hand button, and select "Send To" and then "Desktop (create shortcut)."

Now you have a copy of the Photo Editor icon on your Windows desktop for easy access later.

If you don't have a copy of Photo Editor, or if you are a Mac user, don't despair! The basic editing commands (Crop, Rotate, Resize) are available with any good image-editing software and can usually be found in roughly the same places on each application's menu command bar. If you've purchased a new digital camera, it will have come with image editing software on a CD-ROM. If so, by all means, use it!

OPENING A DIGITAL PICTURE FILE

First, we need to find our digital picture files. I moved copies of the three digital picture files for the small pitcher from my camera to a folder I created on my computer hard drive called "eBay Digital Pictures."

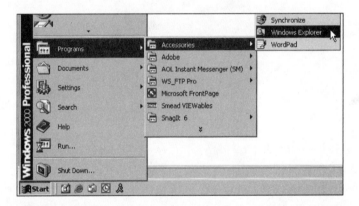

Once you know where the files are located on your computer, you can open them for editing.

There are several ways to open these files for viewing or editing. One way in Windows is to click Start, Accessories, and Windows Explorer to open a Windows Explorer window.

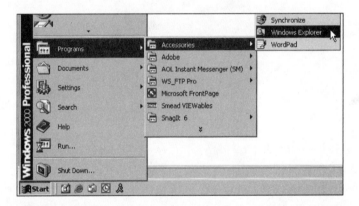

In the Windows Explorer window, navigate to your picture files, then select the file you wish to edit first by hovering your mouse button over the file's name and clicking the right-hand mouse button. Select Open With from the pop-up menu and then Choose Program in order to select the appropriate application from the list of choices presented.

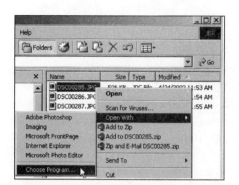

The list of applications on your computer will show in the Open With box.

Another way would be to start Photo Editor or any other image-editing application (by clicking on its shortcut either on your desktop or on "Start, Programs" menu) and use the "File, Open . . ." command on the application's toolbar to bring up an Open dialog box.

Still another way would be to open both Photo Editor and a Windows Explorer window and drag and drop each file from Windows Explorer to the Photo Editor window.

DRAG AND DROP

This would be an excellent place to illustrate a great feature of Windows (and Macs) that most people never use: drag and drop.

Start by placing the image-editing application window and the Windows Explorer window next to each other on your computer screen in such a way that you can see the file you wish to open and the blank space inside the application window (in this example, Photo Editor).

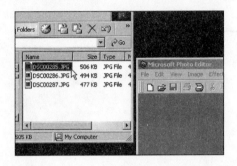

Place your mouse cursor over the file name in Windows Explorer. Hold down the left-hand mouse button. While still holding down the left-hand mouse button, move your cursor over to the application window. You will notice that you are now "dragging" the file name along with the mouse cursor. Don't release the mouse button . . .

. . . until your cursor is completely over the application window. To "drop" the file, release the mouse button.

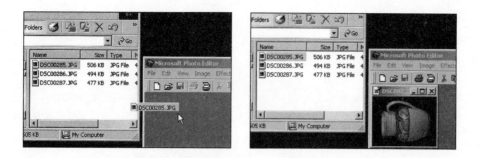

When you do release the mouse button, the file will "drop" into the application window and open.

Regardless of the method you use to open the file, the result is the same: we open our digital picture file in an image-editing application in order to perfect the picture for use on eBay.

Now that we've opened the digital picture file in Photo Editor, let's start editing!

Editing Digital Pictures

ROTATE (AKA FLIP, SPIN, OR TRANSFORM)

Our jug picture was taken in portrait mode, that is, with the camera held at a right angle. The resulting picture shows the item on its side. In order for the picture to make sense when viewed on eBay, we need to rotate it ninety degrees clockwise.

All good image-editing software will have a command for rotating a digital picture. In Photo Editor, the "Rotate . . ." command is found on the submenu under "Image."

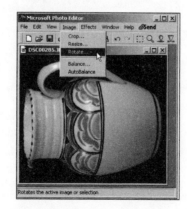

Clicking the "Rotate . . ." command will display the "Rotate" dialog box. This is where you can select exactly how the picture will be rotated: left or right, degrees, etc.

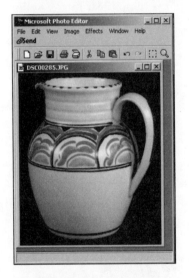

Our digital picture needs to rotate ninety degrees clockwise, which just so happens to be the default setting in Photo Editor. Click OK.

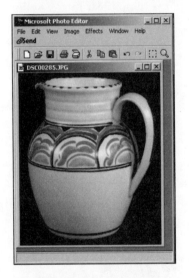

Our digital picture is now right side up. The next step is to crop all extraneous visual information from around the jug.

CROP

Just before we snapped this picture, we framed the picture of the jug so that it nearly filled the frame of the digital viewfinder. Thus there is very little to crop. Still, nearly all digital pictures can benefit from a cropping. In our picture, there is just enough extra black border around the jug for us to crop.

We start by clicking on the Select tool located on the Photo Editor toolbar.

The Select tool lets you use your mouse to "select" an area on the digital picture by creating a box. To start, position your mouse cursor somewhere on the upper left-hand corner of the picture.

While holding down the mouse button, drag the cursor diagonally down toward the right-hand side of the picture.

When you have reached the other corner, release the mouse button. You will see something like the following:

The dotted line has little square nodes in the corners and on the sides of the box. You can change the dimensions and position of the box by dragging these nodes with your mouse cursor. When you have arranged the sides of the box to your liking, click on Image on the menu command bar and select "Crop . . ."

In Photo Editor, this will display a Crop dialog box. Not all image-editing applications have a Crop dialog box. Don't change anything in this box. Accept all of the default settings and click OK.

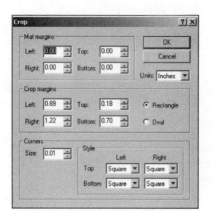

The cropped digital picture!

The next step in the editing process is to resize the digital picture.

RESIZE

If the picture doesn't look too big, why are we resizing?

Notice the little box on the menu bar that shows a percentage. This is the current zoomed view. Photo Editor has automatically "zoomed out" on the view in order that we can see the entire image within the application window without scrolling back and forth. At the moment, we are viewing the digital picture at 25 percent. That's 25 percent of its actual size.

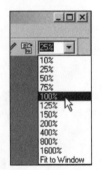

Remember, there are millions of items for sale on eBay. If your digital picture files are so big that they take forever to download onto an eBay shopper's computer, that shopper just might give up waiting and instead decide to walk away from your listing in search of other similar items.

Let's select 100% from the drop-down list of percentages so that we can see just how big the digital picture actually is.

I've reduced the window, but you can clearly see that this digital picture is enormous.

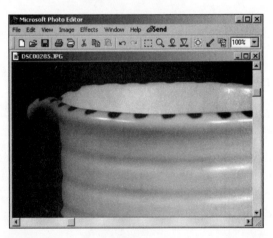

In full screen, only the very top of the jug is viewable. If you were to load this digital picture on your eBay listing, it would take forever to download over a dial-up connection. Remember, the larger the image size, the longer it will take to appear on a bidder's screen.

Let's resize the picture.

Click on Image and then "Resize . . ." on the menu command bar.

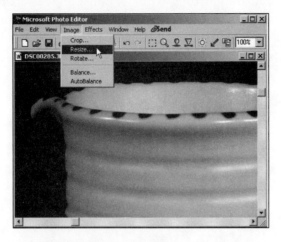

As any command that is followed by ellipses will do, clicking on "Resize . . ." brings up the Resize dialog box.

If the "Units" box is not showing "Pixels," please select it now. When creating digital pictures for viewing over the Web, the standard measurement is always pixels.

Our jug picture is 865 pixels by 1085 pixels. Remember, you should think of a pixel as that dot of light on your computer monitor. Pixel density varies from monitor to monitor, so pixels do not relate in any absolute way to inches or centimeters. However, the number of pixels for height and width of a digital picture are extremely important.

GRIFF'S PIXEL GUIDELINE

After much experimentation, I came up with the following guideline for resizing digital pictures for an eBay listing.

If you keep your digital pictures within a range somewhere between 330 pixels high and 440 pixels wide, your digital pictures will always be large enough to show the complete item in detail (providing you have followed all of the previous steps for digital pictures), yet small enough to download quickly for those bidders with slow dial-up connections.

When faced with huge pixel numbers for Height and Width, I select the larger of the two—1085 for Height—and reduce it to 400.

Notice that you don't have to change the other dimension. All good image-editing software is configured to keep the ratio between height and width constant. When you change one dimension, the other will change to keep the correct proportion.

Changing the Height pixels from 1085 pixels to 400 pixels automatically reduces the Width to 318. This is within the parameters of Griff's Pixel Guideline, so we'll click OK to accept this new size.

Here is the resized digital picture of our jug.

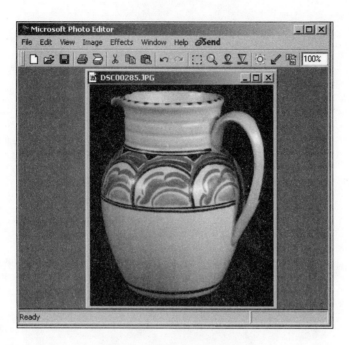

It's a perfectly proportioned picture, if I do say so myself.
Let's save a copy of this priceless work of art.

SAVING AND ARCHIVING YOUR EBAY DIGITAL PICTURES

Once we have edited our digital picture to perfection, we must save it to our computer.

I'm a digital packrat. Pictures, emails, text files . . . I archive most everything sent to me or created on my computer. Unless an image is unusable, I archive *all* of my pictures. Why? Given the low cost of storage on CD-ROM or extra hard drive, it seems foolish to delete perfectly good pictures. Besides, as the mantra of all packrats goes, "You never know when you might need them someday!"

You may not be as obsessively concerned about saving your images as I am, but you should always keep copies of your eBay item pictures for at least three months after your eBay listing ends. And if you are going to save copies of your picture files, you might as well start out right, with a *system*!

First things first. We need to save our magnificently edited digital picture. With the edited digital picture open in your image-editing application, choose File and "Save As . . ."

231

In the resulting Save As dialog box, select a folder on your hard drive for your edited eBay picture. Since we have already created a main folder called "eBay Digital Pictures," I will create a subfolder within this folder for our eBay listing.

To create a folder, click the Create New Folder icon.

Now we must name the folder. If I don't name it, the computer will simply call it "New Folder." Here's the folder-naming convention I use:

My picture folders all begin with the date, followed by a hyphen and a name descriptive enough so that days or weeks or years from now, it will be clear to me what the folder might contain. This folder is going to contain our jug picture and eventually many other pieces of Honiton pottery. Therefore, I will name it "04-25-02-Honiton."

Once I have named the folder, I double-click it to open it.

Remember, we initially set out to save the edited digital picture of our jug, and that is what we do next. In order to save a new file, I have to give it a name. I will rename the file from the name my Sony CyberShot gave it, "DSC00285.JPG," to something more memorable and descriptive, "honiton-pitcher01.jpg."

Before we click the Save button, let's click the button labeled "More>>" (only applicable to Photo Editor).

Nearly every good image-editing application will prompt you, before saving a jpg file, to select a JPEG quality factor. For example, in Photoshop, you are automatically asked to select a quality level between 1 and 10 when you click the Save button. In Photo Editor, if you wish to change the default setting from "high" to something lower, you need to do so before you click Save. Clicking the More>> button on the Photo Editor "Save As . . ." dialog box displays a slider that you can move left to right to change the JPEG quality factor.

Why would you want to change from high quality to lower quality? The higher the quality value for a JPEG digital file, the bigger the file is in kilobytes, the longer it takes to download. You want pictures that snap as quickly as possible into your item description.

When creating digital images for eBay items, lowering the image-quality factor will have little or no discernible effect on the final digital picture. As a rule, I usually reduce the image quality factor to at least a point midway between the lowest and highest qualities (which I have done for this picture). Let's save it to view the change, if any.

There is virtually no change at all in our image. It looks better than ever. But what if there had been a noticeable and consequently unacceptable change in the image's quality? Would we be stuck with it? Not at all! You still have the original image on your hard drive. (Remember, we saved the edited version as a brand-new file.) You would simply start the editing process again with the original digital file.

EXAMPLES OF THE CROP, ROTATE, AND RESIZE COMMANDS IN OTHER SOFTWARE

Adobe Photoshop

Crop
In Photoshop, the "Crop" tool is found on the floating toolbar.

With the Crop tool selected, drag a box around the area to save using the mouse.

Once the box is set, click Image on the Photoshop toolbar and select Crop from the menu list.

Rotate

To Rotate an image in Photoshop, click Image on the toolbar, select Rotate Canvas, and select one of the options.

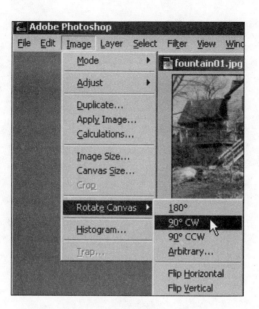

Resize

To resize an image in Photoshop, click Image on the toolbar and select "Image Size . . ."

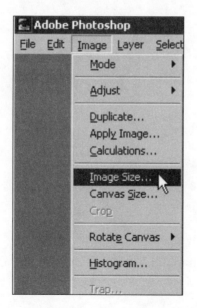

Change the pixel dimensions for either Width or Height.

Image Size

Pixel Dimensions: 2.74M

Width: 1180 pixels

Height: 809 pixels

OK
Cancel
Auto...

Print Size:

Width: 5.9 inches

Height: 4.045 inches

Resolution: 200 pixels/inch

☑ Constrain Proportions
☑ Resample Image: Bicubic

Irfanview

Crop

To select an area of an image to save using Irfanview (a free graphic viewer available for Windows computers), simply hold down the mouse cursor and start drawing a box.

Irfanview's Crop command is located under Edit on the toolbar.

Rotate

To rotate an image in Irfanview, click on Image and then select one of the Rotate options.

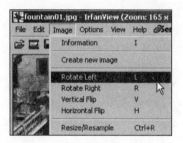

Resize/Resample

To resize an image in Irfanview, click on Image, and Resize/Resample.

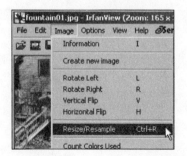

Change the pixel dimension numbers for Width or Height.

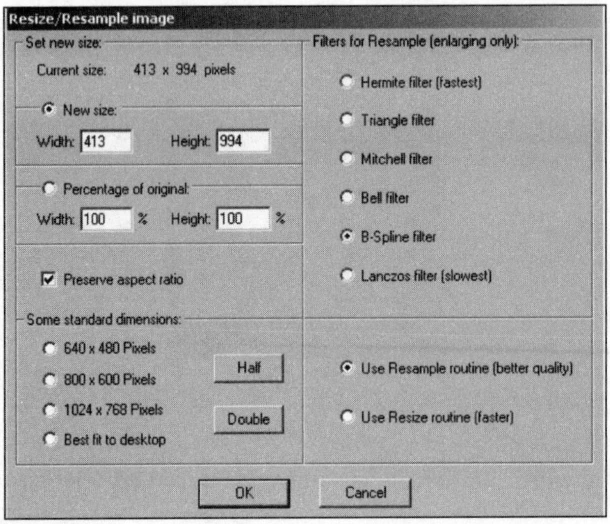

Resize/Resample image

Set new size:

Current size: 413 x 994 pixels

(•) New size:

Width: 413   Height: 994

( ) Percentage of original:

Width: 100 %   Height: 100 %

[✓] Preserve aspect ratio

Some standard dimensions:

( ) 640 x 480 Pixels
( ) 800 x 600 Pixels   [Half]
( ) 1024 x 768 Pixels   [Double]
( ) Best fit to desktop

Filters for Resample (enlarging only):

( ) Hermite filter (fastest)
( ) Triangle filter
( ) Mitchell filter
( ) Bell filter
(•) B-Spline filter
( ) Lanczos filter (slowest)

(•) Use Resample routine (better quality)
( ) Use Resize routine (faster)

[OK]   [Cancel]

Taking good pictures is a skill that anyone with an eye can acquire. There are hundreds of good books on Basic Photography available on- and offline. I urge you to explore the basics of photography. The knowledge and skill will help you create better and better eBay images.

You've now got your perfect pictures captured, edited, named, and saved—ready to go on your eBay listing. Our next task is to compose a good item description worthy of our excellent photo and to put the two together in our first eBay listing.

3

Listing Your Item on eBay

Traditionally, only those artists lucky enough to have a great agent, gallery owner, or patron could count on any semblance of a sustainable career as an artist. An artist's success was limited by the twin evil realities of geography and the unavoidable curse of obscurity.

Starving is never romantic. Artists usually pick up a second line of work—"a day gig"—in order to make ends meet. Trouble is, balancing a day gig and one's art often takes so much energy that both suffer.

However, as artist Keri Lyn Shosted discovered, starving as an artist is not inevitable. eBay can offer an artist instant access to a vast potential customer base from around the globe.

"I went from begging galleries to give my work a shot, to selling full-time—for over three years now on eBay, with a large following of customers and about fifteen shops around the country carrying my line of dog art prints. Not to mention over a hundred commission paintings, all brought to me through the magic of eBay. I even now have a greeting-card company in Canada publishing my work. . . . How did they find me? eBay!"

There are hundreds of artists and craftsmen and -women who have leveraged eBay as a platform for finding eager customers for their work.

"I know that eBay has made what was once impossible a true reality for many other eBay members as well, especially artists. By cutting out the middleman hundred-percent-mark-up gallery, buyers are now able to search thousands of artists and buy direct."

Now that we have our digital pictures, we are finally ready to list our item on eBay.

We've done most of the real work. Our eBay Seller's Account is activated; we've located an item to sell; we've taken and edited digital pictures of the item. Before we actually start the "Sell Your Item" process, we need to create the text for our item description.

A SIMPLE DESCRIPTION

Every item for sale on eBay should have a clear, concise, and comprehensive item description. We could simply type in our description extemporaneously in the box on the "Sell Your Item" form, but I want you to get into the habit of always typing your description into a text editor before you start the listing process. For Windows computers, use Notepad. For Macs, use Simple Text or TextEdit.

NOTE TO MAC USERS: We will use Windows to illustrate our examples. Macintosh users should follow the instructions step by step. The only difference for Mac users will be the name of the text editor and the steps necessary to open the text editor and Web browser. Everything else in this chapter is identical for Windows and for Mac users.

OPENING A TEXT EDITOR

PC users: To start, we open a blank Notepad file. Notepad can be started from the Windows Start menu at Programs, Accessories, Notepad.

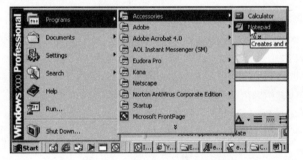

(Mac users: Look on your Hard Drive for a program called Simple Text or Text Edit. Either one will work and will resemble Notepad. You can download text editors for your Mac computer at **www.tucows.com.**)

This will open an Untitled Notepad (or TextEdit or Simple Text) window.

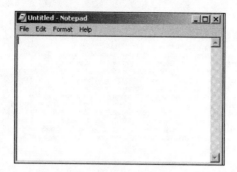

For the remainder of this chapter, everything you type you will type into your Notepad (or for Mac, Simple Text or Text Editor) window. (Please do *not* use Word, Word Pad, or some other application. This exercise will only work perfectly if you use a plain text editor.)

Now, let's start writing our description.

Every good item description should contain the following:

1. A detailed description of the item
2. Your Terms of Service for Payment, Shipping, and Returns
3. Your pictures

We are going to use eBay Picture Services for our pictures, so we don't need to include them in our item description. (We cover other image hosting options in Section Two, Chapter 7—"Advanced Image Hosting Solutions.")

A DETAILED DESCRIPTION

Your item description should include the following item attributes:

Name of the item
Age
Dimensions
Weight (if unusually heavy—for shipping purposes)
Place of origin or manufacture
Condition

Here's what I wrote about our pottery pitcher:

```
Untitled - Notepad                                    _ □ X
File  Edit  Format  Help  Send
Honiton Exton Small Pitcher

I was culling treasure from the china closet and found this
Honiton pitcher, 4 1/2 inches tall, circa 1950's. White clay.
Exton shape. Pitcher is in excellent condition; no cracks,
breaks, chips or stains. Embossed mark on bottom: "Honiton
Potteries Exton England" with a black hand painted "t".

A Brief History of Honiton Pottery: Honiton Pottery was (and
is) located in the town of Honiton in Devon, England. The
pottery was started by Foster and Hunt at the turn of the
19th/20th century. It was purchased by Charles Collard shortly
after WWI. In 1947, Collard sold the pottery to Norman Hull and
Harry Barratt who ran it until 1961 when it was sold to Paul
Redvers. All production ceased in 1997 and the pottery was
shuttered. The premises were recently reopened as pottery and
craft shop.

Payment Terms: I accept and prefer payment be made with a
credit/debit card (via Paypal). I also accept person checks
(item shipped immediately after check has cleared) or money
Orders

Shipping Terms: I will ship this item anywhere to anyone.
International bidders welcome. High bidder pays winning bid
plus USPS priority or global priority shipping and insurance.
US $5, Canada $8,UK  $10, All Others  $15

Refunds, Returns, Regrets: If you win this item and upon
receiving it, are not 100% satisfied, you may return it to me
for a full refund of the winning bid and shipping. (Returning
buyer pays for shipping back to me.)
```

Honiton Exton Small Pitcher

I was culling treasure from the china closet and found this Honiton pitcher, 4½ inches tall, circa 1950's. White clay. Exton shape. Pitcher is in excellent condition; no cracks, breaks, chips or stains. Embossed mark on bottom: "Honiton Potteries Exton England" with a black hand painted "t".

In a short paragraph, I included the history of the pottery. This type of information can help spark interest in new collectors.

A Brief History of Honiton Pottery: Honiton Pottery was (and is) located in the town of Honiton in Devon, England. The pottery was started by Foster and Hunt at the turn of the 19th/20th century. It was purchased by Charles Collard shortly after WWI. In 1947, Collard sold the pottery to Norman Hull and Harry Barratt who ran it until 1961 when it was sold to Paul Redvers. All production ceased in 1997 and the pottery was shuttered. The premises were recently re-opened as pottery and craft shop.

Next I typed in my payment, shipping, and return policies and fees.

Payment Terms: I accept and prefer payment be made with a credit/debit card (via PayPal). I also accept personal checks (item shipped immediately after check has cleared) or money Orders

Shipping Terms: I will ship this item anywhere to anyone. International bidders welcome. High bidder pays winning bid plus USPS priority or global priority shipping and insurance. US $5, Canada $8, UK $10, All Others $15

Refunds, Returns, Regrets: If you win this item and upon receiving it, are not 100% satisfied, you may return it to me for a full refund of the winning bid and shipping. (Returning buyer pays for shipping back to me.)

It pays to be as detailed as possible regarding a buyer's obligations. Buyers don't like surprises. Make sure you provide as clear a picture as possible regarding acceptable payment options, shipping fees, and any other special "Terms of Service" (TOS).

If we were to copy and paste this description into the eBay "Sell Your Item" form, it would turn out like this:

Note how all our blocks of text—our paragraph and line breaks—no longer appear? That's because our description will be viewed through a Web browser and Web browsers don't know how to display line breaks. We have to tell the Web browser where to insert line breaks by using a special text-formatting language called HTML.

BASIC HTML (HYPERTEXT MARKUP LANGUAGE)

(Advanced HTML tips can be found farther on, in Chapter 6—"Advanced HTML.")

HTML is not complex. HTML consists of little bits of text called "tags." An HTML tag contains a "lesser than" sign, a "tag name," and a "greater than" sign.

For this chapter, we are going to learn one simple but important HTML tag:

<P>

The <P> tag is used to indicate a paragraph break (double line break).

Remember, your item description will be viewed as part of a Web page (the eBay Item Description Page for your item), so it has to be treated as a Web page.

Wherever we want a paragraph or double line break to appear in our item description, we need to type in a <P> tag so that an eBay shopper's Web browser will display the text as you intended.

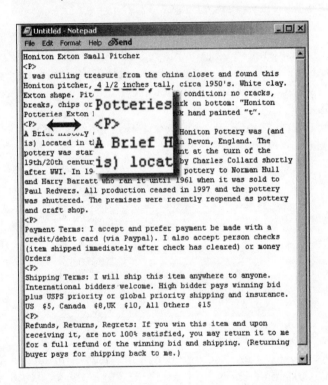

When a Web browser comes across a <P> tag, it will insert a double line break. The tag itself will not display.

It's always wise to save your finished item description text as a file on your computer's hard drive. That way, you always have a copy of it ready on hand to edit and copy and paste into the eBay "Sell Your Item" Web form.

Select File, "Save As . . ." from the Notepad toolbar.

1. In the Save As box, choose a location on your hard drive for the new file. We will use the desktop.
2. In the box labeled "File Name," type in a name (we'll type "itemtext.txt").
3. Click the Save button.

We have set up our eBay Seller Account, created a digital picture of our item, composed our item description, formatted it with HTML <P> tags for paragraphs, and saved it to our hard drive. Now we can go to eBay and start the Sell Your Item process.

THE EBAY "SELL YOUR ITEM" FORM, STEP BY STEP

First, Sign In, if you are not already.

Sign In   ? Need Help?

| New to eBay? | **or** | Already an eBay user? |

If you want to sign in, you'll need to register first.

Registration is fast and **free**.

Register >

eBay members, sign in to save time for bidding, selling, and other activities.

eBay User ID

jimgriff@sover.net

You can also use your registered email.

Password

••••••••••••••

Forgot your password?

Sign In >

☐ Keep me signed in on this computer unless I sign out.

Account protection tips | Secure sign in (SSL)

Navigate to any eBay page. On the top of any eBay page you'll find the trusty old navigation bar.

1. Click the Sell link on the eBay Navigation Bar.
2. In the resulting Sell Your Item: Choose Selling Format window, select the option for "Sell at online Auction."

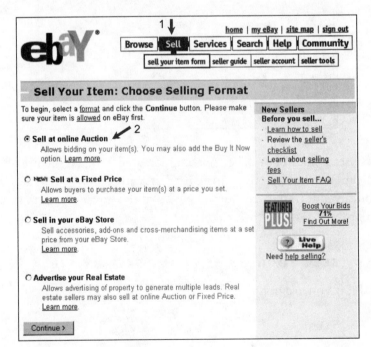

You will have up to four choices for a format; Auction, Fixed Price, eBay Store (if you have already set up an eBay Store), or Real Estate. As it states, eBay Store items are only for fixed or set price items. Make sure that you have selected "Sell at online Auction" and click the Continue button.

This takes us to the Select Category page.

Step 1. Select a Category

Lost your information? Click Refresh. Learn how to stop information loss.

Sell Your Item: Select Category

| ① Category | 2 Title & Description | 3 Pictures & Details | 4 Payment & Shipping | 5 Review & Submit |

If you already know your category number, enter it below.

Click in the boxes below starting with Box 1 until you have found the appropriate category. When the boxes turn gray, click the **Continue** button at the bottom of the page.

Main category
Not sure where to list your item? View descriptions of all top level categories.

1)
```
Antiques ->
eBay Motors
Art ->
Books ->
Business & Industrial ->
Clothing & Accessories ->
```
2)

3)

4)

5)

6)

Click here if you are having trouble viewing the category selector above.

Main category # [   ]

We need to select an appropriate category for our item. We start by selecting Pottery & Glass -> from window one.

Pottery & Glass ->...

1)
```
Movies & Television ->
Music ->
Photo & Optics ->
Pottery & Glass ->
Real Estate ->
Sports ->
```
2)
```
Glass ->
Pottery & China ->
```

Now, we must continue selecting subcategories until we reach a lowest-level category. In Window 2, let's select Pottery & China ->

In Window 3, let's select Pottery ->

In Window 4—since there is no option for "Honiton"—let's select Other.

When you have reached the bottom of the category hierarchy, the remaining windows will gray out.

GRIFF TIP: On the bottom of this page, you'll find a window containing the category number you have selected.

Main **category #** | 86
Number will appear when you have completely selected your category.

If you plan on regularly listing in this category, you should jot this number down. The next time you list an item in this category, you simply enter in the number in this box and the matching category will automatically fill in.

Note, too, that at the bottom of this page, there is also an option for listing the item in a second category-by-category number. This can be an ideal option for those items that might benefit from exposure in two categories. Make sure that the second category relates to the item. For now, we are listing our item in one category.

NOTE: Some older Web browsers or Web browsers that have their Java settings disabled may have trouble displaying the above category selection windows. As time goes on, the eBay web site has become rich with new features and enhancements meant to make navigating and using the site easier. Many of these new features incorporate and rely on either Java, JavaScript, ActiveX controls, or "cookies."

In order to take full advantage of these eBay enhancements, your Web browser must be configured properly.

Some eBay sellers experience difficulties using eBay Picture Services (iPix), the eBay Sign In feature, or other features on eBay. Before you contact eBay Customer Support, you should first try making a few simple changes to some of the settings in your Web browser. In most cases, changing a few browser settings will eliminate the problem.

There are two popular Web browsers in use today: **Internet Explorer** versions and **Netscape** versions. (A third-model Web browser, Opera, though excellent, is not yet popular enough for me to include it in this section—but that could change.)

Changing Settings for Internet Explorer (Version 6.0 and Higher)
1. With an Internet Explorer window open, click on **Tools** on the menu bar and then select **Internet Options** . . .

2. In the **Internet Options** window, select the **Security** tab on the top of the page and then click the **"Custom Level . . ."** button.

3. In the Security Settings box, you'll find a scrollable window. This window contains selectable options for various settings.

4. Make sure you have selected the options for each section as noted below.

ActiveX Controls and Plug-ins

Download signed ActiveX controls: Prompt

Download unsigned ActiveX controls: Disable

Initialize and script ActiveX controls not marked as safe: Disable

Run ActiveX controls and plug-ins: Enable

Script ActiveX controls marked safe for scripting: Enable

Downloads

File Download: Enable

All of the other settings you may leave as they are. Click the **OK** button to return to the Internet Options window and then select the Privacy tab.

Click the **"Advanced . . ."** button. (Note: Your Privacy Tab window may look different than Fig. 4. Ignore the difference and click the **"Advanced . . ."** button.)

Make sure the setting options for Advanced Privacy Settings are as follows:

Click **OK** to return to the Internet Options window.

(You may set **"Third-Party Cookies"** to **Block** if you so desire. You will not need third-party cookies in order to use eBay effectively.)

Select the **Advanced** tab at the top of the Internet Options window to open the Advanced tab view.

There are many options here—we are concerned with only a few, and most of these will have been properly set by default. Begin by scrolling down the window and checking each section as noted below:

Under **Browsing** section, make sure that the option for "Always send URLs as UTF-8" is checked.

Under **Microsoft VM** section, make sure that the options for "Java console enabled" and "JIT compiler for virtual machine enabled" are both checked.

Under **Multimedia** section, make sure that the option for "Show pictures" is checked. (Although not crucial, I also like to make sure that the option for "Enable automatic image resizing" is **not** checked.)

Under the **Security** section, make sure that the options for "Use SSL 2.0" and "Use SSL 3.0" are both checked.

Click Apply, then click OK. Your settings have now been changed for optimal eBay use.

In addition, you can always use the older method of category selection by clicking the link at the bottom of the windows for "Click here if you are having trouble viewing the category selector above." This will take you to a page of top-level categories. Select one and click.

Sell Your Item: Select Category

① Category | 2 Title & Description | 3 Pictures & Details | 4 Payment & Shipping | 5 Review & Submit

Select a top-level category and click the **Continue** button at the bottom of the page.
If you already know your category number, enter it below.

- OR -
Try the enhanced, easier category selector.

○ Antiques	Antique silver, furniture, ceramics, textiles & other décor
○ Art	Paintings, prints, photos, posters, folk art & sculpture
○ eBay Motors	Cars, boats, aircraft, motorcycles, parts & accessories
○ Books	Books rare and recent, magazines & more
○ Business & Industrial	Medical, restaurant, construction equipment & more
○ Clothing & Accessories	Apparel, footwear & accessories
○ Coins	Coins, paper money & numismatic supplies
○ Collectibles	Advertising to historical memorabilia to vintage clothing
○ Computers & Office Products	Hardware, software, office equipment & supplies
○ Consumer Electronics	Audio, games & video equipment
○ Dolls & Bears	Barbies, figures, miniature houses & Cherished Teddies
○ Home & Garden	Baby items, furnishings, tools, food & wine, and pet supplies
○ Jewelry, Gems & Watches	Fine, antique & artisan jewelry, jewelry supplies
○ Movies	DVDs, videos & memorabilia
○ Music	CDs, vinyl, musical instruments & memorabilia
○ Photo & Optics	Digital and film cameras & accessories, binoculars
● Pottery & Glass	China, glass, pottery, porcelain & stoneware
○ Real Estate	Residential, commercial, timeshares & land
○ Sports	Autographs, memorabilia, cards & equipment
○ Stamps	Scripophily, US & world stamps
○ Tickets & Travel	Concerts, events, flights, hotels & luggage
○ Toys & Hobbies	Action figures, bean bag plush, crafts & trains
○ Everything Else	Health & Beauty, Gifts & Occasions, Genealogy, Weird Stuff and More!

Optional - Category Numbers

If you already know the category number(s), enter them below. Then click the **Continue** button

Main category # [   ]   Second category # (optional) [   ]

Double insertion and listing upgrade fees will apply when listing an item in two categories. Final Value fees will **not** be doubled Learn more.

[< Back]   [Continue >]

Click Continue.

On the next page, select a subcategory from each successive box per the instructions above.

Lost your information? Click Refresh . Learn how to stop information loss.

Sell Your Item: Select Subcategory

① Category | 2 Title & Description | 3 Pictures & Details | 4 Payment & Shipping | 5 Review & Submit

Main category (top level you've selected):

[Pottery & Glass ▼]   If you select a different top level category, the sub-categories below will change.

Select your Pottery & Glass subcategory.
Just click in the boxes below from left to right.

1. Glass -->
   Pottery & China -->

2. Porcelain -->
   Pottery -->
   Restaurant Ware
   Stoneware

3. Weller
   Winfield
   Wood & Sons
   Other

4. *** Subcategory selected. ***
   Continue below.

5. *** Subcategory selected. ***
   Continue below.

Click here if you are having trouble viewing the category selector above.
- OR -
Try the enhanced, easier category selector.

Main category # [86]
Number will appear when you have completely selected your category.

Choose a second category (optional)

List your item in two places for greater visibility.   Learn more about listing in
Double insertion and listing upgrade fees will apply Final two categories.
value fees will **not** be doubled
[Click to select a second category ▼]
You will select a subcategory on the next page.

[< Back]   [Continue >]

255

Once you have selected your category, click Continue to rejoin us for step two in the "Sell Your Item" process: "Describe Your Item."

STEP 2. DESCRIBE YOUR ITEM (TITLE AND DESCRIPTION)

Sell Your Item: Describe Your Item

| 1 Category | ② Title & Description | 3 Pictures & Details | 4 Payment & Shipping | 5 Review & Submit |

✱ = Required

Item title ✱

Learn how to write a good item title.

No HTML, asterisks, or quotes. 45 characters maximum.

Item description

Description ✱   Enter either plain text or HTML

Pictures may be added to your listing on the next page.

Enter plain text or add simple HTML tags to change font size, create paragraphs or bulleted lists, add images, and more.

HTML Tip:
Enter <p> to start a new paragraph.

Preview your description

Note: If you are a first-time seller, you may be asked to download a small file on the next page. This file will help you add pictures on eBay. If you have trouble loading the next page, you may change your picture selection method.

< Back   Continue >

Type a title for your item. Your title should be composed entirely of keywords that relate directly to your item. Here's our title.

Sell Your Item: Describe Your Item

| 1 Category | ② Title & Description | 3 Pictures & Details | 4 Payment & Shipping |

Item title ✱
Honiton Pitcher Jug Exton
No HTML, asterisks, or quotes. 45 characters maximum.

"Honiton Pitcher Jug Exton" may not sound elegant, but elegant syntax is not our goal when it comes to creating an item title. Remember that most shoppers on eBay use keywords to search titles in order to find those items for which they are interested.

Some Item Title Tips:

1. Avoid using punctuation or symbols in your titles. They can cause your item to not appear in a title search.
2. In cases where a noun in your title could be plural or singular, type the singular and plural forms if there is enough room.
3. Avoid editorial adjectives like *rare, wonderful, stupendous, gorgeous,* etc. No one wakes up in the morning thinking, *Say, I think I will search eBay for all the "gorgeous" items up for bid or sale.*
4. Usually, articles or prepositions are superfluous in an eBay item title. Use them only if they are absolutely necessary or if there is enough space after you have exhausted all the possible keywords relating directly to your item.

Next we have to supply an item description. We've already created ours in a text file. In order to add it to our description, we must "copy" and "paste" it into the box on the Describe Your Item page. We do this by using the Copy and Paste features that come built into Windows or Mac operating systems.

Cut, Copy, and Paste

I'm always amazed to find out just how many otherwise computer-savvy folks have no idea how to use the three basic text-editing commands:

Cut
Copy
Paste

If you are planning to spend any amount of time using the Internet to sell things, or if you just spend a lot of time at the computer, sending email or writing the great American novel, then you are going to need these three commands. If you are going to sell your merch on eBay, then you will REALLY need them.

Cut, Copy, and **Paste** are the ultimate time savers for moving text from one place to another or creating copies of long pages of text. Let's watch them in action:

The three commands, **Cut, Copy,** and **Paste** can be executed in three ways. The first and most common place to find the commands is under the menu bar **Edit** command for any Windows (or Mac) application. Here is an example of where the commands are usually found in any application using Notepad's **Edit** menu command.

Let's say we want to copy some text from Notepad and paste it into the item description box on the eBay Sell Your Item Page. First we highlight the text in Notepad by clicking the mouse cursor on either side of the text and, while holding down the mouse button, dragging the mouse across the text.

Once the text is highlighted, click **Edit** on the Notepad menu bar and then select **Copy** from the drop-down menu.

What this does is copy the highlighted text to a built-in applet called Clipboard (in Windows and on the Mac). Anything copied to the Clipboard can be pasted into the same or another application. Until some new text is copied to the Clipboard, this text will be available for pasting into any other application any number of times. Let's copy the text into another application—in this instance, we will copy it into the Sell Your Item page's text entry box for the Item Description.

In the example below, I have clicked my cursor so it is blinking inside the box. I then clicked the right-hand button on my mouse and selected Paste from the resulting pop-up menu box.

This will cause the text you copied from Notepad to be pasted into the Description box.

The **Cut** command is similar to the **Copy** command, with one difference—the **Copy** command leaves the original text untouched and copies it to the Clipboard. The **Cut** command "cuts" or removes the instance of the original text and copies it to the Clipboard. The **Cut** command comes in handy when you want to actually move text from one place to another.

As I mentioned earlier, there are three ways to call up the **Cut, Copy,** and **Paste** commands. We have explored one of them—using pop-up menus—but there are two others, one of which is better than the other two. Here are all three ways to reach the editing commands:

1. From the main menu bar
2. From the pop-up menu (reached by clicking the right mouse button)
3. Using keystrokes

Keystrokes are the most efficient way of accessing the basic text-editing commands. In the old, old, old days of DOS (before Windows—yes, there was a time when Windows did not exist!), way before everyone used a pointing device like a mouse, anyone who did a lot of text editing or word processing relied upon these keystroke combinations to do all their basic text editing. There were no other options!

Although it takes a day or so to get used to using keystroke combinations to do text editing, once you are comfortable doing so, you won't ever want to use anything else! Any tip or trick that keeps you from moving your hand over to the mouse and back a hundred times a day not only saves time but also will help prevent repetitive-motion pain or injury.

In order to **Copy** using keystrokes, first select the text you want to copy by placing your mouse cursor to the left of the text. Hold down the right mouse button and drag the cursor to the right (and down if you need to copy more than one line of text), as in the middle figures on page 258.

Once your selected text is highlighted, press and hold down the **Ctrl** (Mac: Command key) key on your keyboard (use your little finger on your left hand. Avoid the bad habit of using two hands for keystroke combinations—it will defeat the whole purpose!)

Keep the **Ctrl** key down and, using your index finger, click the C key once.

This will **Copy** the text to the Windows Clipboard.

Next, select the application and location to where you wish the text to be copied (usually, this means clicking the mouse cursor into a box or blank page so that it is blinking in just the place you want the text to appear). Now, using the keyboard, once again hold down the **Ctrl** key and this time, click the **V** key once.

This keystroke combination (**Ctrl + V**) **Pastes** the text into the application where the mouse cursor is currently active.

Other keystroke combinations include:

Ctrl + X for Cut

The following work for *most* Windows applications but not all!

Ctrl + A for Select All

Ctrl + N for New (window—VERY helpful for opening new Internet Explorer windows)!

Ctrl + S for Save

Try them all and see how much more efficient and quick they are when compared to selecting commands from a menu!

Now we're ready to go back to the Notepad file (or Mac Text Editor/Simple Text file) containing our HTML-formatted item description and click on the Edit, and Select All commands on the text file's menu command bar:

This will highlight all of the text in the file. Once it is highlighted, click on Edit and Copy on the text file's menu command bar like we did in the above exercise.

Go back to the Internet Explorer window showing the eBay Sell Your Item form. Click your mouse cursor anywhere inside the box marked "Description." With the mouse cursor blinking in the Description box, click your mouse's right-hand button and select Paste.

This will paste a copy of the entire item description text into the eBay "Sell Your Item" form "Description" box.

You can preview your description by clicking the link labeled "Preview Your Description." Let's preview ours.

It's plain but it is readable, and readability is the single most important aspect of an item text description layout. Later, in Section Two, Chapter 6—"Advanced HTML," we will learn how to dress up the description with other HTML tags.

NOTE: You could type your item description directly into the Description box on the Sell Your Item form, adding tags <P> tags where needed. However, I suggest that you always type your description in a separate file before you begin the listing process. It is easier to "proof" your description in the bigger Notepad or Mac TextEdit window, and should the text in the Description box erase for some reason (it does happen), you won't have to type it over—you would only need to copy and paste it from the Notepad file.

Click the Continue button to move on to the next step in the listing process.

STEP 3. PROVIDE PICTURES & ITEM DETAILS

This is the page where we will select and add our item pictures. We will also provide our item details by selecting them from the choices.

NOTE: If your computer has never been on this page before, you may see a Security Warning asking you if you want to install and run IPIX Rimfire ActiveX Control. Check the box for "Always trust content from Internet Pictures Corporation" and click the Yes button.

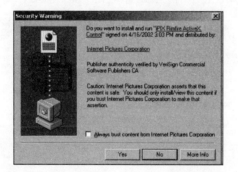

You will not be able to use eBay Picture Services properly if you do not allow the ActiveX Control to download and install on your computer. You have my assurance that the iPix control is safe to download.

Next, we have to select some Item details. If you have an eBay Store, you need to select a Store Category (more on Stores in the next chapter). When I set up my eBay Store, I created a custom store category named "pottery" that fits here.

We also need to select a duration for the listing. The choices are 3, 5, 7, and 10 days. I have selected 7 days. (The 10-day duration costs $.10. All others are free.)

I have a quantity of one item, so I type "1" in the appropriate box. (**NOTE:** Typing any other number will default your listing to a Dutch Auction!)

I also selected

✔ A Starting price of $1
✔ No reserve
✔ A Buy It Now price of $15.

On the next section of this page, I need to enter my regional location information. In the Item Location boxes, I entered the appropriate City and State, Region, and Country.

In the next step, we add our item's digital pictures.

We have two options: eBay Picture Services or "Your Own Web Hosting." We are going to rely on eBay Picture Services for our first listing. Later, in Chapter 7—"Advanced Image Hosting Solutions"—we will go over the finer points of hosting your own images.

NOTE: If the eBay Picture Services tab does not display the six square boxes but instead shows six narrow text boxes, you may need to reconfigure your Web browser's settings. Go to pages 13 and 251.

Remember, we have copies of our edited digital pictures ready to go on our computer's hard drive. To begin the process, make sure the eBay Picture Services tab is selected in the "Add Pictures" section. Click on the first (free!) picture box. This will bring up an "Open" box. Navigate to the image files for the item. Mine are in a subfolder called "04-25-02-honiton" located inside a folder called "eBay Digital Pictures." (I created and named these folders. You should create and name your own folders to your taste.)

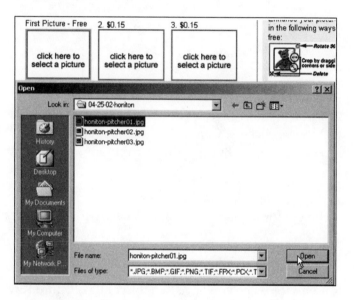

Highlight the first image and click the "Open" button. This will add that picture to the first eBay Picture Services box.

I will now add the other two pictures for our item.

eBay Picture Services | Your own Web hosting
Let eBay host your pictures | Enter your picture URL

To add pictures to your listing:
1. Click in the box below.
2. Find and select your picture. Your picture should now be displayed in the box below.

First Picture - Free   2. $0.15   3. $0.15

4. $0.15   5. $0.15   6. $0.15

click here to select a picture   click here to select a picture   click here to select a picture

Title bar picture: If you add a picture above, your first picture will be displayed at the top of your listing-free.

Picture Layout

⦿ Standard	Free	
○ Slide Show	$0.75	Show multiple views of your item.
○ Supersize Pictures	$0.75	Show more detail with extra large pictures. Submitted pictures must be bigger than 440w x 320h.
○ Picture Pack	$1.00	$1.75 value for only $1.00! Get Gallery, Supersize, and add up to 6 pictures.

NOTE: These digital pictures haven't yet been uploaded to eBay! They have only been selected. Once we click the Continue button on the bottom of this page, the uploading process will begin. But first, we have more information to fill in on this page.

I have accepted the default choice for "Standard Layout."

The other choices for layouts may come in handy for you later. Here's what they do.

Slide Show

This option is useful for when you have two to six eBay Picture Services pictures to display. The images will display one by one in a slide-show format. The viewer can use the buttons below the images to stop the show on any slide of her choice or move back and forth through the images.

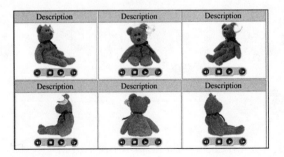

Supersize Pictures

I have often stressed that eBay images need not be larger than 440 pixels wide by 330 pixels tall, but sometimes you may want to provide images that are larger than these dimensions. The supersize option will make small thumbnail pictures of your bigger pictures with a link below each thumbnail for "supersize." A viewer can click the "supersize" link to view the larger images.

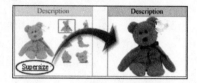

If you simply must provide pictures bigger than these dimensions and you don't want eBay Picture Services to compress them, then you should select this option.

NOTE: Supersize will *not* make small pictures bigger.

Picture Pack

Picture Pack is a bundled feature option with a discount price. For $1 you get a gallery image, six free images, and Supersize. It's a $1.75 value for only $1.00!

In the next section—"Increase your item's visibility"—you can select from several features. Each one can help you promote your item more effectively.

Increase your item's visibility

Gallery picture (this will be displayed as <u>your first picture</u>)
To enter a Gallery picture URL, click the Web hosting tab <u>above</u>

- ○ No Gallery picture
- ● Gallery — $0.25 — Add a picture preview to your listings and search results, and be on display in the Gallery!
- ○ Gallery Featured — $19.95 — Get all the benefits of Gallery plus showcase your item in the Featured section of Gallery.

See examples of <u>Gallery</u> and <u>Gallery Featured</u>.

Listing upgrades - make your item stand out

- ☐ Bold — $2.00 — Attract buyers' attention and set your listing apart -- use **bold**.

See example of a <u>bold</u> listing.

- ☐ Highlight — $5.00 — Make your listing stand out with a colored band.

See example of a <u>highlighted</u> listing.

- ☐ Featured Plus! — $19.95 — Show off your listing in the Featured area of category listings and search results.

See example of <u>Featured Plus!</u> listing.

- ☐ Home Page Featured — $99.95 — Get maximum exposure! Appear in our Featured area and your item may appear on the Home page.

See example of <u>Home Page Featured</u> listing.

Great Gift icon — $1.00 — Let buyers know that your item makes a great holiday or special occasion gift. Add a fun gift icon to your listing.
Not Selected ▼

<u>Learn more</u> about Great Gift icons.

Free page counter

- ○ Do not add a counter
- ● Andale Style `1 2 3 4`
- ○ Green LED `1 2 3 4`
- ○ Hidden `Thanks for looking!`

Only seller can see page views

Andale counters show how often your item has been viewed. <u>Learn more.</u>

Learn more about <u>hidden counters</u>.

`< Back`   `Continue >`

In the first section, we will select to use the Gallery. A Gallery image will cost $.25. eBay stats show that listings with Gallery pictures get more traffic and more bids. It's two bits well spent.

Next, there are other Optional features, which include Bold, Highlight, Featured Plus, and Home Page Featured. All of them can help you better promote your item, depending on the value and type of item you are offering.

The last feature on the page is for a Hit Counter (free). Adding a counter to your item page will show how many unique visitors have visited your listing.

Once you have selected your options (if any), click the Continue button.

At this point, eBay Picture Services will start sending copies of your digital pictures through your Internet connection to the eBay Picture Services Web server back on eBay. You should see a pop-up box indicating that the pictures are being sent. Depending on the speed of your Internet Connection, the upload can take anywhere from a few seconds to a few minutes.

The eBay Picture Services Web server does the rest of the work for you. You don't have to type in URLs for the pictures. You don't have to worry about where the pictures actually are located. Once you are finished with the listing process, your images will display automatically under your item description.

The next displayed page will provide payment and shipping options for you to select for your item.

STEP 4. PAYMENT AND SHIPPING

SPECIAL NOTE: eBay recently acquired the leading online payments provider, PayPal. As of this writing, the eventual integration of PayPal into this section of the "Sell Your Item" form has not been unveiled. The actual page for Step 4 may look different from our example.

We are going to accept credit cards (through PayPal), so I have selected the options stating that I will accept online payments. In addition, I will take checks and money orders, so I have checked those boxes as well.

In the next box, I have selected my shipping terms.

If you know how much your item will cost to ship, enter the information in the "Shipping costs" section. There is also a very helpful option for state sales tax. Your state may require you to collect a sales tax from any buyer who resides in your state. If so, you can select your state from the drop down-box and enter the appropriate percentage for your state. This amount will be added to the total of any bidder who is located in your state.

For this listing, I am offering free shipping and insurance to all continental US buyers. I also need to collect Utah sales tax from any Utah residents who buy from me through eBay.

Next, I can supply payment instructions to the winning buyer.

Here is the complete text I typed into the box:

High Winning Bidder!

Free Shipping and Insurance to any location within the continental US.

If you are located outside of the continental US, please email me with your location so I can provide your shipping costs. Look for the link on this page for "Request a Total."

Thanks!

Griff

I guarantee 100% satisfaction or your money cheerfully refunded upon return of the item.

In the "Ship-to location" section, select the areas of the world to which you will ship your item.

GRIFF TIP: It pays to sell to everyone. Folks from across the globe are using eBay every day. They have cash and they are eager to buy. Don't cut them out!

eBay seller Robert Sachs ("rosachs") has a great holiday selling tip:

EBAY MEMBER TIP: I found a neat little trick to help boost my holiday sales enormously: Free Shipping!

I combined Buy It Now with Free Shipping and came up with a killer offer. If the buyer used Buy It Now, I would zero out the shipping charge. I changed the heading for my listings to be sure to include "FREE SHIP" in each one. My listings, normally set for five days, would close within twenty-four hours! This allowed me to post more without flooding a particular item. And posting more meant more sales!

My normal closing rate for the year 2001 averaged around forty-five percent. My closing rate during November and early December pushed closer to eighty percent, with the vast majority being Buy It Now sales!

Finally, there is the Escrow option. Check the appropriate escrow box.

Escrow	Minimize
⦿ Will not accept escrow (if chosen, the Escrow line doesn't appear in the listing) ○ Will accept escrow on items if the buyer pays the escrow fees. ○ Will accept escrow on items and seller will pay the escrow fees.	Escrow is when a third party holds the buyer's payment in trust until the buyer receives and approves the item from the seller. eBay does not provide escrow services. If you want escrow, you must provide your own.
‹ Back Continue ›	

GRIFF TIP: New sellers of expensive merchandise should consider offering the escrow option, especially since new sellers tend not to have much feedback. You can read more about online escrow in Section One, Chapter 5.

Some bidders may be a bit leery of bidding on items offered by a brand-new seller, especially expensive items. Offering your bidders escrow along with your acceptance of credit card payments can go a long way to instilling bidder confidence.

Once you have finished selecting options, click the Continue button to review the listing before actual submission to the site.

STEP 5: REVIEW AND SUBMIT LISTING

This is an important step! Please don't rush through it. Check each section to make sure that the information is correct.

The first thing to display is your title, description, and pictures.

Sell Your Item: Review & Submit Listing

1 Category 2 Title   3 Pictures   4 Payment   ⑤ Review
          & Description   & Details   & Shipping   & Submit

Step 1: Review your listing

Click an 'Edit page' link to make changes. When you do, you'll be directed to a page where you can make your desired changes.

Honiton Pitcher Jug Exton	Edit title

Description	Edit description

Honiton Exton Small Pitcher

I was culling treasure from the china closet and found this Honiton pitcher, 4 1/2 inches tall, circa 1950's. White clay. Exton shape. Pitcher is in excellent condition; no cracks, breaks, chips or stains. Embossed mark on bottom: "Honiton Potteries Exton England" with a black hand painted "t".

A Brief History of Honiton Pottery: Honiton Pottery was (and is) located in the town of Honiton in Devon, England. The pottery was started by Foster and Hunt at the turn of the 19th/20th century. It was purchased by Charles Collard shortly after WWI. In 1947, Collard sold the pottery to Norman Hull and Harry Barratt who ran it until 1961 when it was sold to Paul Redvers. All production ceased in 1997 and the pottery was shuttered. The premises were recently reopened as pottery and craft shop.

Payment Terms: I accept and prefer payment be made with a credit/debit card (via Paypal). I also accept person checks (item shipped immediately after check has cleared) or money Orders

Shipping Terms: I will ship this item anywhere to anyone. International bidders welcome. High bidder pays winning bid plus USPS priority or global priority shipping and insurance. US $5, Canada $8, UK $10, All Others $15

Refunds, Returns, Regrets: If you win this item and upon receiving it, are not 100% satisfied, you may return it to me for a full refund of the winning bid and shipping. (Returning buyer pays for shipping back to me.)

Edit pictures

1 2 3 4
Free counters powered by Andale!

NOTE: If your description or your pictures do not appear as expected, you may Edit your description or Edit your pictures to fix any problems.

This is exactly how your description and pictures will appear on the live item description page. They look pretty good. Not fancy but clear and concise.

The next section to review contains all the item details.

Listing Summary Table		
Main Category		Edit main category
Pottery & Glass:Pottery & China:Pottery:Other (# 86)		
Second Category		Add second category
Title & Description		Edit title & description
See above for preview of title, Item Specifics and description		
Pictures & Details		Edit pictures & details
Store category	Antiques	
Pictures	3 picture(s) added to your listing See above for preview of pictures	
Duration	7 days	
Quantity	1	
Starting price	$1.00	
Buy It Now	$15.00	
Item location	City, State: Draper, UT Region: UT-Salt Lake City Country: USA	
Optional features	✦ Gallery	
Free page counter	Andale style See above for preview of counter	
Payment & Shipping		Edit payment & shipping
Seller-accepted payment methods	**eBay Payments:** Credit Cards; Electronic Checks; **Other Payment Methods:** Money order or Cashiers check; Personal check; See item description; Other online payment services;	
Payment address	**Jim Griffith** Po box 100 Draper, UT 80001, USA 801-301-3310	
Ship-to locations	Seller ships internationally (worldwide)	
Shipping costs	Seller pays for all shipping costs. Shipping costs not specified	
Payment instructions	High Winning Bidder! Free Shipping and Insurance to any location within the continental US. If you are located outside of the continental US, please email me with your location so I can provide your shipping costs. Look for the link on this page for "Request A Total." Thanks! Griff I guarantee 100% satisfaction or your money cheerfully refunded upon return of the item.	

You can make changes and edits to any of these details before you submit the listing. Simply click the appropriate link for edits or changes and follow the instructions.

The last part of this page shows you the fees for listing this item.

Step 2: Review the fees

Listing fees:		
Insertion fee:		$0.30
Additional pictures:		0.30
Gallery:		0.25
BIN Fee:		0.05
Total listing fee:		**$0.90**

Listing fees are non-refundable. The only exception is the Reserve Price Auction fee, which is refunded automatically if your item sells.

▶ Learn more about fees and credits.

If your item sells, you will be charged a Final Value Fee. This fee is based on a percentage of the final sale price.

Current account balance before adding this item: -$292.57

Step 3: Submit your listing

‹ Back   Submit Listing
Your item will be listed on eBay and the above fees will be charged.

Finally, the moment of truth has arrived. Once you are certain that everything about your listing is accurate, click the Submit button.

Your listing goes "live" to the site immediately after you click the button. The "Congratulations!" page displays a clickable URL that will take you directly to your eBay item page so you can view the live listing.

Sell Your Item: Congratulations

You have successfully listed your item

View your item

Title: Honiton Pitcher Jug Exton

Item # : The item number for your new listing is **2057074428**.

URL: http://cgi.ebay.com/ws/eBayISAPI.dll?ViewItem&item=2057074428

Track items you are selling in My eBay.

Note: Your listing will not show up in the search and category listings pages right away. Listings are updated throughout the day, so yours will be added at the next update. Gallery images may also take a while to appear.

Would you like to sell another item?

Sell a Similar Item		Sell a Different Item
Create a new listing beginning with all the information you just entered.		Create a new listing. Only saved selling preferences will be pre-filled for you.

Revising or ending your listing

You can:

· Revise your item by clicking on the "Revise Item" link on your listing page. Some listings may not be edited. Learn more.

· End your listing early.

· Allow only pre-approved bidders or block specific users from bidding on your items by visiting Bidder Management.

Seller Services

Get additional help. Try Seller Services or visit the Seller Guide.

SQUARE TRADE CERTIFIED **Consider adding the SquareTrade Seal to your listing.** Instantly show your commitment to good business practices & buyer satisfaction with the SquareTrade Seal. Free one-month trial !

The Congratulations page also contains two buttons for those sellers who wish to continue listing items. One is for selling an item similar to the one you just listed. This button will start from the beginning, but the Sell Your Item form will contain most of the information you entered or selected. The second button is for offering a totally different item. It also takes you back to the first Sell Your Item page, but it only prefills fields from your Saved Preferences in "My eBay." ("My eBay" Preferences are explained in Section One, Chapter 3.)

Let's click the URL for our item and see what it looks like!

It looks fabulous, if I do say so myself.

NOTE: Due to the way eBay's system adds items to the search list and to the category lists, you will not be able to use Search features to find your item, or be able to find your item in a category list for approximately ninety minutes.

There's nothing quite like the thrill of satisfaction you feel when you have completed your first eBay listing. Take a moment to relax and savor the accomplishment.

But don't get too relaxed. Your eBay selling tasks are not over. You still have to be available for buyer emails and if the item sells, you will have to accept payment, and pack and ship the item. In the meantime, here are some Seller Troubleshooting tips.

SELLER TROUBLESHOOTING

My eBay Picture Service Images Are Not Showing on the Review Listing page!

This is not a common problem—in fact it is very rare, but it does happen. Usually, this is due to a faulty connection between your computer and eBay. If you notice that your images are not showing up on the "review" page, go back and start the listing process again from the beginning.

Oops! I Need to Change Something in My Listing!

You can make major changes to your listing after it has gone "live" to the site, but only before it actually receives a bid. Since items usually do not receive bids for at least thirty minutes after they are listed, this gives you some time to Revise Your Item.

To make revisions to a live item where no bids have been placed, go to the item description page. Look for and click the link labeled "Revise item" on the top section of the item page next to "Seller Services":

The next page will show the item number for the listing you wish to revise.

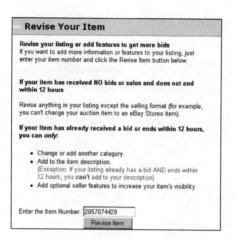

Click the button to go back to the Review & Submit page, where you can change almost anything about your listing.

Revising an Item After Bids Are Received—Add to a Listing

In cases where bids have been received and you need to correct an error, but the error is not so serious as to warrant ending the listing early, you can always add to the listing's description. To do so, go to the "My eBay" Selling tab, scroll down to the bottom of the page, and click the link for "Add to my item description."

Follow the instructions from there.

This feature is very handy for adding information about the item or more pictures of the item after a listing has begun.

I Need to End My Listing Early!

A seller may, at any time and entirely at his discretion, end his listing early. Two reasons for ending a listing early might be that the item was damaged or stolen after the item was listed, or that the seller inadvertently described the item incorrectly.

The link for ending items early is found on the bottom of the Selling page in your "My eBay."

Selling-Related Links

Managing your auctions
Sell your item
Revise my item
Add to my item description
Cancel bids on my item
End my auction early ◀━
Relist my item
Send A Second Chance Offer

When you click this link, it will take you to the following page:

Ending Your Listing Early

Use this form to end your listing early. But remember - lots of bidders wait until the very last minute to bid—You may lose potential buyers by ending your listing early.

If you **have bids** on this listing, or if the **Reserve Price has been met**, you must cancel all bids or sell to the high bidder(s). You may choose on the next page. (Note: This does not apply if you are ending a listing in eBay's Real Estate category using the Ad Format, because no bidding occurs in this format).

The item number: [＿＿＿＿＿＿]

[Continue...]   [Clear form]

If there are active bids on the listing you wish to end early, the system will prompt you to end them first before you end the listing. You should also, as a courtesy, email all bidders whose bids were canceled to inform them of the reason.

Once you have canceled all bids, you can safely end the listing by following the rest of the instructions on the End Your Listing Early page.

I Want to Relist My Item—Using the Relist Feature

Once a listing has ended, the item may be relisted quickly and easily by looking for and clicking the link on the closed listing page for "Relist this item." It's located under the Seller Services section on the top section of the item page.

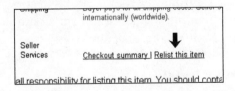

If you are using the Relist feature to relist an item that did not sell on the first go-round, the listing fee for the relisting may be waived if the item sells on the second attempt. When you relist, if your item had a reserve, you will have to lower the reserve price in order for your listing to be eligible for the listing fee credit. If your item did not have a reserve, you will need to lower the opening bid amount in order to qualify for the listing credit.

You can also use the Relist feature to list a new, similar item and save yourself a lot of typing. If you use the Relist feature to sell a similar item, make sure you change the appropriate information (pictures, text, title, etc.) before submitting the listing.

My Bidder Retracted Her Bid! Is This Allowed?

Yes, it is, but only under certain circumstances. If a bidder has made an error in her bid amount, she may retract her bid and reenter the bid correctly. A bidder may also retract due to extraordinary circumstances that place an unreasonable burden on the bidder should he or she win the item.

A bidder may not employ the bid retraction privilege for frivolous reasons, for example, a change of heart or finding the item someplace else for less money.

All bid retractions are tracked on a user's Feedback Profile card.

Chronic bid retractions are routinely investigated by eBay and can result in suspension of the retracting bidder's eBay registration.

The ability to retract a bid is limited by the time left in an item listing and the time between your first bid and the next. Bid retraction rules are explained in detail in Section One, Chapter 7.

My Bidder is Not Responding to Email

How to Contact a Bidder

First, don't panic! Sometimes bidders find themselves unexpectedly pulled away from their computers for a period of time. Bidders can experience crises. Always give your bidder a few days before moving to the next step.

If your buyer hasn't responded to your email within three to five days, then you should attempt to contact him by phone. You can obtain the phone number of any high bidder on your listings by clicking on Search, Find Members.

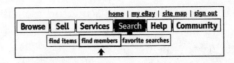

Enter the buyer's User ID in the box provided for Contact Information.

Contact Info
Request a member's contact information

Use this form to request another user's contact information. To better protect the privacy of eBay users, you can only request contact information for eBay users who are involved in your current or recent transactions.* Examples are:

· Sellers can request contact information for all bidders in an active transaction and the winning bidder in a successful, closed transaction.

· Bidders can request contact information for a seller during an active transaction and in a successful, closed transaction if they are the winning bidder.

The information you request will be sent via email to your registered eBay email address. This information can only be used in accordance with eBay's Privacy Policy. The user whose information you are requesting will also receive your contact information. Learn more

*Due to International laws, access to contact information for International users may be limited.

[   ]
User ID of member whose contact information you are requesting

[   ]
Item number of the item you are trading with the above member

[Submit]

(**NOTE:** Only the high bidders and the seller in a single specific eBay transaction can obtain each other's phone numbers.)

Reporting an Unreachable Bidder

If a bidder's phone number is not valid or if an email sent to a bidder is bounced back to you as undeliverable, you should report the bidder to eBay.

Click on the Help link on the eBay Navigation Bar, then click on the link in the pop-up window for Seller Guide. Follow the links to the page for contacting customer support.

My Bidder Backed Out!

Sometimes a winning bidder may back out of a sale. If a bidder contacts you with extenuating circumstances and asks to be relieved of his bidder obligation, you may allow him to do so. Or, if the "back out" is for reasons you consider frivolous or if the bidder does not respond to repeated emails or phone calls, you may want to report him as a Non-Paying Bidder.

In either case, if the transaction is not completed, you can and should file for a Final Value Fee credit.

The process for requesting a FVF credit is part of the Non-Paying Bidder filing process.

Reporting a Non-Paying Bidder / Requesting a Final Value Fee Credit

To start the process, go to the "My eBay" page, click on the Selling tab, scroll down to the bottom of the page, and look for the link for "Non-paying bidder program."

Selling-Related Links

Managing your auctions	Billing/Payment
Sell your item	Update Checkout Preferences
Revise my item	Billing Frequently Asked Questions
Add to my item description	Apply for a eBay Payments
Cancel bids on my item	account
End my auction early	View my eBay Payments account
Relist my item	Apply for an eBay Visa with Cash
Send A Second Chance Offer	Rewards
Feature my item	
Add an Andale counter	**Trust & Safety**
Manage/Edit my Andale counters	Seller Payment Protection
Block or pre-approve certain bidders	Listing policies
eBay Picture Services	Items not allowed
Update selling picture preference	Non-paying bidder program
eBay Seller's Assistant	Trading violations
	Dispute resolution
Selling information	

Requesting a Final Value Fee Credit for a Returned Item

Sometimes you may need to take an item back from a buyer and refund her money. In those cases, you are eligible to receive a Final Value Fee credit. However, in order to do so, you have to go through the Non-Paying Bidder process, following all of the steps as requested.

1. Contact your buyer.
2. Send a payment reminder (optional).
3. File a Non-Paying Bidder Alert. (This is the same for all bidding format listings and Buy It Now.)
4. Request a Final Value Fee credit.

The process begins on the bottom of the "My eBay" page as shown in the previous illustration.

Although the text instructions for the Non-Paying Bidder process do not allude to the mutual return situation, it is an option you can select once you are at Step 4 in the above list.

A SECOND CHANCE OFFER

Sometimes a buyer may back out, leaving you with an unsold item—one for which you have paid insertion and other fees. Instead of relisting the item (and incurring more fees), you might want to try the Second Chance Offer feature.

There are no insertion fees for using the Second Chance Offer feature on an unsold item. In addition, all the normal eBay features like Checkout and Feedback are available to both the buyer and seller in a Second Chance Offer transaction.

A seller can make a Second Chance Offer to a bidder other than the item's winner when:

The winning bidder fails to buy the item.
The seller has a duplicate item for sale but hasn't chosen to run a Multiple Item listing.

Second Chance offers can be sent to any one of the underbidders, if the winning bidder does not complete a purchase (sellers should be sure that everything has been done to resolve the issue with the non-paying, winning bidder before sending a Second Chance Offer), or if a seller has duplicate items. Second Chance offers can be created immediately after a listing ends and for up to sixty days after the end of the listing.

To learn more about the Second Chance Offer feature, click on the Selling tab in the "My eBay" page and scroll down to the section at the bottom of that page for Managing Your Listings.

Look for and click the link labeled "Send a Second Chance Offer."

4

After the Sale

In 1998, Mike Driscoll was selling restaurant equipment and antiques out of an old 1880 home he had recently purchased. On weekends, he would move most of his inventory outside in order to attract roadside attention, and he was lucky if he sold $500 in two days—not nearly enough to survive and certainly not worth the strain of moving furniture in and out of his home shop every weekend.

Then, in 1999, Mike found eBay, started selling, and, in his own words, "fell in love with eBay."

"I now own three computers. I never sat at one until thirteen months ago. I no longer open my front door to my antique store, as I sell all my antiques, and even some restaurant equipment stuff that has sat downstairs in my basement for three years, on eBay."

Today, Mike has an average of 200 items up for sale or bid on eBay. His feedback stands at 4,450 and climbing. He is also a member of the eBay PowerSeller team. eBay has indeed changed his life, but not only in a business sense.

"I sold an item that was not as I described. It was a ice cream syrup pump that I sold as a catsup, mustard, and relish pump."

The buyer contacted Mike to alert him to his error and he immediately obtained the buyer's contact information so that he could quickly refund the buyer's money without even waiting for the item to be returned.

"She surprised me by showing up at my doorstep one day. The rest is history.

"I thank you, eBay, for changing my life! I have never been richer in money, romance, or confidence since finding eBay."

Contacting the Buyer

Your item sold! Congratulations! Now, the after-sale tasks begin.

CONTACTING THE BUYER—DOS AND DON'TS

The first thing you do once one of your items has sold on eBay is to contact the lucky winning buyer by sending her an email invoice or notice. You can always determine the winning buyer for your eBay item by going to the closed item page and clicking on the buyer's User ID:

Seller (Rating)	jimgriff@sover.net (583) ★ me ⟨store⟩
Seller 's Store	**Uncle Griff's Closet** | **Visit my eBay**
	view comments in seller's Feedback Profile | vie
High bid	d•••••••••3 (56) ★
Payment	Money Order/Cashiers Checks. Personal Checks. See item description for payment methods accepted

This will display the buyer's email address:

Email Address and User ID History for: d •••••••••• 3

The email address for this member is: d••••••••••s@hotmail.com

User ID History	Effective Date	End Date
d•••••••••3	Monday, Mar 18, 2002	Present

*** - Parts of prior User IDs that are email addresses are concealed to protect member privacy.

(I've blocked out most of the email address out of respect for this member's privacy.)

You can also set your eBay Sign In preferences so that the email address of a seller or buyer in your transaction displays automatically on the listing page. Go to the Preferences tab in "My eBay":

Scroll down to the Sign In Activities section and click the Modify My Sign In Activities button. (Sign In if requested.)

Sign In Activities

When signed in, you can perform the following activities without entering your User ID and password:

- Bidding and Buying
- Selling
- Keep me signed in on this computer unless I sign out
- See email addresses when viewing User IDs -- if you are involved in a transaction. Learn more.

You have *not* selected the following activities:

Preferred Sign-in Method
- eBay User Id and password

Modify My Sign In Activities

Check the box for "See email addresses when viewing User IDs—if you are involved in a transaction," and click the Save changes button.

Edit your sign in options

Sign in options

☑ Bidding and buying - Remember my User ID and password for bidding and buying
☑ Selling - Remember my User ID and password for selling

☑ Keep me signed in on this computer until I sign out (Available only when you select the eBay preferred sign in method below.)

Note: For your protection, updating personal information or financial information will always require that you enter your User ID and password.

Display Settings

☑ See email addresses when viewing User IDs - if you are involved in a transaction. Learn more

Preferred sign in method

I prefer to sign-in to eBay using:
- ⦿ eBay User ID and password
- ○ Microsoft Passport

Save changes

Now, the email addresses of all sellers of items you have won will display automatically next to their User IDs. In addition, the email addresses of all winning buyers in listings where you are the seller will also display automatically.

Seller (Rating)	jimgriff@sover.net (583) ★ me stores
Seller 's Store	**Uncle Griff's Closet	Visit my eBay Store!** view comments in seller's Feedback Profile	view seller's other
High bid	d••••••••••3 (d••••••••••• s@hotmail.com) (56) ★
Payment	Money Order/Cashiers Checks. Personal Checks. See item description for payment methods accepted

To send your winning buyer an email, you can copy and paste the email address into your email program:

d••••••••••3 (d••••••••••• s@hotmail.com) (56) ★

Money Order/Cashiers Checks. Personal Checks. See item description for payment

Or, if you have a default email client application on your computer, click directly on the buyer's email address. If your email application is properly configured, clicking on an eBay member's email address should open a new email window with the "TO . . ." field automatically populated with the buyer's email address:

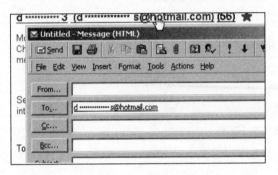

As a professional eBay seller, you should always take the initiative and send an email to the high bidder or buyer of your eBay item immediately after the listing closes.

Nothing is less professional or more annoying to a buyer than receiving an email from a seller containing little or no information or instructions on what to do next. Even if you have stated all terms and instructions explicitly in your listing description, *repeat them in your emails to bidders and buyers.* Some eBay shoppers may have bids out on ten, twenty, or more items and might not recall off the top of their heads your particular payment options, instructions, or general terms. There is nothing to lose and everything to gain by repeating your complete list of terms and options for your buyer. Believe me, we eBay buyers *really* appreciate those sellers who do.

To this end, your email should contain all the information the buyer needs to complete her transaction obligations. This should include:

- Payment options with detailed instructions for each
- Links to payment services wherever possible
- Shipping options and costs
- Your full name, address, and phone number
- Any reminders regarding your terms of sale

Here are some examples:

This is the email that PayPal sends automatically to a winning bidder (you need to configure your PayPal account in order to have these sent).

Congratulations!

Dear jimgriff@sover.net,

You are the winning bidder of my auction!

Auction Details

Auction Title: MAE WEST, LP "Way Out West" MINT w/POSTER

Auction Listing: http://cgi.ebay.com/aw-cgi/eBayISAPI.dll? ViewItem&item=858386367

Winning Bid: 23.50

Number of Items: 1

To pay me quickly and securely with your credit card or checking account, please click the button below.

If you have already sent payment for this item (via PayPal or other means), please disregard this notice.

Paying for Your Auction

I prefer payment through PayPal, which lets me receive your payment instantly and ship your item sooner.

With over 15 million members, PayPal is the #1 payment service on eBay!

For more information on my shipping, insurance, and other policies, or if you would like to pay for this item with a method other than PayPal, please see this auction listing for details.

Thank you,

This is an example of a handwritten email sent by a conscientious eBay seller.

Congratulations!

You have won the bid on this item. The total is:

Bid: $616.01
S&H: $60.00
==================
$676.01 Total

Please read the following notes about payment carefully:

++
We do not accept personal or business checks.
++

If you are a resident of state of Georgia please add 7% tax to Bid amount.
If you have already made your payment just reply that you have.

Thank you.

persianmasterpiece.com

A responsible bidder should and will respond to your email as quickly as he can. In those cases where buyers are slow in responding, do not, I repeat, do not berate, lecture, or criticize them in an email. Always, always, always, maintain your professional poise and courtesy whenever corresponding with a customer.

Your payment reminders should be informative and polite, even if you are informing a customer that you are about to file for a Non-Paying Bidder refund.

Your non-responsive, non-paying buyer may eventually respond with either an apology or a diatribe. If you receive an apology, accept it and move on either with the transaction or, if necessary, with the credit refund process. If you receive a diatribe, avoid responding with a diatribe of your own.

Buyers can find themselves in the most unexpected of circumstances. eBay seller Barry Lamb sent me this amusing tale:

In well over five thousand transactions on eBay, there's one that I'll always remember.

I had a buyer purchase a set of car speakers from me. The first email where she replied to my congratulations email she wrote, "I can't pay you now, I have to go to the hospital." In her second email, she wrote, "I'm having a baby, my boyfriend will send you the money." Her third email: "My boyfriend is an idiot. He didn't send you no money." Then nothing for about four days and then "I have a 6½ pound baby boy, I'm sending it to you."

Boy, was I glad when the payment showed up and NOT the baby.

The rule in brief: There is never a reason or excuse for any seller to behave unprofessionally. You never know what the situation might be on the buyer's end!

SENDING THE ITEM TO THE BUYER

Your duty as an eBay seller is to send the buyer's item to him once payment has been received and cleared. Do not procrastinate! If you only send items once a week, make this fact clear in your listing descriptions and repeat it in your email to the buyer.

Leaving Feedback

Chances are, if you are an eBay seller, you will have previously received feedback as an eBay buyer. You know how important leaving feedback can be. As an eBay seller, you may find many of your buyers are relatively new to eBay and do not quite understand how to leave feedback or, if they do, are not familiar with the protocol of leaving feedback.

Your eBay duty is to help educate your buyers on how eBay Feedback works. eBay User Carolyn Lanzkron has an unusual but effective method of reminding her buyers about the importance of leaving feedback. . . .

EBAY MEMBER TIP: I'm a new seller, and I'm hungry for feedback. I'm hoping my gimmick will help. In the package with the item I put a candy bar, with a wrapper that says, "Thank you for making this eBay transaction such a sweet experience," with my eBay ID. On the back of the candy bar, I put the following: "Ulterior motive disclaimer:

'Now that I've fed you, I'm hoping that you'll feedback! (Pretty Please?)'"

I'm not sure how successful this will be, but the idea is to demonstrate that I'm willing to deliver more than was in the original bargain. . . .

Carolyn is going to be a very successful eBay seller. Not only is she giving a little extra gift to her buyers, she is showing by example how feedback works on eBay.

FEEDBACK—WHO LEAVES IT FIRST?

You, the seller, do. Or you should. In the early days of eBay, the accepted protocol was for the seller to leave feedback immediately upon receiving payment. This has, unfortunately I believe, changed. Many sellers wait until the buyer has left feedback before they will leave him feedback. This may be a safe way of avoiding a possible negative comment, but it is not the best business practice.

The buyer's transaction obligations end when she sends payment for the item. Once the seller receives payment (check has cleared, credit card payment has been transferred to the seller's account, etc.) he should immediately leave appropriate feedback for the bidder. I have found that most sellers who do not receive feedback from their bidders also do not leave feedback first for their bidders.

The seller's transaction obligations are not complete until the buyer has received the item and is satisfied with it. Only then should the bidder be expected to leave feedback.

FEEDBACK—WHAT SHOULD IT SAY?

You have 80 character spaces in which you may type a comment. If the bidder has paid for the item and sent payment quickly, make sure to mention this. Nothing makes bidders happier than to have an eBay seller tell the world that he or she, the bidder, is quick to send payment.

Here are some samples:

"Excellent Transaction. Buyer sent payment immediately."
"A reputable eBay buyer. Always pays fast and is cordial in emails. A+"
"Great to do business with! A definite asset to eBay! WE HIGHLY RECOM-
        MEND!!!"
"Outstanding eBay buyer, sets the ultimate standard. Amazing! . . ."

FEEDBACK—WHAT NOT TO SAY

As a seller, you may run into the occasional "difficult" customer. Unless the buyer has backed out of the sale, you should avoid leaving a negative feedback comment for paying customers. Instead, consider leaving an exuberant neutral or a subdued positive. The customer will get the message.

Either way, avoid using inflammatory language. Regardless of how much you believe the person deserves it, refrain in your feedback comment from calling a customer "a real jerk" or something equally pejorative. Why?

Because calling someone "a jerk" or "an idiot" or worse in his feedback ends up reflecting more on you than the other party. Coarse language is unprofessional and it will put potential customers off doing business with you.

Instead, use unemotional, reasoned comments to let the rest of the community know about the transaction. You have an unpleasant customer who nonetheless sent payment immediately? Leave a positive or, if really deserved, a neutral saying something like:

"Some misunderstanding at first but it all worked out in the end. Thanks!"
or
"Very happy to have finally satisfied this customer. Thank you!"

If a bidder backs out for no reason or is unreachable via email or phone, leave a neutral or negative with a comment along the lines of:

"Not a serious bidder. Recommend avoiding,"
or
"Unable to contact bidder. Avoid bids,"
or
"Bidder refused to complete transaction."

Of course, in all these situations, the bidder can and just might leave you a neutral or negative in kind. Don't sweat it. Your calm and reasoned words will speak volumes about your integrity and professionalism. You can and will weather the occasional retaliatory negative comment. The only words you need to be concerned with are your own.

FUTURE CORRESPONDENCE WITH YOUR EBAY BUYERS

A good customer is an asset to an eBay seller. It's a smart strategy to keep customers coming back to your eBay listings. An effective way to do this is through a mailing list. There are, however, some important concerns about formulating mailing lists of your eBay customers.

Once another eBay buyer has purchased an item from you, you may, in your first emails to her, ask for permission to add her to your mailing list for future eBay listings of interest.

In fact, you mustn't add your eBay customers to your mailing list without their permission. You are also only allowed to email your eBay winning bidders or buyers. You must never email another seller's bidders with solicitations to bid on your items or requests for their permission to place them on your mailing list. These are very serious rules on eBay. Breaking them can result in the suspension of your eBay registration!

Packing and Shipping

Our listing has ended and we have a high bidder. It's time to pack and ship the item.

PACKING

The very last item on the list of your seller obligations is "sale fulfillment," that is, sending the item to the winning buyer.

The ultimate success of your eBay transaction depends on quick and secure fulfillment. How well you pack the item and how quickly you ship it can make all the difference in buyer satisfaction. The most common reasons for buyer-seller disputes are slow or seriously delayed shipping and items damaged in transit due to poor or inadequate packing.

WHEN TO SHIP

The standard protocol on eBay is for the seller to ship the item to the buyer once payment has been received and cleared. Most sellers wait for personal checks to clear before shipping. Nearly all sellers ship immediately upon receiving payment via credit card or money order.

Once you have received payment, it's your duty to get the item packed properly and on its way to the happy buyer.

Speed is important. The most successful eBay sellers send the buyer's merchandise out the very day payment is received. In some cases, sellers have the item packed before the listing has closed so that they can go into action the very second the payment is in their hands. For those bidders who pay via a credit card, this can be mere minutes after the listing has closed.

If you scan through the feedback comments of longtime eBay sellers, you will find that the most common praise is for fast or quick shipping. 'Nuff said?

PACKING—DO IT RIGHT!

You could be the most accommodating, customer-oriented seller in the world. It's all for naught if you pack the item inadequately. No one wants to receive an item damaged in transit. If you take pains to pack your items properly, you will avoid the hassles of having to fill out insurance forms and, more important, placating an unhappy buyer with a refund. Besides, it takes just about as much work to pack an item properly as it does to pack it poorly, so you might as well do it right.

eBay seller Melissa Hornyak provided a great tip on shipping clothing:

EBAY MEMBER TIP: When shipping articles of clothing (mostly what I sell), put the item in a plastic bag and tape it before placing it into the box/envelope/whatever. This protects the item from rain, in case the package ends up sitting on someone's front porch for a while. This saves many a ruined item, and shows the buyer that you are willing to do a little bit extra to make sure that their purchase arrives in the promised condition.

PICTURE IT!

If the item you are packing is extremely fragile or valuable, you may want to take digital or film pictures of the item as you pack it: Whenever I have sold a rare or breakable item, I take two digital pictures of it: one sitting just outside the box into which I am about to pack it and one showing the item sitting in the box before sealing.

Although not absolutely necessary or critical, documenting the packing of the item with pictures could prove to be wise insurance. On the very remote chance that the item is damaged in transit, you will have a record of the item's condition just prior to sealing the package.

I did hear from a seller who actually videos the packing process from start to final sealing for extremely valuable or breakable items.

Again, although this precaution is not necessary, especially for sturdy or less expensive items, you can never overdo documenting the item and the packing process. Better safe than sorry.

MATERIALS—OVERDO IT

When packing, you should always err on the side of caution. Give the item more protection than it may actually need for making the trip safe and sound. For breakables like pottery and glass, *always* double-box (see page 295). For all items, use a box that is at least 25 percent bigger in all dimensions than the item you are packing. For items that could be damaged by moisture, seal them in plastic before sending. Bendable items like old LPs, photographs, autographs, ephemera, and so on, should always be packed sandwiched between stiff boards.

PACKING MATERIALS

Styrofoam Packing Peanuts are probably the most commonly used packing material for eBay items. They are extremely light, so they don't noticeably increase the weight of the package. They are reusable. They work for any size box.

Biodegradable Packing Peanuts are growing in popularity among eBay sellers. They are usually made up of air-puffed corn or potato starch. When wet, they disintegrate harmlessly into the environment.

Excelsior or shredded paper is an inexpensive and abundant source of biodegradable packing material. If you plan on doing a lot of packing and you have access to enough paper (newspaper, old printouts, etc.), you may want to invest in a small paper shredder to make your own excelsior.

BUBBLE WRAP

Bubble-wrapping all your items for shipping is a good strategy. Even when packing in peanuts, the extra layer of bubble wrap helps protect the item from damage. The combination of peanuts or excelsior and sufficient bubble wrap will help guarantee your item arrives at its destination safe and sound.

BOXES AND CONTAINERS

The lion's share of all eBay item shipping is done in plain corrugated boxes. You can buy these from a packaging supplier, from your local post office, from moving companies, and from eBay sellers! You can also pick them up for free from many supermarkets. (For obvious hygiene concerns, avoid picking boxes from Dumpsters. Thank you.)

Regardless of the source, the primary concerns when selecting a box for shipping are condition, size, and strength. The golden rule of packing is to avoid any part of your item touching the sides of the packing container. This means that the box you select for your item should be about 25 percent bigger in all three dimensions than the item you are packing—height, width, and length. A 25 percent difference in size will usually leave adequate room for packing material to fill around the sides, top, and bottom of the item.

WHERE TO GET PACKING SUPPLIES

Here's a suggestion from eBay seller Michael Ford ("heritageharborcollectibles") about where to get free shipping supplies from the USPS Web site. . . .

EBAY MEMBER TIP: Sellers can order any size box, from video size to large boxes designed to hold tons of books . . . sturdy and reliable, delivered fast and for absolutely free. This also includes tape, tons of tape, mailing labels, various customs forms, protective mailers, envelopes—nearly anything and everything you need to ship an item can be gotten at the **www.usps.com** website. It's so easy! Everything you desire will be mailed directly to you for free!

You'll never have to worry again about asking people for boxes, running to the store to grab a package of labels or that always-in-demand tape! It's all free. Usually these are free so you will use the service they are designed for, in most cases, Priority Mail, which is First Class.

If you want to get really thrifty, save your grocery bags. Cut the bottom off of the brown paper grocery bags and you have a free sheet of mailing paper. If your box is bigger, then just cut out several and use the free tape and mailing labels to finish it off. You will save time and money by always looking for ways to reduce shipping costs. There is no need to spend $3 on a pack of labels or $5 on a roll of tape that'll be gone after you wrap a few boxes up. Be smart. You're selling items on eBay to make money; don't let your bottom line get swallowed up by the costs of mailing supplies.

Also, if you do need tape or other various mailing/office supplies, don't pay full price for them. Take advantage of any low-price or dollar stores in your area.

Excellent advice, Mike. Thanks!

eBay is an excellent source of all types of packing materials for great deals. In fact, a handful of eBay sellers have made a full-time business of selling packing materials exclusively! Check out the Shipping and Packing Supplies categories under the main category, Everything Else:

Everything Else > Shipping & Packing Supplies > Other

DOUBLE BOXING

You should double-box extremely fragile items like glass, pottery, or thin metal, or items constructed of delicate materials like paper or papier mâché. Some sellers double-box everything they ship. It does help provide maximum protection against damage or breakage in transit.

Wrap the item in a layer of bubble wrap.

Select a first (inner) box that is at least 25 percent bigger than the item and a second (outer) box that is at least 25 percent bigger than the first box.

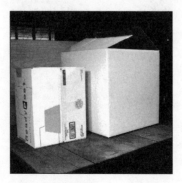

Add a layer of packing material (foam, peanuts, excelsior) to the bottom of the first box. Place the item inside the box.

Fill the spaces between the wrapped item and the box walls with packing material. The item should not touch the box walls at any point. Here is my first box filled to the top.

Seal the first box.

Add a layer of packing material to the bottom of the second box and place the first box inside the second box.

Use packing material to fill in the space between the boxes. Note that there should be at least three inches of space between the two boxes.

Add a layer of packing material to cover the top of the outer box.

Seal the outer box, slap on a label, and you're ready to ship!

PACKING IN A SMOKING HOUSEHOLD

And I don't mean a household that's on fire. Opening a box and having your nose assaulted with the smell of stale cigarette smoke in an unpleasant experience. Tobacco smoke permeates everything it contacts. The smoker is usually un-

297

able to smell this residual odor, but it is painfully apparent to the nonsmoker. Once an item has been "smoked," it is almost impossible to eliminate the smell unless the item is safely washable. For most art and antiques, this is usually not the case.

If you or someone in your household smokes, store your items and packing materials in either a sealed, smoke-free room or in a separate building.

Or maybe it's finally time for the patch!

USED PACKING MATERIALS

Keep your packing materials clean. If you save packing materials for reuse, store them in a dry, smokeless environment.

Saving and reusing packing materials is not only a thrifty habit, it's a "green" duty! By reusing materials, you help extend their usefulness. This is extremely important for materials that may not be easily reclaimable, such as Styrofoam peanuts.

Boxes can usually be used at least twice, if not three or four times, depending on how well they have weathered previous shipping. Always check used corrugated cardboard boxes for fold fatigue before reusing. If the sides of the used box feel soft or floppy, it may be at the end of its safe usefulness. Cover up any old shipping labels. Don't tear them off! Doing so usually results in some of the outer skin of the box coming off as well, which can weaken the structural integrity of the container.

As long as they are kept clean and dry, *packing peanuts* have an indefinite shelf life. Use your judgment. If the peanuts are starting to look funky to you, then they will probably look funky to your buyers. When a batch of peanuts reaches the end of its usefulness, you should take them to your local recycling center for proper disposal.

Excelsior is best used once and then discarded. Paper excelsior is biodegradable and can always be sent your local recycling center or placed in your compost pile.

Bubble wrap is endlessly reusable as long as it's clean and *as long as the bubbles are intact*! Do not use bubble wrap if even just a few of its bubbles have been "popped." It will be just your luck that the place where the bubbles are popped is the very place where your item is damaged in transit. It happens.

PACKING SLIPS AND INVOICES

Using packing slips is one more step to ensuring your item ships safely. In some instances, they are required. It also shows that you are a true eBay professional.

As a bidder, I always appreciate those sellers who include a printout of the item page along with the item. Since I tend to buy a lot on eBay, a copy of the item page always helps me to remember who sent the item, when I bought it, and how much I paid. In the case of similar items, I know to leave feedback for the correct seller.

LABELS

The outside of the package is the first thing your buyer is going to see.

If you want to be perceived as a professional seller, make sure you use professional-looking shipping labels.

Here is a copy of the label I use (when I am not using a USPS preprinted, prepaid label):

I put a "To" and "From" address on the top half of the page. I copy the description bar and one photo from the closed listing and paste it on the bottom half of the page. I save this as a template in Word and simply paste in the new "To" address for every item. I can usually paste in the shipping address a buyer includes in his email. I cut the page in half and tape the top half to the outside of the package. (The photo and description bar help make sure that the right item goes to the right buyer.)

If you have a company or business logo, have adhesive labels made up with your logo and business address in the top left-hand corner or use laser-jet printer labels and print your logo, your return address, and the recipient's address in a clear font like Ariel or Helvetica.

eBay seller Leah Lestina has some good points about packing in general and is happy to share them with you.

EBAY MEMBER TIP: Don't be stingy with bubble wrap.

When packing a box, shake it. If you hear things moving around, you need to add more packing materials.

Make sure the box is folded properly (i.e., the two small ends of the box go in the INSIDE, not the outside) and taped securely.

Don't write the "To" address on top of the packing tape. The party the package is being sent to will be lucky to actually receive the package. (The tape could separate and only a small portion of the address will be left.)

I have to admit—I never thought of that last one. Thanks, Leah!

Shipping

METHODS

Most of the items sold on eBay are small enough to pack and ship through one of the major delivery services:

> USPS (United States Postal Service)
> UPS (United Parcel Service)
> FedEx
> Others (Airborne Express, DHL, etc.)

If you are planning on selling regularly, schlepping boxes back and forth to pickup locations could end up taking much of your day. You will want to open an account with either UPS or FedEx for regular pickup services and invoicing.

USPS does not provide accounts, but they do have a pickup service for a fee of $12.50 per visit. This covers an unlimited number of boxes. For pickup, your packages have to have postage prepaid. The USPS pickup service is available in most Zip Codes, but check their Web site for more information.

USPS offers two solutions for prepaid postage:

> PC Postage (printout postage over the Internet)
> Postage Meters (prints out on a meter)

If you have a postage scale, you can purchase shipping postage over the Internet from USPS. It's very easy.

First you go to the USPS Web site (**www.usps.com**) and look for the link for Click-N-Ship, and follow the instructions from there.

It only took me a minute to register a Click-N-Ship account. It's free. You only pay for postage you purchase. There are no other usage or monthly account fees.

I set up a label for an imaginary parcel to myself from Utah to Vermont. It took all of sixty seconds. I used a credit card to pay for the postage. Here is a copy of the resulting printed label.

Very cool indeed! The label even has a bar code to help expedite shipping! You cut the sheet in half and keep the right-hand side as your receipt. You can then paste or tape the left-hand side onto your package.

Paying for USPS postage over the Internet has another advantage: You can opt for delivery confirmation for no charge. Normally, delivery confirmation costs $.40.

Another postage option is to purchase or lease a postage meter. You then purchase postage by connecting the meter to a phone line, dialing a special number, and downloading postage directly to the meter. Visit the USPS Web site for more information: **www.usps.com** and **www.usps.com/postagesolutions.**

UPS is popular with high-volume sellers. UPS offers a regular pickup service and a wide range of shipping options. You can create an account on the UPS Web site, and just like USPS, you can print UPS postage labels on your computer for your parcels so they are ready for a pickup. UPS also has some shipping supplies. Visit their Web site for more information: **www.ups.com.**

FedEx is also a very popular shipping option, with online shipping tools similar to those of UPS. Account creation can be done on their Web site, **www.fedex.com.**

USPS, UPS, FEDEX . . . WHICH ONE SHOULD I USE?

The three major carriers are fairly competitive when it comes to fees and shipping services. Depending on your location and the type of items you sell, one of the three may work best for you.

Investigate each of the services thoroughly before you pick one. Or, as eBay seller Peter Cini advises, offer your customers *all* of them:

EBAY MEMBER TIP: Empower the customer by offering as many shipping options in your listing as is feasible for your business. Customers love options and it gives them a feeling of control over the outcome.

CRATING AND FREIGHTING

If an item is larger or heavier than the limits set by USPS, UPS, or FedEx, you will have to send it through a shipping company as freight. Large pieces of furniture, art, or machinery are a few examples.

Although it is not always the case, freight items usually need to be crated. Proper crating involves using wood and plywood to create a custom-built box large enough to ship the item safely. Unless you are a whiz with a power saw and don't mind hammering a crate together, you are probably better off handing this chore off to a professional crater/shipper.

NOTE: If your item is too large to ship via standard post or delivery and thus will need to be crated for freight, make certain you state this fact in your item description!

You can usually obtain a good estimate of crating and shipping costs from a local freight company by describing the item size and weight. There are several crating and shipping companies that have Web sites for calculating costs. For example, Craters and Freighters at **http://www.cratersandfreighters.com.**

Whatever the size or weight of your item, do the research before you list and provide as much information about cost, companies, and delivery time as possible.

You can never provide your bidders with too much information!

TOOLS AND SUPPLIES YOU WILL NEED FOR SHIPPING

You should have the following tools and supplies handy:

Printer
Postage scale adequate for parcels
Yardstick or tape measure (in order to weigh and measure the dimensions of each parcel accurately)
Clear packing tape
Packing tape holder/dispenser
Packing materials (bubble wrap, packing peanuts, excelsior, etc.)
Boxes (different shapes and sizes)

CALCULATING COSTS

Nothing pleases customers more than knowing exactly what shipping costs will be *before* they bid. There are many ways to help customers determine costs quickly and accurately.

The easiest way is to simply state shipping costs. Here is a table with shipping costs from an actual eBay listing.

Ship To Location	Shipping (USD)
US	$5
Canada	$8
UK	$10
All Others	$15

This is an ideal solution for small, lightweight items. No calculations to make, no possibility of confusion or mistakes.

> **GRIFF TIP:** Keep your buyers happy! Provide estimated and flat-rate shipping costs as accurately as possible.

IMPORTANT: It is against eBay rules to inflate shipping costs past a reasonable amount (use common sense to determine what constitutes "reasonable.") In addition, your shipping costs cannot be based on the final price of your item, that is, you cannot employ a sliding scale or percentage of the final price to determine shipping.

For larger or heavier items, you may not want to state set shipping fees. Here is one simple way to provide a quick and close shipping-cost estimate for any bidder.

Weigh (and for large parcels, measure) the parcel and provide the information in your listing description along with the Zip Code of the location from where the parcel will be shipped.

Below the information about the size (and weight) of the packed item, place links to the online shipping-costs calculators for each of the services that you offer (USPS, UPS, FedEx, etc.) with instructions on how to calculate costs, based on the bidder's location by Zip or postal code.

This item weighs 1.6 pounds packed. The parcel will be shipped from the following zip code: 84020

www.usps.com

www.ups.com

www.fedex.com

Visit any of the above web sites and use the weight and my zip code along with your zip code to retrieve an estimate of shipping costs location.

Another method is to request the Zip Code of the bidder. Using it, you then calculate the costs yourself. This is a bit more work for you, but it prevents any discrepancies and confusion that might arise if the bidder makes an error when doing the calculations on his own in the previous method.

Here is an example of a seller who uses a special form to collect the Zip Code and email address of the potential bidder. The seller then sends a shipping quote back to the bidder:

Shipping and Payment Info:

Before you bid please take a moment to read our full terms of sale

Winning bidder pays **actual** cost of shipping. Insurance is optional. International bidders, please contact us for a shipping quote before bidding. North Carolina residents add 6.5% sales tax.

Fill in the box below and hit 'send' to receive a shipping quote.

Email:

ZIP/Country:

Send!

To add a form of this type to your item description on your own, you would need to know some fancy HTML formatting. You can also find third-party services online that provide the HTML for forms like this one. I found a really cool free tool called The Zonalyzer at: **http://www.zonalyzer.com/free.html**.

INSURANCE

The best insurance is to overpack your item. Still, even the best-packed items can suffer damage (or worse, loss) in transit.

In order to safeguard the parcel, you should insure it with the carrier. In fact, you should make insurance mandatory for all your eBay sales. In your item description, state something along the lines of "All eBay item parcels will be insured for the selling price."

You can pay for the insurance yourself or pass it on to the buyer as an insurance fee. Whatever the option, always state it explicitly and clearly in your listing description!

Here are the Insurance Rates for USPS parcels:

Insurance Fees	
Insurance coverage desired	Fee in addition to postage
$0.01 to $50.00	$1.30
50.01 to 100.00	2.20
100.01 to 200.00	3.20
200.01 to 300.00	4.20
300.01 to 400.00	5.20
400.01 to 500.00	6.20
500.01 to 600.00	7.20
600.01 to 700.00	8.20
700.01 to 800.00	9.20
800.01 to 900.00	10.20
900.01 to 1,000.00	11.20
1,000.01 to 5,000.00	$11.20 plus $1.00 for each $100 or fraction thereof over $1,000 in desired coverage

There are many ways to insure your packages. For example, USPS has several options. One is actual insurance. Others provide special services to help insure that the intended recipient receives your package. For example, USPS offers various types of delivery and delivery confirmation services:

> Certificate of Mailing
> Certified Mail
> Collect on Delivery (COD)
> Delivery Confirmation
> Insured Mail
> Merchandise Return Service
> Registered Mail
> Restricted Delivery
> Return Receipt
> Return Receipt for Merchandise
> Signature Confirmation
> Special Handling

You can learn more about these services at the USPS Web site.

NOTE: Collecting on a shipping-insurance claim isn't always easy. Each shipper has different criteria that must be met before a claim can be granted. Meet with an authorized representative of the shipping or carrier company and ask for specifics regarding the company's insurance and claims policies.

Keep all documentation regarding the item's condition and the security of the packaging and store it with your insurance and delivery confirmation receipts in a safe place.

LARGE ITEMS

Furniture, machinery, autos, boats, Learjets . . . all of these larger, heavier items need special packing and shipping. Do yourself and your bidders a great service. Before you list the large item, research shipping options from your location. Start with the Yellow Pages under Shipping or Freight. Contact different freight companies and get good estimates or quotes for crating and shipping. Provide this information in your listing description.

It bears repeating: You can never provide your bidders with too much information about shipping costs and options.

INTERNATIONAL SHIPPING CONSIDERATIONS

Customs

For the most part, shipping an item overseas is only slightly more involved than shipping within the US. Normally, shipping overseas will cost more and take longer. All other shipping and insurance considerations are the same as for the US, except you will have to fill out a customs declaration form.

As the sender of an item to a country other than the US, you are responsible for filling out any required US Customs forms. These are available at any post office or from the carrier of your choice (UPS, FedEx, etc.).

Make sure you fill out all forms accurately and honestly.

Sometimes an international bidder will ask you to "fudge" a customs declaration in order to save on any duty (which is paid by the package recipient).

Don't do it.

If a customs official decides to open your package for inspection and determines that your declaration is intentionally inaccurate, you could find yourself in hot water with customs (and customs could also confiscate the item).

These last few chapters have shown eBay Selling basics necessary for every seller—part time to full time. The next chapter will help you find ways to build and grow your eBay business.

5

eBay Business Tips and Tools

Owning and running your own business; what could be more exciting or more fulfilling? How many times have you dreamed of being your own boss? Who among us hasn't come just this close to marching up to that boorish supervisor to announce, "I quit"?

Many new eBay sellers begin as eBay buyers who start a small eBay selling business out of a room of their home. Still other eBay sellers are self-employed business owners who have moved a part or all of the offline business online through eBay. Whether you already own a preexisting business or are starting a new business, using eBay for some or all of your business will help that business grow.

The Family That Trades Together

Laurie Liss ("ixpensive") realized after the birth of her son that she would soon have to quit her career as a flight attendant. Still, she wasn't sure what she could do to keep income coming in. That's when a friend told her to consider selling on eBay.

Laurie's flight attendant job provided her with access to wholesalers across the country, where she regularly bought up discounted designer clothes at bargain prices. Laurie started off on eBay selling some of her "collection" by putting up her first fifty listings.

Everything sold!

Sensing an opportunity, Laurie made regular trips back to her old sources for more merchandise and gradually began increasing her business on eBay. When it became clear to her that, with work and dedication, eBay selling could provide her new family a steady income, she cut back her flight attendant job and devoted herself full-time to selling on eBay.

"eBay has allowed me to become much closer to my family. I am able to take my son to school in the morning, come home and work, and still be home at 3:00 P.M. when he arrives home!"

The rest of Laurie's family were all intrigued by her newfound career and wanted to join in the fun. Laurie taught her mom, Darlene, and sister Hillary ("guccigranny"), as well as her other sisters Joey ("maxxey") and Jaimi ("qtfashion") the finer points of online selling, and in no time they were all selling various lines of women's designer clothing, shoes, and accessories on eBay.

Even Laurie's dad, Arnie ("threads4less"), in partnership with Hillary's husband Jeff Taft got into the act. While the female members of the family were specializing in women's clothing and accessories, Arnie started selling men's designer clothing, completing the Liss retail dynasty.

Recently, Laurie's sister Stefanie ("beautytake-out") joined the family businesses with an eBay business of her own, selling Chinese takeout boxes filled with skin-care and fun items, complete with a fortune cookie in each box. Recently, Laurie ("ixpensive"), Hillary ("guccigranny"), and Arnie ("threads4less") bought houses on the same street in Arizona so they can work on eBay more closely. A true "eBay neighborhood"!

Of course, there are risks. No one can guarantee that every new business venture will be a raging success, but there are potential rewards aplenty for those who at least give it a try.

Here's a small checklist of the things you will need to take your eBay selling from an occasional pastime to a real full-time business:

✔ A business structure
✔ Something to sell
✔ A place from which to sell it (a business location)
✔ A computer
✔ A digital camera
✔ A printer

✔ A bookkeeping system
✔ Office supplies
✔ Packing supplies

The first step is to determine the optimum structure for your eBay business.

Business Structures for eBay Sellers

No business can grow if it cannot be managed. No business can be managed if it cannot be measured. In order for your eBay business to be properly measured, it will need an appropriate business structure.

The short list of possible structures:

> Sole Proprietor
> Partnership
> Corporation

So which business structure is right for you? You should always get professional advice before making any decision as to how you set up your business, but the Internet is the great place to get helpful information quickly (and without cost)!

Look for more information about business structures on the IRS Web site, **www.irs.gov.**

In the search box provided, try searching for:

Publication 334

Tax Guide for Small Business

Read the Introduction page for links to publications for Partnerships, Corporations, S Corporations, Direct Selling, and Record Keeping.

In addition, check out the Small Business Administration Web site at: **http://www.sbaonline.sba.gov.**

Specifically, look for the SBA Small Business Startup Kit.

For more specific information about corporations, try the National Business Incorporators Web site at: **http://www.nationalbusinessinc.com.**

And Now, a Few Words about Taxes

Pay them.

All kidding aside, first, let me state that I am not a tax attorney and that everything I tell you here is from my perspective as a citizen taxpayer and does not necessarily represent the actual word of law.

You Should Contact a Tax Accountant or Tax Attorney
for All Your Tax Liability Questions.

Now that we have that little disclaimer out of the way, let me dispel a popular and rather distressing myth.

There is no such thing as an exemption from tax reporting for "hobby selling," on eBay, or anywhere else for that matter.

Contrary to the beliefs of some eBay sellers with whom I have spoken in the past six years, big or small, successful or not, online and offline—all businesses must report their income to the IRS and the state, where applicable. Yes, eBay seller, that means **you!** In fact, even if you sell only one thing this year, by law you are required to report the income of that sale on your state and federal tax returns.

This doesn't mean that you will necessarily owe taxes on that sale. However, unless you relish risking the unique and exquisite instrument of torture otherwise known as "an audit" and the ensuing wrath of the IRS, heavy fines and penalties, and even possible jail time, you'd better make darned sure that all of your eBay sales are reported to Uncle Sam.

Now, wipe the sweat off your brow and let's get back to our discussion on business structures.

Different business structures use different forms for reporting income from sales. Most sole proprietorships fill out a Schedule C (Profit and Loss) along with their regular form 1040. Partnerships use IRS Form 1065. Corporations must use Form 1120. Some eBay sellers will have to pay their taxes in quarterly estimated installments, depending on their past tax liabilities.

Does all of this sound confusing? Don't worry. It *is* confusing. That's why I strongly suggest that any new or existing eBay business owners inform and educate themselves about their tax-reporting and -filing responsibilities. You can get helpful information on the following Web site, and of course, you should always contact a tax attorney and accountant:

IRS

www.irs.gov.

The IRS Web site is as huge and sprawling as the IRS itself, but it is a whole lot easier to navigate.

YOUR STATE SALES AND INCOME TAX DEPARTMENT WEB SITES

Depending on the state where your business is located, you may be responsible for charging, collecting, reporting, and sending in sales tax. In addition, some local municipalities levy business or inventory taxes or require local businesses to be licensed. How do you determine if you are responsible for collecting sales tax and possibly other taxes? What are your licensing requirements? Most state government Web sites supply all this information along with the necessary forms and applications.

If your state charges a sales tax, you may have to apply for a State Tax Resale Number. You may have to collect sales tax for all eBay sales made to residents of your state. Depending on your state, you may have to file sales tax returns monthly, quarterly, or yearly. If so, you will have to send the collected sales tax funds to the state sales tax department.

Go to **www.google.com** and type in your state name and the phrase *sales tax department*. This will bring up all of the pertinent matches. Find the one for State Sales Tax Department and read up. Or you can look up the phone number for your state tax department in your local yellow pages.

GRIFF TIP: You can usually find your state's official government Web site by typing in **www.your-state.gov;** for example, **www.utah.gov.** If your state name doesn't work, try the abbreviation **www.ca.gov.**

Finally, if your business is growing and you are uncertain as to your liabilities, you should contact a local tax accountant for assistance. It is money well spent.

WHAT TO SELL? SOME IDEAS . . .

It's a common question. I want to start a business online on eBay, but I don't know what to sell.

The possibilities are enormous.

It pays to like what you sell—to have a "feel" for it. Although it is possible to be successful selling a line of wares for which you have absolutely no passion, where's the fun in that? So, let's start off by asking some questions:

What type of merchandise interests you? Do you collect? If so, what? About what types of items or objects or collecting fields are you most knowledgeable?

Many of the more successful eBay sellers I meet in my travels started out as buyers or collectors at first and then started selling on eBay, either out of sheer interest or by necessity. Unless you are filthy rich, collecting as a full-time pastime tends to deplete one's resources rather quickly. In order to keep collecting, many collectors are compelled to sell off lesser pieces of their collection to support their collecting habit. Soon they find themselves bona fide dealer/sellers.

Other sellers don't start out as collectors per se—they might just enjoy shopping at tag or garage sales, picking up items along the way because they are new and cheap or unusual. Many eBay sellers start out this way.

If nothing comes to mind or if you don't collect or have a fancy for certain types of merchandise but you are determined to be a market force on eBay, then you will need to start researching the supply-and-demand situation at both eBay and your local area.

What types of items are readily available in your locale? For example, Vermont is home to the world's best maple syrup (sorry, Canada—Griff's a Vermont boy at heart). Maple syrup is usually cheapest and most plentiful in New England, but it can be extraordinarily difficult to find in other parts of the world. Some savvy Vermont maple syrup producers have realized this and have started offering their maple harvest on eBay with great results.

A few years back, I met a woman in the Midwest who lived close to a factory that made maternity clothing. Many manufacturers routinely offer their seconds at bargain prices or, worse, they toss them into the Dumpster. Most discarded seconds have fairly noticeable flaws, but many of the seconds tossed out are guilty of one or two practically imperceptible imperfections. This plucky woman saw an opportunity. She arranged with the manufacturer to purchase all of their seconds at mere pennies on the dollar. She carefully sifted through the lots, culling out those items whose flaws were inconsequential. She then offered the same merchandise on eBay, as seconds, and soon made a viable business out of the venture.

eBay seller Tim Burnett started out with four items!

My wife and I were trying to work a way of increasing our income, so we decided to try our hand at selling on eBay. We looked for suitable products we could get at *a reasonable price that we could ship easily and possibly would not be widely available. We started off on eBay on a shoestring budget of $15 with four products. We listed our items on eBay for the princely sum of $2.65 (at the time we didn't have a scanner so had to scan our pictures at the local Kinko's for $2.10). Out of the four products, one got six bids and sold much higher than we had guessed, one sold at a reasonable profit, and the other two didn't sell at all. So we had found our market, art supplies.*

At that time the only mode of transport we had was a 1969 VW Camper Bus, which my wife would drive twenty miles each way to work. This left me with a two-mile walk each way to the local post office, which I trudged three times a week to make sure our shipments went out on time. It's now less than six months down the line and we are buying our products direct from the manufacturer, and our eBay sales are going toward building our business. We are planning to introduce many new products in the near future, and it's all thanks to eBay!

If we can start up on a total outlay of less than $20, you can do it too!

In my tenure with eBay I have seen just about anything you can imagine offered for sale. Art supplies, new and vintage clothing, old computers, new kitchenware, auto parts, golf clubs, time-shares, homemade crafts, brand-new electronic equipment, domain names . . . the list is endless.

There are even eBay businesses that offer fresh-baked goods custom made and shipped overnight to your location.

With a little ingenuity and research, you just may find available sources of interesting or unusual products right there in your own neighborhood—products you can then turn around for a potential profit on eBay.

Maybe you cannot think of a single thing to sell. Maybe you could make a business selling things for others on consignment. That's where the eBay Trading Assistants program might help.

TRADING ASSISTANTS

This is a recently introduced program on eBay. Trading Assistants are eBay sellers who sell for others on a consignment or fee basis. There are requirements for joining the Trading Assistant program. You need to have sold at least one item in the last thirty days, have a feedback rating of 49 or higher, and have greater than ninety-seven percent of your feedback as positive. You also must be in good standing with eBay.

If you meet those requirements, you can create a Trading Assistant listing by clicking the Become an Assistant link from the Trading Assistants Directory. Your eBay User ID will then be added to the Trading Assistants directory and will be searchable via your region or location.

Folks in your region who want to sell an item on eBay but are not set up for selling can locate you by searching the Trading Assistant directory. They then contact you and make arrangements for you to sell their item for them on eBay.

To join the directory is a privilege, not a right, and eBay can remove your right to post yourself to the directory. This is something we might do, for example, if clients started complaining about your service as a Trading Assistant.

Including yourself in our Trading Assistants Program directory is a lot like running a classified ad for your services. Trading Assistants are not employees or independent contractors of eBay. Nor does eBay endorse or approve them. Each Trading Assistant runs his or her own independent business free from any involvement by eBay.

As a Trading Assistant, you are free to run your business as you see fit. You may set your own fee schedule and you may limit the types and quantities of items you are willing to sell on consignment. All sales on eBay are under your seller's account. You are charged all eBay fees but are free to pass these fees on to your clients as you see fit. All negotiations are between you and your client.

Selling on consignment on eBay can be a terrific business opportunity. Lots of folks have heard of eBay. Many of them may have things they would like to sell on eBay but either the process is too overwhelming for them or they don't have the time to list their item themselves. That's where you as a Trading Assistant fit in.

You can learn more about the Trading Assistants program on the eBay Web site. Click the Services link on the eBay Navigation Bar. The link for Trading Assistants can be found on the Services page.

BUSINESS LOCATION

You have selected your business structure and you've a pretty good idea of what types of items you are going to sell on eBay. Now it's time to locate a place for your selling.

Selling from Your Home

Home-based selling has several advantages over separate retail-location selling, the most obvious being cost savings of not having to rent and run a separate location. There are also tax advantages. In some cases, you may be able to deduct a percentage of your regular home expenses (rent or mortgage, heat, electricity) as business expenses. You can work in your bathrobe and slippers. You can take coffee and cigarette breaks when you like. (Don't smoke around your merchandise please.) Best of all, if you are a stay-at-home parent, you can keep an eye on the little ones while you work (and once the little ones are able, you can recruit them into your home-business work force).

There are disadvantages to selling from your home, and these will grow exponentially as your eBay business starts to take off. As your business grows, it may become impossible to keep the physical parts of your business from commandeering all of the space in your domicile.

If you don't have the luxury of a second building, select one area of your home for eBay selling. It doesn't have to be much—a spare bedroom or basement or garage. If you cannot give over a complete room, then use a part of a room. For most eBay selling purposes, you will find that a space of roughly four feet deep by eight feet long will be more than adequate. Here is a real-life example of an eBay seller home office sent in by eBay seller Anita ("beachbadge").

Within your home office space, designate separate areas for your computer, for digital photography, for item storage, and for packing and shipping. The key is organization. If you keep your eBay office space strictly organized, you'll be better prepared for any growth of your business and your business will run more efficiently.

Keep pace with your business. Don't cram your growing successful business into a space too small to contain it, else your business itself will suffer. If you are selling from your home and your eBay business is growing in leaps and bounds, you will find that your business takes over your living quarters, often to the detriment of both homelife and business. Although there are no specific warning signs, you will know when it is time to move your eBay home business to a separate and bigger location.

> **GRIFF TIP:** Don't set up your eBay business where there are smokers. Nothing turns off a buyer like opening a package and having stale cigarette smoke come wafting up from the box. If you or anyone in your household smokes, set aside a well-ventilated, smoke-free room for the storage and packing of your eBay items.

Item Storage

Whether you are selling knickknacks or airplanes, merchandise takes up space. Depending on the type, size, and volume of merchandise you plan on selling, you will need an appropriate means of storage. For most cases, simple metal, plastic, or wooden shelving will do (airplanes will need hangar space, of course).

Label and mark all items with an identifying number. This will help prevent mix-ups later.

Avoid wasted storage space. Adapt your shelving or storage system to suit your needs. For example, if your store-bought shelving has shelves spaced every twelve inches and your items are only three inches tall, add more shelves. eBay User "beachbadge" keeps her smaller items on a set of hardware shelves.

eBay seller Karen Gray keeps her fabric items in sealed plastic bins.

YOUR OFFICE EQUIPMENT

There isn't much to say about office equipment that isn't obvious, except maybe good new equipment isn't cheap, so consider used if budget is a concern. New or used, here is a checklist of the equipment you will need for your eBay business.

A computer with an Internet connection. Although you can get by using a four-year-old or older computer, it is best to have the most up-to-date system you can afford. If you can afford it and it is available, get a high-speed Internet connection like DSL or ISDN.

A printer to print out invoices, listing pages, shipping labels, and so on. Again, if you can afford it, purchase two printers—a black and white and a color bubble jet. Print out your listing pages on the color printer and everything else with the black and white.

A digital camera. Buy the best you can afford. I suggest 2.1 megapixels or higher and make sure it has a macro feature for extreme close-ups. Refer to Section Two, Chapter 2, for more information on digital cameras.

A flatbed scanner. You may not use it all the time but when you do need it, you will be glad you have one. Sellers of flat items like comic books, postcards, coins and stamps, etc., simply must have one. Refer to Section Two, Chapter 2, for more information on scanners.

A good desk and chair. Pretty obvious, but I cannot tell you how many eBay seller homes I have been in where the desk was something like an old door on milk crates set too low or too high and the chair was a hard stool—neither item coming close to anything that could be considered ergonomically sound. If you are selling on eBay, you will be sitting in front of a computer for long stretches. Don't harm yourself by sitting incorrectly. Obtain a good desk and the best chair you can afford.

A filing cabinet. Two drawers at least. What with listing pages, invoices, letters . . . you are going to have a lot of paper to file. Keep it organized right from the start.

Good lighting for both the office space and for taking digital pictures.

The other various office necessities like printer paper, labels, and pens are obvious. You can get great deals for office equipment and supplies of all types at . . . hmmm, I wonder where?

BOOKKEEPING

One of the most common and, in some ways, distressing questions I field from both new and seasoned eBay sellers goes something like this: "I sell on eBay primarily as a hobby, so I don't have to keep books, right?"

Wrong.

Whether you're a sole proprietor or multinational corporation—you must keep accurate records of your business activity. As I wrote earlier, you cannot manage what you cannot measure, and no business can survive and thrive without management. Your eBay business is no exception.

Now, don't you wish you had paid better attention during Accounting 101? Not to worry. There are several excellent bookkeeping software programs available that will not only help you track your business but are actually fun to use.

Two popular applications for small businesses are Intuit's QuickBooks and Microsoft's Money. Both applications are excellent tools that allow you to record costs and income, track and manage expenses and accounts receivable, print invoices, and create custom reports to show the state of your business. Most important, come April 15, both applications will help you determine your tax liabilities.

In addition, for the budget conscious, there are also many free and shareware accounting applications. You can find some by going to **www.tucows.com** and searching their application library, using the word *accounting*.

If you sell even one item on eBay, you should create and keep a record of the sale by at the very least saving:

A printout of the item page taken immediately after the listing closes.

A photocopy of the check or money order used to pay for the item (or, if you are using an online payment service to accept credit cards, a printout of the payment page).

A receipt showing your purchase price or cost for the item.

The email and mailing address of the buyer.

WHY KEEP RECORDS? TWO REASONS

Taxes! Even though you might not actually owe taxes on the proceeds of an eBay sale, you are obliged to report the income. Thus for your own peace of mind and to make sure you are in full compliance with all tax laws, create and save a complete record of every eBay sale as well as all your business expenses. They will come in very handy in the event of a tax audit.

If you decide to grow your business, you will need a record of your previous business activity when applying for business loans or establishing business lines of credit.

WHICH BOOKKEEPING METHOD IS RIGHT FOR ME?

There are two basic methods of business accounting: Cash and Accrual.

The Cash method of accounting is the simplest system. Every time you receive payment for an item or pay out an expense, you immediately record it (keep a ledger book or use accounting software). Using the Cash method of accounting, most of your expenses and nearly all of your income are recorded the moment the cash for it is spent or received. The exceptions for expenses would be some capital expenditures for, say, office equipment (computers, printers, etc.) that need to be amortized or depreciated over a period of time.

The Accrual method of accounting is more complex than the Cash method. In brief, when you use the Accrual system, you record sales when they are made, not when the cash for them is actually received or spent.

If your business involves inventory, then you may be required to use the Accrual method of accounting.

There are exceptions. If you sell services instead of items on eBay or if your eBay goods are custom made or if you are an artist or photographer or writer who is selling his own work on eBay, then you might be able to use the Cash method.

Either way, if you are in doubt or have questions consult an expert accountant.

A pair of good online resources are the Business Owners Toolkit, **http://www.toolkit. cch.com**, and of course, the IRS!—**http://www.irs.gov**.

In summary, if you plan on selling regularly on eBay, you really must set up a simple bookkeeping system both to adequately record your business activity and to help your business grow, and it bears repeating—I urge you to educate yourself about your tax and accounting responsibilities both on your own and through the services of a tax accountant or attorney.

USING LISTING MANAGEMENT TOOLS

Keeping Track of Your Listings

Once you get your eBay selling started, the processes for taking digital pictures, and/or writing excellent descriptions, become almost second nature. If you only sell a few items a week, then using the Sell Your Item form with a text file template of your standard payment, shipping, and other terms is probably the easiest way to go. You can also keep track of your listings with "My eBay."

Using "My eBay"

In Section One, Chapter 2, I outlined and described each section of "My eBay." The Selling, Accounts, and Feedback pages of your "My eBay" page are invaluable for managing your eBay listings.

The Selling tab shows you all of your items currently up for sale. It can also show all of your recent (past thirty days) closed listings.

The Accounts tab displays all of your eBay Seller account information including your last invoice and your to-date selling activity, with all fees displayed in a ledger form.

The Feedback tab allows you to view feedback left for you. More important, there is a button on the "My eBay" Feedback page that clicks to a page showing you all the feedback you need to leave for others.

For the low-volume seller, these "My eBay" features may be more than adequate to meet your sales tracking needs.

EBAY SELLER TOOLS

If you are listing ten or more items a week, you will want to employ a listing management tool to make the listing process easier. Listing management tools come in many types. eBay provides two. They are:

- Turbo Lister
- eBay Selling Manager

Each of these tools works in somewhat the same manner. They all eliminate as much repetitive data entry (typing) as possible.

Turbo Lister

Turbo Lister is a relatively new listing management tool created by eBay. It replaces the older, now-retired Mister Lister bulk-uploading tool. It is best suited for those sellers who list ten to thirty items a week, but any seller can use it.

Turbo Lister allows you to create a set of listings offline that you can store as a collection for uploading to eBay at a later time. Turbo Lister also helps to eliminate most of the repetitive typing and feature selection one encounters when using the eBay Sell Your Item form.

Where Do I Get Turbo Lister?

Turbo Lister is available for download on the eBay Services pages. Click on the Services link on the eBay Navigation Bar

and look for the link for Turbo Lister under the header for "Manage Your Items For Sale."

Manage Your Items for Sale

Sellers, from here you can:

- **eBay Seller's Assistant**
  Sell more and save time.
- **Turbo Lister** ←
  List more - easier and faster.
- **Picture Services**
  Add pictures to your listings quickly and easily

Is Turbo Lister free?

Yes, there is no charge for downloading or using Turbo Lister.

Turbo Lister provides all of the following features:

Preview listings before submitting
Schedule when listings will start
Easily create HTML descriptions in a WYSIWYG* interface

Turbo Lister is easy to download, install, and use. Once you have the application installed, click the Turbo Lister icon on your desktop or taskbar:

---

*What You See Is What You Get—no need to know HTML tags. You "draw" your description as you would create a text file in a word processor.

The first time you start Turbo Lister, you will be prompted to configure your user settings. Follow the instructions on the screens as they appear.

Each time you start Turbo Lister, you will be asked to enter your eBay password.

Click the OK button. You will see the main Turbo Lister application window called "Item Inventory."

Each time you create a new listing, it is added to the Item Inventory window.

To create a new listing, click the New button.

You can also click the tiny arrow to the right of the New button, which will present you with the option to create a new item or a new folder.

We will create a new folder later.
Here is the first page for creating our New Item.

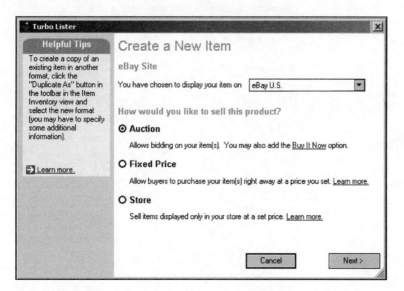

Here we select our listing format. Our listing will be an auction. Once you've selected a format, click the Next button.

TURBO LISTER—STEP 1

On this next screen, we enter our title and choose a category:

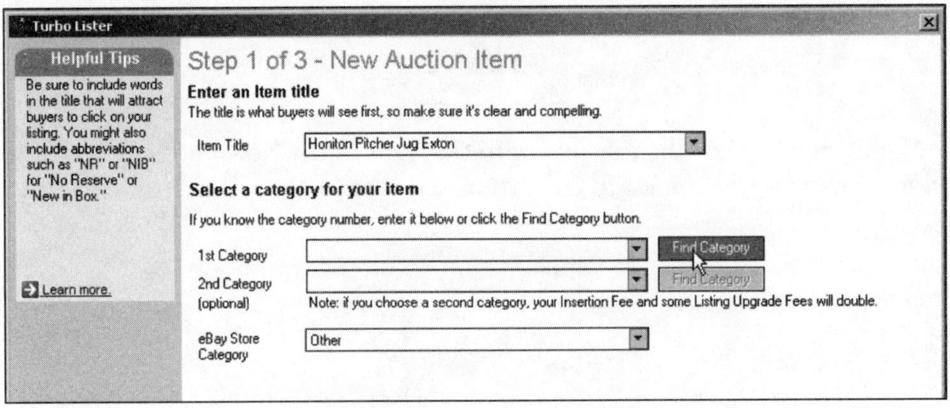

Type in a title and click the button for "Find Category." This will bring up the Select a Category window.

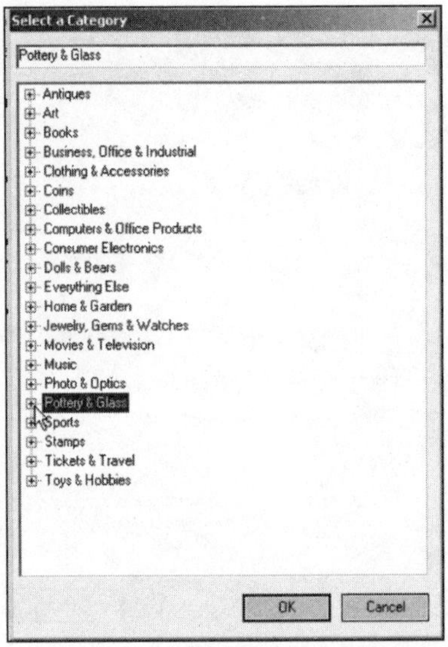

To select a category and then a subcategory, click the little "plus" box to the left of a category name:

Keep clicking till you reach the lowest category of your choice.

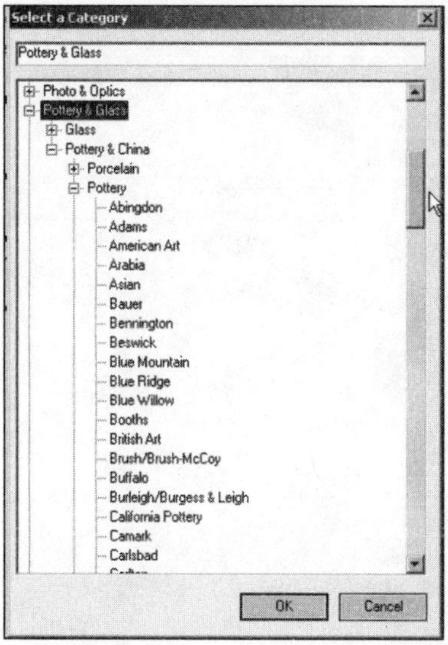

Then click the category to highlight and then click the OK button.

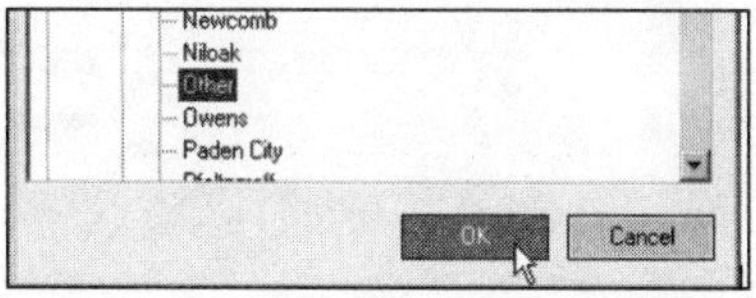

At this stage, you can select a second category. We will stick with one category.

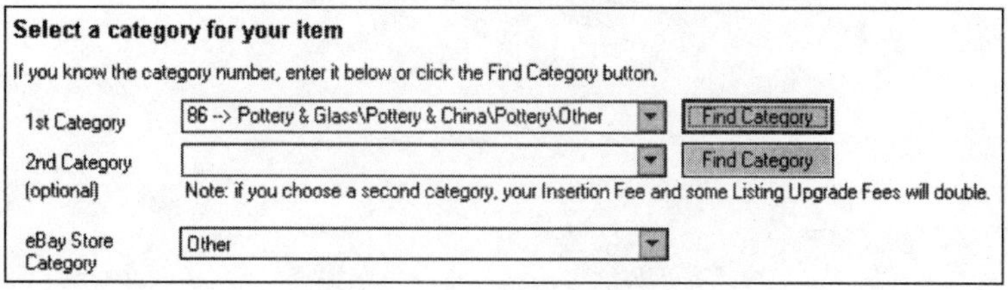

Click the Next button on the bottom of the screen.

TURBO LISTER—STEP 2

This will take us to Step 2 of the Turbo Lister process. In this step, we design the layout and select the pictures for our listing. The window looks like this:

In this window, you can select from a list of theme templates. I have selected "Boutique."

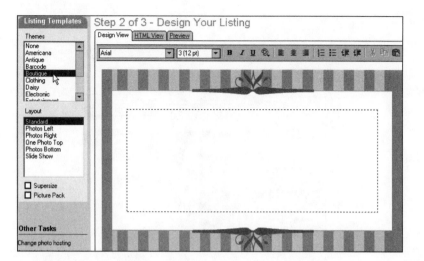

Select other templates to view them. Here are the templates for Barcode:

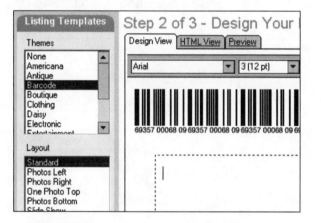

Sports:

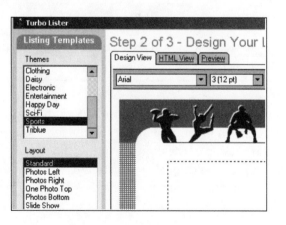

Entertainment:

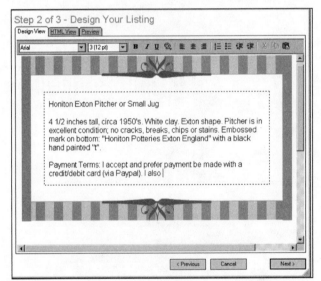

You can also select "None" for a blank template.

The next step is to type the item description directly into the "Design View" window.

Once I have finished typing the description, I can then format it by selecting all or parts of the text with my mouse and using the icon tools on the Turbo Lister Toolbar located at the top of the design window. For example, I will make the top line of my description bold by first selecting it with my mouse so that it is highlighted. (Hold down the mouse button while dragging it across the line of text.)

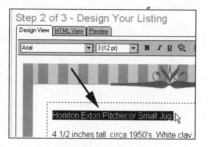

Now select the Bold command icon on the Turbo Lister Toolbar:

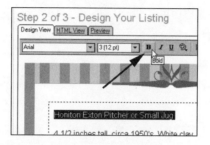

The top line is now HTML formatted to be "Bold."

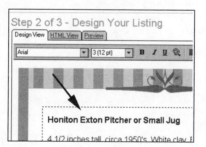

You can view the HTML you just inserted by clicking on the "HTML View" tab.

NOTE: The HTML tag <STRONG> is a "newer" version of the <B> or <BOLD> tag.

GRIFF TIP: The "Design View" window in Turbo Lister a version of something known as a "WYSIWYG" editor. "WYSIWYG" (pronounced "whiz-ee-wig") stands for "What You See Is What You Get." If you are uncomfortable writing out HTML tags by hand, you can use the "Design View" window to type in your description text and to then format it using the icons on the toolbar.

Conversely, if you have already HTML formatted your text by hand (as described in the previous and next chapters), you can copy and paste it into the HTML view window.

GRIFF TIP: First go to the file containing your HTML text. Remember, ours was in a Notepad file.

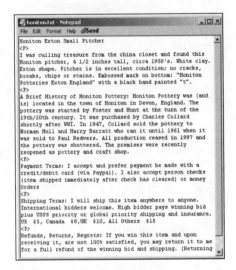

Click Edit, Select All on the Notepad (or Mac Simple Text or Mac Text Edit) application.

Then click Edit, Copy on the menu bar.

Go back to Turbo Lister and click the HTML View tab to display the appropriate window.

Then place your mouse cursor inside the window, under the "<P> </P>," click the mouse's right side button, and select Paste.

Your HTML is now pasted into the Turbo Lister "HTML View" window.

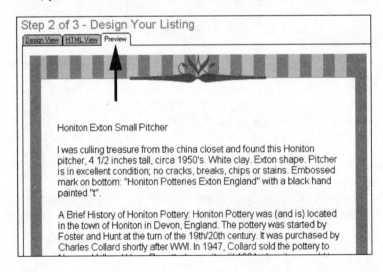

Step 2 of 3 - Design Your Listing

Design View | HTML View | Preview

<P> </P>
Honiton Exton Small Pitcher
<P>
I was culling treasure from the china closet and found this Honiton pitcher, 4 1/2 inches tall, circa 1950's. White clay. Exton shape. Pitcher is in excellent condition; no cracks, breaks, chips or stains. Embossed mark on bottom: "Honiton Potteries Exton England" with a black hand painted "t".
<P>
A Brief History of Honiton Pottery: Honiton Pottery was (and is) located in the town of Honiton in Devon, England. The pottery was started by Foster and Hunt at the turn of the 19th/20th century. It was purchased by Charles Collard shortly after WWI. In 1947, Collard sold the pottery to Norman Hull and Harry Barratt who ran it until 1961 when it was sold to Paul Redvers. All production ceased in 1997 and the pottery was shuttered. The premises were recently reopened as pottery

NOTE: If you're pasting in text that you have previously formatted with HTML, do make sure that you paste it into the HTML view window, not the "Design View" window. If you paste it into the Design View window, your description will show up with the HTML tags showing.

Once you have added your previously formatted item description text, or if, alternatively, you have typed it into the window and formatted it with the tools on the Toolbar, you can see what it will look like by clicking the Preview tab.

Step 2 of 3 - Design Your Listing

Design View | HTML View | Preview

Honiton Exton Small Pitcher

I was culling treasure from the china closet and found this Honiton pitcher, 4 1/2 inches tall, circa 1950's. White clay. Exton shape. Pitcher is in excellent condition; no cracks, breaks, chips or stains. Embossed mark on bottom: "Honiton Potteries Exton England" with a black hand painted "t".

A Brief History of Honiton Pottery: Honiton Pottery was (and is) located in the town of Honiton in Devon, England. The pottery was started by Foster and Hunt at the turn of the 19th/20th century. It was purchased by Charles Collard shortly after WWI. In 1947, Collard sold the pottery to

We can also select a layout for our digital pictures of the item in the Design View of this step (2). The Layout options are listed in a box on the left-hand side of the Turbo Lister Step 2 page. Select an option to view the picture placement inside the description. Here are two options:

Standard

Photos to the left of the description

The other four options are:

Photos to the right of the description
One photo on top (the others in a column below the description)
All photos in one column below the description
SlideShow (photos will display one at a time in one window below the description)

Note that under the options there are two check boxes; one for Supersize and one for Picture Pack. These two options are identical to the same options on the Sell Your Item form.

Supersize is the ideal option for those images that you cannot resize smaller than 440 wide by 320 tall (in pixels). If your images are larger than these dimensions and you want to use eBay Picture Services to host them, eBay Picture Services will resize them down. Most times this doesn't make a big difference in the quality of the images, but occasionally the automatic reduction can seriously degrade the image quality.

Picture Pack is our discount package of services. It includes six pictures, Supersize, and one Gallery image, all for $1.00—a $.75 savings.

The process for selecting images in Turbo Lister using eBay Picture Services is almost identical to selecting pictures for eBay Picture Services in the Sell Your Item form (Section Two, Chapter 3).

Let's select the option for one picture on top. (I always think it is best to have your item picture show up before your item description. "A picture is worth a . . ." Well, you know. . . .)

Click on the box at the top of the listing.

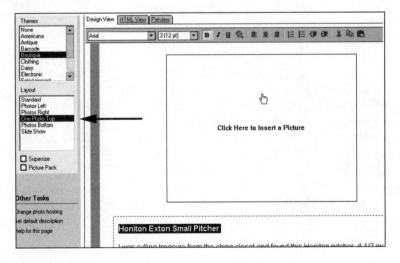

In the Open box locate and select the image(s) on your hard drive.

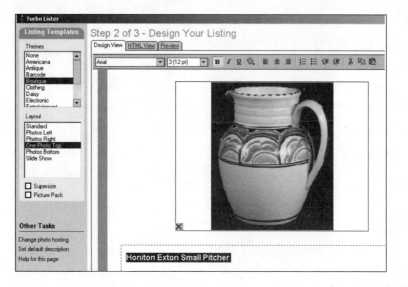

The image will populate the box at the top of the description.

Scroll down to select the other two images (they will go below the description).

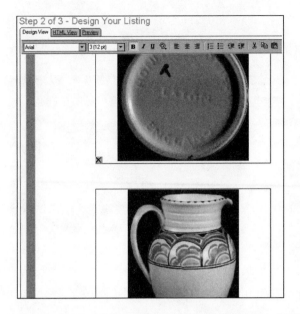

All three images we have added using eBay Picture Services will upload to eBay when we upload the actual listing from Turbo Lister.

NOTE: If you wish to use your own image hosting solution, you need to select the "Change photo hosting" option under "Tasks" located at the bottom left-hand corner of the Step 2 Turbo Lister screen.

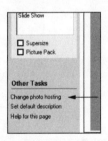

Click the text link. This will erase any eBay Picture Services images you have previously selected.

You have five layout options for hosting images on your own server space.

- None
- Photos Left
- Photos Right
- One Photo Top
- Photos Bottom

Note that the options for Supersize and Picture Pack are grayed out. (They are available only for eBay Picture Services.)

Let's select the option for One Photo Top and click the box to insert our picture.

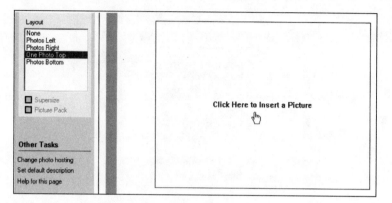

This brings up the following box.

Note that this box is different from the first selection box we saw when using eBay Picture Services. When you host images yourself, you place them somewhere on the Web on a Web server. You need to have the URL (web address) for that hosted image in order to fill in the URL in this box.

I have the URL for a hosted image of this item: **http://www.sover.net/~jimgriff/ images/honiton03.jpg.** I enter it into the box and click Insert.

The picture named "honiton03.jpg," located in **www.sover.net~jimgriff/ images,** now displays in my listing page.

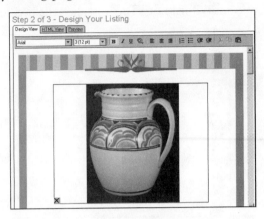

You can learn more about other image hosting solutions in Section Two, Chapter 7—"Advanced Image Hosting Solutions."

Once you have selected your images and layout and have finished formatting your item description text, click the Next button to move on to Step 3.

TURBO LISTER—STEP 3

In this window, we will select all of the other item details.

Each section of this window presents a different aspect of the item's details, including shipping and payment options and instructions and listing upgrades. To change any of the settings, click the "Change" button for that part of the window.

Let's change our payment instructions by clicking on the "Change" button.

In the pop-up box, let's change the instructions.

When finished typing the instructions, click the box labeled "Save for future listings" and then the "OK" button. The changes are now noted in the Step 3 window.

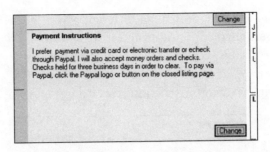

Let's go through the steps for setting a Gallery image.

When you are using eBay Picture Services, the selection is easy.

Click on the "Change" button in the "Listing Upgrades" section of the Step 3 window. In the resulting pop-up box, check the option for "Gallery" and click the button next to it labeled "photo."

Note that the default Gallery image when using eBay Picture Services is the first image you selected for your item description. To substitute this Gallery image for a different one, you have to go back to the window for Step 2.

If you are using your own hosting solution, you can select any URL for your Gallery image simply by typing it into the box that pops up when you select "Listing Upgrades, Photo" next to the checked box for Gallery.

When you have selected all of your Listing Upgrades, review all the other item detail information in Step 3. Click the "Save" button on the bottom of the window to save this listing in your Inventory.

You can now begin creating a new item using the same template and information from the previously created listing. The only changes would be the images and the description. Your terms for shipping, handling, payment options, etc., can stay the same.

Once you have created a number of listings, they will all appear in your Inventory window. To upload them, highlight a selection or all or one of them. Select from the two options: uploading and listing to the site immediately . . .

or uploading and delaying listing for a specified time of your choice. . . .

If you select the second option, you can also select an option for having the item starting times spaced out by an interval between five minutes to one hour.

NOTE: There may be a fee for using the second option. Check the Fee Schedule on the eBay site for more information.

Let's opt to have our four listings "go live" at 9/30/02 at 9:00 P.M. PST. Now we click the "Add to Upload" button down on the lower right-hand corner of the window.

We are nearly done!

Click either button on the bottom of this window to continue. Click the "Go Upload Listings" button to upload the bundle of four listings to eBay. (You can always go back to the Upload window at a later time.)

Here is the Upload window.

Let's calculate the fees for these four listings before we upload them, by clicking Calculate Listing Fee(s).

In order to calculate the fees, Turbo Lister will first check the eBay site for any program updates (so your fee calculations are accurate). You will see a series of windows regarding the status of the updates.

Click the Continue button to download and install any updates.

Turbo Lister will begin downloading updates. Depending on the speed of your Internet connection, the download will take from a minute to several minutes to complete.

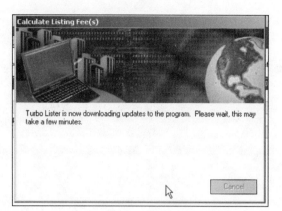

Once it has finished downloading the updates, Turbo Lister will begin retrieving the fees for each listing in the upload batch.

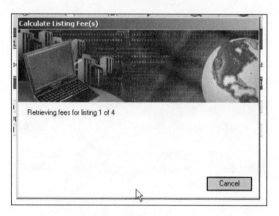

Once you are alerted that the fees have been calculated successfully, click the Close button.

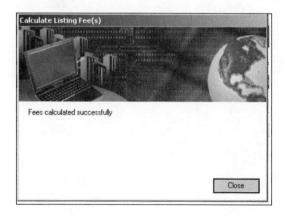

Here is the Upload window for our four items with the fees displayed in the far right-hand column.

To upload the listings to eBay, click the Upload All to eBay button. A status box will show you the progress of the upload for each item.

Remember that we elected to have our listings go live a few hours post-upload. So, once the upload is finished, the status box will include a link labeled "Go to the Pending Listings view . . ."

Click that link to view all the pending listings on eBay. (If we had instead opted to have the listings go live immediately, we would see a link for viewing all the new listings.)

On this page, you can edit or delete any of the listings before they "go live" per the time we selected when we moved them to the upload folder (Sep–30 21:00).

Turbo Lister is an invaluable tool for the high-volume seller. It works like a charm even when listing just one item, if only for the scheduling feature, but the other tools and features make listing one or a hundred items a snap.

SELLING MANAGER

Selling Manager is subscription based, that is, you pay a small monthly fee to use it. Selling Manager provides a comprehensive suite of listing management tools, including: email management, invoicing, feedback alerts, payment status and basic accounting tools, as well as many other features tailor made for the high-volume eBay seller.

Selling Manager works in tandem with Turbo Lister. Together, they provide an excellent bulk-upload and listing-management solution for the full-time eBay seller.

If you are selling a hundred items a week or more, you should give Selling Manager a try.

As of this writing, there is very little information about Selling Manager available to the public, but I did manage to get a few screen shots of the project in progress.

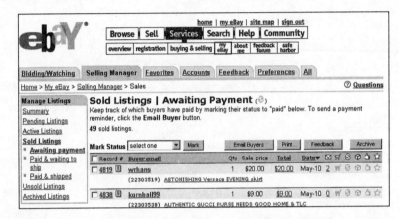

With Selling Manager, you can see all of your pending listings uploaded with Turbo Lister. You can also view your active listings and your sold listings. The sold-listing view will display the payment and shipping status of each item.

The release version of Selling Manager is now available. Click on the link for Services on the eBay Navigation Bar and then click on "buying & selling." The links for Selling Manager's applications and for Turbo Lister will be found there, along with copious Help and FAQ pages that explain how to download, install, and use the products.

You can also subscribe to Selling Manager from the Selling tab on your "My eBay" page.

EBAY STORES

In 2001, eBay introduced a new selling format called eBay Stores. eBay Stores offer the eBay seller a way to promote and market his eBay items to the rest of the world.

If you are a regular eBay seller, there are definite advantages to setting up an eBay Store, especially if you offer a large inventory of various items. You can sell your fixed-price and bidding format items within your eBay Store. You can create up to eleven custom categories in your eBay Store. You can add your own business logo to your eBay Store pages or choose one of eBay's online images. You can talk in depth about your business on your About My Store page.

Before you set up an eBay Store, you must:

- Be registered as an eBay seller by placing your credit card on file.
- Have minimum feedback rating of 20 or be ID Verified ($5 charge).
- Accept credit card payments via an online payment service like PayPal or through a merchant account.

We covered browsing and buying through eBay Stores in Section One, Chapter 3. Setting up an eBay Store is a snap. Go to the eBay home page and click on the link for eBay Stores (located in the box on the top left-hand side of the page).

This will take you to the eBay Stores home page.

On this page, look for and click the link on the top right-hand side of the page for "open your store now."

This takes you to Step 1 for setting up an eBay Store.

1. Pick a name for your store, preferably one that relates in some way to your business or the items you sell.
2. Fill in the Payment Address section. This is the address to which snail mail payments will be sent.
3. Write a short description of your store. This will appear under your store name in the lists of stores as well as at the top of your Store page.
4. List your store specialties.

Scroll down to fill out the next sections.

Custom store categories	Maximum 29 characters each	
optional	Store category 1	Antiques	optional
Create any type of categories you'd like to display in your store (Glass Hearts, Steve's Cars, etc.)	Store category 2	Oriental Rugs	optional
	Store category 3	Textiles	optional
Learn more	Store category 4	Pottery	optional
	Store category 5	Objet d'Art	optional
	Store category 6	Bizarre	optional
	Store category 7	Kitsch	optional
	Store category 8	Oh My	optional
	Store category 9	Why Did I Ever Buy THIS???	optional
	Store category 10	Category 10	optional
	Store category 11	Category 11	optional

Get more attention with these optional features.
Upgrade your store's visibility in eBay Stores!

Select Store Tier	⊙ Basic Store	Your store will appear on the subcategory pages
Learn more	($9.95/month)	where you have items listed. See example
Note: Basic stores are free until 01/01/2002	○ Featured Store ($49.95/month)	Your store will rotate through the Featured section on both the Stores Directory page and the Top Level Category pages where you have items listed. See example

Note: Want to be featured with your logo? Learn more

In an eBay Store, you get to define up to eleven of your own custom categories. I have named nine categories. Whenever you list an item on eBay—whether in your Store or as a regular listing—you will be prompted to select a category for the item from one of your custom eBay Store categories.

Your eBay Store costs $9.95 a month. You can also opt for a Featured Store subscription at $49.95 a month. The Featured Store subscription will put your store in rotation on both the Store Directory and the Top Level Categories where your item is listed.

In the "About Your Store" section, fill in your choices for payment methods, ship-to locations, shipping and handling options, sales tax, return policies, and any additional information you want others to know about your eBay Store.

About Your Store

Store payment methods
required
Choose all that you will accept and enter any additional explanation, if needed.

☑ Money Order/Cashiers Check
☑ Personal Check
☐ Visa/MasterCard
☐ COD (cash on delivery)
☐ American Express
☐ Discover
☑ eBay Online Payments
☐ Other

Additional payment explanation (optional):

    I prefer to accept payment via BillPoint

Maximum 200 characters

Store ship-to locations
required

○ Will ship to United States only
◉ Will ship internationally (worldwide)
○ I will ship to the United States and the following regions only:

  ☐ Canada
  ☐ Europe
  ☐ Australasia
  ☐ Asia
  ☐ South America
  ☐ Africa
  ☐ Mexico and Central America
  ☐ Middle East
  ☐ Caribbean

○ Will arrange for local pickup only (no shipping)

Additional shipping explanation (optional):

Describe any "large item pick up" or international shipping details, for example. Maximum 200 characters

Shipping, Handling
required

☐ Seller Pays Shipping   ☐ Buyer Pays Fixed Amount
☑ Buyer Pays for All Shipping Costs   ☐ See Item Description

Store sales tax
required
Don't collect sales tax? Please leave blank.

[0] % charged in [No Sales Tax ▼]

Additional sales tax explanation (optional):

Maximum 200 characters

Store customer service & return policy
required

    Uncle guarantees 100% satisfaction or your
    money cheerfully refunded upon return of the
    it

Describe any policies such as "satisfaction guaranteed" or "buy as is." Maximum 90 characters

Additional store information
optional

    Watch this space. I won't be selling volumes
    but I have to cull out the barns of mother's
    things someday!

Maximum 200 characters

About Me Page

Note: Your About Me Page will be automatically included in your store. Don't have one? Create one now

Click the Continue button to proceed.

[Continue...]   [Clear form and start over]

Finally, if you haven't done so already, create an eBay About Me page. Your About Me page is a valuable resource for advertising your eBay business. (You'll find instructions for setting up an About Me page later in this chapter.)

Click the "Continue . . ." button. On the next page, you can select the colors and graphics for your eBay Store page.

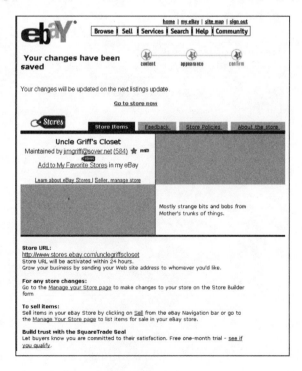

When finished, click the "Save Changes and Publish" button to finish your eBay Store setup.

Your eBay Store is now up and running!

You can learn more about eBay Stores by going to the eBay Stores page as described above and looking for the link labeled "More FAQs."

GRIFF TIP: Items that you list exclusively in your eBay Store will not show up in a regular title search (although they do show up in a title search of eBay Stores). A trick that many sellers use is to list most of their inventory in an eBay Store and always have one or two similar items for sale in a regular (non–eBay Store) listing or Buy It Now. These sellers then cross-promote their eBay Store in their regular listings to help drive traffic to their store items.

EBAY MERCHANDISING MANAGER

There are many cool features that come with an eBay Store, but a real favorite is known as eBay Merchandising. With eBay Merchandising, you have the ability to create and manage cross-promotions of your eBay Store Inventory Items and to promote these items in key buyer locations such as on the Bid Confirmation and Checkout Confirmation pages.

Here's an example of a Bid Confirmation page where the seller is using eBay Merchandising to promote other items he has for sale.

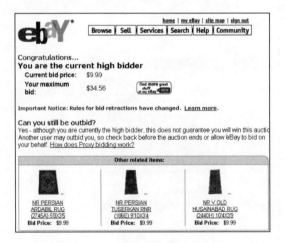

Merchandising can be a great boost for your eBay business. For example, say you are selling digital cameras on eBay and you also have digital camera accessories in your eBay Store. If someone bids or buys one of your digital cameras, you can use eBay Merchandising Manager to have your digital camera accessories show up on the Bid Confirmation or Checkout page both to entice the bidder into purchasing more items from you (she just might need a digital camera bag) and to help lead her to your eBay Store.

To set up eBay Merchandising, go to the Preferences tab of "My eBay" and click the link for "Participate in eBay Merchandising."

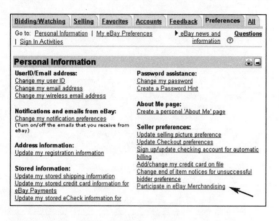

Sign in if requested. On the next page, select the option for "Merchandise My Items" and click the Save Preferences button.

The next step is to create merchandising relationships between your items. Click the link for "create new merchandising relationships."

On this page, you can select the items to cross-merchandise by creating merchandising rules. In Step One, choose the items whose Bid Confirmation or Checkout pages will display other examples of your merchandise. In Step Two, select the items you want to appear as merchandise.

You can edit or delete any of these relationships between your items at any time by returning to Merchandise Manager via the link in My eBay under Preferences.

PROMOTING YOUR EBAY BUSINESS WITH YOUR ABOUT ME PAGE

The eBay About Me page is probably the most underused feature on eBay. I am constantly amazed at how many eBay sellers do not take advantage of this excellent feature.

An About Me page is your eBay home page. Any eBay member can create and maintain an About Me page all on her own.

Building an About Me page is easy. To start, go to the Preferences tab in My eBay and click the link labeled "Create a personal 'About Me' page."

Bidding/Watching	Selling	Favorites	Accounts	Feedback	Preferences	All

Go to: Personal Information | My eBay Preferences ▶ eBay news and Questions
| Sign In Activities information ⑦

Personal Information

UserID/Email address:
Change my user ID
Change my email address
Change my wireless email address

Password assistance:
Change my password
Create a Password Hint

About Me page:
Create a personal 'About Me' page

Notifications and emails from eBay:
Change my notification preferences
(Turn on/off the emails that you receive from
eBay)

Seller preferences:
Update selling picture preference

Follow the instructions from there for creating your About Me page.

You can select from the HTML templates eBay provides to simplify the process or you can enter your own HTML in the text box provided.

GRIFF TIP: If you are creating your own HTML-formatted text for your About Me page using a Web editor like FrontPage, only copy and paste the HTML between and excluding the <body> and </body> tags.

You can talk about practically anything you like on your "About Me" page. You can describe your business, and unlike the restrictions against linking to your Web site from your item page, you *can* link to your own Web site from your About Me page. You can talk about the items you sell (though you mustn't offer items for sale from your About Me page). You can even tell the world about your family, your favorite charities, your hobbies, and your collecting interests.

Once your About Me page is up, you can link to it from your item-listing descriptions with a simple hypertext link along these lines: "Visit my About Me page to learn more about my eBay business."

GROWING YOUR EBAY BUSINESS

You have done everything right so far and your eBay business is now thriving and growing. A growing business is usually most vulnerable once it starts to really take off. Often, an eBay seller will find a successful business strategy and will grab on to it tightly—sometimes so tightly that when the business climate changes, she doesn't. This inflexibility can be deadly to a business.

You can avoid these pitfalls by staying flexible in your business strategies and by always staying one step ahead of the market.

How? It bears repeating. Research! Never take your eye off your competition. Learn what it is that makes them successful or not successful and incorporate the lessons into your own business. Stay ahead of market trends for the items you list.

For example, it is the middle of June and you just got a great deal on a big lot of assorted batteries from a local store that is going out of business. Do you sell the lot off right away? Or do you hold on to it and sell them later? When do you think the demand for batteries is highest, on the Fourth of July or in the month of December? You might have a hunch that maybe your batteries will do better in December, but perhaps you need to turn merchandise over sooner rather than later.

And there are other factors to consider. Who else is currently offering batteries on eBay? What are their starting prices? Are they aggressively marketing them in the middle of the summer? If not, maybe you could offer a portion of them now and reserve the rest of the lot for the upcoming holiday season.

A good business is never static. Stasis is the sure death of any business.

I met an eBay seller a few years ago who was offering a type of item that no other eBay seller was offering at the time. Let's call this seller "Pat." Pat was doing a great business. Pat had an extremely inexpensive source for these items and invested heavily in stocking up her inventory. Buyers interested in these items went to her listings, and since there were no other sellers of this particular item, she had the market cornered. All was profits and bliss until . . .

Eventually, another seller (let's call this seller "Sam") discovered the market in these items simply by doing a little browsing in the eBay category where the items were listed. Sam did some research and discovered Pat's source. Sam began buying from the same source and offered the items at a slightly lower opening bid than Pat. That meant lower margins for Sam, but Sam was banking on making up for the lower margin of profit with a higher volume of sales.

Pat was suddenly faced with competition, and Pat's sales started to slow down. Pat was confronted with a dilemma. If Pat lowered the opening bid prices, it would mean lower profits; but Pat hoped that a higher volume of sales would offset her lower profits, just as Sam had gambled.

So what did Pat do? Nothing. Pat decided that lowering the prices of the items in inventory would be too big a risk, and so Pat chose to wait out Sam's aggressive marketing attack, hoping that the market would expand enough to include both sellers. And it did, at least for a while. But within a few months, other sellers started moving into the same line of merchandise until there were several different sellers of the items.

This was great for buyers, who could now shop by price as well as by item. It was not good for the sellers, as they watched their gross sales drop.

An update: Sam saw the writing on the wall and unloaded his inventory of items for a small loss by dumping them on eBay for a penny opening bid each. Sam then took the cash and went searching for other wares—wares for which there were not many sellers. Pat stuck it out, refusing to adjust prices or to expand the line of eBay merchandise, and was eventually out of business.

The moral of the story: If you choose to move ahead and make the wrong choice, you may fail—but you may also win. If you don't choose to move ahead but instead remain in place, you *will* fail.

THE EBAY "POWERSELLERS" PROGRAM

With the goal of recognizing those sellers who do high-volume sales on eBay, eBay created a program known as PowerSellers.

The PowerSellers program is divided into five levels. Eligibility for each level requires a certain amount of monthly gross merchandise sales (indicated below in parentheses next to the level name).

- Bronze ($1,000–$3,000)
- Silver ($3,000–$10,000)
- Gold ($10,000–$25,000)
- Platinum ($25,000–$150,000)
- Titanium ($150,000+)

There are benefits for those qualifying sellers who join the eBay PowerSellers program:

✔ Membership in the program is free.
✔ All PowerSellers receive a PowerSeller Icon next to their User ID.

✔ Bronze PowerSellers: fast-track 24/7 email support.
✔ Silver PowerSellers: Bronze benefits plus dedicated phone support during business days and hours (PST).
✔ Gold PowerSellers: Silver benefits with the addition of access to a pool of account managers.

✔ Platinum PowerSellers: Gold benefits plus twenty-four-hour/all-week phone support as well as a dedicated Support account manager.

✔ Titanium PowerSellers: Platinum benefits plus initial phone contact from eBay for any listing issues or questions.

✔ The PowerSeller Portal and Forum, which lets all PowerSellers log in and network with other PowerSellers. PowerSellers also enjoy the benefits of a special Recognition and Rewards program.

✔ A Banner Ad Tool to create, target, and monitor their own eBay banner ads.

✔ Exclusive invitations to eBay-sponsored educational or special events.

✔ Monthly newsletters and program updates featuring new products, benefits, and policy updates.

✔ Exclusive PowerSeller offers from eBay designed to help PowerSellers save time and money.

You can find out more about the PowerSellers program requirement, levels, and benefits at: **http://pages.ebay.com/services/buyandsell/powersellers.html**.

You can also navigate to this page by clicking the Services link on the eBay Navigation Bar and then clicking the buying and selling link on the subbar. Scroll down that page and look for the section headed "PowerSellers Program."

Successful Business Practices—Treating Your Customers Like the Priceless Assets They Are

There's a time-honored, golden rule of bricks-and-mortar business that says, "The customer is always right." Actually, there are two rules of business. Rule number one: "The customer is always right." Rule number two: "When the customer is wrong, see rule number one."

eBay sellers with the most successful businesses all apply this rule to each and every customer. During my tenure with eBay Customer Support, I received many emails from sellers embroiled in disputes with their buyers, most of which stemmed from simple misunderstandings due to either an ambiguous email or confusion over an item description or terms. Many, if not most, of these disputes resulted in negative feedback for both buyer and seller, as well as unnecessary additions to the world's already-too-large pool of ill will.

Here are my Seller Tips for nearly trouble-free eBay transactions:

BE EXPLICIT, POLITE, AND PROFESSIONAL
IN YOUR LISTING TERMS

You cannot provide too much information in your item descriptions. Note every quality and every flaw of your item. If you don't have much information, do some research and provide what you find. State your payment and shipping terms with as much detail as possible, in neutral and polite language.

Nothing turns a potential buyer away from your listing faster than a string of harsh rules and regulations for bidders. Not that you shouldn't state your rules, only that you do so in polite and friendly language. Here's an example of text from an actual eBay listing followed by my rewording:

If you have any negative feedback, DO NOT BID! I will not accept any bids from a bidder with negative feedback and I will cancel your bids AND I WILL CONTACT eBAY and you will be thrown off so DON'T BID unless you UNDERSTAND THESE TERMS!

Makes one want to run and hide instead of bid. Wouldn't it sound better this way?

If you have any recent negative feedback, we still want your business. However, please contact us via email so we can discuss the reasons for the negative feedback before you bid. Thanks! We appreciate your cooperation!

DON'T TURN OFF POTENTIAL GOOD BIDDERS
WITH HARSH REGULATIONS AND TERMS

Yes, you can use eBay's Bidder Management Tool to block the bids of an unwanted bidder, but unless you know the User ID of a bidder beforehand, you cannot block him in advance from bidding. Also, using negative feedback alone as a guide to a bidder's reliability or seriousness of intent can be misleading. Each case where negative feedback has been left is different. There may be extenuating circumstances. Give your bidders a chance to explain themselves if necessary. If you are unhappy with a bidder, quietly and without rancor cancel their bid and then add them to your items' blocked list.

PROVIDE A REFUND OPTION FOR YOUR BIDDERS

Although eBay allows you as a seller to adopt an "All-sales-as-is, no-returns-or-refunds" policy, please don't do it. As efficient and fun as the eBay marketplace is, eBay buyers don't have the chance to examine their item with their own hands and eyes until after they have paid for and received it. Even with the most explicit description and pictures, sometimes a well-meaning buyer simply isn't happy with the item once she has received it. Put yourself in a buyer's shoes. Would you want to be stuck with something you bought in good faith but find you don't like once you have received it? Of course not!

In the offline world of retail, returns are an accepted way of life. If you want to succeed on eBay, offer a hundred-percent-satisfaction-guaranteed policy with no such conditions as "I'll take the item back this time, but don't ever bid on my items again!" In fact, if a bidder asks to return an item, not only should you cheerfully agree to take it back, but you should also encourage the bidder to return and shop with you again. Your bidders will love you for it.

For those sellers who will not provide a hundred-percent-satisfaction-guaranteed policy, make sure you spell out your "no returns" policy in clear and concise language within your item description so that your bidders are fully informed before they decide to bid on your item—and, oh, best of luck. You'll need it.

NEVER GET ANGRY

Another fact of life of business is that you will now and then run into the "difficult" customer. I don't mean the non-paying bidder. They are a separate problem dealt with in a separate way. By "difficult," I mean the customer who sends churlish or abrupt, demanding email. We get them all the time with eBay Customer Support. We never respond in kind but instead always respond politely and professionally. We simply ignore any inappropriate or inflammatory language and focus only on the crux of the email, responding to the complaint itself and not to its presentation—no matter how nasty or unpleasant it may be.

You should always do the same. How you respond to an angry customer email reflects directly on you. Think of yourself as the customer support for your eBay business. Do what you can to calm and placate an angry customer. If you are unable to satisfy him, in spite of offering a refund or kind, polite words, send a last email with your regrets and offer of future assistance if needed.

If anyone sends you harassing emails—either in tone or in volume—contact the sender's ISP and forward them a copy of the email with full headers attached. Then add the sender's email address to your email application's spam filter program. Remember, you are under no obligation to open, read, or respond to an email sent to you. If all else fails, delete any and all emails from the sender without opening them.

"What if a customer sends me an email threatening to come find me and do me bodily harm?"

We believe people are basically good. However there are some people out there upon whom one might want to keep a closer eye. The lion's share of email threats are hollow but, if someone menaces you with bodily harm, you may want to contact the local law-enforcement authorities in your and the sender's locale and alert them to the threat.

GO THE EXTRA MILE

Your customers are your most valuable business assets. Treat them like royalty. Always give at least a little more than expected. The most memorable experiences I have had on eBay as a buyer have been with those sellers who have sent refunds for unintentional overcharges for shipping or handling or who have included some small but thoughtful "extra" with the item. Offer free gift wrapping and shipping directly to a gift recipient and you pay for a "confirmation of delivery" option. Again, your goal should be happy customers. Do whatever it takes to reach your goal. Here's what eBay seller Mike Ford has to say on going the extra mile:

EBAY MEMBER TIP: If you are selling an item that requires batteries, you can add a brand-new pack of batteries to the item and tell your potential buyers for that listing. You can increase your sales just by including batteries. . . . You can get a brand-new pack of the batteries (any size) that item requires from top brands like Panasonic and Energizer for as low as $1 for a pack of four at most dollar stores! Be smart! Little things like this will give you the advantage over someone selling the exact same thing.

Or you can find good deals on batteries at eBay.

OFFER AUTHENTICATION SERVICES FOR YOUR ITEMS

If you plan on selling comic books, trading cards, Beanie Babies, stamps, coins, jewelry, or sports autographs or sports memorabilia, you should offer your items preauthenticated or graded by one of the recognized and trusted authentication or grading services on eBay's list of recommended vendors.

Preauthorization or grading will instill confidence in your bidders and establish a sense of security and trust that your item is genuine as described.

You can find a page of all the eBay-reviewed and -approved authentication and grading services by clicking the Services ->buying & selling links on the eBay Navigation Bar. Look at the bottom of that page for the Authentication link under the Trade with Confidence sections.

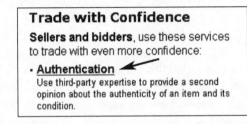

OFFERING ESCROW

If you are a brand-new seller and are offering expensive items, you may want to provide an online escrow option for your bidders. Escrow acts like a trusted middleman between buyer and seller.

Once a listing has ended, the buyer sends payment to the escrow company, who verifies and holds the funds and then notifies the seller, who then sends the merchandise to the buyer. Once the buyer receives, inspects, and accepts the item, she notifies the escrow company, who then sends the payment to the seller.

If the buyer doesn't accept the item, she sends it back to the seller, who inspects the item and alerts the escrow company that the item has arrived in the same condition it was sent. The escrow company then refunds the money to the bidder. Everyone is protected!

eBay's recommended escrow provider is Escrow.com. As of this writing, there is a minimum fee of $22 plus a small percentage fee based on the final bid amount. It is customary for the buyer and seller to split the fees.

Finally, here is what eBay seller Mikmartyka has to say about the road to successful eBay selling:

EBAY MEMBER TIP: Give your buyers more than they expect. Just an example in one area:

I've made quite a few purchases online with major retailers. You pay your money and they ship in seven to ten days.

I control all aspects of my small empire, so when a buyer pays me they have their item in their hands in two to three days. They get their feedback immediately. They get a notice that the item is being shipped, and the tracking number when it applies. Many of my feedback comments are from buyers surprised at how quickly they have their purchases.

There is nothing like a happy and satisfied customer.

PROMOTING YOUR EBAY BUSINESS OFFLINE AND ON YOUR WEB SITE

Most eBay sellers have their own commercial Web sites. You can promote your eBay items on your Web site by including a link. eBay provides links and logos that are preapproved for users.

You can use the links and logos by going to the eBay Site Map and looking under the section for Manage My Items for Sale for the link labeled "Promote your listings with link buttons."

Learn from Your Competition

Your competition is your best teacher. Look for sellers who offer merchandise similar or identical to yours and determine what practices they employ to be successful.

For example, some sellers offer free shipping or they list their items with a low opening bid and no reserves. Others may offer to include extras for the bid price. Sometimes the balance tipper is something as simple as a more detailed description set inside a professional-looking HTML layout or clearer digital pictures.

SPECIAL SELLING CONSIDERATIONS

Selling Cars, Trucks, Boats, etc., on eBay

eBay is becoming the destination of choice online for shoppers looking for new, used, and collector cars as well as trucks, motorcycles, and boats. There are many used-car sellers who have moved some of or their entire inventory to eBay Motors.

Selling a vehicle on eBay is similar to selling any other type of item, with a few extra concerns.

First, the fee schedule is different. The Insertion and Final Value Fees for all passenger vehicles and motorcycles are fixed. It costs $40 to list a passenger or other type of vehicle. It costs $25 to list a motorcycle.

In addition, if the item sells, there's a fixed $40 Final Value Fee for Passenger Vehicles and Other Vehicles; and a $25 Final Value Fee for Motorcycles. Again, this fee applies only when there is a successful high bid on the item.

All other fees are the same as for a standard eBay listing.

Some other tips for selling vehicles:

Take many photos. A car has many sides and facets—inside, outside, and underneath. Make sure that you have a digital image for all views of the vehicle, including: both sides, front, back, inside trunk, under hood, front and back seats, dashboard, and undercarriage. Since eBay Picture Services limits you to six photos, you may want supplement it with another hosting solution. (See Section Two, Chapter 7, for more information on Image Hosting.)

Make sure the vehicle has a clear title and indicate this in the item description.

Be extra explicit in listing the details. Note and picture every imperfection. Include the blue-book values for the same car in various conditions directly above and below the condition of your vehicle.

Be clear about your shipping terms. Most buyers of cars online understand that they will have to pay for shipping the car and that this can often cost several hundred dollars. Make sure to state this clearly in your listing.

When you list the item, you will be prompted to select a category for the vehicle that will also be the title of the item. You can provide a subtitle. Create your subtitle carefully! This is the text that is searched using keywords, so remember to limit your eBay Motors item subtitle to only those keywords that relate to your vehicle. Try to avoid descriptive words like *choice* or *rare* or *Must See,* etc. No one goes to eBay Motors and searches for all the "Must See" items and no one is actually impelled to open your listing because you have ordered them to do so. By using these useless words or phrases, you are effectively wasting space. However, do feel free to use the subtitle for mention of miles on the odometer or maybe as a place to state "no reserve" if there is sufficient space after you enter your keywords (and if the item is indeed a no-reserve item).

SELLING TO INTERNATIONAL BIDDERS

If you are going to sell on eBay, you have to make a decision right off as to whether or not you are going to welcome international eBay buyers to bid on or purchase your items. Let me try to help you make the right decision.

Sell to anyone, anywhere.

Wasn't that easy?

Yes, there are special considerations for selling, accepting payment, and shipping items internationally but don't forget, you are doing business on eBay, the most vibrant and far-reaching marketplace mankind has ever created. eBay is a worldwide phenomenon. There are millions of people around the world ready to shop and buy, and you have to ask yourself, "Do I really want to cut out such a vast potential customer base?"

If my argument has failed to move you, then move on down a few paragraphs to the section marked "I Won't Sell Internationally."

The rest of you savvy businesspeople, follow me. . . .

Don't pay attention to those 'fraidy cats that I just sent to the next page. Selling to international buyers on eBay isn't that difficult. Here are a list of tips and issues to keep in mind.

1. Accept credit cards, and electronic checks, through an online payment service. More and more countries are jumping on the online payment bandwagon. By accepting payment via one of the above methods, you are forgoing the need for cumbersome currency conversion (the credit card company makes the conversion for you and usually at the best possible rate of exchange), and you don't have to worry about clearing checks. In addition, you get paid fast, so you can ship the item fast—making for a happy seller and a happy buyer.

2. Accept international money orders in lieu of checks but, again, offer online payment options for international buyers. You may in fact want to limit all international buyers to online payment only. In any event, never accept cash for any listing—domestic or international.

3. Investigate all shipping options. Go to the USPS, FedEx, UPS, DHL, and Airborne Express Web sites and learn how each one works for international shipping from the US. Then, in your shipping terms, offer your international bidders a choice of those services that you have selected.

4. For large or heavy items: Have a good estimate of the weight and dimensions of the item once it has been packed and post the weight and dimensions in your item description. Include links to your preferred

shipping-services Web sites' rate or postage calculators so that international bidders can calculate the approximate cost for shipping to their country *before* they bid.

5. For smaller, lighter items: Try whenever possible to have a fixed shipping amount for international shipping.

6. When you ship internationally, you will have to fill out a customs form. Familiarize yourself with the various forms (they aren't complicated) and if possible, keep a stack of them handy in your office. **NOTE:** Never deflate the amount of an item's value on a custom declaration when shipping internationally, no matter how hard the buyer insists. See tip number 10 below for more information on detailed payment and shipping terms for international buyers.

7. Make insurance mandatory for all bidders and buyers.

8. Use a packing list, invoice, and envelope as well as a shipping label. Make sure the invoice is complete.

9. Always use tracking or delivery confirmation and always require a signature upon delivery.

10. Finally, make your item description, terms for shipping, payment, and returns as explicit and detailed as possible for both international and domestic buyers—but even more so for international bidders.

I Won't Sell Internationally

And no one can force you to do so. If you are not going to allow international buyers to spend their cash on your items, make sure you state your terms in clear and explicit language that is unavoidable to all.

Do keep in mind that eBay does not (and probably will never) provide a mechanism that automatically blocks international buyers from bidding or buying. Consequently, besides stating your terms in mile-high text in your listing description, you should also check the bidder list for your listings. When you suspect a bidder might be from some other country than the USA, send him an email asking for his location. If he is international, you can cancel his bids and add him to your blocked list.

GRIFF TIP: If you decide to limit your sales to only the US, make sure your terms of service do not offend! Use something along the lines of:

We do not ship to locations outside of the US, nor do we ship to an address that differs from the address a buyer has on his or her eBay registration contact information.

SELLING ON THE EBAY INTERNATIONAL SITES

Most of you reading this are registered at the US eBay site (**www.ebay.com**) but did you know that once you are registered on eBay, regardless of which site you used to register, you can list on any of the several eBay sites—US or international?

There might be a time when you will want to list on an international eBay site. For example, Italians are fanatic philatelists (they collect stamps); specifically, Italian stamps. You may come across some Italian stamps someday and you may realize a higher price if they are listed on the Italian site. Of course, it pays to have some grasp of the language and your description should be in Italian, but these are small obstacles if you use an online translation site like AltaVista's **http://babelfish.altavista.com.**

One more thing—when you list on an international site, you will be paid in the currency of that country. For the Italian site, you would be paid in euros, and your seller's account will be charged fees based on euros (but converted to dollars); so your fees may be at the mercy of the conversion rate between the two currencies at the time the fees are charged.

Happy International Selling!

SELLING LOCALLY

Some sellers are loath to put up very large or very heavy items for bid or sale on eBay due to packing or crating and shipping considerations. However, there is a mechanism that many eBay buyers use to limit their searches to a specific metropolitan area.

When you list your item, you are required to select a Region from a drop-down list of states with city names. Besides being searchable via keyword, item number, seller, and category, your item is also added to that location's Local Trading page.

Bidders can search or browse by region when they are looking for big pieces of furniture, cars, and other large or heavy items and they don't want to pay high crating and shipping costs.

Another use of the Region and Local Trading feature is for items of local interest such as those relating to a local sports team or industry.

We've now covered just about every aspect of selling on eBay that one can imagine. The rest of the chapters in this section cover lots of extra tips, tricks, and skills that can help make you a better eBay seller.

For example, advanced HTML . . .

6

Advanced HTML

In Section Two, Chapter 3, we learned a basic HTML tag for paragraph. This chapter covers several HTML tags that you will find useful in creating a professional eBay Item Description.

Even if you currently use a Web editor to create and format your item description text with HTML, I strongly suggest you read through this chapter. Understanding how HTML works from the bottom up will help you troubleshoot potential HTML snafus later.

Bob Bull ("bobal") is a popular eBay chat-board regular who has found great satisfaction teaching others about HTML. Bob, who is sixty-five, suffers from several serious disabilities.

"I was so lonely staying home alone while my wife, Alice, went to work every day. At one point, I didn't care if I lived or not."

But Bob did not give up, and in April of 1998 he discovered eBay. At first, he bought and sold small lots of items, always watching and learning from other savvy eBay chatters. Bob had a lot of questions about selling, and he began asking for help from other folks on the eBay chat boards. Over time, Bob asked so many questions and garnered so much helpful information that he became an HTML expert, answering "newbie" questions on the chat boards.

"I now live my life on eBay helping others. eBay has changed my life completely. When I can help a new user, I am on top of the world and I feel like my life is still worth living."

Today, Bob is an eBay legend, always ready to help others figure out the ins and outs of selling. And he continues to make new friends every day. As he told me, "No matter how many disabilities you have, you can help make a difference in someone's life."

Once you have finished this chapter, I guarantee that you will experience a great sense of accomplishment. Playing with HTML is fun!

WHAT IS HTML?

HTML (Hypertext Markup Language) is the language of the Internet, specifically, that part of the Internet known as the World Wide Web (or "the Web" for short).

HTML was developed in 1990 by Tim Berners–Lee while working at the European Organization for Nuclear Research (known as CERN, the acronym of its old French name "Centre European pour la Recherche Nucleaire") in Geneva, Switzerland. I wonder if Tim ever imagined his little invention would literally change the world?

HTML is an easy-to-learn, universal formatting language that allows anyone to create pages of text called Web pages, which, when placed on a Web server, can be viewed by anyone else on the Web using any type of computer and a Web browser.

WHAT ARE WEB PAGES?

Web pages are text documents consisting of simple text called ASCII (American Standard Code for Information Interchange). Since all computer systems can read ASCII text, HTML documents can be created and viewed on any type of computer (IBM, Mac, Unix, Linux, etc.). This is what makes the Web accessible to anyone, regardless of what type of computer he or she uses.

WHAT IS THE WEB?

The Web, or World Wide Web, is a vast network of computers that spans the globe. Although they are not technically the same thing, many people use "Internet" and "Web" interchangeably. (The Web is a part of the Internet, which includes email, FTP, etc.)

Anyone with a computer and a connection can access the Web.

There are basically two types of computers on the Web: specially configured computers called "Web servers," and "user" computers (for lack of a better word). Your "user" computer can be a Mac, a PC, a Unix computer, a laptop, a PDA, and so on.

Web servers are where all Web pages are stored. There are hundreds of thousands of Web servers connected to the Web, containing millions and millions of Web pages. There are also millions of people like you across the globe—accessing the Web with their Mac or PC or Linux computer or handheld PDA or cell phone.

There is an extremely important feature of the Web that bears emphasizing: In order for a Web page or picture to be seen by everyone on the Web, the page or picture *must* live on a Web server. The contents of your computer, unless it is a connected Web server, are not viewable on the Web! You can create Web pages or digital pictures on your computer and you can see them in your browser, but until you upload them to a Web server, no one will ever see them. *This includes your eBay pictures!*

GRIFF TIP: Any time the address for a Web page looks like this—

—that is, the address starts with a "C:\ . . ." (or sometimes "File|\\\ . . .), you are viewing a file from your hard drive. No one else will be able to view it.

WHAT IS A WEB BROWSER?

A Web browser is a special type of application designed for viewing Web pages. The two most popular Web browsers are currently Internet Explorer and Netscape Navigator. All of our examples employ Internet Explorer but can easily be adapted to work with Netscape.

A Web browser has the built-in ability to read any text file with the extensions *htm, html,* and *txt.* Web browsers can also read picture files of the type *gif* and *jpg.* Using special "plug-ins," Web browsers can also read Word files, PDF (Portable Document Format), and special multimedia files like Flash graphics.

OH, COME ON, GRIFF. DO I *REALLY* NEED TO KNOW ALL THIS HTML STUFF TO SELL ON EBAY?

Honestly? No, you don't. If you don't mind if your eBay descriptions look something like this:

Description
This lot features an extremely rare "TIN PRE-COINAGE CRAB". Circa 1400, originally used by Chinese as money. Made of tin with Ming Dynasty designs. Used in MALACCA,a very rare item in excellent condition.In very rare occasion, items like these are recovered from the Straits of Malacca seabed. The chinese design has Ming Dynasty influence. (((HISTORY)) In the early 1400, Malacca was a bustling port handling many ships that ply the east asia and the western world.Malacca was the "half way house" where traders from the east would dock,replenish and trade with traders from the west.Malacca was located in a strategic location offering safe and calm waters protected by Straits of Malacca.It was there that the world trading of spices, silk etc took place.In short, it was a "melting pot".Everyone wanted to take control of Malacca.Malacca has a very rich cultural heritage from days of just local natives & Malays,Portuguese came in 1511 and the there was the Dutch,British,Japanese and later independance. The history of this tin animal money started in the wonderful days of the Malacca Empire.After the cowrie shells, some form of money had to be used as Malacca was the trading port.It was discovered that the surrounding area had abundance of tin ore.Tin was considered as a precious metal and the chinese believed that tin brings luck,prosperity and wards off evil spirits.At the entrance of many chinese houses, tin is used to line the walls and columns.This is believed to bring luck to the inhabitants of the house.Tin was chosen as the medium as tin was considered precious,malleable & soft thus easily shaped and tin is widely accepted. This gave birth to the "Tin Animal Money" that you are bidding. This form of money comes in a few denomination, the largest weighing 1 kati and the smallest 1/20kati.The full denomination are 1 kati, 1/2kati, 1/10kati and 1/20kati.The rarest of them are the 1 and 1/2kati.Various animal shapes have been found.To date, 4 distinct animal which is the tortoise,fish,rooster(chicken) and crab(EXTREMELY RARE).Only the tortoise come in 1 & 1/2kati.The others do not have the larger denomination.It was found that each animal comes in several designs and variants.It incorporates design from the Ming Dynasty,brought by the chinese settlers that came from China.So trade was effected using this form of medium of exchange.It must have been a heavy task for the rich to carry around 20katis of tin if he wanted to buy something big. :).... This type of pre-coinage money were only known to us lately in the last 30years.It laid hidden for almost 600 years,unknown to the modern civilisation.They were first discovered by fisherman in an island not far off the coast of the mainland, "Pulau Besar".Over the last 2 decades,a few more were found when excavation works took place in town.Several sites were identified and it was discovered that people lived near to the beach area as the tin money were found there. (((What makes it very rare?))) When the Portuegese conquered Malacca in 1511, like all new government today, they seized all tin animal money and brought in their own.Most were melted down to make their tin Bastardos,dinheiro etc.A new currency was in place.Some that we see today were the ones that got discarded into the sea or rivers. Some were also buried but getting to them is a needle in a haystack.Even if they knew where they were,buildings probably sit on the top of them.The tin animal money is so rare that the local muzium has only a few disfigured items on display. (((Fakes & How to check them?))) Since the item is so rare, many counterfeitors have tried to reproduce these coins.I have seen many that tries to pass off as genuine.There are two simple test that you can deploy (((1)Visual Inspection))) Look for corrosion marks.Tin that sits buried under the seabed or soil will be corroded over the 600years period.All corrosion marks are individual and no 2 pieces are alike.Look for the uneven corrosion marks especially on the edges.Like the walls of old buildings,you will find bits of concrete breaking off especially at the edges.The marks should be uneven and have different colored tones.It is generally grey with a whitish coating.Fresh tin is dark in color. (((2)Scratch Test))) Fresh tin is soft and you can scratch the surface.On the contrary to a genuine tin animal money, it has been sitting under the seabed for 600years.The surface has harden over the centuries,so scratch any of the surface with a key or something sharp.Apply just enough strength for the test.If the surface scratches off, it is probably a recently fabricated item. (((Investment))) Malacca Tin Animal Money is an excellent investment opportunity.Not only for the artistic and esthatic value, it has a heritage,rare and cheap (for now).It is known to the world but no one knows how to get it.It is not something that you can buy in unlimited quantity. What you see in eBay is from my own collection , some passed down by my ancestors. Please feel free to contact me should you need more information on this rare item.Or else, you are encouraged to get more info and pictorial at ------ http://www.collectibles-museum.com/htm_original/coin_introd.htm ---So bid with confidence.An extremely scarce find and will be an excellent addition for only the most discerning and knowlegeable collector. Don't miss out on such an investment opportunity. Guaranteed for authenticity and age.I am asking for a modest reserve on this priceless piece."Buy It Now" would be about the market value.This is also a PRIVATE AUCTION where your identity would be concealed. Cheers Ships Worldwide, Buyer pays for shipping & handling.

You should explore how HTML can make your listing description more professional. At the very least, it helps to know exactly what goes on behind a Web page, since your items will be viewed as Web pages. Plus, learning HTML is fun, as eBay seller Pat Fulton discovered:

Because I can't stand to leave things alone, nor can I see any reason at all for anything to be just plain vanilla, I decided that if I was going to sell on eBay, my item description pages just had to be fancy! Having young males in the house can be very helpful when you want to learn such things, as their youthful minds obviously work in a totally different direction than that of their elderly parents. Of course, as a backup plan, I bought a book on HTML as more often than not, I have no idea at all what the boys are saying when it comes to computer stuff.

Book in hand and son nearby, I bravely dove into HTML. Opening, closing, a <br> here and an <hr> there, tables, fonts, and colors. It was like I'd suddenly turned into Houdini doing magic tricks! Colors, lines, pictures! Amazing!

Of course there were mistakes here and there, and that's where the kid came in handy. "What's wrong with my creation? It's all weird." My son would scrutinize the page, fingers flying, clicking, short-cutting, and scrolling. "You didn't close the table" or "You put the line break in the wrong place again" were the frequent answers.

I finally got that very first item description all written up in HTML, and it had taken me days to do. Things went along very well, and as each item was listed, it sold!

Sound like fun? Let's try it and see!

Creating a Professional eBay Description from Scratch

You don't need special software to create an **HTML** page (or to format your eBay item description)—all you need is a text editor (in Windows that would be **Notepad.** On a Mac, look for a program called Simple Text), a Web browser, and some basic **HTML**. And basic **HTML** is easy!

OPENING A TEXT EDITOR

PC users: To start, we open a blank **Notepad** file. **Notepad** can be started from the Windows **Start** menu at **Programs: Accessories: Notepad:**

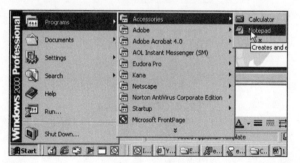

MAC users: Look for and open a program on your hard drive called Simple Text or Text Edit. Follow along with us here, substituting either Mac text editor for Notepad.

Back to Windows . . . this will open an Untitled Notepad window:

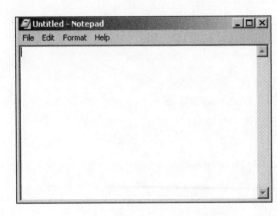

For the remainder of this chapter, everything you type you will type into this Notepad window.

Next, we open up a fresh new **Internet Explorer (IE)** browser window by clicking Start, Programs, and Internet Explorer or by clicking the Internet Explorer icon on your desktop or toolbar.

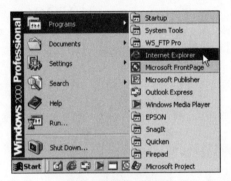

This will open a new IE window.

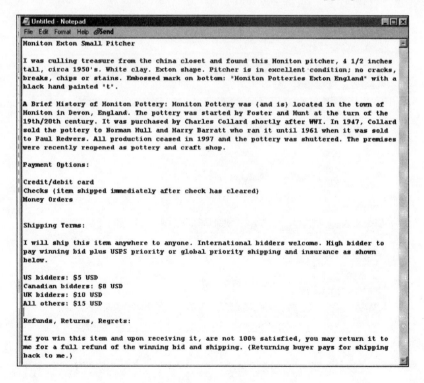

NOTE: I've resized our browser window down for our purposes. Your IE window may be full size. Also, I have typed "about;blank" into the Address window to show a blank (white) page.

This **IE** window is where we will view the text we input into our **Notepad** window. Think of it as our "view" window.

TYPING THE DESCRIPTION

Here we are using the same item description for the small pottery pitcher I photographed in Section Two, Chapter 2. It describes the item by type, age, condition, and size. I also included detailed payment instructions and shipping terms and costs.

IMPORTANT! Notice that whenever I needed to create a new paragraph, I hit the Enter key on my keyboard twice to move down two lines.

GRIFF TIP: Check your spelling! Most text editors like Notepad do not have spell checkers built in; however, there is a quick way to check the spelling of your description text. Click your mouse cursor anywhere inside the Notepad window and then click the right mouse button to display a pop-up menu. Click the menu item Select All.

This will highlight all of the text in the description.

Next, on the Notepad toolbar, click the command for Edit and then Copy.

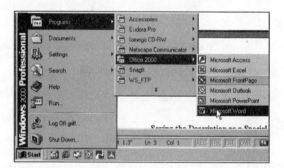

Now, open any application that has a spell checker. In Windows, use Word or Works. In Mac, use any word-processing application. Here, we will use Word.

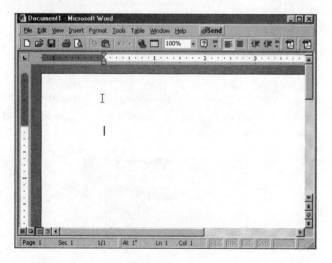

This will open a Microsoft Word window.

Make sure your mouse cursor is blinking somewhere on the blank page shown in the word processor window. Click the Edit command on the toolbar and select Paste.

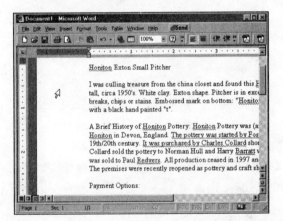

This will paste the entire description into the blank Word file.

On the word processor toolbar, click the menu command for the spell checker. In Word, that would be Tools and then "Spelling and Grammar . . ."

Check each found "error" carefully before accepting the suggested change made by the spell checker! For example, Word thinks the word *Honiton* is an error.

That's because the Word dictionary doesn't have Honiton as a valid entry, but it doesn't mean that the word is incorrect. I will "Add" the word to the dictionary by clicking the Add button. The Word Spelling and Grammar checker next finds a syntax error showing usage of the passive voice.

I agree with this change, so I click the Change button. After I have gone through each found spelling and grammar error, the spelling and grammar checker will tell me the check is complete, so I click OK.

Next, I reverse the copy-and-paste that we did in the beginning of the spell check by clicking the menu command for Edit on the Word toolbar and selecting Select All. This will highlight all the spelling and grammar-checked text of the description. I then click the Edit menu command again and select Copy.

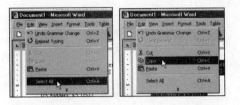

Finally, I return to the Notepad window. The text is still highlighted. I click Edit and Paste and the checked description text pastes over all of the unchecked text.

Now our item description text is all spelled correctly!

"But, Griff," you moan. "Why not just use Word or something like it instead of Notepad in the first place?"

Word and other word-processing applications add their own invisible formatting to all text documents. If we were to type our description in Word and then paste it into the text entry box on the eBay Sell Your Item form, it is possible that this invisible formatting might mess up our HTML. To avoid this, we use a plain text editor like Notepad, which does not add any invisible fancy formatting.

SAVING THE DESCRIPTION AS A SPECIAL TEXT FILE

Now that the content of my description is finished and spell checked, we want to view the description through Internet Explorer. Remember: For this HTML exercise, Notepad is the "input" window and Internet Explorer is the "output" window.

Viewing the text description through Internet Explorer will show us *exactly* how it will look on the eBay Item Description Page for my item when we list it.

But in order to view the text file containing the description in another application, we first must save it to our computer's hard drive. As it stands now, the file exists only in the computer's memory.

Why We Must "Save" First . . .

Computer memory or RAM (Random Access Memory) is divided up into little sections using a special type of addressing plan. For example, when you open an application like Notepad, your computer assigns a block of addresses in its memory where the application loads and waits to do its job. For Notepad, that job is accepting input from your keyboard and displaying it on your computer monitor as words.

Once a set of addresses in RAM is filled with data, nothing else can read or write to those addresses. This is a built-in memory protection mechanism used by all operating systems—Windows, Mac, Unix, etc. If this memory protection were not in place, any program could overwrite data in RAM at any time, making it impossible to use a computer securely.

Here's what happened when we opened Notepad: First, the computer code that makes up Notepad was loaded up from the hard drive into a section of RAM addresses that the computer assigned. Then, we typed in some data (our description), which was also loaded into addresses within the space the computer originally allotted to Notepad when we started it. That data is staring at us from the computer monitor.

We now want to read that data in Internet Explorer, but the rules of computer memory won't let any application read a memory address that is currently in use. The only application that can read the data is one that loaded into that space: Notepad.

In order for another application to read the data from Notepad, we need to first save the data to the hard drive. Once it is saved safely on our hard drive, Internet Explorer can then read that same data by pulling it from the hard drive.

In order to create a computer file that Internet Explorer can read, we need to save the data to the hard drive by selecting File, Save As from the Notepad toolbar.

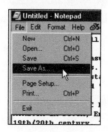

FOLLOW THESE STEPS EXACTLY!

1. Select File and "Save As . . ." from the Notepad toolbar.
2. Choose a location on your hard drive for the new file. We will use the desktop.

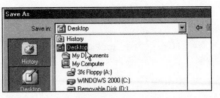

3. In the box labeled "File Name," type "test.html" and in the box labeled "Save as Type," click the arrow on the right of the drop-down box and select All Files. Ignore any box labeled "Encoding."

4. Click the Save button.

NOTE: You have now saved a copy of this file to the hard drive. Note that I said "copy." There is a copy still in RAM. The copy on the hard drive is set in stone. The copy in RAM can be changed while it is open. Both copies have the same file name, in this case, test.html.

By the way, you could name the part of this file before the "dot" anything you like. We chose "test." What is important is what comes after the dot. This must be "html" or our exercise will not work.

Let's open our test.html file in Internet Explorer—our "output" window. Go to your fresh new IE window. Click File, Open.

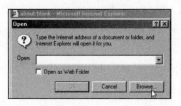

In the next box, click the "Browse . . ." button.

This will bring up an "Open" box. In the box labeled "Look in:" click and select Desktop from the list of choices.

This will display a list of the files on your desktop, filtered so that only HMTL files are displayed. (You will notice that the box for "Files of Type" is set to HTML.)

Look for the file named "test.html" and double-click it.

In the next box, click "OK."

And here's our description, exactly as it would appear on an eBay Item Description Page.

Notice something odd? All of the line and paragraph breaks we placed in our description are gone. If you go back and check the Notepad file, you will see that they are still there. So why are they missing from our description when it is viewed through a Web browser?

Web browsers are built to read all of the text characters on your computer keyboard. However, Web browsers do not recognize the Enter command used in Notepad to break to a new line—so they simply ignore it, running all the text together in one continuous line that breaks only when it reaches the right-hand side of the Web browser window.

Our description is still readable, but it certainly doesn't look professional or easy to parse.

How do we get the Web browser to recognize a line or paragraph break? We need to talk to it in its own language, HTML!

TAGS

HTML is made up almost entirely of bits of text called "tags." The simple syntax for an HTML tag looks like this:

<tag_name>

That's a "lesser than" character, a tag name, and a "greater than" character.

The tag name can be a letter, a combination of letters, or a word. The tag name is also case insensitive, which means it can be upper or lowercase and still be read as the same tag. For visual consistency, we will use uppercase for all of our tag names.

The first tag we will use looks like this:

<P>

"P" is the tag name. No doubt by now you have deduced it stands for "paragraph" (If you followed along in Chapter 3 of this section, you are already familiar with the <P> tag.) We need to type a <P> tag at every location in our description where we wish to insert a paragraph. The <P> tag will tell the browser, "Hey, browser, put a paragraph right here."

Let's type in a paragraph tag for each place in the test.html file where a paragraph appears.

We have inserted the <P> tag in all the right places in our description. To see what these tags "do" to our description when viewed through Internet Explorer, we must resave the file to the hard drive.

Click on File on the Notepad toolbar and then click on Save.

Now go back to the Internet Explorer window and click the icon for "Refresh" on the IE toolbar.

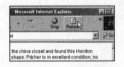

"Magically," where once there were no paragraphs, there are now several!

That's it. That's how HTML works. The <P> tag is just one tag out of many, but almost everything you need to know about HTML from here on is based on this very simple exercise.

You could stop here and use only the <P> tag and your eBay item descriptions will be perfectly readable, if a bit plain. But I have a feeling you won't be satisfied with just the <P> tag.

Let's learn some more tags!

LINE BREAKS

The <P> tag works great for double line breaks, but what about those places where we only want to break to the next line? (For example, our list of payment options.)

> Payment Options:
>
> Credit/debit card Checks (item shipped immediately after check has cleared) Money Orders

Although it's readable, it would be much cleaner if each option item were on a separate line. The tag we need is the **
** or "break" tag. Let's type one in after each of the payment options and the shipping costs in our Notepad file.

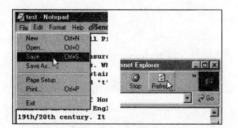

Once we have typed in all of the <BR> tags we need, we must "Save" the changes in Notepad and "Refresh" the Internet Explorer window. From now on, I will refer to these two steps as "Save and Refresh," since we will be saving changes many times in the rest of this chapter.

Here's what our description looks like in Internet Explorer with the added <BR> tags:

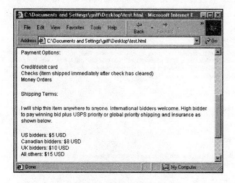

Our payment options and shipping costs are now a lot easier to understand.
So, should we stop here or do you want to learn more tags?
I thought so.

BOLD

I like to emphasize titles and important words in my eBay listing descriptions.
One way to do so is to use the **<B>** tag.

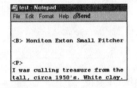

It stands for Bold. Let's add it to the header line at the top of our description.

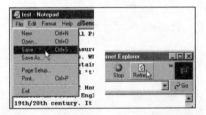

Save and Refresh! ("Save" in Notepad, "Refresh" in Internet Explorer.)

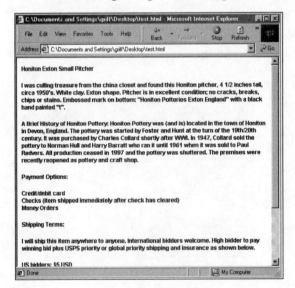

Here's what "Bold" formatting using the **<B>** tag looks like.

Uh . . . so much for bold emphasis. We wanted only the top line of the description to appear bold, but now everything is bold, so nothing stands out! Why did this happen?

When you insert a text-formatting tag, into a text document, the Web browser that reads the document starts the formatting at the exact spot in the text where you placed the particular formatting tag, and it doesn't stop formatting until either it comes to the end of the document or you tell it where to stop.

Clearly, we need to tell the Web browser where to stop with the "Bold." We do this by inserting a close tag. A close tag for a specific tag is the same tag with a forward slash before the name:

</B>

Let's type a bold close tag right after the word *Pitcher*.

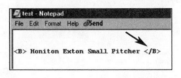

Save and Refresh!

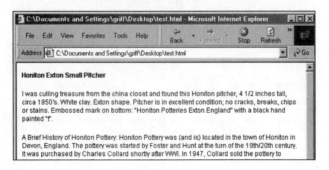

Here's the result in Internet Explorer.

Exactly what we wanted!
Let's add Bold tags to other important words in our description.

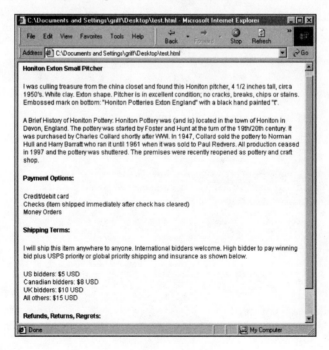

```
<P>
<B>Payment Options:</B>
<P>
Credit/debit card
Checks (item shipped immediately afte
Money Orders
<P>

<B>Shipping Terms:</B>
<P>
I will ship this item anywhere to any
pay winning bid plus USPS priority or
below.
<P>
US bidders: $5 USD <BR>
Canadian bidders: $8 USD <BR>
UK bidders: $10 USD <BR>
All others: $15 USD
<P>
<B> Refunds, Returns, Regrets: </B>
<P>
```

Save and Refresh!

Here's how our eBay item description looks so far. This is exactly how it would look on our eBay listing.

Honiton Exton Small Pitcher

I was culling treasure from the china closet and found this Honiton pitcher, 4 1/2 inches tall, circa 1950's. White clay. Exton shape. Pitcher is in excellent condition; no cracks, breaks, chips or stains. Embossed mark on bottom: "Honiton Potteries Exton England" with a black hand painted "t".

A Brief History of Honiton Pottery: Honiton Pottery was (and is) located in the town of Honiton in Devon, England. The pottery was started by Foster and Hunt at the turn of the 19th/20th century. It was purchased by Charles Collard shortly after WWI. In 1947, Collard sold the pottery to Norman Hull and Harry Barratt who ran it until 1961 when it was sold to Paul Redvers. All production ceased in 1997 and the pottery was shuttered. The premises were recently reopened as pottery and craft shop.

Payment Options:

Credit/debit card
Checks (item shipped immediately after check has cleared)
Money Orders

Shipping Terms:

I will ship this item anywhere to anyone. International bidders welcome. High bidder to pay winning bid plus USPS priority or global priority shipping and insurance as shown below.

US bidders: $5 USD
Canadian bidders: $8 USD
UK bidders: $10 USD
All others: $15 USD

Refunds, Returns, Regrets:

Now our description is starting to look like something. Still, there is so much more we can do to dress it up. For other different emphasis, we can use the **<U>** and **<I>** tags (Underline and Italics).

```
<B>Payment Options:</B>
<P>
Credit/debit card<BR>
Checks (item shipped <U>immediately</U> after chec
Money Orders<BR>
<P>
<B>Shipping Terms:</B>
<P>
I will ship this item <I> anywhere </I> to anyone.
welcome. High bidder to pay winning bid plus USPS
```

Save and Refresh.

Payment Options:

Credit/debit card
Checks (item shipped <u>immediately</u> after check ha
Money Orders

Shipping Terms:

I will ship this item *anywhere* to anyone. Internatior
winning bid plus USPS priority or global priority sh

Here is what the **<I>** and **<U>** tags do in Internet Explorer.

Our description is looking more and more professional. What? You want more? Then more you shall have!

LIST TAGS

There is one tag that comes in very handy when composing an eBay item description. Actually, it's a set of tags that work together to create lists. They are, of course, called the List Tags.

<UL> </UL>

<LI>

Let's use them for our payment options. We will first need to remove the **
** tags we typed in earlier. Then we place an opening **<UL>** tag before the items on the list of payment options and a closing **</UL>** tag after the last payment option on the list. Finally, we place a **<LI>** tag before each option on the list.

```
<UL>
<LI>Credit/debit card
<LI>Checks (item shipped <U>immediately</U> after check has cleared)
<LI>Money Orders
</UL>
```

Save and Refresh!

Here's what our list will look like in our item description.

THE FONT TAG

Up to now, the tags that we have used in our item description have consisted of a name between a lesser-than and a greater-than character. There are some tags that have more than just a name inside the lesser- and greater-than characters. One of them is the **<FONT>** tag.

The **<FONT>** tag is used to change either the size, color, or typeface of text. In order to make these changes, there needs to be more information inside the brackets than just the name, FONT. This information is added after the name using the following syntax:

<name attribute=value>

Looks a little like algebra, but don't panic—it's not complicated. An attribute is some aspect of the name, for example, in HTML, FONT has a few common attributes. Two of the most commonly used are "size" and "color." A value is assigned to an attribute using the "=" equal sign in order to change that particular attribute.

The first attribute we will change using the **<FONT>** tag is **"SIZE."** In HTML, the attribute for **"SIZE"** can take as a value any number from 0 to 7.

<FONT SIZE=6>

To close out the FONT tag, we use a closing tag.

</FONT>

Note that the closing **<FONT>** tag does not include the attribute value pair for **SIZE=6**. Attribute/value pairs are only indicated in the opening tag, never the closing tag.

Let's add it to the title on the top of our item description.

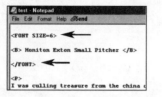

To make it clearer, I have placed the tags above and below the line to be formatted. Let's "Save and Refresh" and view the change in our Web browser.

Amazing, isn't it? Well, there's more! Not only can we change the size, we can change the color of the font as well!

The attribute is **COLOR** and the value can be one of two types. The simplest type of values to use for **COLOR** are common color names like "red," "blue," "green," "orange," "yellow," "purple," "white," "black," etc. Note that some not-so-common color names like "maroon" and "fuchsia" will work, as will some combination words like "lightblue" or "lightgreen." Uncommon names like "bruise," "oatmeal," and "monkeyspit" won't. There is another type of value that uses hexidecimal numbers, which I will tell you more about shortly. For now, we will use a common color name for a value. I'll use "yellow," which will show up gray in our black-and-white illustration.

<FONT SIZE=6 COLOR=yellow>

</FONT>

Note that a tag can have more than one attribute value pair. When adding attribute value pairs, make sure that there is one space and only one space between them. More than one space will "break" the tag and it won't work. Let's add this attribute value pair for COLOR to our item description.

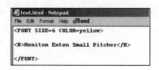

Save and Refresh . . .

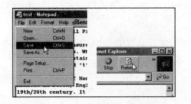

. . . to view the changes in Internet Explorer.

This is the easiest way to indicate a color, but it limits us to a very narrow range of colors. There is, however, another type of value for the **color** attribute that provides literally thousands of colors. It involves a special type of number called *hexidecimal*. Let's talk a little about hexidecimal numbers before we see them in action as a color value.

Our everyday number system is based on a *decimal* system, that is, a numbering system based on 10 (most likely because we have 5 fingers on each hand to work with when counting).

$$1\ 2\ 3\ 4\ 5\ 6\ 7\ 8\ 9\ 0$$

A *hexidecimal* number system is one based on 16 (imagine if humans evolved with eight fingers on each hand. We would most definitely be using a hexidecimal number system instead of the decimal system we have always used).

Since our decimal numbering system only has enough number symbols (10) to accommodate a decimal numbering system, we have to borrow other symbols to make up the difference. Our hexidecimal numbering system uses the digits 0 through 9, plus it "borrows" the first six letters of our alphabet:

$$0\ 1\ 2\ 3\ 4\ 5\ 6\ 7\ 8\ 9\ A\ B\ C\ D\ E\ F$$

The type of hexidecimal system we will use as a value for our **color** attribute has six places, for example:

$$34C8BA$$

We use a six-place hexidecimal number with a pound sign before it as a **color value**, for example:

<font color=#FF33EE>

This number, #FF33EE, as a color value will give you a particular shade and hue of a color. The hexidecimal numbers for a color value are not random, though. Here is how they work:

The six-place hexidecimal color value number can be pictured as three separate two-place values, for example:

FF 33 EE

The three parts of the six-place numbers represent three values for colored light indicated as **RGB** (Red, Green, Blue).

R	G	B
FF	33	EE

The value "FF" represents the strength of the **Red** component of light, the "33" represents the strength of the **Green** component of light, and the "EE" represents the strength of the **Blue** component of light.

The values of the two-place hexidecimal numbers increase in strength from "00" (no value) up to "FF" (highest value). Here is an abridged scale from "00" to "FF."

00 01 02 03 04 05 06 07 08 09 0A 0B 0C 0D 0E 0F 10 11 12 13 14 15 16 17 18 19 1A 1B 1C . . . and on up to . . . 98 99 9A 9B 9C 9D 9E 9F AF BF CF DF EF FF

An interesting fact about light color: Equal amounts of full-strength red, green, and blue light produces white light. A zero value of red, green, and blue light equals black (no light). Therefore:

<font color=#FFFFFF> equals the color **"white"**

<font color=#000000> equals the color **"black"**

With all the other thousands and thousands of colors in between! There are many Web pages on the Internet that display color charts with each color's respective hexidecimal numbers. To find them, go to **www.google.com** and search on the words "HTML color chart."

HTML CHARACTER ENTITIES

Many folks email or ask me at eBay University how to go about inserting a special symbol like ™ into their item description pages or About Me page. It's very easy! Nothing complicated, it's all done with **Character Entities.**

A **character entity** is a small set of keyboard characters, which make up special numeric or text codes that stand for special symbols. When a Web browser then parses these sets of characters, they will display a related special symbol or character not found on your computer keyboard. For example, in order to insert a ™ into your listing description, you would type:

™

That's an ampersand, followed by a pound sign, then a 1, a 5, a 3, and finally a semicolon.

Here are some other popular character entities that rely on numeric codes:

¢ = ¢ (Cent sign)

£ = £ (Pound sterling)

¥ = ¥ (Yen sign)

© = © (Copyright)

® = ® (Registered trademark)

Some character entities utilize ISO Latin 1 codes instead of numeric codes. Here is a good example using the ISO Latin code for "nonbreaking space."

If you type more than one space between words or objects into an HTML document, all Web browsers will ignore any spaces after the first one. For example, if I type

"word   word"

with six spaces between the *words,* the Web page will still display

"word word"

In order to add the extra spaces, we need to insert a special character entity for the "nonbreaking space." It looks like this:

If we type six of these character entities between the two *words:*

"word   word"

We get this:

"word   word"

Another good use of ISO character entities is for displaying actual HTML formatting tags on a Web page.

Let's say you wanted to show someone on one of eBay's chat boards, how to create a hyperlink using HTML. You might type the following into your chat-board post:

<A href=http://www.ebay.com> Visit eBay! </A>

but of course, when others viewed your post, they would see:

Visit eBay!

instead of the actual HTML. That's because the viewers' Web browsers parse and format the text based on the tags you provided. In order to display the actual HTML link tags within a Web browser, you would need to substitute character entities for the "lesser than" and "greater than" tags. Those character entities look like this:

< (which equals the "<" character)

That's an ampersand followed by the lower case letter *L,* the lowercase letter *T,* and finally a semicolon.

> (which equals the ">" character)

That's an ampersand followed by the lowercase letter *g,* the lowercase letter *t,* and finally a semicolon.

By substituting these character entities, you effectively "break" the ability of the Web browser to parse and display the HTML as an actual link. This is good, since your intention is not to create a link, but to *display* the HTML needed in order to create a link!

With the character entity substitutions, you would type:

<A href=http://www.ebay.com> Visit eBay! </A>

and the Web browser would parse this and display it as:

<A href=http://www.ebay.com> Visit eBay! </A>

QUIZ QUESTION!

When I was a regular on the eBay chat forums, I would use this character entity trick to display HTML tags for users who had questions about how to create a link. Other users would notice that I had effectively displayed HTML tags without the tags being parsed by the Web browser. They would ask me, "How did you do that?" I would then show them how. Again, note that if I type what I typed to create the "inactive" HTML link—

<A href=http://www.ebay.com> Visit eBay! </A>

—that the following would display:

<A href=http://www.ebay.com> Visit eBay! </A>

What would one type into her HTML text document in order to display the following text inside a Web browser?

<A href=http://www.ebay.com> Visit eBay! </A>

(HINT! It involves a character entity substitution for one of the characters within the character entities for < and >)

Can you figure it out?

The answer:

In order to display the actual character entity without the Web browser parsing the entity and displaying the character, you substitute a character entity for one of the characters inside the original entity. In this case, we substituted the character entity for ampersand **&** for the & character. This could go on forever in an endless regression of nested character entities, but I will assume you got the point and will spare you the tedium of actually printing out an endless regression of nested character entities, but I will assume you got the point and will spare you the tedium of actually printing out an endless regression of nested character entities but I will assume you got the point and will spare you the tedium of actually printing out an endless regression of nested character entities but I will assume you got the point and will spare you the tedium of actually printing out an endless regression of nested character entities but I will assume you got the point and will spare you the tedium of actually printing out an endless regression of nested character entities . . .

Character entities also come in handy when you need to insert special non-English alphabet characters into your text, for example, *ä* or *ö* (*a* and *o* umlaut).

You can find many complete lists of other numeric-code and ISO Latin 1 HTML Character Entities by going to any good search engine (like my favorite, **www.google.com**) and searching on the phrase "character entities."

You probably never thought you could do so much with a description. You're learning fast!

So far, we've been formatting text. HTML can do much more.

HYPERLINKS

One of the most important features of the Web is the ability to click a text link to "go" to another Web page. The Web would be almost impossible to navigate without these links (imagine having to type in a Web address for every page on the Web you wanted to visit).

Links, or more properly, **Hyperlinks,** are easy to add to your item description. The **tag** for creating a **hyperlink** is the **<A>** tag:

<A>

The *A* stands for **anchor.** The **<A>** tag never stands alone—it always contains an *attribute=value* pair, where the *attribute* is **href** and the *value* is a **URL*** to a file somewhere on the Internet. The opening and closing **<A>** tags surround some text that you have selected to be the actual clickable link.

<A HREF=*some URL***>** type text here that will be the clickable link **</A>**

Let's add a link to the item description. This link will take our bidders to our other eBay listings:

Go to the eBay **Search** page by clicking the Search link on the eBay Navigation bar.

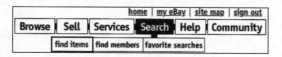

Click the By Seller tab and enter your User ID in the box. I will enter one of my eBay User IDs for our example.

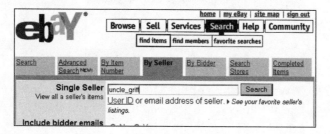

---

* URL stands for **Uniform Resource Locator**—computer geek-speak for "Web address."

Click the Search button. This takes us to the list of current listings by "Uncle_Griff."

Search titles **and** descriptions

Items for Sale by <u>uncle_griff (0)</u> me

View text-only format

0 items found.

All items	Auctions	Buy It Now

Picture hide	Item Title	Price	Bids	Time (Ends PDT)

This seller is not currently offering any items for sale.

There are no listings currently open for "uncle_griff," but no matter—the URL for this page is what we want and it will still work, even if there are no current items for sale.

Find the Address box on the IE menu bar. Click once inside the box to highlight the entire URL (address). Keeping your mouse cursor over the highlighted URL, click the right button on your mouse, and select Copy from the pop-up menu. (Mac users: Use the appropriate key strokes to copy and paste.)

eBay Seller List: uncle_griff - Microsoft Internet Explorer

Back	Forward	Stop	Refresh	Home	»	File

Address API.dll?MfcISAPICommand=ViewListedItems&userid=uncle

Undo
Cut
Copy
Paste
Delete

Browse | Sell | Ser
find items | find

This copies the complete URL in the Address box to the Windows clipboard.

Go back to the item description in the Notepad file. At the end of the second paragraph of our description, before the Payment Options, we'll add the following line of HTML-formatted text:

<A HREF=> Visit my other eBay Items </A>

text.html - Notepad

File   Edit   Format   Help   Send

recently reopened as a pottery and craft shop.
<P>

<A HREF=> Visit my other eBay Items!</A>

<P>

Once you have typed the line of HTML text into the description, place your mouse cursor so that it blinks right between the "=" and the ">" after "**HREF.**"

<A HREF=> Vis

Now, without moving the cursor, click the right mouse button and select Paste from the pop-up menu.

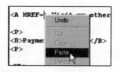

This will paste the entire Search URL into the appropriate space in the **\<A\>** tag:

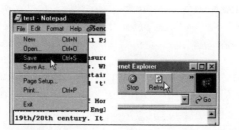

Save and Refresh!

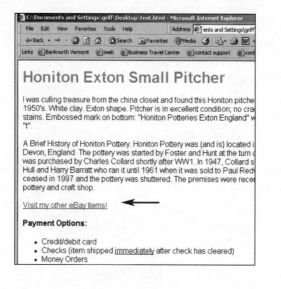

Go to the Internet Explorer window to view the link in the item description.

A FEW IMPORTANT CONSIDERATIONS ABOUT LINKS:

eBay does not allow links from your item description to your personal or commercial Web page. This is an excerpt from the eBay site regarding Links policy:

> *The eBay Item page can contain no URLs or links to, or promotional information about, any off-eBay Web page, including Web sites of the seller or any third party.*
>
> *There are two exceptions to this general rule—the eBay item page may contain a link to information related specifically to that item that:*
>
> > *Gives acknowledgment to a company that provided services related to that listing (such as counters, listing management tools, or payment and mediation services). This acknowledgment may contain both a logo (88 x 33 pixels) and up to ten words of text (HTML font size 3), but only one of those may be clickable.*
> >
> > *Points interested buyers to another Internet page that contains only more information (such as pictures, product specifications, or detailed terms and conditions) about eBay items listed by that seller.*

Just look at our eBay item description. We've gone from a single block of text to a professional-looking layout with a link in just a few minutes!

And you thought this was going to be hard. But wait! There's more. . . .

THE IMAGE TAG

In the previous chapters, when we actually listed our item live to eBay, we relied on eBay Picture Services, since it's a quick, no-fuss way to place digital pictures on your listing.

Still, it's important to know just how digital pictures are "placed" onto an eBay item page.

All Web-page graphics—jpegs, gifs, pictures, icons, etc.—are embedded onto a Web page using the **<IMG>** tag.

The **<IMG>** tag does not have a closing tag. It does not format text; it "does" something, that is, it tells the Web browser to go fetch a copy of a digital picture file somewhere on the Internet. Here's how the **<IMG>** tag works.

The **<IMG>** tag, like the **<FONT>** tag, cannot live on its tag name alone. It needs an attribute/value pair. For the **<IMG>** tag, this attribute/value pair looks like this:

<p align="center"><strong><IMG SRC=<em>url</em>></strong></p>

where *url* is a valid URL that points to either a jpeg or gif file.

Here is a URL that points to a picture of someone you might know.

http://www.unclegriff.com/images/feb-19-02-headshot05.jpg

Let's use it for our listing. Here is the complete URL.

<IMG SRC=http://www.unclegriff.com/images/feb-19-02-headshot05.jpg>

We will place it at the very bottom of our item description in Notepad, "Save and Refresh," and check to see the results.

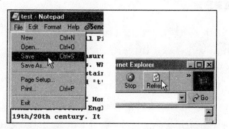

Save and Refresh!

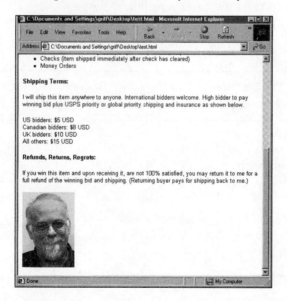

And here's our description with a shot of yours truly.

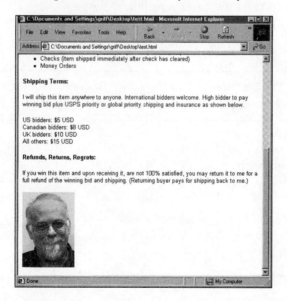

If you know the URL to a picture, you can link to it using the **<IMG>** tag. The linking is the easy part. Placing a digital picture file on a Web server is a bit harder but not impossible. Again, we will use eBay Picture Services when we list our item in the next chapter. I will show examples of using other options for digital picture hosting at the end of the next chapter.

A Note about "Borrowing" Pictures

As I mentioned earlier, if you know the URL for an image file, you can embed it into a Web page (like your eBay Item Description page) by using the **<IMG>** tag. That means it's technically possible to link to any image on the Web. However, this doesn't mean that it's OK to do so without permission.

Never link to another person's or company's images or graphics without first asking their permission. This is especially important on eBay.

CREATING YOUR OWN EXCLUSIVE EBAY GALLERY PAGE IN TEN EASY STEPS!

With just a little copying and pasting, you can add a link in all your eBay item-listing descriptions that will take buyers directly to a page of all your items displayed as an eBay Gallery.

The process involves creating the URL for the link to your own exclusive Gallery page. Follow the instructions below and you'll only have to do these steps one time. The URL for your gallery link will be good for all future eBay item listings.

IMPORTANT: You cannot have a link to your Gallery if you don't opt for Gallery images when you list your items. In order for this link to work, you should *always* opt for a Gallery image from here on.

GRIFF TIP: Studies show that listings with Gallery images get more traffic and consequently more bids. It's two bits well spent.

The Gallery option is located on the "Sell Your Item" form. The option is toward the bottom of the page and looks like this:

> **Increase your item's visibility**
>
> **Gallery picture** (this will be displayed as your first picture)
> To enter a Gallery picture URL, click the Web hosting tab above
>
> ○ No Gallery picture
>
> ◉ Gallery $0.25   Add a picture preview to your listings and search results, and be on display in the Gallery!
>
> ○ Gallery Featured $19.95   Get all the benefits of Gallery plus showcase your item in the Featured section of Gallery.

Here are the steps:

1. Go to the eBay Search link on the top of any eBay page. Search all listings in all categories using your eBay User ID (or some other word or phrase that is unique to you) as a keyword. Make sure to check the box for "Search title and description" and to select the option for "Gallery items only."

The key here is to make sure the text you use is a word or phrase that would appear in the descriptions of your listings only—no one else's.

The obvious choice is your eBay User ID, but . . .

- If your eBay User ID is an email address, try using some other word or phrase.
- Make sure that the word or phrase is unique to your listings.
- If you use a phrase, make sure that you surround it with quotes.

For our example I've used my moniker, "Uncle Griff."

Don't worry if the search comes up empty. We want the URL for the results page, not any actual results.

2. Highlight and copy the URL for the search results page by clicking your mouse once inside the Address box to highlight the text. Then click the mouse's right-hand button and select Copy.

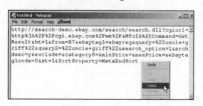

3. Open a new text file (Notepad—or Simple Text or Text Editor, if using a Mac) and paste in the URL from Step 2.

4. Use the pasted URL to create an HTML-formatted link.

In our example, I used the sentence: "Visit a Gallery of all my current eBay items!" I placed the word *Gallery* between the <A> and </A> tags so that it would be the clickable text. This long URL becomes the "value" for the attribute "HREF" so that when someone clicks the word *Gallery,* it will take him to the search results page for all my current listings displayed in Gallery view only.

Save this text file with a recognizable file name for quick access later.

Insert your eBay User ID (or the unique word or phrase used in the keyword search), along with the HTML-formatted link you created in Step 4, into all your future item descriptions.

GRIFF TIP: You can have your eBay Gallery page open up as a brand-new, separate browser window by including the following attribute=value pair after the URL inside the <a href=> tag

target=new_window

For example:

Visit a

<A   HREF=http://search-desc.ebay.com/search/search.dll?cgiurl=http%3A%2F%2Fcgi.ebay.com%2Fws%2F&MfcISAPICommand=GetResult&ht=1&from=R7&ebaytag1=ebayreg&query=%22uncle+griff%22&query2=%22uncle+griff%22&search_option=1&srchdesc=y&exclude=&category0=&minPrice=&maxPrice=&ebaytag1code=0&st=1&SortProperty=MetaEndSort **target=new_window>**

Gallery

</A>

of all my current eBay items for sale!

Make sure to provide **one** space between the end of the URL and the attribute=value

NOTE! This type of link is in full compliance with eBay's View Item Page Links Policy!

As long as you follow each step above (substituting your own unique bit of text for my "uncle griff") and you make sure you include a Gallery image for all your eBay listings, your link to your own, exclusive Gallery page will always work!

TABLE TAGS

Tables are simply grids made up of one or more cells. Here is a typical (non-HTML) four-celled table created in Microsoft Word.

In Web pages (and especially in eBay Item Descriptions) HTML tables come in very handy for creating layouts for text and pictures. We can place tables in our item description by using the **<TABLE>** tag set.

<TABLE> tags never act alone—they are used in sets just like list **<UL>** tags. The other tags that **<TABLE>** needs in order to do its job are **<TR>** (Table Row) and **<TD>** (Table Data).

HTML table cells can contain text, links, or images. **HTML** tables can also have visible or invisible borders. Here is an example of the **HTML** formatting used to create a four-celled table. Each cell contains the word *ebay*:

<TABLE BORDER=1>

<TR> <TD>ebay**</TD> <TD>** ebay**</td> </TR>**

<TR> <TD >ebay**</TD> <TD>** ebay**</td> </TR>**

</TABLE>

The above HTML, when we copy it into our test.html document, save the changes, and then refresh our browser, creates the following table:

Every HTML table starts with a **<TABLE>** tag and ends with a **</TABLE>** tag. **THIS IS EXTREMELY IMPORTANT!** If you use tables in your item description and do not close them with the proper number of **</TABLE>** tags, your item description will not appear in some types of Web browsers!

The **<TABLE>** tag may include *attribute=value* pair for **BORDER=***value*. A *value* of 0 will make the border invisible. Any other *value* will show a border of increasing size. We will use a value of **1**.

Every row in our table is indicated by a **<TR>** and **</TR>** tag. (Again, *TR* stands for "table row.")

Within every set of table row tags **<TR>** and **</TR>**, table cells are created by inserting a **<TD>** and **</TD>** tag for each cell. (To repeat, *TD* stands for "table data.")

TEXT PLACEMENT USING TABLE TAGS

Tables can be useful for laying out text as data in cells. For example, our various shipping costs per location will look better if we place the data in a table. Here's how that section of our eBay item description looks now.

We have four rows of data for each location. Each row contains two parts: one for location and one for cost. Thus, we need a table of four rows with two columns for a total of eight cells. I like to type out the table tags first before typing in the data. Each row starts with an opening <TR> table row tag and ends with a closing </TR> table row tag. In between the <TR> and </TR> for each row, there are two sets of table data tags <TD> </TD>—one for each cell. (Remember, we need two cells for each row.) I am also going to add a fifth row for our headers: "location" and "shipping costs."

<TABLE BORDER=1>

<TR> <TD> </TD> <TD> </TD> </TR>

<TR> <TD> </TD> <TD> </TD> </TR>

<TR> <TD> </TD> <TD> </TD> </TR>

<TR> <TD> </TD> <TD> </TD> </TR>

<TR> <TD> </TD> <TD> </TD> </TR>

</TABLE>

Let's fill in the data for each cell. We *carefully* type it in between each **<TD>** and **</TD>** tag:

<TABLE BORDER=1>

<TR><TD>Ship To Location</TD> <TD>Shipping (USD)</TD></TR>

<TR> <TD>US </TD> <TD>$5 </TD> </TR>

<TR> <TD>Canada </TD> <TD>$8 </TD> </TR>

<TR> <TD> UK </TD> <TD> $10 </TD> </TR>

<TR> <TD>All Others </TD> <TD>$15 </TD> </TR>

</TABLE>

I say carefully because if you type the data in the wrong place, your table will be a mess.

We now type this set of TABLE tags with data into our eBay item description in our Notepad file in place of the original shipping costs.

Save and Refresh!

Here's what our new tabled Shipping costs look like viewed through Internet Explorer.

Data like our shipping costs is much easier to read when it is displayed in a table.

Creating Tables bigger or fancier than a few rows and columns is difficult to do "by hand" without making simple errors created by mistyping a tag name or leaving off a closing tag. If you create HTML tables by hand for your eBay listing description (and I urge you to do so), keep them simple. Two columns and two to five rows should be easy to handle.

PICTURE PLACEMENT USING TABLE TAGS

The following HTML shows an example of how to use a simple two-celled table to align two images in an eBay item description. Between each **<TD>** and **</TD>** tag, there is a complete **<IMG SRC>** tag for a valid digital picture file. (These are digital pictures of our item that I uploaded to a Web server—**www.sover.net**—back in my old home state of Vermont. "How to Upload Digital Pictures" is covered at the end of the next chapter.)

<TABLE BORDER=1>

<TR>

<TD><IMG SRC=http://www.sover.net/~jimgriff/images/honiton03.jpg></TD>

<TD><IMG SRC=http://www.sover.net/~jimgriff/images/honiton04.jpg></TD>

</TR>

</TABLE>

Let's **Paste** the above HTML formatting into our item description before the Payment Options section. Bidders like to see pictures ASAP!

Save and Refresh . . . and here's our item description viewed in Internet Explorer.

There is a very big advantage to embedding digital image files into a table as opposed to without.

When a Web browser gets to an <IMG> tag, it stops loading the rest of the page as the pictures download. For fast Internet connections, this is not a big issue, but for those with slow dial-up connections, the wait can be annoying. Placing your image URLs in an HTML table helps to remedy this problem. Web browsers will load the table and keep loading the rest of the item page while the pictures load into the table cells, allowing the potential bidder to read the rest of the contents of the item description while the pictures download.

OTHER HTML TAGS

To center text or a picture on a Web page, use the **<CENTER>** tags

<CENTER>

</CENTER>

Let's use the **<CENTER>** tag to center my picture on the item description page:

```
<P>
<CENTER>
<IMG SRC=http://www.sover.net/~jimgriff/images/feb-19-02-headshot05.jpg><BR>
Thanks for shopping with Uncle!
</CENTER>
```

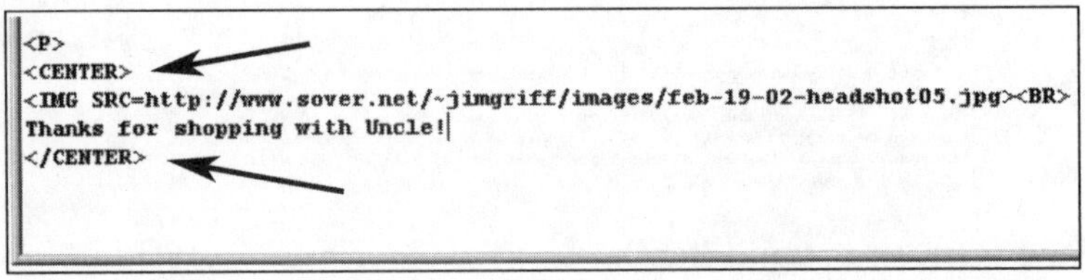

Save and Refresh!

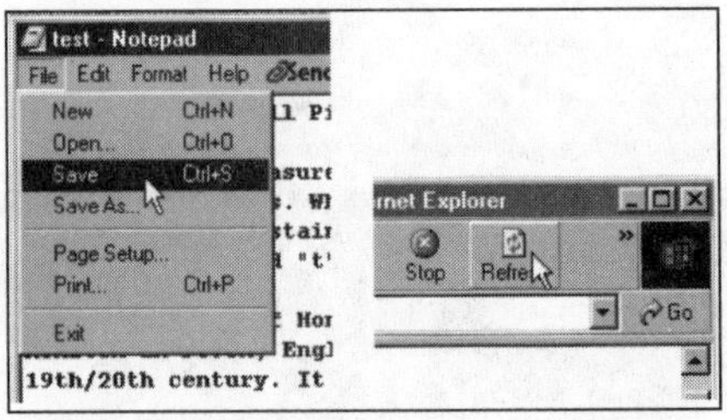

View the changes in Internet Explorer:

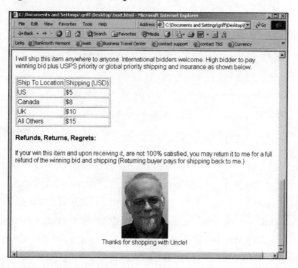

THE HORIZONTAL RULE TAG

The **<HR>** tag places a horizontal rule into the Web page. It comes in handy for separating sections of a Web page or eBay Item Description page.

Let's slip one in our item description to see what it does.

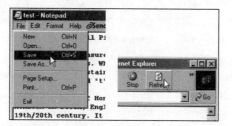

Save and Refresh!

Ta da! A Horizontal Rule!

A Brief History of Honiton Pottery. Honiton Pottery was (and is) located in the town of Honiton in Devon, England. The pottery was started by Foster and Hunt at the turn of the 19th/20th century. It was purchased by Charles Collard shortly after WW1. In 1947, Collard sold the pottery to Norman Hull and Harry Barratt who ran it until 1961 when it was sold to Paul Redvers. All production ceased in 1997 and the pottery was shuttered. The premises were recently reopened as a pottery and craft shop.

Visit my other eBay Items!

Payment Options:

- Credit/debit card
- Checks (item shipped immediately after check has cleared)
- Money Orders

Shipping Terms:

Using simple HTML tags, we've turned a boring, hard-to-read block of text into a polished and professional-looking eBay item description.

There's an additional benefit to creating our eBay item description in a separate text file. We can now save this file and use it over and over again as a template for future eBay listings, effectively avoiding endless retyping of our payment options or shipping and return policies. Saving the description also preserves our layout for future use as well.

That wasn't so difficult, was it? I told you HTML would be a snap. Now that we've finished this chapter, I have to fess up.

Very few sellers actually work through HTML they way we just did. Many eBay sellers purchase predesigned templates with fancy borders, backgrounds, and shapes and simply fill in their text for each listing. Some eBay sellers use specialized applications called Web editors to create their item descriptions. Web editors are like word processors for Web pages. They allow you to create a Web page without typing a single HTML tag.

So why did I put you through this HTML tutorial? Because, if you know how the HTML behind Web pages, and specifically eBay Item Description pages, works, you'll be better prepared to troubleshoot problems as they might arise.

Plus, you have to admit—this has been fun! You've accomplished something solid and useful that you can immediately put to work in your eBay listings.

GRIFF TIP: In the beginning of this chapter, we named our file "test.html." This file can be saved for use as a "template" for future eBay listings. One problem: If we save and close this file and then subsequently click on it to reopen it, it will open in either Internet Explorer or Netscape (depending on which browser you use), not Notepad. We can only make changes in this file when it is open in Notepad. If we open it in Internet Explorer, we won't be able to edit it, since IE is an "output" window and doesn't accept "input."

In Windows, in order to force our "test.html" file to open in Notepad, we need to follow these steps:

Go to your Desktop, hover the mouse cursor over the icon for "test.html," and click the mouse's right-hand button to display a pop-up menu containing special commands.

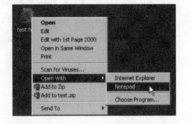

Select "Open With" and then select "Notepad" from the pop-up menus. This will open the test.html file in Notepad.

CREATING YOUR EBAY ITEM DESCRIPTION WITH FRONTPAGE

It is possible to create professional item descriptions without actually hard-copying the HTML around your text. You can use a **Web editor**. My favorite is **Microsoft FrontPage**. It isn't expensive and you can do lots of cool stuff with it.

A Web editor like FrontPage is the Web-page-based equivalent of a word processor. Instead of typing in your HTML tags to achieve some text formatting and then checking the results in a Web browser, you can create your description inside a window in FrontPage exactly the same way you would create and format a document in Microsoft Word.

This is a great way to save time, especially when you are creating complex table structures (for example, nested tables—a real headache to create by hand). There are a few simple steps to follow and a few possible pitfalls to avoid. I will outline them in order below:

First, start FrontPage.

419

(I am assuming you have FrontPage installed on your computer. If not, visit the Microsoft Web site or your local computer/software/office supplies merchant in order to purchase a copy.)

When FrontPage opens, you should see a version of the screen below.

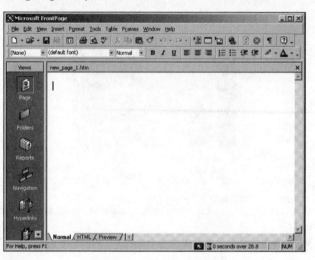

If your copy of FrontPage didn't open a new page by default, click on File . . . New . . . Page to open one.

At the bottom of the main window, there are three tabs for three different screen views. They are marked "Normal," "HTML," and "Preview."

We will type our item description directly into the "Normal" screen.

You use FrontPage the same way you use a word processor. To begin, I will use the Table command to draw a simple, multicelled HTML table. Click on Table, Draw Table on the menu command bar.

Draw a simple table and add cells.

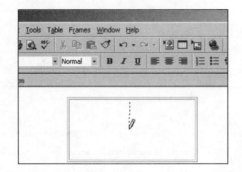

Since this book is not a manual on how to use FrontPage, you'll have to figure out the rest of the commands on your own. If you are familiar with Word (or any other word processor), the commands should be easy to master. (For more information on how to create a page with various colors, tables, cell arrangements, etc., in FrontPage, click the Help link on the FrontPage menu command bar.)

Using the various commands and tools, I created the following item description.

Not bad. Once you have your listing looking exactly like you want it to look, click on the "HTML" tag on the bottom of the FrontPage window.

This will show you an editable "view" of the HTML behind the page you have just created.

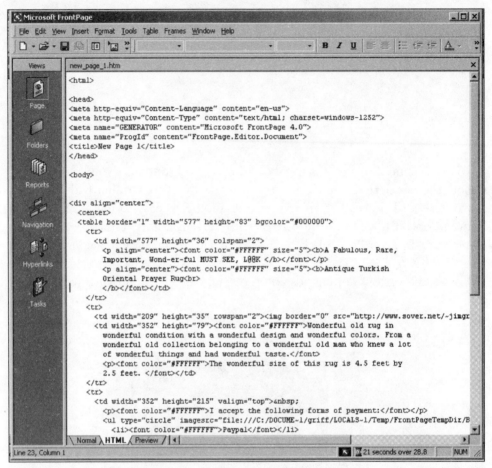

The next step involves highlighting *select* HTML-formatted text on this window to then copy and paste into either a Notepad file or directly into the Text box on the eBay Sell Your Item page. *Do not highlight all of the HTML text on this screen!* Highlight only the text between and excluding the first <body> tag and the closing </body> tag.

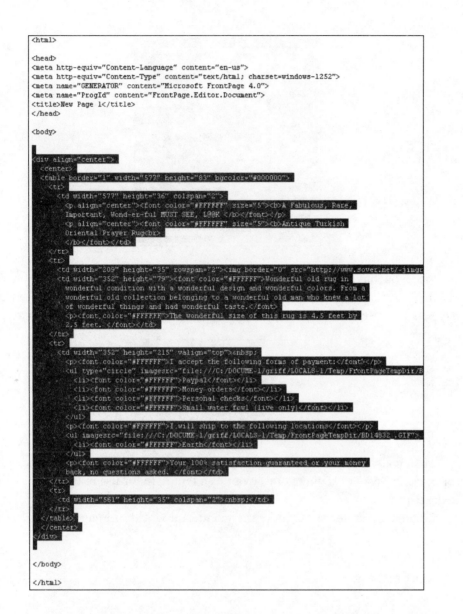

```
<html>

<head>
<meta http-equiv="Content-Language" content="en-us">
<meta http-equiv="Content-Type" content="text/html; charset=windows-1252">
<meta name="GENERATOR" content="Microsoft FrontPage 4.0">
<meta name="ProgId" content="FrontPage.Editor.Document">
<title>New Page 1</title>
</head>

<body>

<div align="center">
  <center>
  <table border="1" width="572" height="83" bgcolor="#000000">
    <tr>
      <td width="577" height="36" colspan="2">
        <p align="center"><font color="#FFFFFF" size="5"><b>A Fabulous, Rare,
        Important, Wond-er-ful MUST SEE, L@@K </b></font></p>
        <p align="center"><font color="#FFFFFF" size="5"><b>Antique Turkish
        Oriental Prayer Rug<br>
        </b></font></td>
    </tr>
    <tr>
      <td width="209" height="35" rowspan="2"><img border="0" src="http://www.sover.net/~jimgr
      <td width="352" height="79"><font color="#FFFFFF">Wonderful old rug in
      wonderful condition with a wonderful design and wonderful colors. From a
      wonderful old collection belonging to a wonderful old man who knew a lot
      of wonderful things and had wonderful taste.</font>
      <p><font color="#FFFFFF">The wonderful size of this rug is 4.5 feet by
      2.5 feet. </font></td>
    </tr>
    <tr>
      <td width="352" height="215" valign="top"> 
      <p><font color="#FFFFFF">I accept the following forms of payment:</font></p>
      <ul type="circle" imagesrc="file:///C:/DOCUME~1/griff/LOCALS~1/Temp/FrontPageTempDir/B
        <li><font color="#FFFFFF">Paypal</font></li>
        <li><font color="#FFFFFF">Money orders</font></li>
        <li><font color="#FFFFFF">Personal checks</font></li>
        <li><font color="#FFFFFF">Small water fowl (live only)</font></li>
      </ul>
      <p><font color="#FFFFFF">I will ship to the following locations</font></p>
      <ul imagesrc="file:///C:/DOCUME~1/griff/LOCALS~1/Temp/FrontPageTempDir/BD14832_.GIF">
        <li><font color="#FFFFFF">Earth</font></li>
      </ul>
      <p><font color="#FFFFFF">Your 100% satisfaction guaranteed or your money
      back, no questions asked. </font></td>
    </tr>
    <tr>
      <td width="561" height="35" colspan="2"> </td>
    </tr>
  </table>
  </center>
</div>

</body>

</html>
```

The caution here is to not copy anything outside of and including the <body> tags. The tags outside of this area can mess up your item description on the eBay page in such a way that some Web browsers won't be able to display the description and even worse, the bid section of the item page!

Copy the highlighted text by right-clicking your mouse button and selecting "Copy."

Once you have copied the HTML between the two <body> tags on the HTML view screen, you can paste it directly into the Description box on the eBay Sell Your Item page (or into any bulk upload software like Turbo Lister).

You can also copy and paste the HTML-formatted text into a Notepad. This is an excellent way of saving your layout as a template for use in future eBay listing descriptions.

In the next chapter, we explore the wonderful world of image hosting.

7

Advanced Image Hosting Solutions

Four years ago, Christopher Spencer was a publicist and personal manager for actors.

"I had a very stressful job working twelve- to fourteen-hour days for unappreciative clients who would whine because they were only making $12,000 a week. I was miserable and unhappy."

Four years ago, Christopher decided to take charge of his life. He started out eBay-selling antiques and collectibles.

"I know virtually nothing about antiques and I don't own any inventory. I work with very honorable and reputable dealers in the L.A. area who provide me with accurate, honest descriptions for the items that I take on consignment. Last year I sold over $400,000 worth of antiques and collectibles on eBay."

Today, Christopher is not only a Gold Level eBay PowerSeller ("borntodeal"), he's also a regular instructor at eBay University seminars.

"I like to teach others how to use the site so that they can make their business better and see the money I am seeing. It is a really fun life!"

eBay Listings and Digital Pictures—Advanced Solutions

For the first-time eBay seller, eBay Picture Services is invaluable. In our earlier example listings, we relied on eBay Picture Services to "host" (upload, store, and display) our digital pictures in our eBay listing. As a digital-picture hosting option, the eBay Picture Services is simple, fast, and most important, the service automatically and seamlessly places our pictures on our listing page.

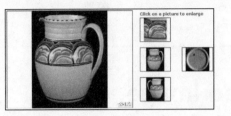

There are other digital picture-hosting solutions that you can employ either in place of, or in combination with, eBay Picture Services.

There are solid advantages to using other hosting solutions: You can add more than six pictures to a listing; you have more options regarding the placement and layout of your item images; and if you are subscribed to an Internet Service Provider, it may not cost you anything extra.

DIGITAL PICTURES—OTHER SOLUTIONS

Before we explore some of these other digital-picture solutions for displaying digital pictures in your eBay listings, we need to examine a few Internet and digital pictures basics.

PICTURES ON A WEB PAGE—HOW DOES THAT WORK?

eBay item pages are Web pages that contain text and images.

To our eyes, the text and images on an eBay item page make up one complete Web-page computer screen, and in fact, though they do "live" together as a single Web page in our Web browser, they didn't start off that way.

Usually, the two major components of a Web page—text and pictures—actually start out as separate files stored in separate locations on the Internet. That is, the text for the Web page is stored on one Web server while the digital-picture files may be stored on another Web server (which could be halfway around the world!).

It's the job of your Web browser to collect copies of all these components and put them together on your computer screen for you to view as one complete page.

I put up a simple Web page to help illustrate how the process of displaying a Web page with images works. If you are near a computer connected to the Internet, go to **http://www.xmission.com/~jimgriff/book/bookexample.html** and follow along. (Make sure you type in the "tilde" character before the username "jimgriff.")

The Web page at the end of the URL above is a single file called "bookexample.html." It looks like this:

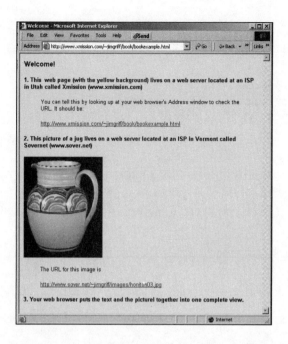

The Web page is actually a simple text file almost exactly like the one we created in the last chapter. (It has a few added HTML tags that are necessary for making a true Web page.)

Here is a copy of the text file I created in Notepad. It contains the HTML-formatted text that makes up our little yellow Web page.

Some of this should look familiar. There are <P> and <B> tags, as well as some new tags not covered. Scroll through the file to find the <img> tag:

```
ISP in Vermont called Sovernet (www.sover.net)</b></p>
<p><img border="0"
src="http://www.sover.net/~jimgriff/images/honiton03.jpg"
width="189" height="236"></p>
```

I have underlined the URL within the <img> tag.

http://www.sover.net/~jimgriff/images/honiton03.jpg

The complete HTML tag is

<img border="0" src="http://www.sover.net/~jimgriff/images/honiton03.jpg" width="189" height="236">

There are attributes inside this <img> tag for "border," "width," and "height" as well as the familiar "src."

The URL after "src" points to a picture file called "honiton03.jpg,"

which "lives" in a folder called "images,"

http://www.sover.net/~jimgriff/images/honiton03.jpg

which is nested inside a folder called "~jimgriff,"

http://www.sover.net/~jimgriff/images/honiton03.jpg

which lives on a Web server called www.sover.net

http://www.sover.net/~jimgriff/images/honiton03.jpg

The **www.sover.net** Web server is physically located at an ISP called Sovernet, which is nestled in the beautiful green mountains of Vermont.

I have an ISP account with Sovernet. As part of that account, I have "space" set aside in my username for storing files. I moved ("uploaded") a copy of the "honiton03.jpg" picture from my computer, over the Internet to the sover.net Web server, using a special type of application on my computer known as an "FTP client." (More on FTP later in this chapter.)

Once I uploaded a copy of the picture file to www.sover.net, I then uploaded a copy of the text file called "bookexample.html" to another Web server called Xmission, which is located in Salt Lake City, Utah. I also have an account with Xmission.

I needed to upload a copy of this text file in order to make it a Web page that can be accessed by anyone on the Internet (like you, if you navigated to it earlier as part of this exercise). Again, we'll explore "uploading" in depth later in this chapter.

The URL for my little yellow Web page is **http://www.xmission.com/~jimgriff/book/bookexample.html.**

The HTML file, "bookexample.html" "lives" inside a subfolder called "book," which is nestled inside another folder called "~jimgriff," which is located on the **www.xmission.com** Web server.

All my components are in place. The picture file lives on a server in Vermont. The little yellow Web page lives on a server in Utah.

Here's what happened when you opened the link **http://www.xmission.com/~jimgriff/book/bookexample.html** in your Web browser.

Your Web browser immediately sent a request through the Internet for the filename located at the end of the URL.

The Web server at Xmission on which the requested file resides then sent a copy of the HTML file back to your computer and it opened up in your Web browser.

The browser then started to "parse" (scan) and convert the HTML-formatted text in the file into viewable text, which is displayed in the Web browser's window.

While parsing the HTML file, the Web browser came across the <IMG> tag for the picture file located in Vermont. The Web browser read the URL.

The computer then sent a request for a copy of the picture file to the location indicated by the URL in the <IMG> tag.

The Web server back in Vermont received and granted the request for a copy of "honiton03.jpg" and sent a copy of the digital picture back to your computer.

The computer hands the copy of the digital picture to the Web browser, which "embeds" the copy of the digital picture file into the exact place on the page where the original <IMG> tag lives.

You have a complete Web page with text and picture in your Web browser!

Every time you open a Web page in your Web browser, this same process occurs. If there are no pictures or files embedded into the page, then only one request is made—for the Web-page HTML file itself. For each image file embedded into the HTML text file, your computer needs to make a request out to the Internet for a copy of the file. This is why a page with several pictures located in different physical locations can sometimes take a while to display completely.

Now that you have a better understanding of how digital pictures are retrieved from the Internet and displayed in your Web browser window, we can explore other digital picture options besides eBay Picture Services.

DIGITAL PICTURE HOSTING (IMAGE HOSTING)

First, some definitions:

Digital picture hosting (otherwise known as "**image hosting**") is the moving ("**uploading**") of a copy of your digital picture file from your computer to a remote Web server on the Internet, where it is stored ("**hosted**") for retrieval by any other Internet user.

The digital picture is then displayed on an item page by typing ("**embedding**") the digital picture Internet address ("**URL**" or Uniform Resource Locator) into the item text. The embedded URL is said to "**reference**" the actual image file.

eBay Picture Services is an automatic image hosting service. You only need to point to a picture on your hard drive and eBay Picture Services does the rest (upload the file to a Web server, host the file, embed the URL for your picture at the bottom of your listing, and display the picture file on your item page).

As I mentioned earlier, there are definite advantages to hosting image files using solutions other than eBay Picture Services. To repeat: You can host more than six pictures; you can place the images wherever you choose inside your item text; and it may not cost you, since you may be paying for the hosting service already!

Hosting an image file is a three-part process:

1. Acquiring hosting space on a Web server
2. Moving copies of your picture files to a Web server
3. Embedding copies of these picture files in your eBay Item Description text by using special HTML to go get the picture file and display it in the item page

The first step is to find hosting space on the Internet.

1. ACQUIRING HOSTING SPACE ON A WEB SERVER

Your ISP

If you are paying an Internet Service Provider (ISP) to access the Internet, you most likely have file hosting space set aside for your use as a part of your service package. For example, if you are an AOL user, you automatically have twelve megabytes set aside on the AOL Web servers for your exclusive use.

As I mentioned, I use an ISP in Vermont called Sovernet. As part of my monthly dial-up access plan, Sovernet provides me with several megabytes of Web server space where I can store my image files.

Most every local-based ISP will provide hosting space. Contact your ISP for more information.

Other Hosting Services

There are many online companies that provide image-hosting services. Most charge a small fee.

You can view a vast list of them by going to **www.google.com** and searching on "image hosting."

2. MOVING COPIES OF YOUR PICTURE FILES TO A WEB SERVER

Once you have acquired space for image hosting, the next step is to upload copies of your digital pictures from your computer to this image-hosting space. The process of moving copies of your digital picture files from your computer to a Web server is called "File Transfer Protocol" or "FTP" for short. Note these two terms—I will use them frequently in the next few pages.

For some ISPs, you will need a special FTP application to move copies of digital picture files from your computer to your Web server space.

Other ISPs (like AOL) have FTP software embedded within their own software, so you don't need a separate FTP application.

In order to move copies of my image files from my computer to my space at Sovernet, I often use something called FTP, which stands for File Transfer Protocol. There are several options for using FTP. You can download one of several popular freeware and shareware FTP client applications from any of the download sites on the Internet.

Try **www.tucows.com** and type in "FTP" as a search for programs to download.

I downloaded and installed an FTP application called "WS_FTP" from the **www.tocows.com** site. I started the application by clicking its icon on my Start menu. This is the "application interface" for the most recent version of "WS_FTP":

Most FTP applications look something like this. FTP applications usually have two windows. The one on the left shows the contents of my computer's hard drive. The one on the right is empty now, but once I connect to sover.net, it will show the contents of my personal Web server space there.

To connect, I clicked the Connect button on the bottom left-hand corner of the application window:

This brings up a dialog box where I can enter a new "site" connection. Sover-net's Web site has all the information I need for establishing an FTP connection.

GRIFF TIP: Your ISP will post on their Web site all the information you need for configuring the FTP connection to your Web server space.

I select the folder for My Sites and then I click the button labeled "Create Site . . ."

On the following screens, I enter the requested information in the spaces provided. I entered a name—Sovernet—for the new profile and opted to have it placed in the folder for "My Sites."

I clicked the Next button and in the next screen, I entered the Host Name (as provided to me by the folks at Sovernet. Again, you must obtain your host name from your ISP).

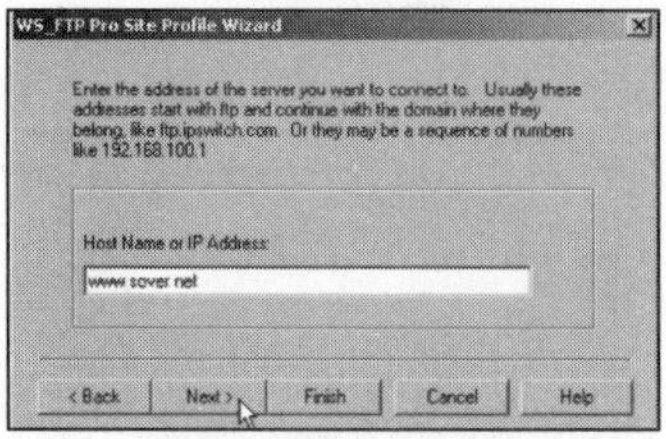

I again clicked Next to move to the next screen to enter my User ID and Password. (Your ISP will tell you if you need an "account.")

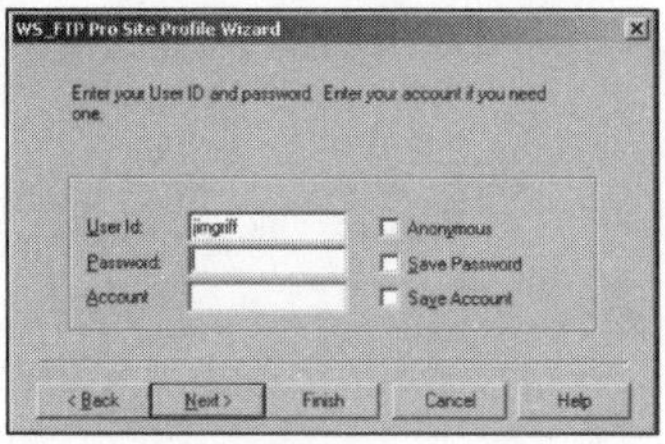

I clicked the Next button to select the server type, which for most cases will be "FTP," and then I clicked Finish.

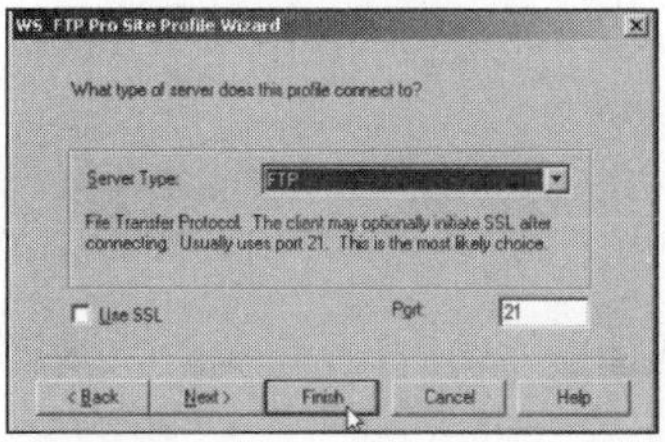

My connection profile is now recorded for quick future access. To connect to my FTP space at Sovernet, I click the Connect button.

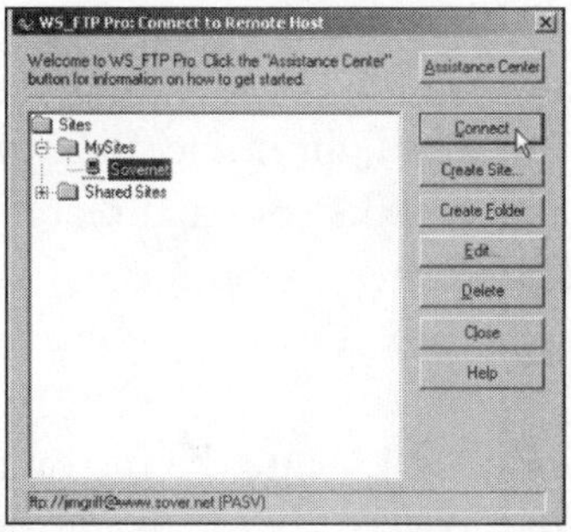

Since I didn't provide my password when I created my profile for Sovernet, the system will prompt me for one before it will complete the connection.

Click Connect and the right-hand FTP window will display the file contents of the remote Web server back in Vermont.

Using this FTP application, I can now create folders or delete folders or files on my Web server space *almost like it was a separate hard drive on my own computer!* I can also move files back and forth from one window to the other. To move a copy of an edited digital picture of my eBay Item from my computer to my Web server space, I locate the file on my hard drive in the left-hand window and either drag and drop it or highlight it and click the right arrow between the windows. I first have to make sure the source directory on my computer and the target directory or folder at sover.net are both open in their windows.

Now I can upload a copy of any file on my computer to my Web server space at Sovernet.

First, in the left-hand window, I locate the file on my computer I wish to up-load (by clicking through the folders and/or using the green arrow to move up one level in the folder hierarchy on my hard drive). The file I am looking for is a picture file called "honiton03.jpg." I find and then highlight the file.

Next I must navigate to the folder into which I want to place the copy of honiton03.jpg. In the right-hand window, I locate and double-click the "images" folder to open it.

Once the "images" folder is open, I can click the right-hand arrow to move copy of the "honiton03.jpg" file from the left-hand window to the right-hand window.

This will tell the FTP application to send a copy of the selected file through the Internet to the "images" folder in the "~jimgriff" directory on the sover.net Web server. A status window shows the progress of the File Transfer.

Once the transfer is complete, a copy of the honiton03.jpg file now lives on the sover.net Web server and is accessible to the entire Internet using the unique URL or address to locate it. In this case, the URL is:

http://www.sover.net/~jimgriff/images/honiton03.jpg

the web server address — my folder — the images folder — the specific filename

I can also check the URL to make sure it is valid by typing it into my Web browser and hitting Enter.

If the image displays, then the URL is correctly typed and valid.

This is a good habit to acquire. Check your picture URLs in a Web browser to make sure they are valid. Better to correct mistakes in a URL before you list the item than have to revise the item after it is listed.

Using Internet Explorer As an FTP Client

A little-known feature of the latest version of Internet Explorer is that is can be used as an FTP client!

If you have FTP space somewhere (check with your Internet Service Provider) and you have a user ID and password, you can use your Internet Explorer Web browser along with a Windows Explorer window to move files to and from your computer and a remote FTP location.

1. Open Internet Explorer.

2. Type the following into the address window, substituting your actual User Name and password for *username* and *password* an your ISP's domain name for *domain.name*.

ftp://username:password@ftp.domain.name

Here is an example: ftp://jimgriff:***********@ftp.sover.net.

(No, I won't tell you my password, thankyouverymuch.)

3. Open Windows Explorer.

4. Position the two windows so that you can drag and drop files back and forth from either window.

5. You can create and delete directories (folders) on your remote FTP space by using the File, New command on the Internet Explorer menu bar.

6. You can also rename, move, and delete files on your FTP space.

HOSTING DIGITAL PICTURE FILES AT AOL

First, you'll need to have an AOL account! So many eBay sellers already do, but the majority of them are unaware that along with their monthly AOL access and AOL email, they are also paying for twelve megabytes of AOL Web space. Twelve MBs of server space can come in real handy for hosting eBay image files.

The steps for uploading your digital pictures onto your space at AOL are easy to find. Open your AOL software and search on keyword "My FTP Space" to bring up the "my ftp space" box (1).

This brings up the My FTP Space window, which is AOL's built-in FTP application. (**NOTE:** You don't need to download and install an application like WS_FTP LE when using your AOL account for hosting.)

Click on See My FTP Space (2) to see the current contents of your AOL FTP space.

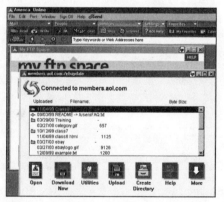

NOTE: AOL's built-in FTP application has only one window.

Using this window, you can create new directories (folders) and you can upload files from your computer to AOL by clicking the icon for "Upload." Let's click Upload to start the process.

Next, you have to type a name for the file. This is an unusual procedure and not how most other FTP applications work. With AOL's FTP procedure, you are in effect creating an empty file on the AOL server and giving the empty file a name into which the file on your computer will be placed once you begin the uploading process. It's confusing. To prevent any mix-ups, I usually type in the same name as the file on my hard drive I want to upload. I suggest you do the same.

I type in the name "honiton03.jpg" and then click Continue. In the "Upload File" window that pops up, I click the Select File icon to choose a file on my hard drive:

This brings up an "Attach File" window. I navigate through my hard drive to the file I wish to upload.

Once I have located the file, I double-click it to Open it. The Path of the file will show up in the File: box on the Upload File window. Next, I click the Send icon:

The file will upload to your FTP space at AOL. A message will alert you when the transfer is complete. Click OK and you are nearly done.

To check if the file was successfully uploaded into the proper directory, I click on the "images" directory to find the file.

There it is!

Whenever I host images or files at AOL, I like to double-check that they were uploaded correctly, so I always recheck the directory into which they were uploaded.

Now, let's test the image in a browser and get its URL. Go to any Web browser, type in the following—**http://members.aol.com/**—and put your AOL user name after the last forward slash. Here's mine: **http://members.aol.com/ebaydale** (see below).

If you haven't previously set up an actual AOL member's hometown Web page, the URL with your AOL user name will display the contents of your AOL FTP space.

If I click the link for the "images" folder, I should see my digital picture named "honiton03.jpg." And there it is:

If I click the image name, it should display the actual digital picture . . .

. . . and it does.

GRIFF TIP: You can usually view the file contents of any Web folder *if* the folder does not contain a file named "index.html." Some Web servers (like **www.xmission.com**) are set up so that the contents of a user's Web folders are not ever readable, even if they do not contain an "index.html" file.

This ability to read the contents of a Web folder can come in very handy should you need to troubleshoot one of your own URLs.

3. EMBEDDING DIGITAL PICTURE FILE URLS IN YOUR EBAY ITEM DESCRIPTION

You have uploaded your item pictures to your own Web server space and you have the URLs (addresses) for each.

The last step in the process is to embed your digital pictures in your item description. You do this by typing, into the item description, the URL for each digital picture you uploaded in Step 2. Each URL is placed inside an HTML <IMG> tag.

In the previous step, I uploaded a file up to my Web server space at Sovernet. Here is the URL for that digital picture:

http://www.sover.net/~jimgriff/images/honiton03.jpg

Here is how the URL looks when used as the value for the attribute "src" inside an <IMG> tag:

<IMG src=http://www.sover.net/~jimgriff/images/honiton03.jpg >

Let's review what happens when the Web browser gets to an <IMG> tag with a URL as the value for an "src" attribute:

<IMG src=http://www.sover.net/~jimgriff/images/honiton03.jpg >

Our URL shows the address location for a file called "honiton03.jpg," which lives in a directory or folder called "images/," which in turn lives inside a directory folder called "~jimgriff/," which in turn lives on a Web server called **www.sover.net.**

GRIFF TIP: Think of any URL as a letter's mailing address, only in reverse. Whereas for a mailing address, the most specific final destination—the name of the recipient of the letter—is always on the top of the address;

Mr. Honiton03 JPG

Image Street

Jimgriff, sover.net, www
----
in a URL, the final destination—the filename—is always at the end of the address:

http://www.sover.net/~jimgriff/images/honiton03.jpg

When the browser gets to the "<IMG" part of the <IMG> tag, it knows that special instructions will follow.

The browser looks next for the "src" attribute and reads, from left to right, the URL after the "equals" sign. The URL tells the browser where on the Internet it needs to send a request for a file. Again, the actual file name is always at the very end of the URL. So reading from left to right, the browser tells the computer to go to a Web server called "sover.net" and ask if there is a file named "honiton02.jpg" in a subdirectory called "images" in a next-level subdirectory called "~jimgriff," and, if there is such a file in such location, would the Web server be so kind as to send a copy of the file back through the Internet to your computer?

If the URL is correct, the Web server "serves" a copy of the digital picture named "honiton03.jpg" through the Internet back to your computer, which passes the file to your Web browser, which then displays the copy of the digital picture by "embedding" it within the Web page at the very spot in the HTML document behind the page where the <IMG> tag appears.

GRIFF TIP: You can quickly find the URL for any picture on the Web by using a special feature in Internet Explorer along with your right mouse button.

Find a picture on the Web. Hover your mouse over the picture and click the right-hand button on your mouse. Select Properties from the pop-up menu:

In the Properties box, there is a field for "Address (URL)." Highlight the URL by holding down your left mouse button and dragging the mouse cursor over the URL itself. Once it is entirely highlighted, click the right mouse button and select Copy.

The URL for the picture is now copied to your Windows (or Mac) Clipboard, ready to paste into any text document.

Using the "Save Picture As . . ." menu option in the same pop-up window,

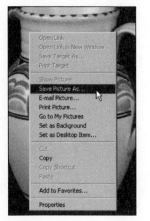

you can save a copy of the digital picture somewhere on your computer!

GRIFF TIP:

Get into the habit of creating all your files in lowercase. "honiton03.jpg" and "honiton03.JPG" are two different files as far as a Web browser is concerned, and one cannot be used to reference the other.

8

Trust and Safety for Sellers

Selling on eBay can be great fun as well as potentially profitable. I hope this book proves to be of some help on your path to successful eBay selling. However, before you start out, there is one area of selling that many sellers don't give due consideration, even after they have been selling on eBay for months years.

THE RULES

Yes, Virginia, there are rules for selling on eBay, and all eBay sellers are expected to become fully acquainted with the rules before they start selling.

As of this writing, "the rules" are better known on eBay as Trust and Safety. We will cover the most common topics of eBay Trust and Safety as they relate directly to sellers. I strongly suggest that you visit the site as soon as possible and read them all in greater detail.

Not all the rules are obvious! There are many procedural ins and outs to eBay selling. It would be foolish for any eBay seller to assume she knows and understands all the rules without reading them carefully.

So, unless you don't mind having your listings ended, receiving warnings for prohibited activity, or having your registration on eBay suspended, possibly forever, then this chapter is an absolute must.

QUESTIONABLE OR PROHIBITED PRACTICES AND ACTIVITIES

All in the eBay community—buyers and sellers alike—are expected to adhere to certain standards of business conduct when using eBay. However, since the typical eBay transaction usually has the buyer sending payment to the seller before goods are shipped, eBay Sellers bear a slightly larger share of responsibility when it comes to staying within the rules.

Most of the rules pertaining to eBay selling are based on good old common sense. Before you initiate some action on eBay—writing out an item description, constructing a terms of service for your buyers, and so on—ask yourself this question: "Will my action provide my listings or my online business with an unfair advantage over other sellers?" If the answer is yes or even maybe, then you need to check the list of policies and offenses on the eBay Rules and Safety page (navigation road map below).

For example, you might think that a great way to promote your business would be to link to your Web site directly off your eBay Item Description page. After all, why shouldn't you take advantage of the traffic that your eBay item is bound to receive? With potentially hundreds of visitors to your eBay listing, a link to your Web site would indeed be to your benefit. However, linking to your Web site from your eBay listing description is strictly prohibited. You may not have realized this, but ignorance will be little comfort when all of your offending listings are ended early by eBay.

Your best protection against having all of your eBay listings ended is to Know The Rules! Safeguard the time and effort you put into listing your items on eBay by reading through all of the eBay selling rules and selling policies before you list an item for bid or sale.

GRIFF TIP: You can navigate to any of the Trust and Safety information and reporting pages by following these steps:

Click the **My eBay** link on top of any eBay page (sign in if required).

Click on the **Selling (or Selling Manager)** tab.

Scroll down to the bottom of the page and under the **Trust and Safety** section, click on the appropriate link for either:

> Seller Payment Protection
> Listing policies
> Items not allowed
> Non-paying bidder program
> Trading violations
> Dispute resolution

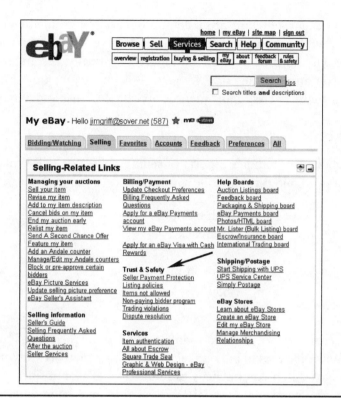

eBay Trust and Safety—a History and Outline

In 1997, we in eBay Customer Support created a special department called Safe-Harbor. SafeHarbor's mission was to explain and apply the rules, processes, and policies governing all eBay members' activity on the eBay site. In the very beginning, the SafeHarbor team had jurisdiction over all potentially prohibited site activity, from bidding and feedback offenses to prohibited items.

In 1999 eBay entered its most frenetic period of explosive growth, and with this growth came whole new areas of prohibited activities and items. The number of new offenses, such as feedback abuse and spam, rose along with the exploding number of new users who registered on eBay each day. It soon became apparent to all of us in customer support and eBay in general that one department alone could not adequately handle these increasingly complex issues and their attendant questions. Thus, in early 1999, a decision was made to split SafeHarbor into four separate departments—SafeHarbor, Community Watch, Fraud, and VeRO.

These four separate teams are made up of specially trained eBay Customer Support reps, with experience in all the particular eBay site rules and policies governing activity on the eBay site and, more specifically, certain eBay member activity both on and off the eBay Web site. All four teams now live under the umbrella of the customer-support meta-team called "Trust and Safety."

SAFEHARBOR

The SafeHarbor team handles reports of selling abuses or seller rule violations, including but not limited to the following areas:

> Shill bidding
> Feedback
> Non-paying bidders
> Contact information
> Spam

Shill Bidding

Simply put, sellers are not allowed to inflate the bid for their items by employing second accounts or agents to bid on their items. This activity is known as **shill bidding**. Not only is shill bidding strictly prohibited on eBay, but since the activity of shill bidding may involve additional activities that may be in violation of local, state, or federal laws, you could find yourself in need of a good bail bondsman.

You can get a fairly good picture of the seriousness of shill bidding by going to **www.google.com** and typing in the phrase, *shill bidding,* Read some of the archived news articles about past shill bidders who are now punching out license plates instead of eBay listings.

Feedback

Certain types of activities are prohibited within the Feedback Forum. For example, you may not post another member's contact information—in part or in whole—within a feedback comment or, for that matter, anywhere else on eBay. This includes, but is not limited to, the other party's first name, phone number, email address, city, or state.

Also, you may not leave profanity or obscenities in another person's feedback file. And using altered spellings or substituting punctuation marks does not excuse the offense, so *as**ole* is as unacceptable as the same word fully spelled out. Besides, rules and policies aside, your words reflect your character. You should choose them with the utmost care, as they are going to tell the world who you are. You may believe the other party in a transaction to be an "as**ole," but don't think for one minute that anyone reading your comment isn't going to say to himself, "Hmmm . . . sounds like this seller is the *real* as**ole."

Finally, if the other party reports such a comment to eBay, we will remove the entire comment and serve a warning to the poster of the offending remark.

The upshot? Leave feedback that you would have others leave for you.

Non-Paying Bidders

Bidders are obligated to follow through with their bids after a listing has closed. The vast majority of bidders are basically good. Sometimes a bidder bids on an item and a real-life crisis takes her away, often to a place where she is unable to make contact with you or pay for the item. It happens.

Other times, a bidder may have intended to pay for the item if he won but suddenly found himself in unexpectedly dire financial straits. This doesn't automatically excuse the bidder from his obligations to follow through on his bid, but you might work out with him a payment schedule or some other solution.

The point? Always give non-paying bidders the benefit of the doubt. If they don't respond to your emails, try calling them. You can obtain their contact information by clicking on the Search link on the top of any eBay page and then clicking the Find Members link that appears on the sub–Navigation bar below Search. Scroll down and enter the bidder's User ID in the box marked Contact Information.

On occasion, a new member will traipse around the site, randomly and frivolously bidding away on things she has no intention of buying. You try to contact her and she ignores your email or you attempt to phone her and she doesn't answer her phone, or worse, the line has been disconnected. These deliberately frivolous bidders are not welcome on eBay.

We cannot hold these bidders upside down and shake the funds out of them. We cannot force them to pay for your item. However, we can show them the exit—but only with your help.

You can help rid eBay of these nuisance bidders by reporting them to eBay through the **Non-Paying Buyer** process. Simply follow the instructions on the **Non-Paying Buyer page: http://pages.ebay.com/help/community/npb.html**.

Each report of non-payment is recorded on a member's account. On the third report, the offending bidder is automatically suspended from the eBay site.

Note that the process has built-in safeguards to prevent sellers who are not basically good (they aren't reading this book, remember) from abusing it. Thus, if you should ever have to use this process, you will note that there are specific steps you must take before you can file a Non-Paying Bidder report. These steps involve attempts to contact the bidder via email, waiting a fair amount of time for a reply, etc.

You may be impatient to file your report ASAP, but we are certain that if the shoe should ever be on the other foot, you would want these safeguards to prevent your being the subject of a hastily filed NBP report that could result in the suspension of your eBay registration.

All of the actual detailed activity that eBay considers reportable to SafeHarbor can be found on the eBay website at: **http://pages.ebay.com/help/community/investigates.html.** You can also use this link to report incidents of possible site violations.

COMMUNITY WATCH

The Community Watch team fields all reports of prohibited items listed on the eBay site, as well as reports of certain specific types of listing-description offenses such as keyword spamming (the inclusion of words or phrases into a listing title or description intended to provide unfair advantage to the listing in search results).

Not all otherwise legal items can be listed on eBay, so don't assume yours is OK. For example, although it is perfectly legal to sell a bear rug in the rest of the USA, it is not legal in California. eBay headquarters are located in California; thus eBay elected to adopt this California law as part of eBay selling rules.

If you are uncertain if your item is allowed on eBay, check out the list of prohibited items on the following eBay Web page: **http://pages.ebay.com/help/community/png-items. html.**

Community Watch also has jurisdiction over the contents of an item description. On the same page as above, you will find a link to a page labeled **Listing policies,** which contains a list of all eBay listing policies and prohibited listing activities: **http://pages.ebay.com/ help/community/png-list.html.**

Note that practically all reports of listings for prohibited items or listings with prohibited activities are sent to eBay by other eBay members.

FRAUD PROTECTION

We (eBay and the eBay community of your fellow buyers and sellers) believe you are basically good. No lip service here. Give yourself a hearty pat on the back. Or a hug.

We really do believe without question that you are basically good. How do we know? Because once your buyer sends payment for an item he has purchased from you on eBay, we just know you are going to speed that item to him. We are dead certain of it. How can we be so certain? Because you are an honest and considerate seller whose primary concerns—in order—are:

Happy, satisfied buyers

Your sterling eBay reputation (as exhibited by your feedback)

The viability and continued success of your eBay business

You, like all basically good sellers, only have the very best of intentions. You, like all basically good sellers, want to avoid disputes with your buyers. Sometimes this becomes extremely difficult to do. Sometimes an item is damaged or lost in the mail. Other times, you might have mistakenly described an item as one thing when it was, unbeknownst to you, quite another thing entirely. No big sin. You didn't mean it. You really thought it was solid gold when it was in fact plated. We are all only human and are all prone to the rare error in attribution. That's why you are going to take that gold-plated-but-mistakenly-sold-as-solid-gold item back and refund the buyer's money.

If any of these unfortunate mishaps should happen to you and your buyer, we are sure that you are going to bend over backward to make it right.

But then there are some other sellers. (They are not reading this book, so we can talk behind their backs.) They are not numerous. In fact, they make up less than .001% of all eBay sellers. But no matter—these sellers are sadly, tragically, *not* basically good. Oh, they were good once. They tried, really they did. But somewhere along the line they decided being basically good wasn't worth all the diligence, the excellent feedback, the happiness of their customers, or the eventual long-term success of their businesses. These sellers, who are not you, who are not basically good, go for the quick return with no concern at all for their buyers' satisfaction or to the end consequences of being not basically good. These sellers say, "Your item was damaged in shipping? Too bad for you. It's not my problem. Your package never arrived? Blame it on the mailman. It's not really solid gold after all? The ad said 'as is' so tough cookies."

Oh, these poor sad sellers. They have no idea what tragic fate awaits them.

Outraged and angry buyers who have tried to get some satisfaction from these sad sellers usually quickly report them to eBay Trust and Safety by filing a fraud complaint.

The Fraud Protection Program provides some financial recourse to defrauded buyers in the way of a payout of up to $200 of the final bid value for the item (less a $25 deductible fee for processing the claim). The criteria for what constitutes fraud on eBay are clear and simple.

1. Paying for an item and never receiving it or
2. Receiving an item that is less than what is described—such as winning a solid gold necklace but receiving a plated one instead

If a seller is found to be at fault in an eBay Fraud Protection case, the seller risks immediate and permanent suspension. Thus it behooves any seller to do whatever it takes to satisfy a filed fraud complaint, including refunding the buyer's money or exchanging the plated gold item with a sold gold example.

We needn't say more on this subject, but you can learn more on your own at **http://pages.ebay.com/help/community/insurance.html.**

THE EBAY VERO PROGRAM (VERIFIED RIGHTS OWNERS)

Offering items that infringe upon an owner's trademark, copyright, or other intellectual property rights is strictly prohibited on eBay.

Believe it or not, some sellers (again, not you, of course) find sources for infringing items and offer them on eBay. For example, chic handbags with the Fendi label brand name and trademark that are not genuine Fendi. Or a wristwatch that was made offshore somewhere but is inaccurately and dishonestly labeled as a well-known brand name.

Important note! These items, if not manufactured by the trademark holder, are infringing on the trademark holder's rights and the seller of said infringing items can be suspended from eBay for offering them. In addition, sellers of infringing items run the serious risk of civil or criminal prosecution.

When I first started with eBay back in 1996, I would occasionally field reports from concerned eBay members about fake brand-name watches on the site. They were easy to spot. The sellers of such items would use words like *faux* (French for "false") or *not* in their titles. I would quickly remove these items from the site and send the sellers a stern warning about the consequences of future activity of this sort.

More times than not, the offending seller would respond with surprise that what he was doing was in any way wrong. "But I was not being dishonest! I stated that they were fakes/knockoffs/copies/reproductions! I demand that you reinstate my listing."

At which point I would reply that our decision was final but that they were free to contact the trademark holder and ask them for their opinion.

Property rights are not limited to trademarks or name brands. Copyrights cover all sorts of intellectual property, including but not limited to video, film, music, software, and books.

If you are a trademark or copyright holder, you may want to join the VeRO program yourself! You can read more about the VeRO Program in greater detail by going to **http://pages.ebay.com/help/community/vero-program.html.**

DISPUTE RESOLUTION

Some buyer and seller disputes are, to a great extent, no-fault disputes, that is, no real fraud was intended on the part of either the seller or the buyer. Something just went terribly, horribly wrong. This is where dispute resolution comes in handy.

eBay's third-party provider of choice for dispute resolution (at the time of this writing) is Square Trade: **http://www.squaretrade.com**. Square Trade is an independent service that provides a neutral place where a buyer and seller can work out their dispute online efficiently and effectively.

We've covered the most common topics regarding Trust and Safety issues that relate directly to sellers. There are more policies to read on the **Trust and Safety Overview** pages accessible either by following the links provided in this chapter or via the following roadmap.

Click the Help link on the eBay Navigation Bar at the top of any eBay page.

Click the link for "Seller Guide" in the pop-up window.

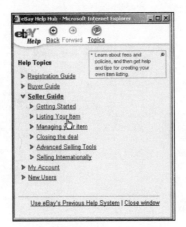

Click the link for "Listing Your Item."

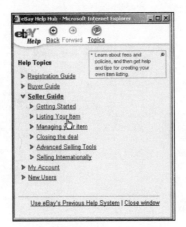

Click the link for "Is My Item Allowed?"

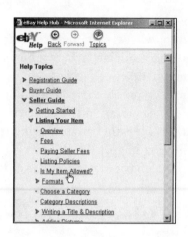

The resulting page contains information and links regarding prohibited items, listing polices, and the VeRO program, as well as a link for contacting Trust and Safety (customer support) via email.

Is My Item Allowed?

Prohibited, questionable, and infringing items

As an eBay user, you're ultimately responsible for making sure that buying or selling your item (s) is legal in the eyes of the law.

Take these steps to find out if your item can be listed on eBay:

* First, review eBay's listing policies. These guidelines will help you list items properly and understand what's allowed on eBay.
* If you're still unsure about listing your particular item, look over the list below. These guidelines and policies are designed to help you trade safely on eBay. Remember that:
  1. **Prohibited** means that these items may not be listed on eBay.
  2. **Questionable** means that items may be listed under certain conditions.
  3. **Potentially infringing** means that items may be in violation of certain copyrights, trademarks, or other rights. For your protection, some items here are not allowed ("prohibited"), regardless of their legality, because they almost always violate copyright or trademark laws.

Prohibited
Alcohol
Animals and Wildlife Products
Catalog and URL Sales
Counterfeit Currency and Stamps
Counterfeit Items
Credit Cards
Drugs & Drug Paraphernalia
Embargoed Goods and Prohibited Countries
Firearms
Fireworks
Government IDs and Licenses
Human Parts and Remains
Links
Lockpicking Devices
Lottery Tickets
Mailing Lists and Personal Information

Questionable
Artifacts
Autographed Items
Batteries
Contracts and Tickets
Electronics Equipment
Event Tickets
Food
Freon
Hazardous Materials
International Trading - Buyers
International Trading - Sellers
Mature Audiences
Offensive Material
Pesticides
Police-Related Items
Pre-Sale Listings
Slot Machines
Used Clothing
Used Medical Devices
Weapons & Knives
Wine

Plants and Seeds
Postage Meters
Prescription Drugs and Devices
Recalled Items
Satellite and Cable TV Descramblers
Stocks and Other Securities
Stolen Property
Surveillance Equipment
Tobacco
Travel

Special
Real Estate

Potentially Infringing (copyright & trademark)
Academic Software
Anti-circumvention Policy
Authenticity Disclaimers
Beta Software
Bootleg Recordings
Brand Name Misuse
Comparison Policy
Contracts and Tickets
Downloadable Media
Faces, Names and Signatures
Games Software
Importation of Goods into the United States
Misleading Titles
Mod Chips
Movie Prints
OEM Software
Recordable Media
Replica and Counterfeit Items
Promotional Items
Unauthorized Copies

Important Notes:

Even if you offer to give away for "free" (rather than sell) a prohibited, questionable, or infringing item, this will not relieve you of potential liability. This applies to both seller and buyer.

This list is updated from time to time and is incorporated by reference into the User Agreement. Notice of updates to this list will be posted on the Announcement Board on the eBay Web site on the day of the change. These guidelines do not constitute legal advice and do not pertain to any particular company's practices. When in doubt, check with law enforcement agencies, a lawyer, the law, or with a copyright, trademark, or other rights owner for clarification. eBay has also adopted certain policies regarding prohibited items, regardless of the legality of the item.

Why did eBay end my listing early?

If eBay ends your auction early because it violates one of our stated policies, you deserve to be properly informed. Therefore, eBay will notify both the seller and bidders via email when an auction has been ended. For additional information, visit the Why Did eBay End My Auction Early? page.

Reporting prohibited, questionable, or infringing items to eBay

* Descriptions and image guidelines: Community members can report listings that use their copyrighted text or images without permission.
* Contact Rules & Safety: Community members can report prohibited, questionable, and infringing items to eBay.
* Verified Rights Owner (VeRO) Program: Intellectual property owners can report items that allegedly infringe on their rights. See a list of VeRO Program member pages.
* Digital Millennium Copyright Act (DMCA) Registered Agent

9

Help!

How to Get Assistance at eBay

Although this book should prove to be a useful tool for using eBay, there is a seemingly infinite number of topics and potential issues regarding how to use eBay, and it would be impossible for one book to cover them all in detail.

Not to despair! The eBay Web site is a virtual treasure trove of valuable information, tips, answers, and clarifications. However, just as with any treasure, one has to hunt a little in order to find it. I hope that this last chapter will serve as a handy road map for finding answers to nearly any question, issue, complaint, or concern you might have about eBay.

Here are a few starting points for finding help, information, and general eBay knowledge right on the eBay Web site.

LIVE HELP

eBay Customer Support recently initiated a project called "Live Help" in order to quickly respond to new customer queries. "Live Help" works similarly to an Instant Messenger service. You—the brand-new eBay member—click the icon for "Live Help," which brings up a messaging window. For those unfamiliar with the instant-messaging format, the concept is simple. You type your query into the window, and within moments an expert eBay support representative responds. Then the two of you conduct an online conversation using text in real time.

Currently, eBay Live is intended primarily as a resource for new eBay buyers and sellers with questions about registration, bidding, and selling, along with some basic computer and Internet technical questions. For the moment, it is not an ideal tool for finding answers to questions regarding SafeHarbor, Community Watch, Fraud Protection, eBay policy, user-to-user disputes, or the eBay VeRO program. However, this may change in the future.

Here's the process, step-by-step.

1. Locate a Live Help icon. They usually can be found on those pages frequented by new users, such as the eBay home page, the "Registration" form, and the "Sell Your Item" form.

2. Depending on how your Web browser is configured, you may see an alert to accept a cookie.

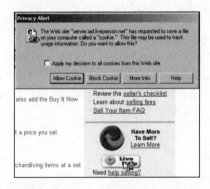

You must accept this cookie in order to use Live Help. (If your Web browser is configured to reject cookies, see the section for "Cookies" on page 13.)

3. In the next window, you type in a "chat" name. It can be just about anything. You also select a topic from the drop-down list.

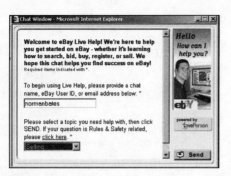

I have selected "Selling," but there is a topic "Other," for other questions. Click the Send button to begin the chat session.

4. Type your question into the box at the bottom of the next window. Once a support rep is free, he or she will respond.

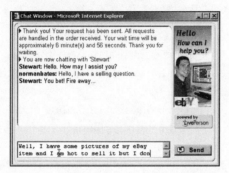

You can then continue to chat until your question is answered to your satisfaction.

5. When you are finished with your Live Help session, click the "X" on the upper right hand-corner of the Live Help window to close it.

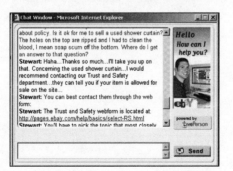

6. You may see a survey window. Do take the time to let eBay know what you thought of the chat session.

CLICK HERE TO "LEARN MORE"

A quick perusal of any eBay Web page, especially those pages where one can "do" something like register, search, list an item for sale, bid, and so on, will show small links labeled "learn more" sprinkled throughout the page. I am constantly amazed at how little use these valuable links receive.

The eBay Web site is chock-a-block with reams and reams of helpful information, tips, knowledge, clarification, explanations, tutorials, etc. The key, of course, is finding this information.

If you are at a place within eBay and you are confused or unsure about how to proceed, look for and click the "learn more" links related to that topic or question. For example, on the Sell Your Item form, there are four separate selling formats. Each one has a related "learn more" link.

Clicking the link for "learn more" under the Advertise your Real Estate option brings up a window with more information about the format.

There are "learn more" links covering practically any and every eBay-related topic you could imagine. Sometimes the links are labeled with a keyword related to the topic. For example, on the top of the same Sell Your Item page, there are links that explain selling formats and what items are not allowed to be sold at eBay.

Sell Your Item: Choose Selling Format

To begin, select a format and click the **Continue** button. Please make sure your item is allowed on eBay first.

Clicking them brings up the appropriate information pages.

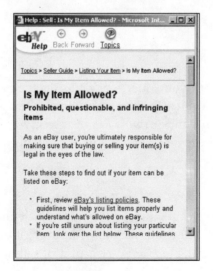

CONTACTING EBAY CUSTOMER SUPPORT

If the information provided on any eBay pop-up Help page doesn't adequately answer your question, scroll down to the bottom of the pop-up window displayed and look for a link that states: "If you have not found the information you are looking for, please ask a question."

This link is located at the bottom of just about every single eBay Help page. If you click it, you will see a Web form for sending an email to eBay Customer Support.

Fill out the form with your question. Be as detailed as possible! Include all pertinent information. You can expect a response from an eBay Customer Support rep in as little as an hour or two, or up to twenty-four hours and more, depending on the number of emails waiting in queue before yours.

"MY EBAY"

Your "My eBay" Bidding/Watching, Selling, Accounts, and Preferences pages all contain numerous links. For example, on the bottom of the Selling tab, there are selling-related links covering nearly every aspect of selling at eBay, including:

Canceling a bid
Ending an auction early
Blocking bidders
Preapproving bidders
Filing for a Final Value Fee Credit
And more

Selling-Related Links

Managing your auctions
Sell your item
Revise my item
Add to my item description
Cancel bids on my item
End my auction early
Relist my item
Send A Second Chance Offer
Feature my item
Add an Andale counter
Manage/Edit my Andale counters
Block or pre-approve certain bidders
eBay Picture Services
Update selling picture preference
eBay Seller's Assistant

Selling information
Seller's Guide
Selling Frequently Asked Questions
After the auction
Seller Services

Billing/Payment
Update Checkout Preferences
Billing Frequently Asked Questions
Apply for a eBay Payments account
View my eBay Payments account
Apply for an eBay Visa with Cash Rewards

Trust & Safety
Seller Payment Protection
Listing policies
Items not allowed
Non-paying bidder program
Trading violations
Dispute resolution

Services
Item authentication
All about Escrow
Square Trade Seal
Graphic & Web Design - eBay Professional Services

Help Boards
Auction Listings board
Feedback board
Packaging & Shipping board
eBay Payments board
Photos/HTML board
Mr. Lister (Bulk Listing) board
Escrow/Insurance board
International Trading board

Shipping/Postage
Start Shipping with UPS
UPS Service Center
Simply Postage

eBay Stores
Learn about eBay Stores
Create an eBay Store
Edit my eBay Store
Manage Merchandising Relationships

If you have a selling, buying, account, or preferences-related question, check the bottom of the appropriate tab page in your "My eBay" before sending an email to customer support.

OTHER MEMBERS

eBay members are an invaluable source of eBay-related knowledge. Lucky for us, most expert eBay members are more than happy to dispense their wisdom, free of charge!

I have mentioned the chat boards in previous chapters, but it bears repeating here that the smartest eBay members in the world hang out on one or more of the many eBay chat boards.

You can find the chat boards under Community and Chat on the eBay Navigation Bar.

Click on any of the topics to begin. I will select Packing & Shipping.

Each "title" is a separate thread started by either an eBay member or, in some cases, an eBay employee. Anyone—registered eBay member or not—can read the contents of any of the threads. Only registered members can start a thread or post responses to a thread. In order to start a thread or post a response, a member must first log in with her registered eBay User ID and password.

To read a thread, simply click on its title. Let's check out the thread for "Media Mail is cheapest."

eBay > Community > Discussion Boards > Board Policies > Packaging & Shipping >   Board log in

MEDIA MAIL IS CHEAPEST (Report)
nuttyjoicel (7) mp (view author's auctions)
4:54am October 22, 2002

I learned from a friend at the post office that the cheapest way to mail a cd, book, video any type of media, it is MEDIA MAIL. It generally costs approxametly $1.40 to $1.90 depending where you ship to in the US. Outside the US is about $2.35 to $3.65. (Prices are for 1lb or 2lb packages.)
Usually received in 3 days. You can get a print out at the post office that explains exactly everything that is allowed under MEDIA MAIL.

paintpower (452) ⭐ mp (view author's auctions)
5:08am October 22, 2002 (#1 of 6) (Report)

Don't count on your Media Mail being delivered in 3 days. Priority usually doesn't even get delivered in that time. Media Mail can take up to a month to get delivered if it gets stuck in some sorting facility. Just be sure to tell your buyers it will be slow so they won't be emailing you every 3 days looking for their package. You mentioned outside the US ... I don't believe Media Mail is available outside the US.

dr_pepper_junkie (29) ⭐ (view author's auctions)
5:44am October 22, 2002 (#2 of 6) (Report)

Note the "Board log in" link in the upper right-hand corner. If you want to post a query or answer, you need to click this link and log in first. Follow the instructions from there.

The members who hang out on these topic-specific chat boards provide a great service to other members. It's a subject near and dear to my heart, since I got my start at eBay by answering questions on the first eBay chat board. The tradition continues!

GLOSSARY

About Me: Your eBay About Me page is your very own personal eBay home page wherein you can talk about your family, your collecting interests, your eBay business. Any registered eBay User can create and maintain an About Me page at eBay. Go to your "My eBay" page and click the tab for Preferences. Look for the link on the bottom of the page for "Create a personal 'About Me' page."

Ad Format Listings: Ad Format listings are advertisements for products or services rather than auction-style listings. Since no transaction occurs on eBay for Ad Format listings, no feedback can be left for these listings. At the time of this writing, Ad Format listings are only available in the eBay Real Estate category.

Announcements Board (News and Events): A special bulletin board where eBay posts timely information such as announcements of new features, site and policy updates, changes to existing features or policies, or notices of system downtime. If you're a regular eBay user, it's a good idea to check the Announcements Board daily. Simply click the Announcements link at the very bottom of any eBay page.

Bid Cancellation: The cancellation of a bid by a seller. Sellers may cancel the bid of any user with whom they would be uncomfortable completing a transaction. A seller can cancel bids by clicking on the Selling tab in their "My eBay" page. There is a link for "Cancel a Bid" under the Managing Your Auctions section of links.

Bid Increment: The bid increment is the amount by which a bid will be raised each time the current bid is outdone. It is predetermined based on the current high bid. Here is how increments are determined:

Current Price	Bid Increment
$0.01—$0.99	$0.05
$1.00—$4.99	$0.25
$5.00—$24.99	$0.50
$25.00—$99.99	$1.00
$100.00—$249.99	$2.50
$250.00—$499.99	$5.00
$500.00—$999.99	$10.00
$1,000.00—$2,499.00	$25.00
$2,500.00—$4,999.00	$50.00
$5,000.00 and up	$100.00

Bid Retraction: A cancellation of the bid by the bidder. Users should exercise this option only in unusual circumstances. This is because when you place a bid, you are in a binding contract with the seller in many states. To retract a bid, go to your "My eBay" Bidding/Watching page and look for the link labeled "Retract a Bid" under the Buying—Related Links heading at the bottom of that page.

Bid History: The list of bidders for an item. You can view the current list of bidders for any item by going to that item's description page and clicking on the link in the top section of the page for Bid History.

Bidder Search: A search for all the items upon which a user has placed bids. Click the Search link on the eBay navigation bar located at the top of any eBay page. Then click on the tab for By Bidder. Enter the bidder's User ID and click Search.

Bidding: The act of placing a bid on a listed item. A bid is an amount you are willing to pay for an item. You can learn more about bidding strategies and the types of listing bids by clicking on the Help link on the eBay navigation bar located at the top of any eBay page. Follow the links from there for Buying Guide>Buying an Item>Bidding.

Big Ticket Items: Items with bids of $5,000 or more. Listings with bids at that level automatically appear in the Big Ticket listings in the first update after the first $5,000 bid has been made for an item. To view all Big Ticket items, click on the Browse link on the eBay Navigation Bar located at the top of any eBay page. Then click the Categories link. There is no fee for placement in the Big Ticket list. The only way an item is listed in the Big Ticket pages is by our system's record of bids that have actually been placed.

eBay Stores: eBay's seller storefront solution. Any eBay seller can open an eBay Store. The eBay Store format is perfectly suited for sellers who wish to offer fixed price inventory in customizable store categories. To learn more about eBay Stores, click on the link labeled eBay Stores in the box labeled Specialty Sites located on the top of the eBay Home page.

Buy It Now: eBay's fixed-price format. Buy It Now listings can be purchased for a fixed price as opposed to bidding for the item and waiting till the listing closes. The option for employing Buy It Now format belongs to the seller. There are three permutations of a Buy It Now listing: Buy It Now only for a regular listing, Buy It Now only for an eBay Store item and Buy It Now used in combination with a proxy bidding format. In the combination format, the Buy It Now option disappears once a bid has been submitted or, if a reserve is used, once the reserve is met.

Category Listings: Items for bid or for sale at eBay are listed within a category or subcategory. One can browse an individual category or subcategory and view all the listings in that category by title and for some listings, by Gallery image as well.

Checkout: eBay's built-in after-the-sale tool for buyers and sellers. Bidders can click on the Checkout button and complete the transaction from there, including sending payment to the seller. Sellers select the option for eBay Checkout when they list an item.

Completed Search: A search of the results of listings that have ended. This is a useful tool if you want to find out the approximate selling price of an item or its value in the marketplace. To get to the Completed Search box, click on the Search link located on the eBay navigation bar and then click the tab for Advanced Search.

Contact Information: The information about you that you provide upon registering at eBay. eBay contact information includes your name, address, and phone number. eBay registered users can only request contact information for other eBay users who are involved in a current or recent transaction either as bidder or seller. Examples are:

- Sellers can request contact information for all bidders in an active transaction and the winning bidder in a successful, closed transaction.
- Bidders can request contact information for a seller during an active transaction and in a successful, closed transaction if they are the winning bidder.

Customer Support: eBay offers customer support through several channels:

✔ Online Help Text
Click on the Help link located on the eBay Navigation Bar found at the top of any eBay page and follow the links from there.

✔ Live Online Help
Live, one-on-one support with an eBay Customer Support representative via an "instant messenger" format.

✔ Online Tutorials
Several terrific real-time, interactive tutorials can be found at **http://pages.ebay.com/education/,** including registering, selling, buying, and How eBay Works.

✔ Email
eBay Customer Support is also accessible via email through one of the various email Web forms on the eBay site. Click on the Help link located on the eBay Navigation Bar found at the top of any eBay page. Select "Use eBay's Previous Help System" and follow the links from there.

✔ Other eBay Members
eBay provides more than eighty chat forums based on topic. They are an excellent source of eBay information from both other experienced eBay members and eBay chat board employees who are usually available for guidance and answers somewhere within one of the various chat forums. Click on the Community link on the eBay Navigation Bar and follow the links from there to the chat boards.

Dutch Auction: Also referred to as a Multiple Item Auction, the Dutch Auction format is perfectly suited for selling quantities of identical items in one listing. A seller selects the Dutch Auction Format when he lists the item, by entering a number of 2 or higher in the Quantity box on the Sell Your Item form. A bidder in a Dutch Auction can specify the number of items he is interested in and the price he is willing to pay. In the end, all winning bidders will pay the same price: the lowest successful bid. Thus it is possible to bid one amount and end up paying less than that bid amount (if your bid is not the lowest successful bid). Learn more about Dutch Auctions by clicking the Help link on the eBay navigation bar located on the top of any eBay Web page.

eBay-o-rama: A shop online where anyone can purchase totally cool eBay-branded merchandise like hats, mugs, T-shirts, bags, and limited edition eBay collectibles. You can find eBay-o-rama under the Community link on the eBay Navigation Bar.

eBay Picture Service: eBay's own image hosting tool and service, provided to eBay users in conjunction with iPix. With one click, sellers can opt to use the eBay Picture Service when they are listing an item for bid or sale. The process for selecting and uploading images using the eBay Picture Service is so easy to follow, it is the perfect solution for new eBay sellers who are confused or intimidated by the whole digital picture process.

Escrow: eBay sellers have the option of providing their bidders with an online escrow service. Escrow can be a valuable tool for the brand-new seller of high ticket items since it extends a layer of security to the buyer. In brief, the buyer sends payment to the escrow account created for the item. The seller sends the buyer the goods. The buyer receives and inspects the item and informs the escrow service that the goods are acceptable. The escrow service pays the seller from the escrow account. The service charges a fee, and the seller and bidder can negotiate as to how the fee will be shared. You can learn more about escrows on eBay service by clicking the Help link on the eBay Navigation bar. In the pop-up window, click Buyer Guide, Trusting the Seller and then Escrow.

Featured Listings: Special sections of eBay where items are more prominently displayed. Sellers can elect from three types of Featured Listings:

Featured Plus: Item is featured on the first pages of the category into which the seller listed it.

Home Page Featured: Item is featured in the main Featured Listings section. Listings in this section are randomly selected for intermittent appearance on the eBay home page.

Gallery Featured: Item's Gallery picture is featured on the top of the page for the category's Gallery view.

Feedback: Comments made by one user about the trading experience with another person. Feedback comments are posted for the eBay community to see and are organized by a rating system. Learn more about eBay's Feedback system by clicking the Feedback Forum link under the Services link on the eBay navigation bar.

Final Value Fee: Fee paid by a seller to eBay for the completion of the auction. The fee is calculated as a percentage of the final selling price. Final value fees are stepped, rather than calculated at a flat rate. You can view the Final Value Fee schedule by clicking the Seller Guide link under Services on the eBay navigation bar. On the resulting page, click the link for Fees.

Gallery: eBay's patented way of presenting a thumbnail picture of a seller's item next to its title in the category list. The seller provides the JPEG image for the Gallery when she lists her item. eBay formats and displays the thumbnail "Gallery" image next to the item's title in that item's category list of titles.

Gift Icon: A small icon of a wrapped present box. Sellers can include this icon on their listing to make it stand out and indicate that the item would make a great gift.

Hot Items: When a non-reserve item receives more than thirty bids we mark that item with a match icon to signify it as a hot item in search results.

ID Verify: The ID Verify feature helps verify a user's personal information, which is cross-checked against consumer and business databases for consistency. ID Verify uses a third party to check the information a user provides and verifies that information for accuracy. After successfully completing the verification, the user will receive an ID Verify icon in their Feedback Profile.

They will also be permitted to sell items and bid on Sothebys.com.

Indefinite Suspension: An indefinite suspension is a suspension of a user's privilege to use the eBay site for more than sixty days with no definite reinstatement date. Indefinite suspensions are generally reserved for the more serious violations of eBay rules, or for repeated violations of eBay rules.

Insertion Fee: Nominal fee paid by a seller to initially list an item for auction on eBay. The fee is calculated either by the opening bid price or the reserve price.

Item Lookup: Searching by item number. (eBay assigns a unique item number to each listing.) To search by item number, click the Search link on the top of any eBay page and then click the tab for Item Number.

Live Help: eBay's new Customer Support feature, which utilizes a real-time chat format similar to popular instant messaging programs. The user types his question in the box and a customer support rep responds. It's fast and as close to a live audio conversation as possible. It's also the perfect help solution for folks with one phone line. The user doesn't have to log off the Internet in order to speak with an eBay rep. To use Live Help, look for and click the Live Help icon on the eBay site (sporadically on the home page).

Live Auctions: eBay Live Auctions provide bidders with a real-time format for some specially listed and announced Live Auctions. These auctions take place in a real, live setting with an auctioneer and a bidding crowd. In an eBay Live Auction, a bidder can place absentee bids, bid against the floor or just watch the auction from their computer as it unfolds. You can find upcoming and currently running Live Auctions:

1. From search results, where eBay Live Auctions items are identifiable via this icon:

2. At **www.ebayliveauctions.com**
3. From links on the **www.sothebys.com** site
4. From promotional links on the eBay home page and listings

Maximum Bid: A keystone of the Proxy Bidding system (see Proxy Bidding). A bidder decides the absolute maximum amount he is willing to pay for an item and submits it as a maximum bid which the eBay system then executes on behalf of the bidder against any other bids up until such time as someone else bids an amount greater than the first bidder's maximum bid.

Merge: Merge is an eBay internal administrative process for combining two or more User IDs (including feedback scores and comments). Once accounts are merged into one account, the old User IDs are no longer active. For example, you cannot use the old User IDs to leave feedback or respond to feedback comments left for you.

If you'd like to request a merge, you must meet the following requirements:

- Proof that you are the owner of the old and new User ID. For example, the contact information on your old User ID needs to match with the new User ID.
- No bidding or listing activity using any of your old User IDs within the last sixty days.
- Confirmed registration of the old and new User IDs.
- No seller fees owed on your old User IDs (zero balance).
- Use the same billing currencies (dollars or pounds, etc.) on the old and new User IDs.

You can only merge a maximum of two old User IDs into one. Your newly combined User ID cannot be merged again into yet another User ID.

All requests for merges are initially made through the email Web forms on the eBay site at: **http://pages.ebay.com/help/basics/select-support.html.**

MIB: Stands for Mint In Box. Used by sellers to describe items that come inside their original box and may also mean that the item was never removed from box. Consult seller for more information if needed.

Minimum Bid: The smallest amount that can be entered as a first bid for a specific listing. The seller determines the minimum bid amount. It is displayed on a listing page as an amount next to the First Bid field.

MOC: Stands for Mint On Card. Used by sellers of items that are still on the card used with their original packaging. Refers mostly to small toys and other mass produced collectibles.

"My eBay": An invaluable tool available to all eBay registered users. Your "My eBay" page can help you keep track of all your eBay buying, selling, and related activities on one special page, viewable only by you. With your "My eBay" page, you can keep track of your favorite categories, view the items you're currently selling and bidding on, and check your most recent account balance and feedback. You can also update your contact information or change your User ID on this page. To view and customize your "My eBay" page, click the link for "My eBay" at the top of any eBay page.

NARU: An acronym for Not A Registered User—used to define suspended eBay members.

Navigation Bar: A graphic with clickable links on the top of every eBay page, the eBay navigation bar is an all-purpose portal to just about every other eBay Web page. If you cannot find a topic or answer to your question or if you are looking for a specific information page on eBay, the best place to start is on the eBay navigation bar.

New: The term "New" refers to items listed during the past twenty-four hours. Both a category list and a search list of results can be sorted for viewing new items first. New items are indicated by the sun icon next to their titles in a category or search list of results.

Non-Paying Bidder Policy: Bidders are expected to follow through with their transaction obligations. Bidders who don't are subject to the eBay Non-Paying Bidder (also referred to as NPB) policy. A seller of an item for which the bidder has not paid can apply for a Final Value Fee credit. As part of the credit process, the seller provides a reason for the request. If the reason is one of several relating to bidder non-performance, the seller is requested to follow a few simple steps to first attempt to reach a solution with the bidder and, if the attempts are unsuccessful, the NPB system awards the credit to the seller and applies a mark against the Non-Paying Bidder's account. If the bidder garners three marks, the bidder's account is suspended.

OOP: An acronym for Out of Print. Used primarily but not exclusively by book dealers.

Outbid: When, during proxy bidding, a new bidder bids more than a previous high bidder's maximum bid amount, the previous bidder has been outbid.

PayPal: eBay's online payment service. **www.paypal.com.**

PIC: Specifically the camera icon, which appears next to the titles of those eBay listings for which the seller has provided a picture. The camera or PIC icon only appears next to the title of those listings where the seller has either used the eBay Picture Service or has provided a URL for a picture in the box provided on the Sell Your Item form. The lack of a camera or PIC icon does not necessarily mean that the seller didn't supply a picture in their listing description. They may have not used eBay Picture Service or typed in a picture URL in the box provided but instead embedded image URLs within their item description.

PowerSellers: An eBay program that recognizes those sellers who have achieved a certain level of sales performance. PowerSellers are indicated by the PowerSeller icon next to an eBay member's User ID. In addition to reaching certain sales levels, a PowerSeller must have at least a 100 feedback rating (98 percent or more positive). PowerSellers can also use the eBay PowerSeller logo in their item descriptions. To learn more about the eBay PowerSeller program, click the Services link on the eBay navigation bar. Then click the link for Buying and Selling. Look on the resulting page for the link labeled "PowerSellers."

Private Listings: Sellers can elect to have their listing formatted as a Private Listing. In a Private Listing, all bidders' email addresses are hidden on the item screen or the bidding history screen. Only the seller and the high bidder are notified via email when the listing is over. The Private Listing option is not available for Dutch Auctions.

Proxy Bidding: The bidding system used by eBay for all non–Dutch Auction listings. A bidder submits a maximum bid, which, if it is an amount on increment above the current high bid, is accepted and executed against the current high bid. The higher of the two bids becomes the current high bid. The proxy bidding system works on behalf of the bidder by executing their maximum bid against all subsequent bids in amounts no smaller than the current bid increments (which are based on the current amount of the high bid). For more information on the Proxy Bidding system, click on the Help link on the eBay navigation bar and then select the topics in the following order: Buyer Guide>Buying an Item> Bidding>Proxy Bidding.

Registered User: In order for people to use eBay to buy, sell, and post to chat forums, they must first be a Registered User. To register at eBay, click the Register Now button on the top of the eBay home page.

Relisting: Sellers may quickly relist an unsold item at eBay by clicking on the Relist Item link on the closed item's item description page.

Reserve Price Listing: Those listings for which the seller has indicated a specific, hidden amount—the reserve—below which the item will not sell. A reserve amount is separate from the Minimum Bid. For example, a reserve listing can have a minimum bid of $.01 or more and a reserve of $50. Bidders may bid on the item starting at a penny but the listing will not be considered a binding sale unless and until someone bids an amount equal to or greater than the reserve amount. Bidders can easily tell if a listing is using a reserve by checking for text next to the amount in the Currently field. If the seller has used a reserve and the reserve has not been met, the text will read "reserve not met." Once the reserve price in a reserve listing has been met, the text indication next to the amount in the Currently field will change to "reserve met." Only the seller knows the reserve amount of her listing.

Retracting a Bid: Bidders are allowed, under certain circumstances, to retract their bids from an open listing. (Bid retraction is not possible for a closed listing.) To read more about Bid Retracting (both policies and procedure) click on the Help link on the eBay navigation bar located at the top of any eBay page. In the resulting pop-up window, click the links in order for Buyer Guide > Buying an Item > Retracting a Bid.

SafeHarbor: eBay's Trust and Safety department. SafeHarbor fields reports of site abuse and helps educate all eBay members about the do's and don'ts of selling, buying, and chat conduct on eBay. To view the SafeHarbor charter, go to **http://pages.ebay.com/help/community/investigates.html**.

Search: The page at eBay from which an eBay member can search for items using one of six different types of search:

Title Search
Advanced Search
By Item Number
By Seller
By Bidder
Search Stores
Completed Items

To view the various search types, click on the Search link located on the eBay navigation bar on the top of any eBay page.

Secure Server: A special type of server and server connection used for sensitive or confidential information like credit-card numbers and contact information. Secure servers use a special type of data transmission encryption called Secure Socket Layer, or SSL for short. eBay provides SSL technology as an option for users to send their credit card and contact information to eBay. Look for the SSL link on the page or look for the yellow padlock on the bottom bar of Internet

Explorer. The yellow padlock indicates the currently viewed page is secured with SSL technology.

Seller Search: One of the search options on the Search page (see Search, above), which provides the ability for any eBay member to view all the current and recent listings for a single seller.

Shades: A special icon that appears next to a User ID for a new user registration or for an eBay registration for which the seller has recently changed the User ID. In each case, the shades icon appears next to the User ID for thirty days.

Shilling: The act of sellers bidding up their own items with either a second eBay registration or the registration of a friend, associate, or family member. Shill bidders risk permanent suspension from eBay.

Sniping: Placing a bid for an item in the last minutes or even seconds of a listing.

SSL: Acronym for Secure Socket Layer. See Secure Server, above.

Star Icons: eBay has created a list of special colored star icons in order to recognize eBay members with certain levels of feedback.

Yellow star represents a Feedback Profile of 10 to 99.
Turquoise star represents a Feedback Profile of 100 to 499.
Purple star represents a Feedback Profile of 500 to 999.
Red star represents a Feedback Profile of 1,000 to 4,999.
Green star represents a Feedback Profile of 5,000 to 9,999.
Yellow shooting star represents a Feedback Profile of 10,000 to 24,999.
Turquoise shooting star represents a Feedback Profile of 25,000 to 49,999.
Purple shooting star represents a Feedback Profile of 50,000 to 99,999.
Red shooting star represents a Feedback Profile of 100,000 or higher.

Starting Price: See Minimum Bid.

Support Boards: Special bulletin boards where eBay users post questions and get answers from the Customer Support staff. Click on the Community link on the eBay navigation bar and then click the link for Chat Forums.

Title Search: A popular search feature. To use Title Search, enter keywords most likely to appear in the title of the item for which you are searching. The Search function will return a list of items that match your keywords. To return a larger list of results, Title Search can be expanded to include titles and descriptions.

User Agreement: The User Agreement outlines the terms of use for eBay service. All registered users must agree to these terms before they can bid on or list items or use any other eBay service. The eBay User Agreement can be viewed at any time by clicking the SafeHarbor (Rules and Safety) link on the very bottom of the eBay home page. This will take you to the Rules and Safety page. Click the link there for User Agreement.

User Discussion Boards: Special threaded chat boards, grouped by discussion topics, where users can discuss issues, ideas, and questions and answers with other users. To reach the User Discussion Boards, click on the link for Community on the eBay navigation bar and select the link for Chat Forums.

User ID: A unique nickname chosen by an eBay user when he registers. The eBay User ID can be used interchangeably with your email address at eBay.

INDEX